435

READING
FORWARD

READING

FORWARD

An Approach to Writing

edited by **Josephine J. Curto** *and* **Frances A. MacLeod**

MIAMI-DADE JUNIOR COLLEGE

WADSWORTH PUBLISHING COMPANY, INC.
BELMONT, CALIFORNIA

COPYRIGHTS AND ACKNOWLEDGMENTS

PART 1

Morton Mott-Smith, "This Mechanical World." From *Reading through Précis* by Mabel A. Bessey and I. P. Coffin (New York: Appleton-Century-Crofts, 1934). Reprinted by permission of the publisher.

William Feather, "A Business Man's Philosophy." Reprinted by permission of the author.

James Truslow Adams, "Our Lawless Heritage." Copyright © 1928 by The Atlantic Monthly Company. Reprinted with permission.

Walter Van Tilburg Clark, "A Case for Law." From *The Ox-Bow Incident* by Walter Van Tilburg Clark. Copyright 1940 by Walter Van Tilburg Clark. Reprinted by permission of Random House, Inc.

O. Henry, "Guessed Everything Else." From *Postscripts* by O. Henry. Copyright 1923 by Harper & Brothers; renewed 1951 by Sara Coleman Porter. Reprinted by permission of Harper & Row, Publishers, Incorporated.

Anton Chekhov, "Out of Sorts." "Out of Sorts" is reprinted with the permission of Charles Scribner's Sons from *Russian Silhouettes* by Anton Tchekoff, translated by Marian Fell. Copyright 1915 Charles Scribner's Sons; renewal copyright 1943 Olivia Fell Vans Agnew.

Mark Twain, "Dr. McDowell." From *The Autobiography of Mark Twain*, edited by Charles Neider. Copyright © 1959 by The Mark Twain Company. Reprinted with the permission of Harper & Row, Publishers.

Christopher Morley, *Thursday Evening*. Copyright 1922, 1950, by Christopher Morley. By permission of the estate of Christopher Morley.

Robert Benchley, "The Children's Hour." From *The Benchley Roundup*, selected by Nathaniel Benchley. Copyright 1936 by Robert C. Benchley. Reprinted with the permission of Harper & Row, Publishers.

Lincoln Steffens, "I Get a Colt to Break In." From *The Autobiography of Lincoln Steffens*, copyright, 1931, by Harcourt, Brace & World, Inc.; renewed, © 1959, by Peter Steffens. Reprinted by permission of the publishers.

Edward Bok, "Just Because I Want to Play." Copyright © 1920 by The Atlantic Monthly Company. Reprinted with permission.

William E. Barrett, "Señor Payroll." Reprinted from *Southwest Review*, Autumn 1943. Copyright © 1943 by Southern Methodist University Press. Reprinted by permission of Harold Ober Associates Incorporated.

PART 3

PREFACE

Reading Forward *is a compilation of material designed to be used in writing classes. A word, therefore, may be in order to explain what is expected of a Reader that should help people to write.*

We believe that it should not be another conventional essay anthology. Students are not inclined to relate the content of formalized essays to their own experience. Since the literary essay appeals to a more mature taste than other prose writing, the student writer may better derive his stimulus from other forms that appeal to him more directly. Hence, various prose forms have been included.

The arrangement is almost casual. It is assumed that the book will be used under different conditions in which there will be a great variety of purpose and individuality of interest, as well as diversity of background. It represents, therefore, divergent reading experiences to serve for motivation, for background, for preparation, and for thought. It does not pretend to offer models of style, though all of the selections are well written. Although it has no real subject or chronological order, it does have a discernible pattern. It is a miscellany containing various literary pieces that are curious and interesting, but not necessarily useful; it contains short stories, myths, legends, scraps of history, excerpts from longer works, and gleanings from periodicals. What, one may ask, does all of this have to do with student writing?

We have kept in mind our needs and conditions at the Miami-Dade Junior College. Many of the selections are brief enough to read and to discuss in a single class period. They are provocative enough that the student's writing motivated by the reading should not be a restatement of the content but an expression of his personal thinking on that or a related subject. They may supplement the student's experiences. They may challenge him in areas not explored and may even stimulate leisure reading. We think that the student's involvement in interests is necessary if his writing is to be effective and interesting.

Since we like to believe that students will find most of their ideas for themselves, we have included few exercises or suggestions for study. Also with a liberal book of this kind, we believe that teachers will prefer to give their own instructions.

J.J.C.
F.A.M.

ix

CONTENTS

1.

4.

FROM SENSITIVITY TO STATURE   231

FROM CURIOSITY TO COMPREHENSION

Curiosity is the quality of mind from which the pleasure of learning stems. It is also the property that leads to the solving of riddles and the uncovering of realities. Much of our everyday curiosity is so reflexive and transient that it leaves no impression. It is developed through the senses: one hears a noise, sees a light, receives countless impressions that a glance will satisfy below the level of consciousness. If, on the contrary, the glance becomes conscious, as when a person looks at the sky long enough to decide that there will be rain to prevent an outing, he has used his curiosity to comprehend, to understand.

Zest for living results from curiosity. It leads to the kind of learning that is pursued for its own sake and not for any practical use one expects to make of it. It leads also to human progress. The first of our ancestors to emerge from the cave, after a sojourn there of some 30,000 years, was probably impelled by curiosity. The explorers of the sea risked falling over the edge of the horizon or being devoured by monsters because their desire to know was stronger than their fears. The poet Browning extended his curiosity about life to the wish that he might "taste the whole" of death.

The selections that follow may add something to your general store of information, but that is not the main intention. They are somewhat random writings that may incite attention or inquiry for its own sake. Comprehension is not entirely a matter of intellectual apprehension. It includes awareness of many things, trivial as well as significant, and many types of appreciation. It involves humor and empathy. It does not necessarily come when too conscientiously sought for. It may develop through the informal reading that is pursued for curiosity's sake. With curiosity, with genuine interest, will come *understanding; there is nothing truer than that in one way or another we learn those things that we really wish to know.*

Enthusiastic curiosity need not mean a retreat from textbooks. It is, however, a human quality with which we are born and which at every stage of development should be fostered and encouraged; for it is the high road to comprehension.

THE HATTER'S SIGN

Thomas Jefferson

A journeyman hatter, a companion of Dr. Franklin, on commencing business for himself, was anxious to get a handsome sign-board, with a proper inscription. This he composed himself, as follows: "John Thompson, *Hatter, makes and sells hats for ready money,*" with the figure of a hat subjoined. But he thought he would submit it to his friends for their amendments. The first he showed it to thought the word "hatter" tautologous, because followed by the words "makes hats," which showed he was a hatter. It was struck out. The next observed that the word "makes" might as well be omitted, because his customers would not care who made the hats; if good, and to their mind, they would buy, by whomsoever made. He struck that out also. A third said he thought the words "for ready money" were useless; as it was not the custom of the place to sell on credit, every one who purchased expected to pay. These, too, were parted with, and the inscription then stood, "John Thompson sells hats." "Sells hats!" says his next friend; "why, who expects you to give them away? What, then, is the use of the word?" It was struck out, and "hats" was all that remained attached to the name of John Thompson. Even this inscription, brief as it was, was reduced ultimately to "John Thompson," with the figure of a hat subjoined.

THIS MECHANICAL WORLD

Morton Mott-Smith

When man emerged from the barbaric to the civilized state, and began to build great cities, temples, and pyramids of stone, it became necessary to transport and lift heavy burdens. Two of the earliest and most effective devices for these purposes were the wheel and the crowbar. We see them depicted on the most ancient monuments. The one diminishes resistance, the other multiplies force. Civilization could hardly have begun without them.

OEDIPUS AND THE SPHINX

Laius, king of Thebes, was warned by an oracle that there was danger to his throne and life if his new-born son should be suffered to grow up.

He therefore committed the child to the care of a herdsman, with orders to destroy him; but the herdsman, moved with pity yet not daring entirely to disobey, tied up the child by the feet, and left him hanging to the branch of a tree. In this condition the infant was found by a peasant, who carried him to his master and mistress, by whom he was adopted and called Oedipus, or Swollen-foot.

Many years afterwards Laius being on his way to Delphi, accompanied only by one attendant, met in a narrow road a young man, also driving in a chariot. On his refusal to leave the way at their command, the attendant killed one of his horses, and the stranger, filled with rage, slew both Laius and his attendant.

The young man was Oedipus, who thus unknowingly became the slayer of his own father.

Shortly after this event, the city of Thebes was afflicted with a monster which infested the high-road. It was called the Sphinx. It had the body of a lion, and the upper part of a woman. It lay crouched on the top of a rock, and arrested all travellers who came that way, proposing to them a riddle, with the condition that those who could solve it should pass safe, but those who failed should be killed. Not one had yet succeeded in solving it, and all had been slain. Oedipus was not daunted by these alarming accounts, but boldly advanced to the trial. The Sphinx said:—

> "Tell me, what animal is that
> Which has four feet at morning bright,
> Has two at noon, and three at night?"—PRIOR

Oedipus replied, "Man, who in childhood creeps on hands and knees, in manhood walks erect, and in old age with the aid of a staff." The Sphinx was so mortified at the solving of her riddle that she cast herself down from the rock and perished.

The gratitude of the people for their deliverance was so great that they made Oedipus their king, giving him in marriage their queen Jocasta. Oedipus, ignorant of his parentage, had already become the slayer of his father; in marrying the queen, he became the husband of his mother.

These horrors remained undiscovered, till at length Thebes was afflicted with famine and pestilence, and, the oracle being consulted, the double crime of Oedipus came to light.

Jocasta put an end to her own life, and Oedipus, seized with madness, tore out his eyes.

He then wandered away from Thebes, dreaded and abandoned by all except his daughters. These faithfully adhered to him, till, after a tedious period of miserable wandering, he found the termination of his wretched life.

THE EXECUTION OF HANNAH DAGOE

The Newgate Calendar

We have adduced many instances of the hardness of heart, and contempt of the commandments of God, in men who have undergone the last sentence of the law; but we are of opinion that in this female will be found a more relentless heart, in her last moments, than any criminal whom we have yet recorded.

Hannah Dagoe was born in Ireland, and was one of that numerous class of women who ply at Covent Garden Market, to the exclusion of poor Englishwomen.

She became acquainted with a poor and industrious woman of the name of Eleanor Hussey, who lived by herself in a small apartment, in which was some creditable household furniture, the remains of the worldly goods of her deceased husband. Seizing an opportunity, when the owner was from home, this daring woman broke into Hussey's room, and stripped it of every article which it contained.

For this burglary and robbery she was brought to trial at the Old Bailey, found guilty, and sentenced to death.

She was a strong masculine woman, the terror of her fellow-prisoners, and actually stabbed one of the men who had given evidence against her; but the wound happened not to prove dangerous.

On the road to Tyburn she showed little concern at her miserable state, and paid no attention to the exhortations of the Romish priest who attended her.

When the cart in which she was bound was drawn under the gallows she got her hands and arms loose, seized the executioner, struggled with him, and gave him so violent a blow on the breast as nearly knocked him down. She dared him to hang her, and took off her hat, cloak, and other

parts of her dress, and disposed of them among the crowd, in despite of
him. After much resistance he got the rope about her neck, which she
had no sooner found accomplished, than, pulling a handkerchief, bound
round her head, over her face, she threw herself out of the cart, before
the signal was given, with such violence that she broke her neck and
died instantly, on the 4th of May, 1763.

THE KEY OF DEATH

The "Key of Death" is apparently a large key which is shown
among the weapons at the arsenal at Venice.
It was invented by Tibaldo, who, disappointed in love, designed this
instrument for the destruction of his rival.
The key is so constructed that the handle may be turned around, reveal-
ing a small spring, which being pressed, a very fine needle is driven with
considerable force from the other end. This needle is so very fine, that the
flesh closes over the wound immediately, leaving no marks, but the death
of the victim is almost instantaneous.

A BUSINESS MAN'S PHILOSOPHY

William Feather

Whether we realize it or not, we are all influenced by our
immediate surroundings. We do more and better work on a bright day
than on a gloomy one. We read with greater satisfaction in an easy chair
than on a hard bench.

In St. Louis is a school attended by 500 young men. In former days
the dining hall was generally a scene of bedlam. There was loud talk,
shuffling of feet, clatter of dishes, throwing of scraps of food, and announcements bawled through megaphones. Then the school was trans-
ferred to a new group of buildings erected in the suburbs. The dining
halls were designed with the same care as the library and chapel. There
are stone-mullioned windows, leaded glass, and graceful hammer-beam

ceilings. Today a meal in one of those halls is as orderly as the morning assembly. No rules are posted, no penalties announced. The dignity of the building did the trick.

OUR LAWLESS HERITAGE

James Truslow Adams

Respect for law is a plant of slow growth. If, for centuries, laws have been reasonably sound, and impartially and surely enforced by the lawful authorities, respect for law as law will increase. If, on the other hand, laws are unreasonable or go counter to the habits and desires of large parts of the population, and are not enforced equitably or surely, respect for law will decrease. On the whole, the first supposition applies to the history of England for three hundred years and the second to our own.

A CASE FOR LAW

Walter Van Tilburg Clark

Davies knew how he was, and let him cool. Then he said, without looking up, "Legal action's not always just, that's true."

"You're damn shootin' it ain't."

"What would you say real justice was, Bill?"

Winder got cautious. "Whadya mean?" he asked.

"I mean, if you had to say what justice was, how would you put it?"

That wouldn't have been easy for anyone. It made Winder wild. He couldn't stand getting reined down logical.

"It sure as hell ain't lettin' things go till any sneakin' cattle thief can shoot a man down and only get a laugh out of it. It ain't that, anyway," he defended.

"No, it certainly isn't that," Davies agreed.

"It's seein' that everybody gets what's coming to him, that's what it is," Winder said.

Davies thought that over. "Yes," he said, "that's about it."

"You're damn shootin' it is."

"But according to whom?" Davies asked him.

"Whadya mean, 'according to whom'?" Winder wanted to know, saying "whom" like it tasted bad.

"I mean, who decides what everybody's got coming to him?"

Winder looked at us, daring us to grin. "We do," he said belligerently.

"Who are we?"

"Who the hell would we be? The rest of us. The straight ones."

Gabe was standing up and looking at us again, with his hands working. Winder saw him.

"Sit down, you big ape," he yelled at him. "I told you once this is none of your business." Gabe sat down, but kept watching us, looking worried. Winder felt better. It pleased him to see Gabe mind.

Davies said, "Yes, I guess you're right. It's the rest of us who decide."

"It couldn't be any other way," Winder boasted.

"No; no, it couldn't. Though men have tried."

"They couldn't get away with it."

"Not in the long run," Davies agreed. "Not if you make the 'we' big enough, so it takes in everybody."

"Sure it does."

"But how do we decide?" Davies asked, as if it were troubling him.

"Decide what?"

"Who's got what coming to him?"

"How does anybody? You just know, don't you? You know murder's not right and you know rustlin's not right, don't you?"

"Yes, but what makes us feel so sure that they aren't?"

"God, what a fool question," Winder said. "They're against the law. Anybody . . ." Then he saw where he was, and his neck began to get red. But Davies wasn't being just smart. He let his clincher go and made his point, mostly for Gil and me, that it took a bigger "we" than the valley to justify a hanging, and that the only way to get it was to let the law decide.

"If we go out and hang two or three men," he finished, "without doing what the law says, forming a posse and bringing the men in for trial, then, by the same law, we're not officers of justice, but due to be hanged ourselves."

"And who'll hang us?" Winder wanted to know.

"Maybe nobody," Davies admitted. "Then our crime's worse than a murderer's. His act puts him outside the law, but keeps the law intact. Ours would weaken the law."

"That's cuttin' it pretty thin," Gil said.

He'd let himself in. Davies turned to him. "It sounds like it at first," he said earnestly, "but think it over and it isn't." And he went on to prove how the greater "we," as he called it, could absorb a few unpunished criminals, but not unpunished extra-legal justice. He took examples out of history. He proved that it was equally true if the disregard was by a ruler or by a people. "It spreads like a disease," he said. "And it's infinitely more deadly when the law is disregarded by men pretending to act for justice than when it's simply inefficient, or even than when its elected administrators are crooked."

"But what if it don't work at all," Gil said; and Winder grinned.

"Then we have to make it work."

"God," Winder said patiently, "that's what we're tryin' to do." And when Davies repeated they would be if they formed a posse and brought the men in for trial, he said, "Yeah, and then if your law lets them go?"

"They probably ought to be let go. At least there'll be a bigger chance that they ought to be let go than that a lynch gang can decide whether they ought to hang." Then he said a lynch gang always acts in a panic, and has to get angry enough to overcome its panic before it can kill, so it doesn't ever really judge, but just acts on what it's already decided to do, each man afraid to disagree with the rest. He tried to prove to us that lynchers knew they were wrong; that their secrecy proved it, and their sense of guilt afterward.

"Did you ever know a lyncher who wasn't afraid to talk about it afterward?" he asked us.

"How would we know?" Winder asked him. "We never knew a lyncher. We'll tell you later," he added, grinning.

I said that with the law it was still men who had to decide, and sometimes no better men than the rest of us.

"That's true," Davies said, "but the poorest of them is better fitted to judge than we are. He has three big things in his favor: time, precedent, and the consent of the majority that he shall act for them."

I thought about it. "I can see how the time would count," I said.

He explained that precedent and the consent of the majority lessened personal responsibility and gave a man more than his own opinion to go on, so he wasn't so likely to panic or be swung by a mob feeling. He got warmed up like a preacher with real faith on his favorite sermon, and at the end was pleading with us again, not to go as a lynching party, not to weaken the conscience of the nation, not to commit this sin against society.

"Sin against society," Winder said, imitating a woman with a lisp.

"Just that," Davies said passionately, and suddenly pointed his finger at Winder so Winder's wry, angry grin faded into a watchful look. Davies' white, indoor face was hard with his intensity, his young-looking eyes shining, his big mouth drawn down to be firm, but trembling a little, as if he were going to cry. You can think what you want later, but you have to listen to a man like that.

"Yes," he repeated, "a sin against society. Law is more than the words that put it on the books; law is more than any decisions that may be made from it; law is more than the particular code of it stated at any one time or in any one place or nation; more than any man, lawyer or judge, sheriff or jailer, who may represent it. True law, the code of justice, the essence of our sensations of right and wrong, is the conscience of society. It has taken thousands of years to develop, and it is the greatest, the most distinguishing quality which has evolved with mankind. None of man's temples, none of his religions, none of his weapons, his tools, his arts, his sciences, nothing else he has grown to, is so great a thing as his justice, his sense of justice. The true law is something in itself; it is the spirit of the moral nature of man; it is an existence apart, like God, and as worthy of worship as God. If we can touch God at all, where do we touch him save in the conscience? And what is the conscience of any man save his little fragment of the conscience of all men in all time?"

GUESSED EVERYTHING ELSE

O. Henry

A man with a long, sharp nose and a big bundle which he carried by a strap went up the steps of the gloomy-looking brick house, set his bundle down, rang the bell, and took off his hat and wiped his brow.

A woman opened the door and he said:

"Madam, I have a number of not only useful but necessary articles here that I would like to show you. First, I want you to look at these elegant illustrated books of travel and biography, written by the best authors. They are sold only by subscription. They are bound in ——"

"I don't care to see them. We have sm——"

"Small children only, eh? Well, Madam, here are some building blocks that are very instructive and amusing. No? Well, let me show you some beautiful lace window curtains for your sitting room, handmade and a great bargain. I can ——"

"I don't want them. We have sm——"

"Smoking in the house? It won't injure them in the least. Just shake them out in the morning and I guarantee not a vestige of tobacco smoke will remain. Here also I have a very ingenious bell for awakening lazy servants in the morning. You simply touch a button and ——"

"I tell you we have sm——"

"Have smart servants, have you? Well, that is a blessing. Now, here is a clothes line that is one of the wonders of the age. It needs no pins and can be fastened to anything—fence, side of the house, or tree. It can be raised or lowered in an instant, and for a large washing is the most convenient and labor-saving invention that ——"

"I say we have small ——"

"Oh, you have a small family. Let's see, then I have here a ——"

"I'm trying to tell you," said the woman, "that we have smallpox in the family, and ——"

The long-nosed man made a convulsive grab at his goods and rolled down the steps in about two seconds, while the woman softly closed the door just as a man got out of a buggy and nailed a yellow flag on the house.

THE FIRST STEAMSHIP TO CROSS THE ATLANTIC

It was under the American flag that the first steam vessel crossed the Atlantic Ocean. The *Savannah*, built at New York by Francis Pickett, was a vessel of three hundred tons burden, and was still on the stocks when Mr. William Scarborough, a wealthy merchant of Savannah, Ga., who had conceived a fancy for trying the effect of steam navigation on the high seas, bought her as she stood. She had a fuel-storage capacity of 75 tons of coal and 25 cords of wood, and her wheels were so constructed as to be removable in rough or stormy weather. She was launched August 23d, 1818, and began her first outside voyage, a trip from New York to Savannah, on Sunday, March 28th, 1819. Stephen Vail, of Morristown, N. J., furnished her engines. Savannah was reached on Tuesday, April 6th. Scarborough and McKinnee were the consignees, and they advertised extensively for passengers and freight to make the trans-Atlantic voyage in her, to start May 20th; there were no responses; the people everywhere were enthusiastic, but few were confident enough to risk either life or property in such an undertaking. On the 20th of May she started as advertised. She did not venture upon the high seas, however, until the 25th. Her voyage thenceforward was uneventful until June 16th, when the Irish coast was sighted. On the 17th, Lieut. Bowin, of the king's cutter "Kite," boarded the "*Savannah,* under the impression, from the smoke rising out of her smoke-stack, that she was a ship on fire." On the 20th, the wheels were shipped and the sails furled, and she ran "into the river Mersey, and at 6 p. m. came to anchor off Liverpool, with the small bower anchor," according to the log. Afterward the vessel visited Copenhagen, Stockholm, Cronstadt, St. Petersburg and other foreign ports. Captain Rogers tried to dispose of the ship to the King of Sweden, but that negotiation failing, she started for home again, reaching the city of her name on Tuesday, Nov. 30th, 1819, and, although they had rough weather, Captain Rogers writes, "not a screw, bolt or rope-yarn parted." It should be added that the actual voyage out from land to land consumed twenty-two days, on only fourteen of which the engines were used. Mr. Scarborough died in 1838; it is not recorded that he ever repeated his experiment in steam navigation. Capt. Rogers died at the age of forty-two, after considerable service as steamboat captain on the great Pedee River, in South Carolina.

✳

OUT OF SORTS

Anton Chekhov

Simon Pratchkin, a commissioner of the rural police, was walking up and down the floor of his room trying to smother a host of disagreeable sensations. He had gone to see the chief of police on business the evening before, and had unexpectedly sat down to a game of cards at which he had lost eight roubles. The amount was a trifle, but the demons of greed and avarice were whispering in his ear the accusation that he was a spendthrift.

"Eight roubles—a mere nothing!" cried Pratchkin, trying to drown the voices of the demons. "People often lose more than that without minding it at all. Besides, money is made to spend. One trip to the factory, one visit to Piloff's tavern, and eight roubles would have been a drop in a bucket!"

"It is winter; horse and peasant—"

monotonously murmured Pratchkin's son Vania, in the next room.

"Down the road triumphant go—triumphant go—"

"Triumphant!" Pratchkin went on, pursuing the train of his thoughts. "If he had been stuck for a dozen roubles he wouldn't have been so triumphant! What is he so triumphant about? Let him pay his debts on time! Eight roubles—what a trifle! That's not eight thousand roubles. One can always win eight roubles back again."

"And the pony trots his swiftest
For he feels the coming snow—
For he feels the coming snow."

"Well, he wouldn't be likely to go at a gallop, would he? Was he supposed to be a race-horse? He was a hack, a broken-down old hack! Foolish, drunken peasants always want to go at breakneck speed, and then, when they fall into an ice-hole, or down a precipice, someone has to haul them out and doctor them. If I had my way, I'd prescribe a kind of turpentine for them that they wouldn't forget in a hurry! And why did I lead a low card? If I had led the ace of clubs, I wouldn't have fallen into a hole myself—"

"O'er the furrows soft and crumbling
Flies the sleigh so free and wild—
O'er the furrows soft and crumbling—"

"Crumbling—crumbling furrows—what stuff that is! People will let those writers scribble anything. It was that ten-spot that made all the trouble. Why the devil did it have to turn up just at that moment?"

"When a little boy comes tumbling—comes tumbling
Down the road; a merry child—a merry child."

"If the boy was running he must have been overeating himself and been naughty. Parents never will put their children to work. Instead of playing, that boy ought to have been splitting kindling, or reading the Bible—and I hadn't the sense to come away! What an ass I was to stay after supper! Why didn't I have my meal and go home?"

"At the window stands his mother,
Shakes her finger—shakes her finger at the boy—"

"She shakes her finger at him, does she? The trouble with her is, she is too lazy to go out-of-doors and punish him. She ought to catch him by his little coat and give him a good spanking. It would do him more good than shaking her finger at him. If she doesn't take care, he will grow up to be a drunkard. Who wrote that?" asked Pratchkin aloud.

"Pushkin, papa."

"Pushkin? H'm. What an ass he is! People like that simply write without knowing themselves what they are saying."

"Papa, here's a peasant with a load of flour!" cried Vania.

"Let someone take charge of it!"

The arrival of the flour failed to cheer Pratchkin. The more he tried to console himself, the more poignant grew his sense of loss, and he regretted those eight roubles as keenly as if they had in reality been eight thousand When Vania finished studying his lesson and silence fell, Pratchkin was standing gloomily at the window, his mournful gaze fixed upon the snow-drifts in the garden. But the sight of the snowdrifts only opened wider the wound in his breast. They reminded him of yesterday's expedition to the chief of police. His spleen rose and embittered his heart. The need to vent his sorrow reached such a pitch that it would brook no delay. He could endure it no longer.

"Vania!" he shouted. "Come here and let me whip you for breaking that window-pane yesterday!"

DR. McDOWELL

Mark Twain

Dr. McDowell—the great Dr. McDowell of St. Louis—was a physician as well as a surgeon; and sometimes in cases where medicines failed to save, he developed other resources. He fell out once with a family whose physician he was and after that they ceased to employ him. But a time came when he was once more called. The lady of the house was very ill and had been given up by her doctors. He came into the room and stopped and stood still and looked around upon the scene; he had his great slouch hat on and a quarter of an acre of gingerbread under his arm and while he looked meditatively about he broke hunks from his cake, munched them, and let the crumbs dribble down his breast to the floor. The lady lay pale and still, with her eyes closed; about the bed, in the solemn hush, were grouped the family softly sobbing, some standing, some kneeling. Presently the doctor began to take up the medicine bottles and sniff at them contemptuously and throw them out of the window. When they were all gone he ranged up to the bed, laid his slab of gingerbread on the dying woman's breast and said roughly:

"What are the idiots sniveling about? There's nothing the matter with this humbug. Put out your tongue!"

The sobbings stopped and the angry mourners changed their attitudes and began to upbraid the doctor for his cruel behavior in this chamber of death; but he interrupted them with an explosion of profane abuse and said:

"A pack of snuffling fat-wits! Do you think you can teach me my business? I tell you there is nothing the matter with the woman—nothing the matter but laziness. What she wants is a beefsteak and a washtub. With her damned society training, she ——"

Then the dying woman rose up in bed and the light of battle was in her eye. She poured out upon the doctor her whole insulted mind—just a volcanic irruption, accompanied by thunder and lightning, whirlwinds and earthquakes, pumice stone and ashes. It brought the reaction which he was after and she got well. This was the lamented Dr. McDowell, whose name was so great and so honored in the Mississippi Valley a decade before the Civil War.

THURSDAY EVENING

Christopher Morley

The scene is a small suburban kitchen in the modest home of Mr. *and* Mrs. Gordon Johns. *A meal has recently been cooked, as is shown by a general confusion of pots and pans and dishcloths. Along the back wall we see an icebox standing in the corner, an oil range, and two shelved cabinets, one containing groceries and household sundries, the other dishes and glassware. Some baby linen and very small shirts (such as would be suitable for a child of about ten months) are hanging on a clotheshorse near the stove. A door in the right wall leads out to the back porch; there are two windows in this wall, one each side of door. A door in the left wall leads to dining room. Near the icebox is a door opening on back stairs, which ascend to upper parts of the house. Below the dining-room door is a sink and oilcloth-covered drainboard or shelf beside it. In the center of stage a small table covered with oil-cloth. A kitchen chair in corner, near porch door.*

When the scene opens, GORDON *and* LAURA *are carrying in soiled dishes through dining-room door. They come in and out several times, making methodical arrangements for cleaning up. They pile the dishes on the shelf by the sink.* GORDON *takes dishpan from a hook under the sink, and fills it with hot water from the kettle on the stove.* LAURA, *who is an attractive little person, aged about twenty-three, is in that slightly tense condition of a young hostess who has had a long and trying day with house and baby, and has also cooked and served a dinner for four.*

GORDON: All right, Creature, just wait till I light my pipe and we'll polish this up. (*Lights pipe and rolls up shirt sleeves.*)

LAURA (*taking an apron from chair in corner*): Put this on first. That's the only decent pair of trousers you've got.

(*Enter* MRS. SHEFFIELD, *carrying dishes.*)

MRS. SHEFFIELD: Now you children run along and take it easy. I'll do all this.

LAURA: No, no, Mother. You go and talk to Mrs. Johns. (*Pointedly*) Don't let her come in here.

MRS. SHEFFIELD (*ultramaternally*): Poor baby, she's tired. You've been on your feet all day. Now let Mother wash up for you. That was a big dinner to cook.

LAURA: No tireder than you are, Mother, darling. You cooked lunch.

GORDON: Both of you clear out; I can get this done in no time.

MRS. SHEFFIELD (*patting* LAURA's *cheek*): Busy with the baby all afternoon, and then cooking such a delicious dinner— Dearie, won't you let Mother do this for you?

LAURA: There isn't room in this kitchen for everybody—

(*Enter* MRS. JOHNS, *carrying dishes.*)

MRS. JOHNS: Gordon, you and Laura go and rest. Let the two grand-mothers—

GORDON: Now listen, little people, this is my job. I always wash up on Thursday evenings—

MRS. JOHNS: You go and read your newspaper. I can see you're all fagged out after that long day in the office—

MRS. SHEFFIELD (*to* LAURA): *Please* go and lie down, baby. You're *so* tired.

LAURA *(with waning patience)*: You two go and amuse yourselves; Gordon and I'll attend to this. *(They gently eject the two mothers-in-law.)*

GORDON: Come on, now, the good old system! *(He takes the small table from center of stage, and puts it carefully midway between sink and dish cabinet. Takes chair from corner and sets it beside table. LAURA sits down on chair and wipes silverware and dishes as he hands them to her after washing.)*

LAURA: The silver first, while the water's clean.

GORDON: Right. We make a pretty good team at this, don't we?

LAURA *(holds up a small silver jug)*: That darling old cream jug. Mother used that when she was a little girl.

GORDON: I love our little Thursday-evening suppers. I think they're more fun than any other night.

LAURA: I'm glad, Gordie.

GORDON: We get better grub on Thursdays, when Ethel goes out, than we ever do when she's in.

LAURA: I tried to have everything specially nice tonight. Some visitors are very critical.

GORDON: It was lovely. I'm afraid it was hard for you, Creature, to have Mother come just now. *(A short pause.)* Especially when *your* mother was here.

LAURA: Didn't she know Mother was here?

GORDON: No. I hadn't told her. You see, your mother is here so much more often. I didn't know your mother would still be here. I was afraid Mother might be a little hurt—

LAURA: Mother helps me a great deal. I think it's a queer thing if a wife can't have her mother stay with her once in a while—

GORDON *(aware of danger, changes the subject)*: Ye Gods, Ethel has cracked the Copenhagen platter. *(LAURA is silent.)* That's one of the set Mother gave us when we were married.

LAURA: It's a stock pattern. You can get another at any department store.

GORDON: I'll bet Ethel didn't empty the icebox pan before she went. I never saw a cook yet who could remember to do that—

LAURA: If you had to go out and hunt for them, you wouldn't be so particular. She's better than no one.

GORDON *(goes to icebox and removes a large, brimming pan from under it)*: What did I tell you! *(The water slops over from pan as he carries it gingerly to sink and empties it. He replaces the pan under icebox.)*

LAURA: You'd better heat some more water. You've poured that ice water into the dishpan.

GORDON *(getting a little peevish; refills kettle and puts it on stove)*: It's perfectly absurd not having any pantry to keep the icebox in. In here, the heat of the stove melts the ice right away. (*Goes back to icebox and slams its doors shut.*) Of course, she never keeps the doors properly closed. (*He returns to sink and resumes dishwashing.*) It's a funny thing.

LAURA: What is?

GORDON: Why, that a presumably intelligent person can't understand the doors of an icebox are meant to be kept tight shut, to save ice. What does she suppose those little clamps are for? (LAURA *is silent. There is a pause, while* GORDON *scrapes portions of food off the soiled plates. He examines some of these plates rather carefully, and picks out several large pieces of meat, lettuce, butter, etc., which he puts on one plate at one side. Then he seems to resume his good humor and relights his pipe.*) Well, it's jolly to have both the grandmothers here together, isn't it?

LAURA: Gordon, dear, put the silver away in the sideboard before it gets wet again. (*He gathers up silver from the table in front of her and exits into dining room.* LAURA *steps out on the porch, and returns, bringing garbage can, which she puts down by the sink. She begins to wash dishes, and sees the plate of odds and ends which* GORDON *has carefully put to one side. She scrapes its contents into the garbage pail. While she is washing,* GORDON *enters.*)

GORDON: Now, Creature, let me do that. You don't want to spoil those pretty hands. (*Takes them, with an attempt to be affectionate.*)

LAURA: I guess it isn't any worse for them than washing the baby's things.

GORDON: Come on, old man, let *me*. (*Gently removes her from sink, and pushes her to the chair by the table. She sits down and wipes dishes as he hands them to her.*) It doesn't take long when there are two of us.

LAURA: Gordie, these dishes aren't properly clean. You can't get that grease off without hot water.

GORDON: I guess that kettle's hot by now. (*To stove, feels water in kettle.*) Give it a minute longer. (*Stands by stove and puffs at his pipe. In a moment of false security, he foolishly reopens a dangerous topic.*) You know, I'm a little worried about Mother.

LAURA (*putting away dishes*): Why?

GORDON: I don't think she's as well as usual. She hardly ate any of her salad.

LAURA (*turns as though about to say something, but checks herself and pauses a moment. This time it is she who tries honorably to avert the gathering storm*): Oh, Gordie, I forgot to tell you! Junior drank out of a cup today—the first time!

GORDON: He did! The little rascal!

LAURA: Look, here's the cup. (*Shows a small silver cup.*)

GORDON (*affectionately, putting his arm around her*): Well, well. (*Looks at cup.*) What cup is that? I don't seem to remember it—

LAURA: Why—Mother brought it with her. She used it when she was a baby.

GORDON: Where's that nice old christening mug of mine? I think Junior would like to use that once in a while, too.

LAURA: I put it away, dear. I was afraid Ethel might dent it.

GORDON (*takes kettle from stove, goes back to sink*): I hope Mother isn't feeling poorly. I noticed at supper—

LAURA: When hot meat is served, refined people usually call it *dinner*—

GORDON (*looks at her cautiously, and suddenly seems to realize that they are on the edge of an abyss*): Now, honey, you're tired. You go and rest; I'll finish up here.

LAURA: No, thank you. I like to see that everything gets cleaned up properly. Someone might come snooping out here, and then there'd be hints about my housekeeping. Of course, I'll admit I wasn't brought up to be a cook—

GORDON (*seeks inspiration by relighting his pipe, and takes up a handsome silver coffeepot*): One thing I never can make out is how to prevent coffee grounds from going down the sink. (*He talks desperately, trying to tide over the mutually realized danger point.*) Perhaps if I could invent some kind of a little coffee-ground strainer I'd make our fortune. That coffee was delicious, Creature.

LAURA: Take care of that urn; it's one of the few handsome things we have.

GORDON: It *is* a beauty.

LAURA: Jack Davis gave it to me—

GORDON (*puts it down with distaste*): I guess I'd better attend to the garbage.

LAURA (*nervously*): It's all fixed.

GORDON: I always like Thursdays because that's one evening Ethel doesn't get a chance to throw away about five dollars' worth of good food.

LAURA: I fixed the garbage. You can put the pail outside.

GORDON (*hunting among plates on the shelf beside sink*): Where's that plate I put here? There was a lot of perfectly good stuff I saved—

LAURA (*blows up at last*): Well, if you think I'm going to keep a lot of half-eaten salad your mother picked over—

GORDON (*seizes garbage pail, lifts it up to the sink and begins to explore its contents. His fuse also is rapidly shortening*): My Lord, it's no wonder we never have any money to spend if we chuck half of it away in waste. (*Picking out various selections.*) Waste! Look at that piece of cheese, and those potatoes. You could take those things, and some of this meat, and make a nice economical hash for lunch—

LAURA: It's a wonder you wouldn't get a job as a scavenger. I never *heard* of a husband like you, rummaging through the garbage pail.

GORDON (*blows up*): Do you know what the one unforgivable sin is? The sin against the Holy Ghost? It's *waste!* It makes me wild to think of working and working like a dog, and half of what I earn just thrown away by an ignorant cook. Look at this, just look at it! *(Displays a grisly object.)* There's enough meat on that bone to make soup. And ye gods, here's that jar of anchovy paste! *(Holds it up.)* I thought you got that for me as a little treat. I wondered where it had gone to. Why, I hadn't eaten more than just the top of it.

LAURA: Well, you left it, and it got mildewed.

GORDON: Scrape it off. A little mildew won't hurt anybody. There'll be mildew on my bank account if this kind of thing goes on. *(Still examining garbage pail.)* Look here, about half a dozen slices of bread. What's the matter with *them*, I'd like to know.

LAURA: I think it's the most disgusting thing I ever heard of. To go picking over the garbage pail like that. You attend to your affairs and I'll attend to mine.

GORDON: I guess throwing away good, hard-earned money is my affair, isn't it?

LAURA: You're always quick enough to find fault. I know Ethel's careless, but she's the best I can get out here in this godforsaken suburb. Maybe you'll be good enough to find me a better servant. A well-trained girl wouldn't work in this old dump, where there isn't even gas. You don't seem to know when you're lucky. You come back at night and find your home well cared for and me slaving over a hot dinner, and do you ever say a word of thanks? No, all you can think of is finding fault. I can't imagine how you were brought up. Your mother—

GORDON: Just leave my mother out of it. I guess she didn't spoil me the way yours did you. Of course, I wasn't an only daughter—

LAURA: I wish you had been. Then I wouldn't have married you.

GORDON: I suppose you think that if you'd married Jack Davis or some other of those jokers you'd never have had to see the inside of a kitchen—

LAURA: If Junior grows up with your disposition, all I can say is I hope he'll never get married.

GORDON: If he gets married, I hope it'll be to some girl who understands something about economy—

LAURA: If he gets married, I hope he'll be man enough not to be always finding fault—

GORDON: Well, he *won't* get married! I'll put him wise to what marriage means, fussing like this all the time—

LAURA: Yes, he *will* get married. He *shall* get married!

GORDON: Oh, this is too absurd—

LAURA: He *shall* get married, just to be a humiliating example to his father. I'll bring him up the way a husband *ought* to be.

GORDON: In handcuffs, I suppose—

LAURA: And his wife won't have to sit and listen to perpetual criticism from his mother—

GORDON: If you're so down on mothers-in-law, it's queer you're anxious to be one yourself. The expectant mother-in-law!

LAURA: All right, be vulgar. I dare say you can't help it.

GORDON: Great Scott, what did you think marriage was like, anyway? Did you expect to go through life having everything done for you, without a little hard work to make it interesting?

LAURA: Is it necessary to shout?

GORDON: Now let me tell you something. Let's see if you can ratify it from your extensive observation of life. Is there anything in the world so cruel as bringing up a girl in absolute ignorance of housework, believing that all her days she's going to be waited on hand and foot, and that marriage is one long swoon of endearments—

LAURA: There's not much swooning while you're around.

GORDON: Why, I believe you actually think your life is wrecked if you aren't being petted and praised every minute. You pretend to think marriage is so sacred and yet you're buffaloed by a few greasy dishes. I like my kind of sacredness better than yours, and that's the sacredness of common sense. Marriage ought not to be performed before an altar, but before a kitchen sink.

LAURA (*furiously*): I ought to have known that oil and water won't mix. I ought to have known that a vulgar, selfish, conceited man couldn't make a girl happy who was brought up in a refined family. I was a Sheffield, and why I ever became a Johns is more than I can imagine. Johns—I suppose that's camouflage for Jones. You're too common, too ordinary, to know when you're lucky. You get a charming, aristocratic wife and expect her to grub along like a washerwoman. You try to crush all the life and spirit out of her. You ought to have married an icebox— that's the only thing in this house you're really attentive to.

GORDON: Now listen—

LAURA (*will not be checked*): Talk about being spoiled—why, your mother babies you so, you think you're the only man on earth. (*Sarcastically.*) Her poor, overworked boy, who tries so hard and gets all fagged out in the office and struggles so nobly to support his family! I wonder how you'd like to run this house and bear a child and take care of it and shuffle along with an ignoramus for a maid and then cook a big dinner and be sneered at and never a word of praise. All you can think of is picking over the garbage pail and finding fault—

GORDON (*like a fool*): I didn't find fault. I found some good food being wasted.

LAURA: All right, if you love the garbage pail better than you do your wife, you can live with it. (*Flings her dish towel on the floor and exits into dining room.*)

(GORDON *stands irresolutely at the sink, and makes a few gloomy motions among the unfinished dishes. He glares at the garbage can. Then he carefully gathers those portions of food that he had chosen as being still usable, contemplates them grimly, then puts them on a plate and, after some hesitation, puts the plate in the icebox. He takes the garbage can and puts it outside the porch door. He returns into the kitchen, but then a sudden fit of anger seizes him.*)

GORDON: It's always the way! (*Tears off apron, throws it on the floor, and goes out on porch, slamming door.*)

(*After a brief pause, the door at the rear, opening onto the back stairs, is cautiously opened, and MRS. SHEFFIELD enters quietly. She takes one swift look around the disordered kitchen, pick up dish towel and apron from the floor, and sets to work rapidly to clean up. Then the back-stairs door is again opened in the same stealthy way, and MRS. JOHNS enters. The two ladies seem to take each other's measure with instinctive shrewdness, and fall into a silent, business-like team play in putting things to rights. MRS. JOHNS takes charge at the sink, and the remaining dishes spin under her capable hands. MRS. SHEFFIELD takes them from her, rapidly polishes them, and puts them away on the shelves. There is unconscious comedy in the trained precision and labor-saving method of their actions, which are synchronized so that every time MRS. JOHNS holds out a washed dish, MRS. SHEFFIELD is moving back from the cabinet, ready to receive it. They work like automatons. For perhaps two minutes not a word is said, and the two seem, by searching side glances, to be probing each other's mood.*)

MRS. JOHNS: If it wasn't so tragic I'd laugh. (*A pause, during which they work busily.*)

MRS. SHEFFIELD: If it wasn't so comic I'd cry. (*Another pause.*) I guess it's my fault. Poor Laura, I'm afraid I *have* spoiled her.

MRS. JOHNS: *My* fault, I think. Two mothers-in-law at once is too much for any young couple. I didn't know you were here, or I wouldn't have come.

MRS. SHEFFIELD: Laura is so dreadfully sensitive, poor child—

MRS. JOHNS: Gordon works so hard at the office. You know he's trying to get promoted to the sales department, and I suppose it tells on his nerves—

MRS. SHEFFIELD: If Laura could afford to have a nurse to help her with the baby, she wouldn't get so exhausted—

MRS. JOHNS: Gordon says he wants to take out some more insurance, that's why he worries so about economy. It isn't for himself; he's really very unselfish—

MRS. SHEFFIELD (*a little tartly*): Still, I do think that sometimes—(*They pause and look at each other quickly.*) My gracious, we'll be at it ourselves if we don't look out!

(*She goes to the clotheshorse and rearranges the garments on it. She holds up a Lilliputian shirt, and they both smile.*)

MRS. JOHNS: That darling baby! I hope he won't have poor Gordon's quick temper. It runs in the Johns family, I'm afraid. I was an Armstrong before I married Gordon's father. I didn't know what temper was until I married—either my own or his.

MRS. SHEFFIELD: I was a Thomson—Thomson without the *p*, you know, from Rhode Island. All families are hot tempered. All husbands' families, anyway.

MRS. JOHNS: Gordon's father used to say that Adam and Eve didn't know when they were well off. He said that was why they called it the Garden of Eden.

MRS. SHEFFIELD: Why?

MRS. JOHNS: Because there was no mother-in-law there.

MRS. SHEFFIELD: Poor children, they have such a lot to learn! I really feel ashamed, Mrs. Johns, because Laura is an undisciplined little thing, and I'm afraid I've always petted her too much. She had such a lot of attention before she met Gordon, and was made so much of, it gave her wrong ideas.

MRS. JOHNS: I wish Gordon was a little younger; I'd like to turn him up and spank him. He's dreadfully stubborn and tactless—

MRS. SHEFFIELD: But I'm afraid I *did* make a mistake. Laura was having such a good time as a girl, I was always afraid she'd have a hard awakening when she married. But Mr. Sheffield had a good deal of money at that time, and he used to say, "She's only young once. Let her enjoy herself."

MRS. JOHNS: My husband was shortsighted, too. He had had to skimp so that he brought up Gordon to have a terror of wasting a nickel.

MRS. SHEFFIELD: Very sensible. I wish Mr. Sheffield had had a little more of that terror. I shall have to tell him what his policy has resulted in. But really, you know, when I heard them at it, I could hardly help admiring them. (*With a sigh.*) It brings back old times!

Mrs. Johns: So it does! (*A pause.*) But we can't let them go on like this. A little vigorous quarreling is good for everybody. It's a kind of spiritual laxative. But they carry it too far.

Mrs. Sheffield: They're awfully ingenious. They were even bickering about Junior's future mother-in-law. I suppose she's still in school, who-ever she may be!

Mrs. Johns: Being a mother-in-law is almost as painful as being a mother.

Mrs. Sheffield: I think every marriage ought to be preceded by a treaty of peace between the two mothers. If they understand each other, every-thing will work out all right.

Mrs. Johns: You're right. When each one takes sides with her own child, it's fatal.

Mrs. Sheffield (*lowering her voice*): Look here, I think I know how we can make them ashamed of themselves. Where are they now?

Mrs. Johns (*goes cautiously to dining-room door, and peeps through*): Laura is lying on the couch in the living room. I think she's crying—her face is buried in the cushions.

Mrs. Sheffield: Splendid. That means she's listening with all her ears. (*Tiptoes to window.*) I can't see Gordon, but I think he's walking around the garden—

Mrs. Johns (*quietly*): If we were to talk a little louder he'd sit on the back steps to hear it—

Mrs. Sheffield: Exactly. Now listen! (*They put their heads together and whisper; the audience does not hear what is said.*)

Mrs. Johns: Fine! Oh, that's fine! (Mrs. Sheffield *whispers again, in-audibly.*) But wait a moment. Don't you think it would be better if *I* praise Laura and *you* praise Gordon? They won't expect that, and it might shame them—

Mrs. Sheffield: No, no! Don't you see— (*Whispers again, inaudibly.*)

Mrs. Johns: You're right. Cunning as serpents and harmless as doves— (*They carefully set both doors ajar.*)

Mrs. Sheffield: I only hope we won't wake the baby— (*They return to the task of cleaning up, and talk very loudly, in pretended quarrel.*)

Mrs. Johns: Where do these dessert plates go?

Mrs. Sheffield: On this shelf.

Mrs. Johns: You're here so much more often than I, naturally you know Laura's arrangements better.

Mrs. Sheffield: It's a lucky thing I *am* here. I don't know what poor Laura would do without me at such a dreadful time—

Mrs. Johns: *Poor* Laura! I should say she's very fortunate, such a good husband—

MRS. SHEFFIELD: I think it's rather sad for a girl who has had as much as she has to come down to this—

MRS. JOHNS: It's perfectly wonderful how Gordon has got on in business—

MRS. SHEFFIELD: He ought to, with such a lovely home, run like a clock—

MRS. JOHNS: Yes—an alarm clock.

MRS. SHEFFIELD: Well, I'm not going to see my daughter's happiness ruined—

MRS. JOHNS: I always knew he'd make some girl a fine husband—

MRS. SHEFFIELD: Perhaps. But he seems to have picked the wrong girl. Laura has too much spirit to be bullied—

MRS. JOHNS: Well, perhaps it was all a mistake. Poor Gordon, he works so hard. I believe his hair is going white over his ears already.

MRS. SHEFFIELD: Stuff! That's lather from where he shaved this morning. He's too slovenly to wash it off.

MRS. JOHNS: It isn't right that a young man should have to slave the way he does—

MRS. SHEFFIELD (*apparently in a passion*): Do you think that business slavery can compare to household slavery? I think it's heart-rending to see an attractive girl like Laura shut up in a poky little house doing drudgery and tending a baby. Think of it, having to take care of her own baby! Why, it's an outrage. If Gordon was half a man, he'd get her a trained baby nurse so she wouldn't have to *look* at the poor little thing—

MRS. JOHNS (*scathingly*): Yes, how sad that Gordon should have to entrust his son to amateur care when it needs scientific attention.

MRS. SHEFFIELD: Poor darling Laura—she never ought to have had a baby.

MRS. JOHNS: Gordon is too intellectual to be bothered with these domestic details. He ought to be able to concentrate on his work.

MRS. SHEFFIELD (*coming close to* MRS. JOHNS, *feigning great rage, but grimacing to show it is merely acting*): Well, if you don't think my daughter is good enough for your son, I can always take her home with *me*. I guess I can find room for her and we can put the child in an institution. (*Both nearly laugh, but recover themselves.*)

MRS. JOHNS: Don't worry. *I'll* take the child. He's a Johns anyway, not a Sheffield. And you just watch Gordon, when he's relieved of all this family worry and quarreling. He'll make his mark in the world. He's too fine to be tied down by a wife that doesn't understand him.

MRS. SHEFFIELD: Oh, how happy Laura will be to hear this. My sweet, clever, attractive, economical, sensible little girl, free at last. Her married life has been a nightmare. That great, hulking, selfish man has tried to trample all the joy out of her. He shan't do it.

MRS. JOHNS: I never heard of a young husband as self-sacrificing as Gordon. I don't believe he *ever* goes out for an evening with other men, and he *never* spends anything on himself—

MRS. SHEFFIELD: I think the way Laura runs her little home is just wonderful. See how she struggles to keep her kitchen in order—this miserable, inconvenient little kitchen—no gas, no pantry, no decent help. I think it's *terrible* she has had to put up with so much— (*They pause, and listen at the dining-room door. The kitchen is now spick and span. MRS. JOHNS makes a gesture to indicate that LAURA is taking it all in, off stage.*)

MRS. JOHNS: Well, then, it's all settled.

MRS. SHEFFIELD: Yes. As Laura's mother, I can't let her go on like this. A husband, a home, and a baby—it's enough to ruin any woman.

MRS. JOHNS: It's only fair to both sides to end it all. I never heard of such brutal hardships. Gordon can't fight against these things any longer. Throwing away a soupbone and three slices of bread! I wonder he doesn't go mad.

MRS. SHEFFIELD: We've saved them just in time. (*They look at each other knowingly, with the air of those who have done a sound bit of work. Then they stealthily open the door at the rear, and exeunt up the back stairs.*)

(*There is a brief pause; then the dining-room door opens like an explosion, and LAURA bursts in. She stands for a moment, wild-eyed, stamps her foot in a passion. Then she seizes one of the baby shirts from the rack, and drops into the chair by the table, crying. She buries her head in her arms, concealing the shirt. Enter GORDON, from porch. He stands uncertainly, evidently feeling like a fool.*)

GORDON: I'm sorry, I—I left my pipe in here. (*Finds it by the sink.*)

LAURA (*her face still hidden*): Oh, Gordie, *was* it all a mistake?

GORDON (*troubled, pats her shoulder tentatively*): Now listen, Creature, don't. You'll make yourself sick.

LAURA: I never thought I'd hear such things—from my own mother.

GORDON: I never heard such rot. They must be mad, both of them.

LAURA: Then you were listening, too—

GORDON: Yes. Why, they're deliberately trying to set us against each other.

LAURA: They wouldn't have *dared* speak like that if they had known we could hear. Gordon, I don't think it's *legal*—

GORDON: I'm afraid the law doesn't give one much protection against one's mothers.

LAURA (*miserably*): I guess she's right. I *am* spoiled, and I *am* silly, and I *am* extravagant—

GORDON: Don't be silly, darling. That's crazy stuff. I'm *not* overworked, and even if I were I'd love it, for *you*—

LAURA: I don't *want* a nurse for Junior. I wouldn't have one in the house. (*Sits up, disheveled, and displays the small shirt she had been clutching.*) Gordon, I'm *not* an amateur! I love that baby and I *am* scientific. I keep a chart of his weight every week.

GORDON: Yes, I know, ducky, Gordon understands. Soon we'll be able to buy that scale you want, and we won't have to weigh him on the meat balance.

LAURA: *Nobody* can take away my darling baby—

GORDON: It was my fault, dear. I *am* obstinate and disagreeable—

LAURA: I'll speak to Ethel about the garbage—

GORDON: Ethel's all right. We're lucky to have her.

LAURA: Gordon, you mustn't work too hard. You know you're all I have (*a sob*) since Mother's gone back on me.

GORDON (*patting her*): I think it's frightful, the things they said. What are they trying to do, break up a happy home?

LAURA: We *are* happy, aren't we?

GORDON: Well, I should say so. Did you ever hear me complain? (*Takes her in his arms.*)

LAURA: No, Gordie. It was cruel of them to try to make trouble between us; but, perhaps, some of the things they said—

GORDON: Were true?

LAURA: Well, not exactly true, dear, but—interesting! Your mother is right, you *do* have a hard time, and I'll try—

GORDON (*stops her*): No, *your* mother is right. I've been a brute—

LAURA: I'm lucky to have such a husband— (*They are silent a moment.*)

GORDON: I suppose you'll think it an awful anticlimax—

LAURA: What, dear?

GORDON: Suppose we have something to eat?

LAURA (*happily*): Good idea. Quarreling always makes me hungry. (*They go to the icebox.*) I didn't really get any supper to speak of; I was worrying about everything so—

GORDON (*opening icebox*): You mean *dinner*, honey—among refined people!

LAURA: Don't be a tease. Come on, we'll have a snack— (*She discovers* GORDON's *plate of leftovers.*)

GORDON: Throw out that junk—I was idiotic to save it.

LAURA: No, Gordie, you were quite right. We must save everything we can. Four or five heads of lettuce would make a new shirt for Junior.

GORDON (*bewildered*): Lettuce?

LAURA: I mean, if we saved that much, it would make enough money to buy him a new little vest. He's getting so *enormous—* *(She puts plate of leftovers on the table, with some other cold food.)*

GORDON: There, now, this is better. *(They sit down at table.)*

LAURA *(thoughtfully)*: You know, Gordie, we mustn't let them know we heard them.

GORDON: No, I suppose not. But it's hard to forgive that sort of talk.

LAURA: Even if they did say atrocious things, I think they really love us—

GORDON: We'll be a bit cold and standoffish until things blow over.

LAURA *(complacently)*: If I'm ever a mother-in-law, I shall try to be *very* understanding—

GORDON: Yes, Creature. Do you remember why I call you Creature?

LAURA: Do I not?

GORDON: There was an adjective omitted, you remember.

LAURA: Oh, Gordie, that's one of the troubles of married life. So many of the nice adjectives seem to get omitted.

GORDON: Motto for married men: Don't run short of adjectives! You remember what the adjective was?

LAURA: Tell me.

GORDON: *Adorable.* It was an abbreviation for Adorable Creature. *(Holds her. They are both perfectly happy.)* I love our little Thursday evenings.

LAURA *(partly breaks from his embrace)*: Sssh! *(Listens.)* Was that the baby?

THE CHILDREN'S HOUR

Robert Benchley

I don't want to be an alarmist, but I think that the Younger Generation is up to something. I think that there is a plot on foot.

I base my apprehension on nothing more definite than the fact that they are always coming in and going out of the house, without any apparent reason. When they are indoors, they sit for a while without doing anything much. Then they suddenly decide to go out again for a while. Then they come in again. In and out—in and out.

Of course, this applies only to Saturdays and vacation time. I don't know what they do at school but presumably they stay put. They can't just wander in and out of classrooms and school buildings as they do at home.

This foot-loose tendency is most noticeable during spring and summer vacations. Let us say that two or three of them leave the house right after breakfast. In answer to the question: "Where are you going this morning?" they say: "Oh, just around."

In half an hour they are back, with possibly three others. They don't talk. They just come in. Sometimes they sit down in various attitudes of abandon. Sometimes they walk slowly around the room. Sometimes they just stand and lean against the wall. Then, after perhaps five minutes of this, they start outdoors again in a body.

This goes on all day. Each time they return, they have two or three new ones with them, but there seems to be no reason why fresh members have come. They don't act as if it made any difference to them *where* they were. They do not even appear to enjoy each other's company very much. They are very quiet about it all, except for slamming the screen door. It is ominous.

All that I can figure out is that they are plotting a revolution. When they go out, I think that they work secretly on laying cement foundations for gun-bases, or even lay mines. Then they come indoors to look around and see if the old folks have begun to suspect anything yet. Assuring themselves that all is well, someone gives the signal and they are off again to their plotting.

I don't think that anyone but mothers and fathers of adolescent families will know what I mean, but I have spoken to several parents about it and they have all noticed the same thing. There is a restlessness abroad among the Young Folk, but it is a quiet, shambling sort of restlessness which presages a sudden bugle call some day, at which they will all spring into action.

All that I ask is that they let me in on their plans. It would help if they were noisier about the thing and did a little yelling now and then. It's this constant coming in and going out of the house like slippered Moslems fomenting a revolt that gets me down.

All I hope is that they start something—anything—before I am too old to run.

I GET A COLT TO BREAK IN

Lincoln Steffens

Colonel Carter gave me a colt. I had my pony, and my father meanwhile had bought a pair of black carriage horses and a cow, all of which I had to attend to when we had no "man." And servants were hard to get and to keep in those days; the women married, and the men soon quit service to seize opportunities always opening. My hands were pretty full, and so was the stable. But Colonel Carter seemed to think that he had promised me a horse. He had not; I would have known it if he had. No matter. He thought he had, and maybe he did promise himself to give me one. That was enough. The kind of man that led immigrant trains across the continent and delivered them safe, sound, and together where he promised would keep his word. One day he drove over from Stockton, leading a two-year-old which he brought to our front door and turned over to me as mine. Such a horse!

She was a cream-colored mare with a black forelock, mane, and tail and a black stripe along the middle of her back. Tall, slender, high-spirited, I thought then—I think now—that she was the most beautiful of horses. Colonel Carter had bred and reared her with me and my uses in mind. She was a careful cross of a mustang mare and thorough-bred stallion, with the stamina of the wild horse and the speed and grace of the racer. And she had a sense of fun. As Colonel Carter got down out of his buggy and went up to her, she snorted, reared, flung her head high in the air, and, coming down beside him, tucked her nose affectionately under his arm.

"I have handled her a lot," he said. "She is as kind as a kitten, but she is as sensitive as a lady. You can spoil her by one mistake. If you ever lose your temper, if you ever abuse her, she will be ruined forever. And she is unbroken. I might have had her broken to ride for you, but I didn't want to. I want you to do it. I have taught her to lead, as you can see; had to, to get her over here. But here she is, an unbroken colt; yours. You take and you break her. You're only a boy, but if you break this colt right, you'll be a man—a young man, but a man. And I'll tell you how."

Now, out West, as everyone knows, they break in a horse by riding out to him in his wild state, lassoing, throwing, and saddling him; then they let him up, frightened and shocked, with a yelling broncho-buster astride of him. The wild beast bucks, the cowboy drives his spurs into him, and off they go, jumping, kicking, rearing, falling, till by the weight of the man, the lash, and the rowels, the horse is broken—in body and spirit. This was not the way I was to break my colt.

"You must break her to ride without her ever knowing it," Colonel Carter said. "You feed and you clean her—you; not the stable man. You lead her out to water and to walk. You put her on a long rope and let her play, calling her to you and gently pulling on the rope. Then you turn her loose in the grass lot there and, when she has romped till tired, call her. If she won't come, leave her. When she wants water or food, she

will run to your call, and you will pet and feed and care for her." He
went on for half an hour, advising me in great detail how to proceed. I
wanted to begin right away. He laughed. He let me lead her around to
the stable, water her, and put her in the stable and feed her.

There I saw my pony. My father, sisters, and Colonel Carter saw me
stop and look at my pony.

"What'll you do with him?" one of my sisters asked. I was bewildered
for a moment. What should I do with the little red horse? I decided at
once.

"You can have him," I said to my sisters.

"No," said Colonel Carter, "not yet. You can give your sisters the pony
by and by, but you'll need him till you have taught the colt to carry you
and a saddle—months; and you must not hurry. You must learn patience,
and you will if you give the colt time to learn it, too. Patience and control.
You can't control a young horse unless you can control yourself. Can you
shoot?" he asked suddenly.

I couldn't. I had a gun and I had used it some, but it was a rifle, and I
could not bring down with it such game as there was around Sacramento—
birds and hares. Colonel Carter looked at my father, and I caught the
look. So did my father. I soon had a shotgun. But at the time Colonel
Carter turned to me and said:

"Can't shoot straight, eh? Do you know what that means? That means
that you can't control a gun, and that means you can't control yourself,
your eye, your hands, your nerves. You are wriggling now. I tell you that
a good shot is always a good man. He may be a 'bad man' too, but he is
quiet, strong, steady in speech, gait, and mind. No matter, though. If
you break in this colt right, if you teach her her paces, she will teach
you to shoot and be quiet."

He went off downtown with my father, and I started away with my
colt. I fed, I led, I cleaned her, gently, as if she were made of glass; she
was playful and willing, a delight. When Colonel Carter came home with
my father for supper, he questioned me.

"You should not have worked her today," he said. "She has come all
the way from Stockton and must be tired. Yes, yes, she would not show
her fatigue; too fine for that, and too young to be wise. You have got to
think for her, consider her as you would your sisters."

Sisters! I thought; I had never considered my sisters. I did not say that,
but Colonel Carter laughed and nodded to my sisters. It was just as if he
had read my thought. But he went on to draw on my imagination a
centaur; the colt as a horse's body—me, a boy, as the head and brains of
one united creature. I liked that. I would be that. I and the colt: a centaur.

After Colonel Carter was gone home I went to work on my new horse.

The old one, the pony, I used only for business: to go to fires, to see my friends, run errands, and go hunting with my new shotgun. But the game that had all my attention was the breaking in of the colt, the beautiful cream-colored mare, who soon knew me — and my pockets. I carried sugar to reward her when she did right, and she discovered where I carried it; so did the pony, and when I was busy they would push their noses into my pockets, both of which were torn down a good deal of the time. But the colt learned. I taught her to run around a circle, turn and go the other way at a signal. My sisters helped me. I held the long rope and the whip for signaling), while one of the girls led the colt; it was hard work for them, but they took it in turns. One would lead the colt round and round till I snapped the whip; then she would turn, turning the colt, till the colt did it all by herself. And she was very quick. She shook hands with each of her four feet. She let us run under her, back and forth. She was slow only to carry me. Following Colonel Carter's instructions, I began by laying my arm or a surcingle over her back. If she trembled, I drew it slowly off. When she could abide it, I tried buckling it, tighter and tighter. I laid over her, too, a blanket, folded at first, then open, and, at last, I slipped up on her myself, sat there a second, and as she trembled, slid off. My sisters held her for me, and when I could get up and sit there a moment or two, I tied her at a block, and we, my sisters and I, made a procession of mounting and dismounting. She soon got used to this, and would let us slide off over her rump, but it was a long, long time before she would carry me.

That we practiced by leading her along a high curb where I could get on as she walked, ride a few steps, and then, as she felt me and crouched, slip off. She never did learn to carry a girl on her back; my sisters had to lead her while I rode. This was not purposeful. I don't know just how it happened, but I do remember the first time I rode on my colt all the way round the lot and how, when I put one of the girls up, she refused to repeat. She shuddered, shook and frightened them off.

While we were breaking in the colt a circus came to town. The ring was across the street from our house. Wonderful! I lived in that circus for a week. I saw the show but once, but I marked the horse-trainers, and in the mornings when they were not too busy I told them about my colt, showed her to them, and asked them how to train her to do circus tricks. With their hints I taught the colt to stand up on her hind legs, kneel, lie down, and balance on a small box. This last was easier than it looked. I put her first on a low big box and taught her to turn on it; then got a little smaller box upon which she repeated what she did on the big one. By and by we had her so that she would step up on a high box so small that her four feet were almost touching, and there also she would turn.

The circus man gave me one hint that was worth all the other tricks put together. "You catch her doing something of herself that looks good," he said, "and then you keep her at it." It was thus that I taught her to bow to people. The first day I rode her out on the streets was a proud one for me and for the colt, too, apparently. She did not walk, she danced; perhaps she was excited, nervous; anyhow I liked the way she threw up her head, champed at the bit, and went, dancing, prancing down the street. Everybody stopped to watch us, and so, when she began to sober down, I picked her up again with heel and rein, saying, "Here's people, Lady," and she would show off to my delight. By constant repetition I had her so trained that she would single-foot, head down, along a country road till we came to a house or a group of people. Then I'd say, "People, Lady," and up would go her head, and her feet would dance.

But the trick that set the town talking was her bowing to anyone I spoke to. "Lennie Steffens' horse bows to you," people said, and she did. I never told how it was done; by accident. Dogs used to run out at us and the colt enjoyed it; she kicked at them sometimes with both hind hoofs. I joined her in the game, and being able to look behind more conveniently than she could, I watched the dogs until they were in range, then gave the colt a signal to kick. "Kick, gal," I'd say, and tap her ribs with my heel. We used to get dogs together that way; the colt would kick them over and over and leave them yelping in the road. Well, one day when I met a girl I knew, I lifted my hat, probably muttered a "Good day," and I must have touched the colt with my heel. Anyway, she dropped her head and kicked—not much; there was no dog near, so she had responded to my unexpected signal by what looked like a bow. I caught the idea and kept her at it. Whenever I wanted to bow to a girl or anyone else, instead of saying "Good day," I muttered "Kick, gal," spurred her lightly, and—the whole centaur bowed and was covered with glory and conceit.

Yes, conceit. I was full of it, and the colt was quite as bad. One day my chum Hjalmar came into town on his Black Bess, blanketed. She had had a great fistula cut out of her shoulder and had to be kept warm. I expected to see her weak and dull, but no, the good old mare was champing and dancing, like my colt.

"What is it makes her so?" I asked, and Hjalmar said he didn't know, but he thought she was proud of the blanket. A great idea. I had a gaudy horse blanket. I put it on the colt, and I could hardly hold her. We rode down the main street together, both horses, and both boys, so full of vanity that everybody stopped to smile. We thought they admired, and maybe they did. But some boys on the street gave us another angle. They, too, stopped and looked, and as we passed, one of them said, "Think you're hell, don't you?"

Spoilsport!

We did, as a matter of fact; we thought we were hell. The recognition of it dashed us for a moment; not for long, and the horses paid no heed. We pranced, the black and the yellow, all the way down J Street, up K Street, and agreed that we'd do it again, often. Only I said, we wouldn't use blankets. If the horses were proud of a blanket, they'd be proud of anything unusually conspicuous. We tried a flower next time. I fixed a big rose on my colt's bridle just under her ear and it was great—she pranced downtown with her head turned, literally, to show off her flower. We had to change the decorations from time to time, put on a ribbon, or a bell, or a feather, but, really, it was not necessary for my horse. Old Black Bess needed an incentive to act up, but all I had to do to my horse was to pick up the reins, touch her with my heel, and say, "People"; she would dance from one side of the street to the other, asking to be admired. As she was. As we were.

I would ride down to my father's store, jump off my prancing colt in the middle of the street, and run up into the shop. The colt, free, would stop short, turn, and follow me right up on the sidewalk, unless I bade her wait. If anyone approached her while I was gone, she would snort, rear, and strike. No stranger could get near her. She became a frightened, frightening animal, and yet when I came into sight, she would run up to me, put her head down, and as I straddled her neck, she would throw up her head and pitch me into my seat, facing backwards, of course. I whirled around right, and off we'd go, the vainest boy and the proudest horse in the State.

"Hey, give me a ride, will you?" some boy would ask.

"Sure," I'd say, and jump down and watch the boy try to catch and mount my colt. He couldn't. Once a cowboy wanted to try her, and he caught her; he dodged her forefeet, grabbed the reins, and in one spring was on her back. I never did that again. My colt reared, then bucked, and, as the cowboy kept his seat, she shuddered, sank to the ground, and rolled over. He slipped aside and would have risen with her, but I was alarmed and begged him not to. She got up at my touch and followed me so close that she stepped on my heel and hurt me. The cowboy saw the point.

"If I were you, kid," he said, "I'd never let anybody mount that colt. She's too good."

That, I think, was the only mistake I made in the rearing of Colonel Carter's gift-horse. My father differed from me. He discovered another error or sin, and thrashed me for it. My practice was to work hard on a trick, privately, and when it was perfect, let him see it. I would have the horse out in our vacant lot doing it as he came home to supper. One evening, as he approached the house, I was standing, whip in hand, while the colt, quite free, was stepping carefully over the bodies of a lot of girls, all my sisters and all their girl friends. (Grace Gallatin, later Mrs. Thompson-Seton, was among them.) My father did not express the admiration I expected; he was frightened and furious. "Stop that," he called, and he came running around into the lot, took the whip, and lashed me with it. I tried to explain; the girls tried to help me explain.

I had seen in the circus a horse that stepped thus over a row of prostrate clowns. It looked dangerous for the clowns, but the trainer had told me how to do it. You begin with logs, laid out a certain distance apart; the horse walks over them under your lead, and whenever he touches one you rebuke him. By and by he will learn to step with such care that he never trips. Then you substitute clowns. I had no clowns, but I did get logs, and with the girls helping, we taught the colt to step over the obstacles even at a trot. Walking, she touched nothing. All ready thus with the logs, I had my sisters lie down in the grass, and again and again the colt stepped over them. None was ever touched. My father would not listen to any of this; he just walloped me, and when he was tired or satisfied and I was in tears, I blubbered a short excuse: "They were only girls." And he whipped me some more.

My father was not given to whipping; he did it very seldom, but he did it hard when he did it at all. My mother was just the opposite. She did not whip me, but she often smacked me, and she had a most annoying habit of thumping me on the head with her thimbled finger. This I resented more than my father's thoroughgoing thrashings, and I can tell why now. I would be playing Napoleon and as I was reviewing my Old Guard, she would crack my skull with that thimble. No doubt I was in the way; it took a lot of furniture and sisters to represent properly a victorious army; and you might think as my mother did that a thimble is a small weapon. But imagine Napoleon at the height of his power, the ruler of the world on parade, getting a sharp rap on his crown from a woman's thimble. No. My father's way was more appropriate. It was hard. "I'll attend to you in the morning," he would say, and I lay awake wondering which of my crimes he had discovered. I know what it is to be sentenced to be shot at sunrise. And it hurt, in the morning, when he was not angry but very fresh and strong. But you see, he walloped me in my own person; he never humiliated Napoleon or my knighthood, as my mother did. And I learned something from his discipline, something useful.

I learned what tyranny is and the pain of being misunderstood and wronged, or, if you please, understood and set right; they are pretty much the same. He and most parents and teachers do not break in their boys as carefully as I broke in my colt. They haven't the time that I had, and they have not some other incentives I had. I saw this that day when I rubbed my sore legs. He had to explain to my indignant mother what had happened. When he had told it his way, I gave my version: how long and cautiously I had been teaching my horse to walk over logs and girls. And having shown how sure I was of myself and the colt, while my mother was boring into his silence with one of her reproachful looks, I said something that hit my father hard.

"I taught the colt that trick, I have taught her all that you see she knows, without whipping her. I have never struck her; not once. Colonel Carter said I mustn't and I haven't."

And my mother, backing me up, gave him a rap: "There," she said, "I told you so." He walked off, looking like a thimble-rapped Napoleon.

⌄ JUST BECAUSE I WANT TO PLAY

Edward Bok

The real trouble with the American business man is that in many instances he is actually afraid to let go because, out of business he would not know what to do. For years he has so immersed himself in his business to the exclusion of all other interests that at fifty or seventy he finds himself a slave to his business, with positively no inner resources. Retirement from the one thing that he does know would leave a man useless to himself, his family, and his community; worse than useless, as a matter of fact, for he would become a burden to himself and a nuisance to his family. You rarely ever find a European or English business man reaching a mature age devoid of outside interests; he always lets the breezes of other worlds blow over his mentality when he is in affairs, with the result that, when he is ready to retire from business, he has other interests to fall back upon. This is rarely the case with the American business man. It is becoming more frequent that we see American men retiring from business and devoting themselves to other interests, and their number will undoubtedly increase as time goes on and we learn the lessons of life with a richer background. But one cannot help feeling regretful that the number is not growing larger more rapidly.

EXTRAORDINARY WAGER

The London Morning Post says a wager came off, the terms of which were as follows:—

"I will bet any man one hundred pounds that he cannot make a million strokes with pen and ink within a month." They were not to be mere dots or scratches, but fair down strokes, such as form the child's first lesson in writing. A gentleman accepted the challenge. The month allowed was the lunar month, of only twenty-eight days; so that, for the completion of the undertaking, an average of thirty-six thousand strokes per diem was required. This, at sixty per minute, or three thousand six hundred per hour,—and neither the human intellect nor the human hand can be expected to do more,—would call for ten hours' labor in every four and twenty. With a proper feeling of the respect due to the observance of the Sabbath, he determined to abstain from his work on the Sundays; and by this determination, he diminished by four days the period allowed him; at the same time, by so doing, he increased the daily average of his strokes to upwards of forty-one thousand. On the first day he executed about fifty thousand strokes; on the second, nearly as many. But at length, after many days, the hand became stiff and weary, the wrist swollen, and it required the almost constant attendance of some assiduous relation or friend to besprinkle it, without interrupting its progress over the paper, with a lotion calculated to relieve and invigorate it. On the twenty-third day, the million strokes, exceeded by some few thousands, "to make assurance doubly sure," are accomplished; and the piles of paper that exhibit them testify that to the courageous heart, the willing hand, and the energetic mind, nothing is impossible. These interesting papers are not placed in the archives of the Royal Society, of which their author is a fellow, but were claimed and received by the person who paid the wager.

SEÑOR PAYROLL

William E. Barrett

Larry and I were Junior Engineers in the gas plant, which means that we were clerks. Anything that could be classified as paper work came to the flat double desk across which we faced each other. The

Main Office downtown sent us a bewildering array of orders and rules that were to be put into effect.

Junior Engineers were beneath the notice of everyone except the Mexican laborers at the plant. To them we were the visible form of a distant, unknowable paymaster. We were Señor Payroll.

Those Mexicans were great workmen; the aristocrats among them were the stokers, big men who worked Herculean eight-hour shifts in the fierce heat of the retorts. They scooped coal with huge shovels and hurled it with uncanny aim at tiny doors. The coal streamed out from the shovels like black water from a high-pressure nozzle, and never missed the narrow opening. The stokers worked stripped to the waist, and there was pride and dignity in them. Few men could do such work, and they were the few.

The Company paid its men only twice a month, on the fifth and on the twentieth. To a Mexican, this was absurd. What man with money will make it last fifteen days? If he hoarded money beyond the spending of three days, he was a miser—and when, Señor, did the blood of Spain flow in the veins of misers? Hence, it was the custom of our stokers to appear every third or fourth day to draw the money due to them.

There was a certain elasticity in the Company rules, and Larry and I sent the necessary forms to the Main Office and received an "advance" against a man's pay check. Then, one day, Downtown favored us with a memorandum:

"There have been too many abuses of the advance-against-wages privilege. Hereafter, no advance against wages will be made to any employee except in a case of genuine emergency."

We had no sooner posted the notice when in came stoker Juan Garcia. He asked for an advance. I pointed to the notice. He spelled it through slowly, then said, "What does this mean, this 'genuine emergency'?"

I explained to him patiently that the Company was kind and sympathetic, but that it was a great nuisance to have to pay wages every few days. If someone was ill or if money was urgently needed for some other good reason, then the Company would make an exception to the rule.

Juan Garcia turned his hat over and over slowly in his big hands. "I do not get my money?"

"Next payday, Juan. On the twentieth."

He went out silently and I felt a little ashamed of myself. I looked across the desk at Larry. He avoided my eyes.

In the next hour two other stokers came in, looked at the notice, had it explained and walked solemnly out; then no more came. What we did not know was that Juan Garcia, Pete Mendoza, and Francisco Gonzalez had spread the word, and that every Mexican in the plant was explaining the order to every other Mexican. "To get money now, the wife must be sick. There must be medicine for the baby."

The next morning Juan Garcia's wife was practically dying, Pete Mendoza's mother would hardly last the day, there was a veritable epidemic among children, and, just for variety, there was one sick father. We always suspected that the old man was really sick; no Mexican would otherwise have thought of him. At any rate, nobody paid Larry and me to examine private lives; we made out our forms with an added line describing the "genuine emergency." Our people got paid.

That went on for a week. Then came a new order, curt and to the point: "Hereafter, employees will be paid ONLY on the fifth and the twentieth of the month. No exceptions will be made except in the cases of employees leaving the service of the Company."

The notice went up on the board, and we explained its significance gravely, "No, Juan Garcia, we cannot advance your wages. It is too bad about your wife and your cousins and your aunts, but there is a new rule."

Juan Garcia went out and thought it over. He thought out loud with Mendoza and Gonzales and Ayala, then, in the morning, he was back. "I am quitting this company for different job. You pay me now?"

We argued that it was a good company and that it loved its employees like children, but in the end we paid off, because Juan Garcia quit. And so did Gonzalez, Mendoza, Obregon, Ayala and Ortez, the best stokers, men who could not be replaced.

Larry and I looked at each other; we knew what was coming in about three days. One of our duties was to sit on the hiring line early each morning, engaging transient workers for the handy gangs. Any man was accepted who could walk up and ask for a job without falling down. Never before had we been called upon to hire such skilled virtuosos as stokers for handy-gang work, but we were called upon to hire them now.

The day foreman was wringing his hands and asking the Almighty if he was personally supposed to shovel this condemned coal, while there in a stolid, patient line were skilled men—Garcia, Mendoza, and others—waiting to be hired. We hired them, of course. There was nothing else to do.

Every day we had a line of resigning stokers, and another line of stokers seeking work. Our paper work became very complicated. At the Main Office they were jumping up and down. The procession of forms showing Juan Garcia's resigning and being hired over and over again was too much for them. Sometimes Downtown had Garcia on the payroll twice at the same time when someone down there was slow in entering a resignation. Our phone rang early and often.

Tolerantly and patiently we explained: "There's nothing we can do if a man wants to quit, and if there are stokers available when the plant needs stokers, we hire them."

Out of chaos, Downtown issued another order. I read it and whistled. Larry looked at it and said, "It is going to be very quiet around here."

The order read: "Hereafter, no employee who resigns may be rehired within a period of 30 days."

Juan Garcia was due for another resignation, and when he came in we showed him the order and explained that standing in line the next day would do him no good if he resigned today. "Thirty days is a long time, Juan."

It was a grave matter and he took time to reflect on it. So did Gonzalez, Mendoza, Ayala and Ortez. Ultimately, however, they were all back—and all resigned.

We did our best to dissuade them and we were sad about the parting. This time it was for keeps and they shook hands with us solemnly. It was very nice knowing us. Larry and I looked at each other when they were gone and we both knew that neither of us had been pulling for Downtown to win this duel. It was a blue day.

In the morning, however, they were all back in line. With the utmost gravity, Juan Garcia informed me that he was a stoker looking for a job.

"No dice, Juan," I said. "Come back in thirty days. I warned you."

His eyes looked straight into mine without a flicker. "There is some mistake, Señor," he said. "I am Manuel Hernandez. I work at the stoker in Pueblo, in Santa Fe, in many places."

I stared back at him, remembering the sick wife and the babies without medicine, the mother-in-law in the hospital, the many resignations and the rehirings. I knew that there was a gas plant in Pueblo, and that there wasn't any in Santa Fe; but who was I to argue with a man about his own name? A stoker is a stoker.

So I hired him. I hired Gonzalez, too, who swore that his name was Carrera, and Ayala, who had shamelessly become Smith.

Three days later the resigning started.

Within a week our payroll read like a history of Latin America. Everyone was on it: Lopez and Obregon, Villa, Diaz, Batista, Gomez, and even San Martín and Bolívar. Finally Larry and I, growing weary of staring at familiar faces and writing unfamiliar names, went to the Superintendent and told him the whole story. He tried not to grin, and said, "Damned nonsense!"

The next day the orders were taken down. We called our most prominent stokers into the office and pointed to the board. No rules any more.

"The next time we hire you hombres," Larry said grimly, "come in under the names you like best, because that's the way you are going to stay on the books."

They looked at us and they looked at the board; then for the first time in the long duel, their teeth flashed white. "Si, Señores," they said.

And so it was.

BROTHERING FISH

William Beebe

You are standing on a metal ladder in water up to your neck. Something round and heavy is slipped gently over your head, and a metal helmet rests upon your shoulders. Thus were the knights of old helmeted by their squires for the grim business of war. Instead of a slotted vizor, however, you find two large frames of glass before your eyes. Turning your head, you see emerald waves breaking upon the distant beach of ivory, backed by feathery palms waving in the sunlight against the sky of pure azure.

You wave good-by to your grinning friend at the pump, and slowly descend, climbing down step by step. For a brief space of time the palms and the beach show intermittently through waves which are now breaking over your very face. Then the world changes. There is no more harsh sunlight, but delicate blue-greens with a fluttering of shadows everywhere. Huge pink and orange growths rise on all sides—you know they are living corals, just as you know that the perfect clouds in the sky visible in the earliest light of dawn from Darjeeling are not clouds, but the snow peaks of the distant Himalayas. The first little people of this strange realm greet you—a quartet of swimming rainbows—four gorgeously tinted fish who rush up and peer in at you. You reach out for them, and they vanish.

Now your feet touch ground, and you walk slowly about on the cleanest white sand in the world. An ostrich feather of a sea-plume as tall as yourself sweeps against you; it is royal purple and might well be some weird fern from Mars. On a mound of sand you gently seat yourself, sand colored crabs and small fish skittering just out of the way. You lean against a fretwork of purest marble while at your elbow is a rounded table of lapis lazuli on which are blossoming three flowers—flowers unearthly and which lean toward you of their own free will. Their petals are resplendent in hues of gold and malachite, and are fluted and fringed like some rare and unknown orchid. You reach forward to pluck one, and, faster than the eye can follow, the blossoms disappear beneath the fur of lapis velvet from which they seemed to sprout.

Dozens of fishes, all strange, all graceful and beautiful, play about you, nibbling at the coral, rushing toward the sponge which you have lifted from its place, hoping for some disturbed titbit. When you sit quietly, they gather closer and peer in through the glass at you again and again. Their absurd mouths forever open and close, and if you are a good lip-reader, you cannot fail to decipher the syllables which seem to issue in watery waves. They say, "Oh! Oh! Brother! Brother! Oh! Oh!" And you answer them in kind, speaking from the safe, dry, airy room of your helmet. They are so friendly, so curious, so utterly unlike the nervous, useless-lived inmates of our aquariums.

Your attention swings from wonders to marvels and back again. You begin to say things to yourself, gasps of surprise, inarticulate sounds of awe; you are troubled with a terrible sense of loss that (as the case may be) twenty, thirty, or fifty years of your life have passed and gone without your knowing the ease of entry into this new world. Are you under water? There is no sense of wetness; the air you breathe is, if anything, better than that in the motor-boat rocking overhead. You hold up your hand and see little washerwoman's wrinkles on the soles of your fingers, and you realize you are where you are. A great blue enameled fish glides past, then suddenly stands straight upon his head and mumbles something; a skein of fairy lace drifts against your helmet, to your friends in the boat it is merely a school of jelly-fish.

Only a moment has passed since you left the world overhead, or was it many hours? A gentle tug comes along the hose, and you resent this reminder of an existence which you had almost forgotten. But you rise and half walk, half float to the swaying ladder, and regretfully mount it. You find that you have been down forty minutes and another impatient adventurer is waiting to take your place. You had planned to tell the others all about it, but you suddenly find yourself wordless. You exclaim something bromidic which sounds like Marvellous! Great! Wonderful, then relapse futilely into silence and look helplessly into the distance where the emerald waves still break and the palms wave as if fairyland had not intervened in your life since you saw them last.

All I ask of each reader is this—Don't die without having borrowed, stolen, purchased, or made a helmet of sorts, to glimpse for yourself this new world. Books, aquaria, and glass-bottomed boats are, to such an experience, only what a time-table is to an actual tour, or what a dried, dusty bit of coral in the whatnot of the best parlor is to this unsuspected realm of gorgeous life and color existing with us today on the selfsame planet Earth.

WHY GO TO COLLEGE?

Robert M. Hutchins

Most American parents want to send their children to college. And their children, for the most part, are anxious to go. It is an American tradition that there is something about a college that transforms an ordinary infant into a superior adult. Men and women who have been to college sometimes suspect that this is not the case, but they seldom say so. They are alumni, and, as such, it is their life work to maintain the tradition that college—their college anyway—is the greatest place in the world.

College is the greatest place in the world for those who ought to go to college and who go for the right reasons. For those who ought not to go to college or who go for the wrong reasons, college is a waste of time and money.

Who should go to college? In order to answer this question, we might well begin by deciding who should not. My experience with college, as student, teacher and commencement orator, convinces me that the following persons should not go to college:

Children whose parents have no other reason for sending them than that they can afford to.

Children whose parents have no other reason for sending them than to get them off their hands for four years.

Children whose characters are bad and whose parents believe that college will change them for the better.

Children who have no other reason for going to college than to avoid work or have a good time for four years.

Children who have no other reason for going to college than to have a stadium in which to demonstrate their athletic ability.

Children who have no other reason for going to college than the notion that it will help them achieve social or financial success in later life.

These children should be kept at home, or they should be sent to a country club, a trade school, or a body-building institute. There is, or should be, no place for them in an institution whose only excuse for existing is the training of the mind.

If we may then proceed to the original question—"Who should go to college?"—I submit the following answer:

Anyone should go to college who has demonstrated both an aptitude and a desire for more education than he has been able to get in elementary and high school.

PRELUDE TO REUNION

Oliver La Farge

The room was furnished with what the college issued: a desk, placed dead center under the overhead light, a table, three wooden chairs, a bed, a bureau, and an empty fireplace, the brick floor of which was free of ashes and cigarette butts. One shelf of the bookcase was almost filled with textbooks, a one-volume edition of Shakespeare, and a Bible. On the table were two notebooks and a dictionary, a cup and saucer, a plate, and a small electric stove with a sauce-pan on it. A calendar and two pine cones had been arranged on the mantelpiece in an effort at decoration. There was a framed photograph of a middle-aged woman on the bureau, and two neckties hung from a corner of the mirror. The room looked as if its occupant had moved in that afternoon and would leave tomorrow.

The boy paced slowly, methodically, between the fireplace and the bookcase. Passing the window, he caught the smell of the night—the new, disturbing mildness of spring—and he could hear voices below on the campus. He was tall, thin, fair-haired, with too much Adam's apple and too long a nose. He was not thinking, he was stringing out the time before he should decide to take a walk.

In a few moments he would put on a necktie and coat and go downstairs. As he stepped outside, he would feel a faint anticipation, a nameless, automatic stirring of hope, which he would quickly discount by a defensive reflex, a moment of pain never admitted. Then he would stroll. If he met fellows who sat in his classes, he would walk a little faster until he passed them, but sometimes even so they would remember him and nod, or say "Hello" or even "Hello, Matterson." He would say "Hello" and go on by, letting them continue their appointed ways. His own pace, too, would be a declaration that he was going somewhere.

By one route or another he would come to the Women's School. Here his walk would be a swinging, unhesitating stride. He would not turn his head, he would just go on through, but his eyes would take in a wide range, the groups of girls and the pairs of girls and fellows. Last week, the first night of the warm weather, a man who sat next to him in biochemistry passed him with a girl. He said, "Hi, Matterson. Sparking?" He'd answered, "Hello, Newman. Just scouting," and Newman and the girl had laughed.

They were all just kids, really—as old as he, but nothing had taught them seriousness. His brain could run rings around them. He wasn't interested in their eternal play.

Beyond the School he would come out into the town, buy a paper, and then return to his room, the room he was walking up and down now, not thinking anything much except that it was time, perhaps, to go out and get a paper.

A firm knock on his door brought him up sharp. He moved to open it, then stood back and called, "Come in!"

The visitor, who entered rather self-consciously, was a well-dressed boy of medium height, neither fair nor dark, with a scrubbed, healthy face.

"Matterson?" he said. "I'm Bill Farraday. May I come in?"

"Hello. Sit down." His anger at himself for being so tense added to his stiffness.

"I live in this entry, 2 B."

Matterson knew well enough, as he knew that Farraday had his letter in hockey and was a candidate for class marshal. He nodded, watchful.

Farraday arranged himself with an effect of relaxation for which the chair was not well adapted. He looked around the room, said "Nice," then broke off. The thin boy understood; it wasn't a nice joint. Seeing that his visitor was ill at ease, he felt a shade more comfortable.

"Looks like spring had really come, doesn't it?" Farraday said. He became more assured at the sound of his own voice. "Here the winter's over, and this is the first time I've been up here." Matterson listened, guarded, protecting himself. "This college is so damn big you can't hope to know everyone, but I'd promised myself to meet all the men in this entry. You know how it is. You get tied up in so many things and the first thing you know the ice has melted and the ball team's coming out of the cage."

Matterson said, "Yeah."

"Where do you come from? You're not from around here, are you?"

"Vermont."

"Well! Why did you pick to come here?"

"I'm going into analytical chemistry and I wanted to be under MacPherson."

"Oh. Oh, yeah, sure." Farraday paused again, then took off as if from a cue. "You had a scholarship?"

"Not to start with; the first two years I worked my way. Then I got the Bernstein." He was proud of that; it was the best there was in science for undergraduates. "Now I'm hoping for the Marlin Fellowship if I can get my *magna cum* all right."

Farraday looked vaguely uncomfortable. The look passed. "Good for you. I admire a guy like you and I'm glad I came up." Again his flow of talk became smooth. His voice had a flattering frankness. "Yeah, when I get out of here I'll go to Wall Street, and I guess that twenty years from now I'll just be another bond salesman living the old country-club life, and I'll be bragging about how I used to know you. I've had it easy and you've had it tough."

The Vermonter felt an unfamiliar warmth run through him. "It's been tough sometimes," he said. He hesitated, then added with an effort, "I saw you shoot that long goal against Colmouth."

"Oh, that was just luck." Farraday was visibly pleased. He pulled out a pack of cigarettes. "Smoke?"

"No, thanks."

"Oh. Do you mind—"

"Go ahead."

"Come down to my room sometime, won't you? Sling the bull, you know. I generally have a little beer on hand—or ginger ale."

"I like beer." Matterson considered explaining that he didn't smoke on account of the expense, then decided not to.

Farraday brightened. "That's fine. I mean it. Drop in."

"Thanks." He wanted to say more, but didn't know how.

"Say, a man like you, working your way along, and then getting fellowships and things—I'd like your slant on this endowment business."

Matterson had read the ballyhoo with a mounting sense of discomfort. The University was driving for extra endowment and the Senior Class Committee had voted a graduation gift of fifteen thousand dollars, which would mean a little over twenty dollars a member. The gift was getting a big play from the Endowment Fund's publicity bureau in going after the graduates.

"Well," he said, "I guess it's a good idea."

"Yeah, I think so, too. Our tuition fees don't cover the cost of our education. When you average it up—the men on scholarship and things— the University gives us nearly a thousand dollars." Farraday caught himself up. "Of course," he said hastily, "that's what you expect the old place to do—help the men like you who really have brains. It's part of a university's proper function." He looked around. "Got an ash tray?"

"Chuck it in the fireplace."

Farraday threw the butt, then pulled out the pack again. "I guess I'm smoking a lot right now. What with finals coming on and all the boning up to do and one thing and another, I get kind of nervous." He lit up. "This endowment business on top of the rest has me about daffy. You see, I'm in charge of this entry and we're short on our quota. I dunno how it is, some of the fellows don't seem to appreciate what the old school does for them. I guess I'm a rotten collector; it kind of burns me up to get after a man if he isn't willing." He gave a short, unreal laugh. "Yeah, I hate doing it. I've upped my share to fifty bucks, though God knows, I guess it means the sheriff will be after me, what with the old unpaid bills and all." He made the last statement with a smile, as one man speaking to another of a common problem.

Matterson just watched him, saying nothing.

"I've got you down for five bucks," Farraday said. "Of course, it's up to you. You know what you can afford, spreading it over the next two months."

Matterson continued staring at him. Out of a swirl inside himself he said quietly, without a shade of defiance in his tone, "You can put me down for ten."

"Why, say, that's great. Say, that's the real spirit, Matterson. Wait till I tell some of the other men that, the ones who've been holding out." He pulled at his cigarette, held it a moment, threw it in the fireplace. "Yeah, that's great. Well, look, I've go to get after some of the others now." He rose. "Don't forget to drop in on me sometime."

Matterson said, "Sure. Thanks."

Farraday answered heartily, "Thanks to you. Well, so long. Be seeing you."

"So long."

Matterson sat and stared at the long-awaited, casual disorder of the two cigarette stubs in the fireplace. Then he stood with his hands in his pockets. Ten dollars was catastrophic. Double what the rich boy thought him good for—pride stiffened in him, covering the pain of a warm moment betrayed. More slowly than usual, he tied his necktie, put on his coat, and went out.

∨ PUNCTUATION AND MEANING

Harry Shaw

Edgar Allen Poe was hardly exaggerating when he said: "Even where the sense is perfectly clear, a sentence may be deprived of half its force—its spirit—its point by improper punctuation."

When you talk you do not depend upon words alone to tell your listener what you mean. Facial and bodily gestures can and do add much to the words themselves: you shrug a shoulder, wiggle a finger, raise an eyebrow, wink, clasp hands, bend forward or backward, grin or grimace, stamp your foot, nod or shake your head. The tone and stress of your voice can and do influence the meaning of words you speak: you yell or whisper; speak calmly or angrily; lower or raise your voice at the end of a statement or a question. Meaning in talk is affected by pauses and halts which are often as significant as the words themselves. . . .

Similarly, when we write we cannot expect words alone to make clear to our reader what we have or think we have in mind. The pauses, stresses, and inflections which occur in speech must be represented in writing by various marks of punctuation if meaning is to be fully clear. The needs of the eye are quite different from those of the voice and ear.

Punctuation came into existence solely for the purpose of making clear the meaning of written words. Every mark of punctuation is a sort of shorthand device or road sign provided to help the reader along his way.

The relationship between parts of a sentence is revealed by word order; words in an English sentence have meaning largely because of their position. . . . In written English, various marks of punctuation both suggest and indicate the grouping and relationship required to convey meaning clearly. . . .

Correct punctuation is organic, not merely mechanical and arbitrary. . . . By *organic* is meant "belonging to, an essential part of." . . . Correct punctuation is itself a form of communication. And communication is, or should be, the primary purpose of all writing. . . .

✓ WHICH

James Thurber

The relative pronoun "which" can cause more trouble than any other word, if recklessly used. Foolhardy persons sometimes get lost in which-clauses and are never heard of again. My distinguished contemporary, Fowler, cites several tragic cases, of which the following is one: "It was rumoured that Beaconsfield intended opening the Conference with a speech in French, his pronunciation of which language leaving everything to be desired . . ." That's as much as Mr. Fowler quotes because, at his age, he was afraid to go any farther. The young man who originally got into that sentence was never found. His fate, however, was not as terrible as that of another adventurer who became involved in a remarkable which-mire. Fowler has followed his devious course as far as he safely could on foot: "Surely what applies to games should apply to racing, the leaders of which being the very people from whom an example might well be looked for . . ." Not even Henry James could have successfully emerged from a sentence with "which," "whom," and "being" in it. The safest way to avoid such things is to follow in the path of the American author, Ernest Hemingway. In his youth he was trapped in a which-clause one time and barely escaped with his mind. He was going along on solid ground until he got into this: "It was the one thing of which, being very much afraid—for whom has not been warned to fear such things—he . . ." Being a young and powerfully built man, Hemingway was able to fight his way back to where he had started, and begin again. This time he skirted the treacherous morass in this way: "He was afraid of one thing. This was the one thing. He had been warned to fear such things. Everybody has been warned to fear such things." Today Hemingway is alive and well, and many happy writers are following along the trail he blazed.

What most people don't realize is that one "which" leads to another. Trying to cross a paragraph by leaping from "which" to "which" is like Eliza crossing the ice. The danger is in missing a "which" and falling in. A case in point is this: "He went up to a pew which was in the gallery, which brought him under a colored window which he loved and always quieted his spirit." The writer, worn out, missed the last "which"—the one that should come just before "always" in that sentence. But supposing he had got it in! We would have: "He went up to a pew which was in the gallery, which brought him under a colored window which he loved and which always quieted his spirit." Your inveterate whicher in this way gives the effect to tweeting like a bird or walking with a crutch, and is not welcome in the best company.

It is well to remember that one "which" leads to two and that two "whiches" multiply like rabbits. You should never start out with the idea that you can get by with one "which." Suddenly they are all around you. Take a sentence like this: "It imposes a problem which we either solve, or perish." On a hot night, or after a hard day's work, a man often lets himself get by with a monstrosity like that, but suppose he dictates that sentence bright and early in the morning. It comes to him typed out by his stenographer and he instantly senses that something is the matter with it. He tries to reconstruct the sentence, still clinging to the "which," and gets something like this: "It imposes a problem which we either solve, or which, failing to solve, we must perish on account of." He goes to the water-cooler, gets a drink, sharpens his pencil, and grimly tries again. "It imposes a problem which we either solve or which we don't solve and..." He begins once more: "It imposes a problem which we either solve, or which we do not solve, and from which..." The more times he does it the more "whiches" he gets. The way out is simple: "We must either solve this problem, or perish." Never monkey with "which." Nothing except getting tangled up in a typewriter ribbon is worse.

⟋ THE CURTAIN IS THE PICTURE

About the year 455 B.C., an improved style of painting was introduced in Athens by a celebrated painter named Zeuxis. The aim of this new style was illusion of the senses. Zeuxis soon acquired great wealth by his paintings, and was very ostentatious in the display of it. The same vanity is shown by the fact that, after he had reached the summit of his fame, he no longer sold, but gave away, his pictures, as being above all price.

He was a great master of color: and in this lay the secret of his success, and of that of his school; for it rendered his paintings so accurate and lifelike that they amounted to illusion. This is exemplified in the story told of him and Parrhasius. As a trial, these artists were appointed to paint each a picture. That of Zeuxis represented a bunch of grapes; and so naturally was it represented, that the birds came and pecked at it.

After this proof, Zeuxis, confident of success, called upon his rival to draw aside the curtain that concealed his picture. "The curtain is the picture," replied Parrhasius; and Zeuxis was obliged to acknowledge himself vanquished, for though he had deceived birds, Parrhasius had deceived him.

⟋ WHAT IS LITERATURE?

Edwin Greenlaw

Literature is the record of the adventures of the soul of man as he struggles to understand himself and the world in which he lives. It is one of the chief sources of right enjoyment and of right thinking.

In it we find not merely a subject to be studied in school as a series of lessons, but a means of satisfying our curiosity about life, of living more lives than one. It opens a world of fancy and imagination into which we go at will just as Ali Baba or Aladdin could enter the world of magic by using a charm. It opens a world of heroic action, through which the desire to do worthy things may be born in us. It opens a world of sympathy and service because it shows how men have sought for realization of their highest ideals through service to their fellows. And it brings enrichment through knowledge of the world of Nature, a perception of the beauty of Nature and of the way in which Nature serves man as the genius of the lamp served Aladdin. Poetry, drama, story, all writing that men have preserved because of its beauty or its enduring worth, these are means for recreation and for growth. By reading, man is lifted far above the realm in which animals pass their lives, and is taught how to crowd into his brief years enjoyment and experience that make rich his life and multiply his powers.

TWO VIEWS ON CENSORSHIP

John Ciardi and Walter Lippmann

John Ciardi: I am not well disposed, let me say, to banning any book. I believe that parents who have reared their children in sympathy, and yet within a sense of this world as it goes, have nothing to fear from what the children read. And it is always likely—it seems, in fact, certain—that any statute framed to suppress pornography will be used to suppress the work of serious writers. It is, I believe, socially irresponsible to let moral indignation bring about statutes that cannot, by their nature, be responsibly phrased to cover all cases. The only consequence of such statutes is that the good will be damned with the bad—a clear affront to the legal principle that it is better for a hundred guilty persons to go free than to punish one innocent person. These, I submit, are ponderable reasons for opposing legal censorship of any sort, and I must take them to be sufficient.

Walter Lippmann: ... There can be no real doubt, it seems to me, that the movies and television and the comic books are purveying violence and lust to a vicious and intolerable degree. There can be no real doubt that public exhibitions of sadism tend to excite sadistic desires. Nor can there be any real doubt that there is a close connection between the suddenness of the increase in sadistic crimes and the vogue among mass media...

Censorship is no doubt a clumsy and usually a stupid and self-defeating remedy for such evils. But a continual exposure of a generation to the commercial exploitation of the enjoyment of violence and cruelty is one way to corrode the foundations of a civilized society. For my part, believing as I do in freedom of speech and thought, I see no objection in principle to censorship of the mass entertainment of the young. Until some more refined way is worked out of controlling this evil thing, the risks of our liberties are, I believe, decidedly less than the risks of unmanageable violence.

WE CAPTURE GORILLAS ALIVE

Martin Johnson

[The most convenient and safest place for you to study wild animals is the zoo. Of all the cages the greatest attraction to the visitors is the section containing monkeys and apes. Whenever you see a gorilla, the largest and most powerful of the apes, you may be sure that it was born near the equator in West Africa. How it may have been forced to leave its tropical home, even though it is much stronger than any man, is made clear in the following selection.]

I had lost all faith in the native method of capturing gorillas. I doubt if a native ever caught a big one alive, and I was beginning to look with pessimism on our chances of taking one of the apes when the eventful day dawned. About twenty miles from camp we stopped to address some natives.

"Have you seen any gorillas?" I inquired in a makeshift language.

"Why, yes," one answered, "we just heard them at the side of the road."

We got out of the car, listened, and, sure enough, heard the animals not more than a hundred feet above us. With porters toting the cameras we began climbing up the hillside. The bamboo was not so thick as that to which we had been accustomed, and wide trails led in every direction. The thought struck me that this spot must have been the headquarters of all the gorillas on the mountain.

In five minutes we were upon the pack, but they saw us as soon as we saw them and hied themselves away. Following, we lost track of them, but kept on going, never wandering far from the road. Catching the tell-tale sounds of another pack, I called a halt and crept warily forward alone with my camera. I had negotiated only about a hundred feet when the gorillas sensed my presence and began to scream. Throwing all caution to the winds, I dashed headlong in their direction. I could hear the rest of my party following. I came upon two youngsters at the foot of a tree and kept on toward them, my hand camera ready to spin.

This maneuver on my part astonished the apes to such a degree that they completely lost their heads and instead of running away, leaped into a tree about a foot in diameter at the base and about eighty feet high. The animals were climbing hand over hand up in the branches when the other members of the party appeared. Here was a new situation, with the apes above us this time, in a position from which they could not escape. I decided to try my own system of capturing gorillas. There were two other vine-clad trees near by into which I feared the animals might leap; so I ordered my boys to cut down everything around the tree in which our quarry was trapped.

I set off in the direction in which the other members of the pack had scooted, expecting not to find them. But the old silverback, apparently worried about the two youngsters in the tree, rushed at me as I broke my way through the brush. Like all of the gorilla charges we had faced, this, too, was merely a bluff. I got a good look at the silverback.... He was the biggest gorilla I ever saw.

Carrying a camera and accompanied by Lew and Dick, armed with elephant guns, I took up the chase of the big silverback. He charged and retreated, stamping up and down in the jungle on stiff legs. Five times he came at me, screeching with frenzy, while I was busily taking pictures. Then, abandoning his attempt to protect the youngsters, the old fellow ran away uttering invectives and lamentations.

He didn't escape us, however. We kept right on his trail until we saw him with seven others. He acted as a rear guard as the others retreated, charging at us when we neared the pack. I never saw a gorilla so enraged as this one, and was really apprehensive for our safety. The silverback shrieked his hate and defiance. He picked up bamboo sticks and broke them, screaming ferociously during the entire time and prancing about on stiffened legs. As we cautiously proceeded, however, he gave ground, continuing toward his pack.

We reached a donga and saw the gorilla cross a small stream on a fallen log. Lew counted ten of them, but I paid no attention to that. My mind was on the big fellow. I crossed the log after him. He made one more charge and then disappeared with the rest of the pack into the jungle too dense for us to travel through. It was keen fun, the brush with this silverback. I was confident that his rushes were only bluffs to cover the retreat of his fellows and that he would not complete a charge. I made some good film of him. As I indicated before, gorilla hunting has more thrills to the square inch and is more exciting than any other sport I know of.

We returned to our gorilla tree and found the boys working feverishly to clear the ground below. They, too, were filled with enthusiasm and eagerness over our plans to attempt a capture. DeWitt was back on the road, enlisting natives to aid us. Shortly he returned with twenty men, and we put them to work at assisting with the clearing.

While this was in progress, I took pictures of the gorillas and also studied them. I began to sympathize with the youngsters. They really looked pathetic, sitting up there watching every move we made. They climbed as high as they could, clung to the branches and stared down, wondering what would happen next.

An hour was consumed in taking pictures with various lenses and cameras before stopping off for lunch. The black boys cleared a hundred-foot circle around the tree and cut out a two-hundred-foot space where we knew it would fall when we chopped it down. We now prepared for a battle, often imagined in fiction—the hand-to-hand struggle between gorillas and man.

I set up a motion picture camera for Osa to use during the capture. DeWitt and I put on all the coats we could find and donned gloves. The boys got all of the tarpaulin and blankets from the motorcar. We then formed in a circle about the spot on which the top of the tree would fall. The stage all set, I gave the signal that started two axmen hewing at the tree trunk.

The tree swayed, began to crack, and fell with a roaring thump as branches were crushed against the ground. The gorillas, falling with arms clasped about each other, were stunned, and before they knew what was happening, we were upon them. Bukari, the gun boy, won the honors of the day, capturing one of the animals single-handed. The tree was still groaning from the crash when he dived in. He grabbed a gorilla and had it wrapped helplessly in a tarpaulin before the brute knew what was up. A dozen boys were on the other animal, tangling him up in blankets and tarpaulins. The capture was accomplished so quickly that I had no chance to do anything but shout orders. DeWitt likewise was left out of the action, our black boys being too quick for him. Dick and Lew were all over the place taking pictures with the cameras.

It was as pretty a bit of action as I have ever hoped to see and lasted only a minute. With the gorillas helpless, a dozen boys clinging to their heads, Bukari and Orangi bound them hand and foot with ropes. We then removed the tarpaulin and blankets. . . .

After being tied, the gorillas made little effort to escape. They were frightened, and all of their vaunted fighting spirit was chilled. The poor brutes looked at us with pleading eyes. They were amazed and confounded by this sudden turn of events. The animals were beauties, in perfect condition without a scratch or a scar upon them. Each weighed more than a hundred pounds. They were the largest ever captured. And our boys escaped from the battle without a scratch or a bruise. It was a splendid piece of work on the part of all concerned. The animals were then trussed on poles and, with eight boys to the pole, carried to our motorcar.

All of our cars have sides and ends enclosed with heavy, expanding metal. Back in camp, we put the brutes into one of the machines, and all that was necessary for a perfect cage were a few cross logs back of the driver's seat. A dozen boys clung to each gorilla as we untied their hands and feet and tossed them into the cage. The captives made no effort to escape and took the situation in a very philosophic manner. We gave them a pan of water, and they drank immediately. They went after some green corn and sweet potatoes we placed in the cage as though they were famished. I was astonished to see them eat and drink so soon after their frightening experience.

The remainder of the day was spent in camp looking at the gorillas and patting ourselves on the back because of the capture. Every face expressed the same thought: "How did we ever manage to catch two of them as big and strong as these?" However, they were in the cage, and we knew that we had effected the most unusual and interesting capture, from a scientific standpoint, ever made. If we succeeded in getting these animals to America, alive, we realized, we would have very valuable subjects for all students interested in anthropology.

We held a big celebration in camp that evening. I gave our boys, who had behaved admirably, much back-sheesh and passed out tea, sugar, and cigarettes all around. . . .

All night long gorillas were about the camp, beating on their chests and calling to the captives. Our prisoners answered them. The conversation continued for hours. This was proof that the apes did have a sort of language, but in this there is nothing unusual. Nearly all animals have some means of oral communication with each other, even your dogs and cats at home. What was striking about this night-time gathering of the gorillas was the sense of loyalty they displayed. Instinctively they knew where to find the missing members of the family, and they were vitally concerned about the fate of the two held in the cage. During the night

Osa and I walked along the road and heard gorillas in the bamboo. This was a rare occurrence as these apes nearly always sleep in the night hours. I was up a half dozen times during the night to look at the gorillas. This restlessness was due partly to pride of possession, but I will confess that I had visions of a mass attack upon us by the remaining animals in search of revenge. Each time I visited the cage I found DeWitt there. He was just as proud of the capture and as much concerned about the welfare of the new acquisition as I was.

We could have made a capture much sooner than we did had we followed the usual method practiced. The approved system of catching dangerous beasts is to shoot the mothers and grab the babies. We caught these gorillas, however, without causing injury to man or beast, which was something to boast about.

MR. CARLOS WILSON

Norman Douglas

I used to meet my friend at luncheon and tea-time (that is, whisky-and-soda) when sun helmets could be removed; and, of course, for dinner. In the morning and afternoon he was at work while I perambulated the country alone in all directions, with one eye, towards evening, on that sun which sank with such pedantic regularity and threatened to leave me in sudden darkness at the mercy of some other leopard unless I hurried home. Those sunsets I shall long remember; such tumultuous conflagrations I never saw. Altogether, my solitary strolls at Arusha were a tonic; one could strike fresh roots in this unfamiliar environment. A favourite spot was a wooded hill to the south of Arusha; there was a path to the summit from where you looked across leagues of country to the majestic dome of Kilimanjaro glittering with snow. At the foot of this hill, to the west, lay a patch of forest full of birds and butterflies, all of them new to me; there I often went, when too lazy to climb. Another hill bordered on that level tract, once possibly a lake, where I think they now have a golf-course. Yet another was the one marked "Kibwesi" on the map; it stands about fifteen hundred feet above Arusha, and this was a more arduous undertaking. I was there only twice, but the view southwards over the tawny plain dotted with eminences great and small—parasitic craters, maybe, of Meru—was worth the trouble. It suggested a lunar landscape.

Of lions I saw only the tracks: three of them had been round a friend's house on the previous night, after his donkey; of elephants I saw only the dung; of rhinos only a head: it came, still warm, from somewhere near Moshi. They are none too rare, and shortly before my arrival two Europeans, Mrs. Green and Captain Atkins, were killed within an hour by the same beast—not a bad morning's work for the rhino. Here is a lion story from the local press: "When the whisky was making its round, a well-known Rhodesian sportsman described how he unexpectedly came face to face with a huge lion. He was so surprised that he hadn't even time to raise his gun. *I stood there helpless*, he said, *rooted to the ground. The lion growled and then sprang at me. I thought my last hour had come, and closed my eyes. But, no, the lion misjudged his distance and went clean over my head. My wits returned to me and I got safely away.* After a sip of whisky, he added: *A week later I returned to the same spot and there was the same lion—practising short jumps!*

There is a plain about six miles from Arusha where you may see game in abundance, antelopes of various kinds, troops of zebras, wildebeeste, ostriches, giraffes. Giraffes are tall, but you do not expect them to look at you over the top of a tree. These particular trees being full-grown and built according to the European model, it is a puzzling illusion; only on approaching nearer do you perceive that they are not half the height of ours. The giraffe meanwhile saunters away with that singular gait, like a sailing ship in a breeze.

SMALL-TOWN UNITY

John Steinbeck

It is wonderful the way a little town keeps track of itself and of all its units. If every single man and woman, child and baby, acts and conducts itself in a known pattern and breaks no wall and differs with no one and experiments in no way and is not sick and does not endanger the ease and peace of mind or steady unbroken flow of the town, then that unit can disappear and never be heard of. But let one man step out of the regular thought or the known and trusted pattern, and the nerves of the townspeople ring with nervousness and communication travels over the nerve lines of the town. Then every unit communicates to the whole.

THE FAMILY WHICH DWELT APART

E. B. White

On a small, remote island in the lower reaches of Barnetuck Bay there lived a family of fish folk by the name of Pruitt. There were seven of them, and they were the sole inhabitants of the place. They subsisted on canned corn, canned tomatoes, pressed duck, whole wheat bread, terrapin, Rice Krispies, crabs, cheese, queen olives, and homemade wild-grape preserve. Once in a while Pa Pruitt made some whisky and they all had a drink.

They liked the island and lived there from choice. In winter, when there wasn't much doing, they slept the clock around, like so many bears. In summer they dug clams and set off a few pinwheels and salutes on July 4th. No case of acute appendicitis had ever been known in the Pruitt household, and when a Pruitt had a pain in his side he never even noticed whether it was the right side or the left side, but just hoped it would go away, and it did.

One very severe winter Barnetuck Bay froze over and the Pruitt family was marooned. They couldn't get to the mainland by boat because the ice was too thick, and they couldn't walk ashore because the ice was too treacherous. But inasmuch as no Pruitt had anything to go ashore for, except mail (which was entirely second class), the freeze-up didn't make any difference. They stayed indoors, kept warm, and ate well, and when there was nothing better to do, they played crokinole. The winter would have passed quietly enough had not someone on the mainland remembered that the Pruitts were out there in the frozen bay. The word got passed around the county and finally reached the Superintendent of State Police, who immediately notified Pathé News and the United States Army. The Army got there first with three bombing planes from Langley Field, which flew low over the island and dropped packages of dried apricots and bouillon cubes, which the Pruitts didn't like much. The newsreel plane, smaller than the bombers and equipped with skis, arrived next and landed on a snow-covered field on the north end of the island. Meanwhile, Major Bulk, head of the state troopers, acting on a tip that one of the Pruitt children had appendicitis, arranged for a dog team to be sent by plane from Laconia, New Hampshire, and also dispatched a squad of troopers to attempt a crossing of the bay. Snow began falling at sundown, and during the night three of the rescuers lost their lives about half a mile from shore, trying to jump from one ice cake to another.

The plane carrying the sled dogs was over southern New England when ice began forming on its wings. As the pilot circled for a forced landing, a large meat bone which one of the dogs had brought along got wedged in the socket of the main control stick, and the plane went into a steep dive and crashed against the side of a powerhouse, instantly killing the pilot and all the dogs, and fatally injuring Walter Ringstead, 7, of 3452 Garden View Avenue, Stamford, Conn.

Shortly before midnight, the news of the appendicitis reached the Pruitt house itself, when a chartered autogiro from Hearst's International News Service made a landing in the storm and reporters informed Mr. Pruitt that his oldest boy, Charles, was ill and would have to be taken to Baltimore for an emergency operation. Mrs. Pruitt remonstrated, but Charles said his side did hurt a little, and it ended by his leaving in the giro. Twenty minutes later another plane came in, bearing a surgeon, two trained nurses, and a man from the National Broadcasting Company, and the second Pruitt boy, Chester, underwent an exclusive appendectomy in the kitchen of the Pruitt home, over the Blue Network. This lad died, later, from eating dried apricots too soon after his illness, but Charles, the other boy, recovered after a long convalescence and returned to the island in the first warm days of spring.

He found things much changed. The house was gone, having caught fire on the third and last night of the rescue when a flare dropped by one of the departing planes lodged in a bucket of trash on the piazza. After the fire, Mr. Pruitt had apparently moved his family into the emergency shed which the radio announcers had thrown up, and there they had dwelt under rather difficult conditions until the night the entire family was wiped out by drinking a ten-per-cent solution of carbolic acid which the surgeon had left behind and which Pa Pruitt had mistaken for grain alcohol.

Barnetuck Bay seemed a different place to Charles. After giving his kin decent burial, he left the island of his nativity and went to dwell on the mainland.

SPLIT CHERRY TREE

Jesse Stuart

"I don't mind staying after school," I says to Professor Herbert, "but I'd rather you'd whip me with a switch and let me go home early.

Pa will whip me anyway for getting home two hours late."

"You are too big to whip," says Professor Herbert, "and I have to punish you for climbing up in that cherry tree. You boys knew better than that! The other five boys have paid their dollar each. You have been the only one who has not helped pay for the tree. Can't you borrow a dollar?"

"I can't," I says. "I'll have to take the punishment. I wish it would be quicker punishment. I wouldn't mind."

Professor Herbert stood and looked at me. He was a big man. He wore a gray suit of clothes. The suit matched his gray hair.

"You don't know my father," I says to Professor Herbert. "He might be called a little old-fashioned. He makes us mind him until we're twenty-one years old. He believes: 'If you spare the rod you spoil the child.' I'll never be able to make him understand about the cherry tree. I'm the first of my people to go to high school."

"You must take the punishment," says Professor Herbert. "You must stay two hours after school today and two hours after school tomorrow. I am allowing you twenty-five cents an hour. That is good money for a high school student. You can sweep the schoolhouse floor, wash the blackboards, and clean windows. I'll pay the dollar for you."

I couldn't ask Professor Herbert to loan me a dollar. He never offered to loan it to me. I had to stay and help the janitor and work out my fine at a quarter an hour.

I thought as I swept the floor, "What will Pa do to me? What lie can I tell him when I go home? Why did we ever climb that cherry tree and break it down for anyway? Why did we run crazy over the hills away from the crowd? Why did we do all of this? Six of us climbed up in a little cherry tree after one little lizard! Why did the tree split and fall with us? It should have been a stronger tree! Why did Eif Crabtree just happen to be below us plowing and catch us in his cherry tree? Why wasn't he a better man than to charge us six dollars for the tree?"

It was six o'clock when I left the schoolhouse. I had six miles to walk home. It would be after seven when I got home. I had all my work to do when I got home. It took Pa and me both to do the work. Seven cows to milk. Nineteen head of cattle to feed, four mules, twenty-five hogs, firewood and stove-wood to cut, and water to draw from the well. He would be doing it when I got home. He would be mad and wondering what was keeping me!

I hurried home. I would run under the dark, leafless trees. I would walk fast uphill. I would run down the hill. The ground was freezing. I had to hurry. I had to run. I reached the long ridge that led to our cow pasture. I ran along this ridge. The wind dried the sweat on my face. I ran across the pasture to the house.

I threw down my books in the chip-yard. I ran to the barn to spread fodder on the ground for the cattle. I didn't take time to change my clean school clothes for my old work clothes. I ran out to the barn. I saw Pa spreading fodder on the ground to the cattle. That was my job. I ran up to the fence. I says, "Leave that for me, Pa. I'll do it. I'm just a little late."

"I see you are," says Pa. He turned and looked at me. His eyes danced fire. "What in th' world has kept you so? Why ain't you been here to help me with this work? Make a gentleman out'n one boy in th' family and this is what you get! Send you to high school and you get too onery fer th' buzzards to smell!"

I never said anything. I didn't want to tell why I was late from school. Pa stopped scattering the bundles of fodder. He looked at me. He says, "Why are you gettin' in here this time o' night? You tell me or I'll take a hickory withe to you right here on th' spot!"

I says, "I had to stay after school." I couldn't lie to Pa. He'd go to school and find out why I had to stay. If I lied to him it would be too bad for me.

"Why did you haf to stay atter school?" says Pa.

I says, "Our biology class went on a field trip today. Six of us boys broke down a cherry tree. We had to give a dollar apiece to pay for the tree. I didn't have the dollar. Professor Herbert is making me work out my dollar. He gives me twenty-five cents an hour. I had to stay in this afternoon. I'll have to stay in tomorrow afternoon!"

"Are you telling me th' truth?" says Pa.

"I'm telling you the truth," I says. "Go and see for yourself."

"That's jist what I'll do in th' mornin'," says Pa. "Jist whose cherry tree did you break down?"

"Eif Crabtree's cherry tree!"

"What was you doin' clear out in Eif Crabtree's place?" says Pa. "He lives four miles from th' county high school. Don't they teach you no books at that high school? Do they jist let you get out and gad over th' hillsides? If that's all they do I'll keep you at home, Dave. I've got work here fer you to do!"

"Pa," I says, "spring is just getting here. We take a subject in school where we have to have bugs, snakes, flowers, lizards, frogs, and plants. It is biology. It was a pretty day today. We went out to find a few of these. Six of us boys saw a lizard at the same time sunning on a cherry tree. We all went up the tree to get it. We broke the tree down. It split at the forks. Eif Crabtree was plowing down below us. He ran up the hill and got our names. The other boys gave their dollar apiece. I didn't have mine. Professor Herbert put mine in for me. I have to work it out at school."

"Poor man's son, huh," says Pa. "I'll attend to that myself in th' morning'. I'll take keer o' 'im. He ain't from this county nohow. I'll go down there in th' mornin' and see 'im. Lettin' you leave your books and galavant all over th' hills. What kind of a school is it nohow! Didn't do that, my son, when I's a little shaver in school. All fared alike too."

"Pa, please don't go down there," I says, "just let me have fifty cents and pay the rest of my fine! I don't want you to go down there! I don't want you to start anything with Professor Herbert!"

"Ashamed of your old Pap are you, Dave," says Pa, "after th' way I've worked to raise you! Tryin' to send you to school so you can make a better livin' than I've made.

"I'll straighten this thing out myself! I'll take keer o' Professor Herbert myself! He ain't got no right to keep you in and let the other boys off jist because they've got th' money! I'm a poor man. A bullet will go in a professor same as it will any man. It will go in a rich man same as it will a poor man. Now you get into this work before I take one o' these withes and cut the shirt off'n your back!"

I thought once I'd run through the woods above the barn just as hard as I could go. I thought I'd leave high school and home forever! Pa could not catch me! I'd get away! I couldn't go back to school with him. He'd have a gun and maybe he'd shoot Professor Herbert. It was hard to tell what he would do. I could tell Pa that school had changed in the hills from the way it was when he was a boy, but he wouldn't understand. I could tell him we studied frogs, birds, snakes, lizards, flowers, insects. But Pa wouldn't understand. If I did run away from home it wouldn't matter to Pa. He would see Professor Herbert anyway. He would think that high school and Professor Herbert had run me away from home. There was no need to run away. I'd just have to stay, finish foddering the cattle, and go to school with Pa the next morning.

I would take a bundle of fodder, remove the hickory-withe band from around it, and scatter it on rocks, clumps of green briers, and brush so the cattle wouldn't tramp it under their feet. I would lean it up against the oak trees and the rocks in the pasture just above our pigpen on the hill. The fodder was cold and frosty where it had set out in the stacks. I would carry bundles of the fodder from the stack until I had spread out a bundle for each steer. Pa went to the barn to feed the mules and throw corn in the pen to the hogs.

The moon shone bright in the cold March sky. I finished my work by moonlight. Professor Herbert really didn't know how much work I had to do at home. If he had known he would not have kept me after school.

He would have loaned me a dollar to have paid my part on the cherry tree. He had never lived in the hills. He didn't know the way the hill boys had to work so that they could go to school. Now he was teaching in a county high school where all the boys who attended were from hill farms.

After I'd finished doing my work I went to the house and ate my supper. Pa and Mom had eaten. My supper was getting cold. I heard Pa and Mom talking in the front room. Pa was telling Mom about me staying in after school.

"I had to do all th' milkin' tonight, chop th' wood myself. It's too hard on me atter I've turned ground all day. I'm goin' to take a day off tomorrow and see if I can't remedy things a little. I'll go down to that high school tomorrow. I won't be a very good scholar fer Professor Herbert nohow. He won't keep me in atter school. I'll take a different kind of lesson down there and make 'im acquainted with it."

"Now, Luster," says Mom, "you jist stay away from there. Don't cause a lot o' trouble. You can be jailed fer a trick like that. You'll get th' Law atter you. You'll jist go down there and show off and plague your own boy Dave to death in front o' all th' scholars!"

"Plague or no plague," says Pa, "he don't take into consideration what all I haf to do here, does he? I'll show 'im it ain't right to keep one boy in and let the rest go scot free. My boy is good as th' rest, ain't he? A bullet will make a hole in a schoolteacher same as it will anybody else. He can't do me that way and get by with it. I'll plug 'im first. I aim to go down there bright and early in the mornin' and get all this straight! I aim to see about bug larnin' and this runnin' all over God's creation huntin' snakes, lizards, and frogs. Ransackin' th' country and goin' through cherry orchards and breakin' th' trees down atter lizards! Old Eif Crabtree ought to a-poured th' hot lead to 'em instead o' chargin' six dollars fer th' tree! He ought to a-got old Herbert th' first one!"

I ate my supper. I slipped upstairs and lit the lamp. I tried to forget the whole thing. I studied plane geometry. Then I studied my biology lesson. I could hardly study for thinking about Pa. "He'll go to school with me in the morning. He'll take a gun for Professor Herbert! What will Professor Herbert think of me! I'll tell him when Pa leaves that I couldn't help it. But Pa might shoot him. I hate to go with Pa. Maybe he'll cool off about it tonight and not go in the morning."

Pa got up at four o'clock. He built a fire in the stove. Then he built a fire in the fireplace. He got Mom up to get breakfast. Then he got me up to help feed and milk. By the time we had our work done at the barn, Mom had breakfast ready for us. We ate our breakfast. Daylight came and we could see the bare oak trees covered white with frost. The hills were white with frost. A cold wind was blowing. The sky was clear. The sun would soon come out and melt the frost. The afternoon would be warm with sunshine and the frozen ground with thaw. There would be mud on the hills again. Muddy water would then run down the little ditches on the hills.

"Now, Dave," says Pa, "Let's get ready fer school. I aim to go with you this mornin' and look into bug larnin', frog larnin', lizard and snake larnin', and breakin' down cherry trees! I don't like no sicha foolish way o' larnin' myself!"

Pa hadn't forgot. I'd have to take him to school with me. He would take me to school with him. We were going early. I was glad we were going early. If Pa pulled a gun on Professor Herbert there wouldn't be so many of my classmates there to see him.

I knew that Pa wouldn't be at home in the high school. He wore overalls, big boots, a blue shirt and a sheepskin coat and a slouched black hat gone to seed at the top. He put his gun in its holster. We started trudging toward the high school across the hill.

It was early when we got to the county high school. Professor Herbert had just got there. I just thought as we walked up the steps into the schoolhouse, "Maybe Pa will find out Professor Herbert is a good man. He just doesn't know him. Just like I felt toward the Lambert boys across the hill. I didn't like them until I'd seen them and talked to them. After I went to school with them and talked to them, I liked them and we were friends. It's a lot in knowing the other fellow."

"You're th' Professor here, ain't you?" says Pa.

"Yes," says Professor Herbert, "and you are Dave's father."

"Yes," says Pa, pulling out his gun and laying it on the seat in Professor Herbert's office. Professor Herbert's eyes got big behind his black-rimmed glasses when he saw Pa's gun. Color came into his pale cheeks.

"Jist a few things about this school I want to know" says Pa. "I'm tryin' to make a scholar out'n Dave. He's the only one out'n eleven youngins I've sent to high school. Here he comes in late and leaves me all th' work to do! He said you's all out bug huntin' yesterday and broke a cherry tree down. He had to stay two hours atter school yesterday and work out money to pay on that cherry tree! Is that right?"

"Wwwwy," says Professor Herbert, "I guess it is."

He looked at Pa's gun.

"Well," says Pa, "this ain't no high school. It's a bug school, a lizard school, a snake school! It ain't no school nohow!"

"Why did you bring that gun?" says Professor Herbert to Pa.

"You see that little hole," says Pa as he picked up the long blue fortyfour and put his finger on the end of the barrel, "a bullet can come out'n that hole that will kill a schoolteacher same as it will any other man. It will kill a rich man same as a poor man. It will kill a man. But atter I come in and saw you, I know'd I wouldn't need it. This maul o' mine could do you up in a few minutes."

Pa stood there, big, hard, brown-skinned, and mighty beside of Professor Herbert. I didn't know Pa was so much bigger and harder. I'd never seen Pa in a schoolhouse before. I'd seen Professor Herbert. He'd always looked big before to me. He didn't look big standing beside of Pa.

"I was only doing my duty," says Professor Herbert, "Mr. Sexton, and following the course of study the state provided us with."

"Course o' study," says Pa, "what study, bug study? Varmint study? Takin' youngins to th' woods and their poor old Ma's and Pa's at home a-slavin' to keep 'em in school and give 'em a education! You know that's dangerous, too, puttin' a lot o' boys and girls out together like that!"

Students were coming into the schoolhouse now.

Professor Herbert says, "Close the door, Dave, so others won't hear."

I walked over and closed the door. I was shaking like a leaf in the wind. I thought Pa was going to hit Professor Herbert every minute. He was doing all the talking. His face was getting red. The red color was coming through the brown, weather-beaten skin on Pa's face.

"I was right with these students," says Professor Herbert. "I know what they got into and what they didn't. I didn't send one of the other teachers with them on this field trip. I went myself. Yes, I took the boys and girls together. Why not?"

"It jist don't look good to me," says Pa, "a-takin' all this swarm of youngins out to pillage th' whole deestrict. Breakin' down cherry trees. Keepin' boys in atter school."

"What else could I have done with Dave, Mr. Sexton?" says Professor Herbert. "The boys didn't have any business all climbing that cherry tree after one lizard. One boy could have gone up in the tree and got it. The farmer charged us six dollars. It was a little steep, I think, but we had it to pay. Must I make five boys pay and let your boy off? He said he didn't have the dollar and couldn't get it. So I put it in for him. I'm letting him work it out. He's not working for me. He's working for the schoo!"

"I jist don't know what you could a-done with 'im," says Pa, "only a-larruped 'im with a withe! That's what he needed!"

"He's too big to whip," says Professor Herbert, pointing at me. "He's a man in size."

"He's not too big fer me to whip," says Pa. "They ain't too big until they're over twenty-one! It jist didn't look fair to me! Work one and let th' rest out because they got th' money. I don't see what bugs has got to do with a high school! It don't look good to me nohow!"

Pa picked up his gun and put it back in its holster. The red color left Professor Herbert's face. He talked more to Pa. Pa softened a little. It looked funny to see Pa in the high-school building. It was the first time he'd ever been there.

"We were not only hunting snakes, toads, flowers, butterflies, lizards," says Professor Herbert, "but, Mr. Sexton, I was hunting dry timothy grass to put in an incubator and raise some protozoa."

"I don't know what that is," says Pa. "Th' incubator is th' new-fangled way o' cheatin' th' hens and raisin' chickens. I ain't so sure about th' breed o' chickens you mentioned."

"You've heard of germs, Mr. Sexton, haven't you?" says Professor Herbert.

"Jist call me Luster, if you don't mind," says Pa, very casual-like.

"All right, Luster, you've heard of germs, haven't you?"

"Yes," says Pa, "but I don't believe in germs. I'm sixty-five years old and I ain't seen one yet!"

"You can't see them with your naked eye," says Professor Herbert. "Just keep that gun in the holster and stay with me in the high school today. I have a few things I want to show you. That scum on your teeth has germs in it."

"What," says Pa, "you mean to tell me I've got germs on my teeth!"

"Yes," says Professor Herbert. "The same kind as we might be able to find in a living black snake if we dissect it!"

"I don't mean to dispute your word," says Pa, "but I don't believe it. I don't believe I have germs on my teeth!"

"Stay with me today and I'll show you. I want to take you through the school anyway! School has changed a lot in the hills since you went to school. I don't guess we had high schools in this county when you went to school!"

"No," says Pa, "jist readin', writin', and cipherin'. We didn't have all this bug larnin', frog larnin', and findin' germs on your teeth and in the middle o' black snakes! Th' world's changin'."

"It is," says Professor Herbert, "and we hope all for the better. Boys like your own there are going to help change it. He's your boy. He knows all of what I've told you. You stay with me today."

"I'll shore stay with you," says Pa. "I want to see th' germs off'n my teeth. I jist want to see a germ. I've never seen one in my life. 'Seein' is believin',' Pap allus told me."

Pa walks out of the office with Professor Herbert. I just hoped Professor Herbert didn't have Pa arrested for pulling his gun. Pa's gun has always been a friend to him when he goes to settle disputes.

The bell rang. School took up. I saw the students when they marched in the schoolhouse look at Pa. They would grin and punch each other. Pa just stood and watched them pass in at the schoolhouse door. Two long lines marched in the house. The boys and girls were clean and well dressed. Pa stood over in the schoolyard under a leafless elm, in his sheepskin coat, his big boots laced in front with buckskin, and his heavy socks stuck above his boot tops. Pa's overalls legs were baggy and wrinkled between his coat and boot tops. His blue work shirt showed at the collar. His big black hat showed his gray-streaked black hair. His face was hard and weather-tanned to the color of a ripe fodder blade. His hands were big and gnarled like the roots of the elm tree he stood beside.

When I went to my first class I saw Pa and Professor Herbert going around over the schoolhouse. I was in my geometry class when Pa and Professor Herbert came in the room. We were explaining our propositions on the blackboard. Professor Herbert and Pa just quietly came in and sat down for a while. I heard Fred Wurts whisper to Glenn Armstrong, "Who is that old man? Lord, he's a rough-looking scamp." Glenn whispered back, "I think he's Dave's Pap." The students in geometry looked at Pa. They must have wondered what he was doing in school. Before the class was over, Pa and Professor Herbert got up and went out. I saw them together down on the playground. Professor Herbert was explaining to Pa. I could see the prints of Pa's gun under his coat when he'd walk around.

At noon in the high-school cafeteria Pa and Professor Herbert sat together at the little table where Professor Herbert always ate by himself. They ate together. The students watched the way Pa ate. He ate with his knife instead of his fork. A lot of the students felt sorry for me after they found out he was my father. They didn't have to feel sorry for me. I wasn't ashamed of Pa after I found out he wasn't going to shoot Professor Herbert. I was glad they had made friends. I wasn't ashamed of Pa. I wouldn't be as long as he behaved. He would find out about the high school as I had found out about the Lambert boys across the hill.

In the afternoon when we went to biology Pa was in the class. He was sitting on one of the high stools beside the microscope. We went ahead with our work just as if Pa wasn't in the class. I saw Pa take his knife and scrape tartar from one of his teeth. Professor Herbert put it on the lens and adjusted the microscope for Pa. He adjusted it and worked awhile. Then he says: "Now Luster, look! Put your eye right down to the light. Squint the other eye!"

Pa put his head down and did as Professor Herbert said. "I see 'im," says Pa. "Who'd a ever thought that? Right on a body's teeth! Right in a body's mouth. You're right certain they ain't no fake to this, Professor Herbert?"

"No, Luster," says Professor Herbert. "It's there. That's the germ.

Germs live in a world we cannot see with the naked eye. We must use the microscope. There are millions of them in our bodies. Some are harmful. Others are helpful."

Pa holds his face down and looks through the microscope. We stop and watch Pa. He sits upon the tall stool. His knees are against the table. His legs are long. His coat slips up behind when he bends over. The handle of his gun shows. Professor Herbert pulls his coat down quickly.

"Oh, yes," says Pa. He gets up and pulls his coat down. Pa's face gets a little red. He knows about his gun and he knows he doesn't have any use for it in high school.

"We have a big black snake over here we caught yesterday," says Professor Herbert. "We'll chloroform him and dissect him and show you he has germs in his body, too."

"Don't do it," says Pa. "I believe you. I jist don't want to see you kill the black snake. I never kill one. They are good mousers and a lot o' help to us on the farm. I like black snakes. I jist hate to see people kill 'em. I don't allow 'em killed on my place."

The students look at Pa. They seem to like him better after he said that. Pa with a gun in his pocket but a tender heart beneath his ribs for snakes, but not for man! Pa won't whip a mule at home. He won't whip his cattle.

"Man can defend hisself," says Pa, "but cattle and mules can't. We have the drop on 'em. Ain't nothin' to a man that'll beat a good pullin' mule. He ain't got th' right kind o' a heart!"

Professor Herbert took Pa through the laboratory. He showed him the different kinds of work we were doing. He showed him our equipment. They stood and talked while we worked. Then they walked out together. They talked louder when they got out in the hall.

When our biology class was over I walked out of the room. It was our last class for the day. I would have to take my broom and sweep two hours to finish paying for the split cherry tree. I just wondered if Pa would want me to stay. He was standing in the hallway watching the students march out. He looked lost among us. He looked like a leaf turned brown on the tree among the treetop filled with growing leaves.

I got my broom and started to sweep. Professor Herbert walked up and says, "I'm going to let you do that some other time. You can go home with your father. He is waiting out there."

I laid my broom down, got my books, and went down the steps.

Pa says, "Ain't you got two hours o' sweepin' yet to do?"

I says, "Professor Herbert said I could do it some other time. He said for me to go home with you."

"No," says Pa. "You are goin' to do as he says. He's a good man. School has changed from my day and time. I'm a dead leaf, Dave. I'm behind. I don't belong here. If he'll let me I'll get a broom and we'll both sweep one hour. That pays your debt. I'll hep you pay it. I'll ast 'im and see if he won't let me hep you."

"I'm going to cancel the debt," says Professor Herbert. "I just wanted you to understand, Luster."

"I understand," says Pa, "and since I understand, he must pay his debt fer th' tree and I'm goin' to hep 'im."

"Don't do that," says Professor Herbert. "It's all on me."

"We don't do things like that," says Pa, "we're just and honest people. We don't want somethin' fer nothin'. Professor Herbert, you're wrong now and I'm right. You'll haf to listen to me. I've larned a lot from you. My boy must go on. Th' world has left me. It changed while I've raised my family and plowed th' hills. I'm a just and honest man. I don't skip debts. I ain't larned 'em to do that. I ain't got much larnin' myself but I do know right from wrong atter I see through a thing."

Professor Herbert went home. Pa and I stayed and swept one hour. It looked funny to see Pa use a broom. He never used one at home. Mom used the broom. Pa used the plow. Pa did hard work. Pa says, "I can't sweep. Durned if I can. Look at th' streaks o' dirt I leave on th' floor! Seems like no work a-tall fer me. Brooms is too light 'r somethin'. I'll jist do th' best I can, Dave. I've been wrong about th' school."

I says, "Did you know Professor Herbert can get a warrant out for you for bringing your pistol to school and showing it in his office! They can railroad you for that!"

"That's all made right," says Pa. "I've made that right. Professor Herbert ain't goin' to take it to court. He likes me. I like 'im. We just had to get together. He had the remedies. He showed me. You must go on to school. I am as strong a man as ever come out'n the hills fer my years and th' hard work I've done. But I'm behind, Dave. I'm a little man. Your hands will be softer than mine. Your clothes will be better. You'll allus look cleaner than your old Pap. Jist remember, Dave, to pay your debts and be honest. Jist be kind to animals and don't bother th' snakes. That's all I got agin th' school. Puttin' black snakes to sleep and cuttin' 'em open."

It was late when we got home. Stars were in the sky. The moon was up. The ground was frozen. Pa took his time going home. I couldn't run like I did the night before. It was ten o'clock before we got the work finished, our suppers eaten. Pa sat before the fire and told Mom he was going to take her and show her a germ sometime. Mom hadn't seen one either. Pa told her about the high school and the fine man Professor Herbert was. He told Mom about the strange school across the hill and how different it was from the school in their day and time.

Suggestions for Study

1. After you have read "Guessed Everything Else," relate one or more of your experiences as (or with) a door-to-door salesman. Which people who sell from door to door are best (worst) treated?

2. What use does Dr. McDowell make of psychology?

3. Is Benchley's humor in "The Children's Hour" too exaggerated? Write a sketch describing a younger member of your family.

4. Does "Prelude to Reunion" seem to depict accurately the relationship between wealthy and poor students?

5. After reading "Split Cherry Tree," write an incident in which you place one of your parents at college or high school, sitting in your desk. Show how he or she would react to the material being presented, the instructor's humor or lack of it, and the "new fangled" ideas of present-day education.

6. Explain how "The Family Which Dwelt Apart," an engaging satire, employs cause and effect.

Composition Topics

1. My Favorite Means of Travel

2. The Water Sport That I Know Best

3. Tips on How to Sell

4. Mom and the Salesman

5. Who Plays Sick?

6. My Little Brother Has the Stomach Ache Every Day Except Saturday and Sunday

7. Why Teachers Grow Weary

8. Is "College Life" Necessary?

9. Living in Isolation

10. The Doctor's Waiting Room

FROM PAST

TO PRESENT

In one of his many lectures about education, Cardinal Newman (1801-1890) of England said that a fine mind is one which takes a sound view "of old and new, past and present, far and near, and which has an insight into the influence of all these one on another; without which there is no whole and no center." Past to present covers a formidable time span. Thus, readings in this section are understandably only a mere suggestion of the boundless eclectic possibilities. Let us consider just three of the selections.

The showpiece of "Venetian Pageant" was the rich vessel Bucentaur. Does it occur to you that this was doubtless an ancestor of the ornate floats ridden by parade queens at Homecoming? (In English of the past, float meant a ship, a boat.) Now, a short mention of Captain John Davis and his uncomfortable adventures. As is so well known, the latter half of the 1500s was a time of intense English exploration and exploitation by Frobisher, Hawkins, Drake, and others throughout all available parts of the world. For the audience at home, accounts of these travels were made the more exciting by hearty exaggeration — for instance, Captain Davis's account of the voracious worms. But even in the news of today some crew member occasionally sights a sea monster. Finally, the selection "The Mound Builders" may make one a bit contemplative of time. We can look at any one of America's great cities today and feel that the mound builders existed across an abyss of history too wide to fathom. Yet between each of the single days stretching from the past into the present, there were no gulfs; each merged into the next, with changes for the most part as imperceptible to those who lived them as those between our own yesterdays and tomorrows.

Literature of the past is a means of exploring many contemporary problems. It places them in perspective. For, notwithstanding contemporary science and technology, the *basic human condition varies little from nation to nation or age to age. Those who create the future translate activities of the past into constructive and productive ideas of the present.*

THE MOUND BUILDERS

In the central part of North America, along the valleys of the Mississippi and the Ohio rivers, from the Gulf of Mexico to the Great Lakes, there are remains of the works of an extinct race of people, now known as the "Mound Builders." Very little is known of their history, except that they were a people akin to those who settled in Mexico and Central America, and that they were a very different race of people from the North American Indians.

They are generally considered the aborigines of this continent, which is fast proving itself to be as old as, if not older than, the eastern continent.

At what time these people made their appearance in North America, and erected the mounds from which they are named "Mound Builders," is uncertain, and can never, perhaps, be fully ascertained; but antiquarians who have investigated these wonderful monuments assure us that they have full proof that the builders enjoyed a high state of civilization, were expert agriculturists, good mathematicians, adepts in the arts, and devotees of some form, or of different forms, of religious faith.

Of these mounds, or tumuli, it is said that ten thousand are found in the State of Ohio alone. Some of these have evidently been built as mausoleums, others for defense, still others as altars on which to offer sacrifices; but it is difficult to assign a reason for those built in the shape of various animals, such as alligators, buffaloes, eagles, serpents, etc.

Several of these mounds cover many hundred acres of ground. One near Newark, O., forms a perfect circle a mile in circumference, and twenty feet high. It is large enough to accommodate the county fair of the Agricultural Society; and upon it, beech, maple, and hickory trees have grown luxuriantly, showing, it is believed, that the erection of this mound far antedates the time of Columbus. In the same county is the "Alligator Mound," which is two hundred and fifty feet long, and fifty feet wide. The famous "Serpent Mound," on Brush Creek, Adams County, O., is more than one thousand feet in length: the embankment is five feet high, and has a base of thirty feet at the centre of the body, diminishing slightly toward the head and tail. In West Viriginia, there stands a sepulchral mound, which is seventy feet in vertical height, and has a circumference of nine hundred feet.

In the mounds of Ohio, there is frequently a combination of a square and two circles; and, wherever found, they correspond in this respect, that the sides of the squares measure exactly one thousand and eighty feet, and the adjacent circles have a circumference of seventeen hundred and eight hundred feet respectively.

In the construction of the military mounds, still greater mathematical skill is shown. They are erected on high ground, and often in groups extending several miles, and all connected one with another.

Such of the sepulchral mounds as have been excavated are found to contain human bones; but they crumble into dust when exposed to the air, so that no estimate of the size or national characteristics of the race can be formed. In the figures of heads on the pottery, and especially on clay pipe-bowls found in the mines, there is a strong resemblance to the sculptured heads found in the ruins in Yucatan.

It is thought that the Aztecs, found in Mexico by Cortez; and the ancient Peruvians, whose empire was destroyed by Pizarro, may have been remnants of the Mound Builders, who were driven south by invading hordes (such as our Indian tribes) from the other continent across Behring's Strait; but this is all conjecture.

In the Mississippi Valley, the mounds are very numerous; and it is said that some of them, as is shown by the growth of trees and by the excavation of antique articles, cannot be less than two thousand years old. One of these represents a man with two heads; the body being fifty feet long, and twenty-five feet across the breast.

Who the Mound Builders were remains to be answered; yet, so long as the mounds exist, they testify to the fact that, at a very remote age, a race of people, now extinct, was in possession of this country, from the frozen lakes of the North to the Gulf of Mexico, and from Vermont to the Rocky Mountains.

THE FIRST ACCOUNT OF CHINA

Marco Polo, the celebrated traveller, born at Venice about 1254, gave to the world the first correct account of China. In 1271 he started on a tour through Asia, finally reaching China in 1275, which was then known in Europe as Cathay, supposed to comprise the entire "Far East" of the world.

The Emperor of China received him, and soon gave him important offices in the government, making him governor of a large city, which position he held for three years.

The emperor, however, would not allow him to leave the empire, as it was closed to all foreigners; and for sixteen years he was an honored prisoner of the emperor. He finally managed to escape on board a ship which was carrying the emperor's daughter to Persia, where she was to become the king's wife. After nine months Polo went from Persia to the Black Sea, and finally returned to Venice in 1295.

He had almost forgotten his native language; and his friends would not believe his story, even when he showed the rich presents he had received from the Emperor of China. He entered the navy, and was taken prisoner in a war with Genoa: during five years' imprisonment he prepared an account of his travels, and gave to the world the first correct description of China. His book was published, and created an immense excitement among learned men, who did not hesitate to affirm it to be pure fiction.

After his liberation he returned to Venice, was abjured by his friends, and even on his death-bed was urged to retract his falsehoods.

He died in 1323, aged seventy years.

Subsequent Venetian travellers and Roman-Catholic missionaries verified many of Polo's statements; then came a reaction of public opinion, and the wonderful accuracy of Polo's history became the theme of universal praise. His work became of inestimable value as a guide in geographical research; by it the Portuguese were led to sail round the Cape of Good Hope, and Columbus to make his discoveries in the western hemisphere.

The book was translated into all foreign languages, but not into English until 1844.

Marco Polo was long remembered in China; and a bust of him is still to be seen in one of the temples of Canton, where great men figure as social idols.

CAPTAIN JOHN DAVIS RETURNS TO ENGLAND

G. B. Harrison

Captain John Davis hath returned with some few of his men to Cornwall on the 16th, being but the poor remainder of the company of seventy-six that had left Plymouth on 26th August, 1591, on board the *Desire* with Mr. Thomas Cavendish's fleet.

After losing sight of Mr. Cavendish, their General, on the night of the 20th May, 1592, they had returned to Port Desire, being now in very miserable case, the shrouds all rotten, without pitch, tar or nails, and living only upon seals and mussels. Here they remained hoping for sight of the General until 6th August, when they made for the Straits of Magellan, and there stayed, in the deep of winter, with but little victual and not enough clothing to defend the extremity of the winter's cold. In these seas they were lamentably driven by storms until on 25th October they came to an island named Penquin Island. There the boat was sent on shore, which returned laden with birds' eggs; and the men said that the penquins were so thick that the ships might be laden with them. The Captain, therefore, sent some of the men ashore whilst he sailed the ship up a river in the mainland, where she was run aground and made fast to the shore with running ropes moored to stakes. Here nine of their men were slain by savages, but the rest remained feeding on eggs, penquins, young seals, gulls, and other birds. In this place they found a herb called scurvy grass which so purged the blood that it took away all kinds of swelling, of which many had died, and restored them to perfect health of body.

In this labour they stayed until 22nd December, in which time they had dried 20,000 penquins on the island, of which 14,000 were taken on board, but not being able to fetch the rest by reason of the dangerous tides, they shaped course for Brazil. On 30th January, 1593, they landed at the Isle of Placencia, hoping to surprise the Portugals, but when they came to the houses they were all burnt, so that they thought no man remained on the island. Then the Captain went to the gardens and brought thence fruits and roots for the company, and all laboured to put the water casks in order.

The 5th February at night many of the men dreamed of murder and slaughter, and the Captain likewise having dreamed very strangely himself, gave straight charge that those who went on shore should take weapons with them. All the forenoon they laboured in quietness, but when it was ten o'clock, the heat being now extreme, they came to a rock near the woods' side (for all this country was nothing but thick woods) and there they boiled some cazavi roots and dined. After dinner some slept, some washed themselves in the sea, all being stripped to their shorts, and no man keeping a watch. Suddenly as they were thus sleeping and sporting, having gotten themselves into a corner out of sight of the ship, there came a multitude of Indians and Portugals upon them, and slew them sleeping; only two escaped, one very sorely hurt, one unharmed, who ran to the ship.

With all speed the boat was manned and landed to succour the men, but they found them all slain, and laid naked in a rank, with their faces upward and at a cross set by them. Moreover, they saw in the river two very great pinnaces full of men. So the next day, choosing rather to fall into the hands of the Lord than into the hands of men, they cast off in great distress, having only eight tuns of water in bad casks.

And now as they came near to the sun the dried penquins began to corrupt and there bred in them a most loathsome and ugly worm of an inch long, which so mightily increased and devoured the victuals that there was in reason no hope of avoiding famine; for there was nothing they did not devour, only iron, cloths, boots, shoes, hats, shirts, stockings, and for the ship they did so eat the timbers that there was great fear lest they should gnaw through her side. In this woeful case after passing the equinoctial toward the north, the men began to fall sick of a monstrous disease so that their ankles and whole bodies began to swell, and some to grow raging mad, and perished thus in most loathsome and furious pain, so that all but sixteen died, and of these but five were able to move, and upon them only stood the labour of the ship.

Thus as lost wanderers upon the sea, it pleased God that they arrived at Bearhaven in Ireland the 11th of June, and there ran the ship on shore, where the Captain left the master and three or four of the company, and within five days after, he and certain others passed in an English fishing boat to Padstow in Cornwall.

THE BAD MAN

O. Henry

A bold, bad man made a general display of himself in a Texas town a few days ago. It seems that he'd imbibed a sufficient number of drinks to become anxious to impress the town with his badness, and when the officers tried to arrest him he backed up against the side of a building and defied arrest. A considerable crowd of citizens, among whom were a number of drummers from a hotel close by, had gathered to witness the scene.

The bad man was a big, ferocious-looking fellow with long, curling hair that fell on his shoulders, a broad-brimmed hat, a buckskin coat with fringe around the bottom, and a picturesque vocabulary. He was flourishing a big six-shooter and swore by the bones of Davy Crockett that he would perforate the man who attempted to capture him.

The city marshal stood in the middle of the street and tried to reason with him, but the bad man gave a whoop and rose up on his toes, and the whole crowd fell back to the other side of the street. The police had a conference, but none of them would volunteer to lead the attack.

Presently a little, wizened, consumptive-looking drummer for a Connecticut shoe factory squeezed his way through the crowd on the opposite side of the street to have a peep at the desperado. He weighed about ninety pounds and wore double glass spectacles. Just then the desperado gave another whoop and yelled:

"Gol darn ye, why don't some of ye come and take me? I'll eat any five of ye without chawin', and I ain't hungry either—whoopee!"

The crowd fell back a few yards further and the police turned pale again, but the skinny little man adjusted his spectacles with both hands, and stepped on to the edge of the sidewalk and took a good look at the bad man. Then he deliberately struck across the street at a funny hopping kind of a run right up to where the terror stood.

The crowd yelled at him to come back, and the desperado flourished his six-shooter again, but the little man went straight up to him and said something. The crowd shuddered and expected to see him fall with a forty-five bullet in him, but he didn't. They saw the desperado lower his pistol and run his hand in his pocket and hand something to the little man.

Then the desperado walked sheepishly down the sidewalk, and the little man came back across the street.

"Bad man?" he said. "I guess not. He wouldn't hurt a fly. That's Zeke Skinner. He was raised on the farm next to me in Connecticut. He's selling some kind of fake liver medicine, and that's his street rig he's got on now. I loaned him eight dollars in Hartford nine years ago, and never expected to see him again. Thought I knew his voice. Pay? I reckon he paid me. I calculate I always collect what's owing to me."

Then the crowd scattered and the twelve policemen headed Zeke off at the next corner and clubbed him all the way to the station house.

THE BUCCANEERS

The buccaneers were a celebrated association of sea robbers, or pirates, called also "Brethren of the Coast," who for nearly two centuries, from the second quarter of the sixteenth century to the end of the seventeenth, maintained themselves in the Caribbean Seas, and waged a

constant warfare against the Spaniards in the West Indies. The buccaneers were Europeans, chiefly natives of Great Britain and France, who
first associated together about 1524. The arrogant assumption by the
Spaniards (on account of a bull issued by the Pope) of a divine right
to the whole New World was not, of course, to be tolerated by the enter-
prising mariners of England and France; and the enormous cruelties
practised by the Spaniards upon all foreign interlopers, of which the
history of that time is full, naturally led to an association for mutual
defence, particularly among the English and French.

The fundamental principles of their policy—for they in course of time
formed distinct communities—were close mutual alliance, and mortal war
with all that was Spanish. Their simple code of laws bound them to
share the common necessaries of life; locks and bars were proscribed, as
an insult to the general honor; and every man had his comrade who stood
by him when alive, and succeeded to his property after his death.

When they were not hunting Spaniards, or being hunted themselves,
their chief occupation and means of subsistence was the chase.

From the flesh of wild animals they made their "boucan," or cured
meat, and sold the skins and tallow to Dutch traders.

The name buccaneer is derived from the Caribbee word "boucan," the
French calling it "boucanier," from which the English derive our present
"buccaneer."

The history of these men embraces narratives of cruelty and bloodshed
unsurpassed in the annals of crime.

It has, however, not a few stories of high and romantic adventure, of
chivalrous and brilliant generalship.

Among the great captains whose names figure most prominently in the
records of buccaneering are the Frenchman Montbar, surnamed "The
Exterminator," and his countryman Peter Dieppe, surnamed "The Great."

Pre-eminent, however, among them all was the Welshman Henry
Morgan, who organized fleets and armies, took strong cities, and displayed throughout the genius of a born commander. He led the way for
the buccaneers to the Southern Ocean, by his daring march, in 1670, across
the Isthmus of Panama to the city of that name, which he took and
plundered after a desperate battle.

He was knighted by Charles II, and became deputy governor of
Jamaica. The war between France and Britain, after the accession of
William III, dissolved the ancient alliance of the French and English
buccaneers. The last great event in their history was the capture of
Carthagena, in 1697, where the booty was enormous.

After the peace of Ryswick (1697), and the accession of the Bourbon,
Philip V., to the Spanish crown (1701), they finally disappeared.

MAMMON AND THE ARCHER

O. Henry

Old Anthony Rockwall, retired manufacturer and proprietor of Rockwall's Eureka Soap, looked out the library window of his Fifth Avenue mansion and grinned. His neighbour to the right—the aristocratic clubman, G. Van Schuylight Suffolk-Jones— came out to his waiting motor-car, wrinkling a contumelious nostril, as usual, at the Italian renaissance sculpture of the soap palace's front elevation.

"Stuck-up old statuette of nothing doing!" commented the ex-Soap King. "The Eden Musee'll get that old frozen Nesselrode yet if he don't watch out. I'll have this house painted red, white, and blue next summer and see if that'll make his Dutch nose turn up any higher."

And then Anthony Rockwall, who never cared for bells, went to the door of his library and shouted "Mike!" in the same voice that had once chipped off pieces of the welkin on the Kansas prairies.

"Tell my son," said Anthony to the answering menial, "to come in here before he leaves the house."

When young Rockwall entered the library the old man laid aside his newspaper, looked at him with a kindly grimness on his big, smooth, ruddy countenance, rumpled his mop of white hair with one hand and rattled the keys in his pocket with the other.

"Richard," said Anthony Rockwall, "what do you pay for the soap that you use?"

Richard, only six months home from college, was startled a little. He had not yet taken the measure of this sire of his, who was as full of unexpectednesses as a girl at her first party.

"Six dollars a dozen, I think, dad."

"And your clothes?"

"I suppose about sixty dollars, as a rule."

"You're a gentleman," said Anthony, decidedly. "I've heard of these young bloods spending $24 a dozen for soap, and going over the hundred mark for clothes. You've got as much money to waste as any of 'em, and yet you stick to what's decent and moderate. Now I use the old Eureka—not only for sentiment, but it's the purest soap made. Whenever you pay more than 10 cents a cake for soap you buy bad perfume and labels. But 50 cents is doing very well for a young man in your generation, position, and condition. As I said, you're a gentleman. They say it takes three generations to make one. They're off. Money'll do it as slick as soap grease. It's made you one. By hokey! It's almost made one of me. I'm nearly as impolite and disagreeable and ill-mannered as these two old

Knickerbocker gents on each side of me that can't sleep of nights because I bought in between 'em."

"There are some things that money can't accomplish," remarked young Rockwall, rather gloomily.

"Now, don't say that," said old Anthony, shocked; "I bet my money on money every time. I've been through the encyclopedia down to Y looking for something you can't buy with it; and I expect to have to take up the appendix next week. I'm for money against the field. Tell me something money won't buy."

"For one thing," answered Richard, rankling a little, "it won't buy one into the exclusive circles of society."

"Oho! won't it?" thundered the champion of the root of evil. "You tell me where your exclusive circles would be if the first Astor hadn't had the money to pay for his steerage passage over?"

Richard sighed.

"And that's what I was coming to," said the old man, less boisterously. "That's why I asked you to come in. There's something going wrong with you, boy. I've been noticing it for two weeks. Out with it. I guess I could lay my hands on eleven millions within twenty-four hours, besides the real estate. If it's your liver, there's the *Rambler* down in the bay, coaled, and ready to steam down to the Bahamas in two days."

"Not a bad guess, dad; you haven't missed it far."

"Ah," said Anthony, keenly; "what's her name?"

Richard began to walk up and down the library floor. There was enough comradeship and sympathy in this crude old father of his to draw his confidence.

"Why don't you ask her?" demanded old Anthony. "She'll jump at you. You've got the money and the looks, and you're a decent boy. Your hands are clean. You've got no Eureka soap on 'em. You've been to college, but she'll overlook that."

"I haven't had a chance," said Richard.

"Make one," said Anthony. "Take her for a walk in the park, or a straw ride, or walk home with her from church. Chance! Pshaw!"

"You don't know the social mill, dad. She's part of the stream that turns it. Every hour and minute of her time is arranged for days in advance. I must have that girl, dad, or this town is a blackjack swamp forevermore. And I can't write it—I can't do that."

"Tut!" said the old man. "Do you mean to tell me that with all the money I've got you can't get an hour or two of a girl's time for yourself?"

"I've put it off too late. She's going to sail for Europe at noon day after to-morrow for a two years' stay. I'm to see her alone to-morrow evening for a few minutes. She's at Larchmont now at her aunt's. I can't go there.

But I'm allowed to meet her with a cab at the Grand Central Station to-morrow evening at the 8:30 train. We drive down Broadway to Wallack's at a gallop, where her mother and a box party will be waiting for us in the lobby. Do you think she would listen to a declaration from me during that six or eight minutes under these circumstances? No. And what chance would I have in the theatre or afterward? None. No, dad, this is one tangle that your money can't unravel. We can't buy one minute of time with cash; if we could, rich people would live longer. There's no hope of getting a talk with Miss Lantry before she sails."

"All right, Richard, my boy," said old Anthony, cheerfully. "You may run along down to your club now. I'm glad it ain't your liver. But don't forget to burn a few punk sticks in the joss house to the great god Mazuma from time to time. You say money won't buy time? Well, of course, you can't order eternity wrapped up and delivered at your residence for a price, but I've seen Father Time get pretty bad stone bruises on his heels when he walked through the gold diggings."

That night came Aunt Ellen, gentle, sentimental, wrinkled, sighing, oppressed by wealth, in to brother Anthony at his evening paper, and began discourse on the subject of lovers' woes.

"He told me all about it," said brother Anthony, yawning. "I told him my bank account was at his service. And then he began to knock money. Said money couldn't help. Said the rules of society couldn't be bucked for a yard by a team of ten-millionaires."

"Oh, Anthony," sighed Aunt Ellen, "I wish you would not think so much of money. Wealth is nothing where a true affection is concerned. Love is all-powerful. If he only had spoken earlier! She could not have refused our Richard. But now I fear it is too late. He will have no opportunity to address her. All your gold cannot bring happiness to your son."

At eight o'clock the next evening Aunt Ellen took a quaint old gold ring from a moth-eaten case and gave it to Richard.

"Wear it to-night, nephew," she begged. "Your mother gave it to me. Good luck in love she said it brought. She asked me to give it to you when you had found the one you loved."

Young Rockwall took the ring reverently and tried it on his smallest finger. It slipped as far as the second joint and stopped. He took it off and stuffed it into his vest pocket, after the manner of man. And then he 'phoned for his cab.

At the station he captured Miss Lantry out of the gadding mob at eight thirty-two.

"We mustn't keep mamma and the others waiting," said she.

"To Wallack's Theatre as fast as you can drive!" said Richard loyally.

They whirled up Forty-second to Broadway, and then down the white-starred lane that leads from the soft meadows of sunset to the rocky hills of morning.

At Thirty-fourth Street young Richard quickly thrust up the trap and ordered the cabman to stop.

"I've dropped a ring," he apologized, as he climbed out. "It was my mother's, and I'd hate to lose it. I won't detain you a minute—I saw where it fell."

In less than a minute he was back in the cab with the ring.

But within that minute a crosstown car had stopped directly in front of the cab. The cabman tried to pass to the left, but a heavy express wagon cut him off. He tried the right, and had to back away from a furniture van that had no business to be there. He tried to back out, but dropped his reins and swore dutifully. He was blockaded in a tangled mess of vehicles and horses.

One of those street blockades had occurred that sometimes tie up commerce and movement quite suddenly in the big city.

"Why don't you drive on?" said Miss Lantry, impatiently. "We'll be late."

Richard stood up in the cab and looked around. He saw a congested flood of wagons, trucks, cabs, vans and street cars filling the vast space where Broadway, Sixth Avenue and Thirty-fourth Street cross one another as a twenty-six inch maiden fills her twenty-two inch girdle. And still from all the cross streets they were hurrying and rattling toward the converging point at full speed, and hurling themselves into the struggling mass, locking wheels and adding their drivers' imprecations to the clamour. The entire traffic of Manhattan seemed to have jammed itself around them. The oldest New Yorker among the thousands of spectators that lined the sidewalks had not witnessed a street blockade of the proportions of this one.

"I'm very sorry," said Richard, as he resumed his seat, "but it looks as if we are stuck. They won't get this jumble loosened up in an hour. It was my fault. If I hadn't dropped the ring we—"

"Let me see the ring," said Miss Lantry. "Now that it can't be helped, I don't care. I think theatres are stupid, anyway."

At 11 o'clock that night somebody tapped lightly on Anthony Rockwall's door.

"Come in," shouted Anthony, who was in a red dressing-gown, reading a book of piratical adventures.

Somebody was Aunt Ellen, looking like a grey-haired angel that had been left on earth by mistake.

"They're engaged, Anthony," she said, softly. "She has promised to marry our Richard. On their way to the theatre there was a street blockade, and it was two hours before their cab could get out of it.

"And oh, brother Anthony, don't ever boast of the power of money again. A little emblem of true love—a little ring that symbolized unending and unmercenary affection—was the cause of our Richard finding his happiness. He dropped it in the street, and got out to recover it. And before they could continue, the blockade occurred. He spoke to his love and won her there while the cab was hemmed in. Money is dross compared with true love, Anthony."

"All right," said old Anthony. "I'm glad the boy has got what he wanted. I told him I wouldn't spare any expense in the matter if—"

"But, brother Anthony, what good could your money have done?"

"Sister," said Anthony Rockwall, "I've got my pirate in a devil of a scrape. His ship has just been scuttled, and he's too good a judge of the value of money to let drown. I wish you would let me go on with this chapter."

The story should end here. I wish it would as heartily as you who read it wish it did. But we must go to the bottom of the well for the truth.

The next day a person with red hands and a blue polka-dot necktie, who called himself Kelly, called at Anthony Rockwall's house, and was at once received in the library.

"Well," said Anthony, reaching for his cheque-book, "it was a good bilin' of soap. Let's see—you had $5,000 in cash."

"Paid out $300 more of my own," said Kelly. "I had to go a little above the estimate. I got the express wagons and cabs mostly for $5; but the trucks and two-horse teams mostly raised me to $10. The motormen wanted $10, and some of the loaded teams $20. The cops struck me hardest—$50 I paid two, and the rest $20 and $25. But didn't it work beautiful, Mr. Rockwall? I'm glad William A. Brady wasn't onto that little outdoor vehicle mob scene. I wouldn't want William to break his heart with jealousy. And never a rehearsal, either! The boys was on time to the fraction of a second. It was two hours before a snake could get below Greeley's statue."

"Thirteen hundred—there you are, Kelly," said Anthony, tearing off a check. "Your thousand, and the $300 you were out. You don't despise money, do you, Kelly?"

"Me?" said Kelly. "I can lick the man that invented poverty."

Anthony called Kelly when he was at the door.

"You didn't notice," said he, "anywhere in the tie-up, a kind of a fat boy without any clothes on shooting arrows around with a bow, did you?"

"Why, no," said Kelly, mystified. "I didn't. If he was like you say, maybe the cops pinched him before I got there."

"I thought the little rascal wouldn't be on hand," chuckled Anthony. "Good-by, Kelly."

THE RETURN TO FAVOR

William Dean Howells

He never, by any chance, quite kept his word, though there was a moment in every case when he seemed to imagine doing what he said, and he took with mute patience the rakings which the ladies gave him when he disappointed them.

Disappointed is not just the word, for the ladies did not really expect him to do what he said. They pretended to believe him when he promised, but at the bottom of their hearts they never did or could. He was gentle-mannered and soft-spoken, and when he set his head on one side, and said that a coat would be ready on Wednesday, or a dress on Saturday, and repeated his promise upon the same lady's expressed doubt, she would catch her breath and say that now she absolutely must have it on the day named, for otherwise she would not have a thing to put on. Then he would become very grave, and his soft tenor would deepen to a bass of unimpeachable veracity, and he would say, "Sure, lady, you have it."

The lady would depart still doubting and slightly sighing, and he would turn to the customer who was waiting to have a button sewed on, or something like that, and ask him softly what it was he could do for him. If the customer offered him his appreciation of the case in hand, he would let his head droop lower, and in a yet deeper bass deplore the doubt of the ladies as an idiosyncrasy of their sex. He would make the customer feel that he was a favorite customer whose right to a perfect fidelity of word and deed must by no means be tampered with, and he would have the button sewed on or the rip sewed up at once, and refuse to charge anything, while the customer waited in his shirt-sleeves in the small, stuffy shop opening directly from the street. When he tolerantly discussed the peculiarities of ladies as a sex, he would endure to be laughed at, "for sufferance was the badge of all his tribe," and possibly he rather liked it.

The favorite customer enjoyed being there when some lady came back on the appointed Wednesday or Saturday, and the tailor came soothingly forward and showed her into the curtained alcove where she was to try on the garments, and then called into the inner shop for them. The shirt-sleeved journeyman, with his unbuttoned waistcoat-front all pins and threaded needles, would appear in his slippers with the things barely basted together, and the tailor would take them, with an airy courage, as if they were perfectly finished, and go in behind the curtain where the lady was waiting in a dishabille which the favorite customer, out of reverence for the sex, forbore to picture to himself. Then sounds of volcanic fury would issue from the alcove. "Now, Mr. Morrison, you have lied to me again, deliberately *lied*. Didn't I tell you I *must* have the things perfectly ready today? You see yourself that it will be another week before I can have my things."

"A week? Oh, madam! But I assure you—"

"Don't talk to me any more! It's the last time I shall ever come to you, but I suppose I can't take the work away from you as it is. *When* shall I have it?"

"Tomorrow. Yes, tomorrow noon. Sure!"

"Now you know you are always out at noon. I should think you would be ashamed."

"If it hadn't been for sickness in the family I would have finished your dress with my own hands. Sure I would. If you come here tomorrow noon you find your dress all ready for you."

"I know I won't, but I will come, and you'd *better* have it ready."

"Oh, sure."

The lady then added some generalities of opprobrium with some particular criticisms of the garments. Her voice sank into dispassionate murmurs in these, but it rose again in her renewed sense of the wrong done her, and when she came from the alcove she went out of the street door purple. She reopened it to say, "Now, remember!" before she definitely disappeared.

"Rather a stormy session, Mr. Morrison," the customer said.

"Something fierce," Mr. Morrison sighed. But he did not seem much troubled, and he had one way with all his victims, no matter what mood they came or went in.

One day the customer was by when a kind creature timidly upbraided him. "This is the third time you've disappointed me, Mr. Morrison. I really wish you wouldn't promise me unless you mean to do it. I don't think it's right for you."

"Oh, but sure, madam! The things will be done, sure. We had a strike on us."

"Well, I will trust you once more," the kind creature said.

"You can depend on me, madam, sure."

When she was gone the customer said: "I wonder you do that sort of thing, Mr. Morrison. You can't be surprised at their behaving rustily with you if you never keep your word."

"Why, I assure you there are times when I don't know where to look, the way they go on. It is something awful. You ought to hear them once. And now they want the vote." He rearranged some pieces of tumbled goods at the table where the customer sat, and put together the disheveled leaves of the fashion-papers which looked as if the ladies had scattered them in their rage.

One day the customer heard two ladies waiting for their disappointments in the outer room while the tailor in the alcove was trying to persuade a third lady that positively her things would be sent home the next day before dark. The customer had now formed the habit of having his own clothes made by the tailor, and his system in avoiding disappointment was very simple. In the early fall he ordered a spring suit, and in the late spring it was ready. He never had any difficulty, but he was curious to learn how the ladies managed, and he listened with all his might while these two talked.

"I always wonder we keep coming," one of them said.

"I'll tell you why," the other said. "Because he's cheap, and we get things from a fourth to a third less than we can get them anywhere else. The quality is first rate, and he's absolutely honest. And, besides, he's a genius. The wretch has *touch*. The things have a style, a look, a hang! Really it's something wonderful. Sure it iss," she ended in the tailor's accent, and then they both laughed and joined in a common sigh.

"Well, I don't believe he means to deceive anyone."

"Oh, neither do I. I believe he expects to do everything he says. And one can't help liking him even when he doesn't."

"He's a good while getting through with her," the first lady said, meaning the unseen lady in the alcove.

"She'll be a good while longer getting through with *him*, if he hasn't them ready the next time," the second lady said.

But the lady in the alcove issued from it with an impredictable smile, and the tailor came up to the others, and deferred to their wishes with a sort of voiceless respect.

He gave the customer a glance of good-fellowship, and said to him, radiantly: "Your things all ready for you, this morning. As soon as I—"

"Oh, no hurry," the customer responded.

"I won't be a minute," the tailor said, pulling the curtain of the alcove aside, and then there began those sounds of objurgation and expostulation, although the ladies had seemed so amiable before.

The customer wondered if they did not all enjoy it; the ladies in their patience under long trial, and the tailor in the pleasure of practicing upon it. But perhaps he did believe in the things he promised. He might be so much a genius as to have no grasp of facts; he might have thought that he could actually do what he said.

The customer's question on these points found answer when one day the tailor remarked, as it were out of a clear sky, that he had sold his business; sold it to the slippered journeyman who used to come in his shirt-sleeves, with his vest-front full of pins and needles, bringing the basted garments to be tried on the ladies who had been promised them perfectly finished.

"He will do your clothes all right," he explained to the customer. "He is a first-rate cutter and fitter; he knows the whole business."

"But why—why—" the customer began.

"I couldn't stand it. The way them ladies would talk to a person, when you done your best to please them; it's something fierce."

"Yes, I know. But I thought you liked it, from the way you always promised them and never kept your word."

"And if I hadn't promised them?" the tailor returned with some show of feeling. "They *wanted* me to promise them—they made me—they wouldn't have gone away without it. Sure. Everyone wanted her things before everyone. You had got to think of that."

"But you had to think of what they would say."

"Say? Sometimes I thought they would *hit* me. One lady said she had a notion to slap me once. It's no way to talk."

"But you didn't seem to mind it."

"I didn't mind it for a good while. Then I couldn't stand it. So I sold."

He shook his head sadly; but the customer had no comfort to offer him. He asked when his clothes would be done, and the tailor told him when, and then they were not. The new proprietor tried them on, but he would not say just when they would be finished.

"We have a good deal of work already for some ladies that been disappointed. Now we try a new way. We tell people exactly what we do."

"Well, that's right," the customer said, but in his heart he was not sure he liked the new way.

The day before his clothes were promised he dropped in. From the curtained alcove he heard low murmurs, the voice of the new proprietor and the voice of some lady trying on, and being severely bidden not to expect her things at a time she suggested. "No, madam. We got too much work on hand already. These things, they will not be before next week."

"I told you tomorrow," the same voice said to another lady, and the new proprietor came out with an unfinished coat in his hand.

"I know you did, but I thought you would be better than your word, and so I came today. Well, then, tomorrow."

"Yes, tomorrow," the new proprietor said, but he did not seem to have liked the lady's joke. He did not look happy.

A few weeks after that the customer came for some little alterations in his new suit.

In the curtained alcove he heard the murmurs of trying on, much cheerfuller murmurs than before; the voice of a lady lifted in gladness, in gayety, and an incredible voice replying, "Oh, sure, madam."

Then the old proprietor came out in his shirt-sleeves and slippers, with his waistcoat-front full of pins and neeedles, just like the new proprietor in former days.

"Why!" the customer exclaimed. "Have you bought back?"

"No. I'm just here like a journeyman already. The new man he want me to come. He don't get along very well with his way. He's all right; he's a good man and a first-class tailor. But," and the former proprietor looked down at the basted garment hanging over his arm, and picked off an irrelevant thread from it, "he thinks I get along better with the ladies."

THE GREAT FIRE OF HAMBURG

Of all the phenomena attending the great fire at Hamburg, Germany, in May, 1842, the most impressive was the simultaneous ringing, for a time, of all the great bells in the city, by the currents of air which the fire produced. Each of the large churches rang on its own chimes its funeral knell. The magnificent church of St. Nicholas, erected in the 12th century, and covering a space 370 by 140 feet, had a square tower surmounted by a spire,—in all 360 feet high. A writer in the *Westminster Review* says: "When this spire began to burn, its appearance was that of a magnificent torch in the midst of a wide-spreading sea of fire; and, as the flames climbed toward the pinnacle, every eye in Hamburg was directed to the church, and all personal anxieties were forgotten for the moment in the interest excited by the approaching catastrophe. That interest was painfully increased when the chimes of the tower began mournfully to perform its funeral dirge. The last tones of the bells, untuned by the expansion from the heat, came upon the ear as a cry of suffering, and it was a relief to the spectators when it ceased. The sheets of copper with which the sides of the spire were plated, were seen to peel off and, glowing with a red heat, floated away in the air. Soon after, it inclined from the perpendicular, and fell, with a tremendous crash, to the ground."

St. Peter's, a church valued for its architectural beauty as well as for its being a relic of the 12th century, made a hard fight for its life. It had a lofty tower, surmounted by a pyramid, and contained many beautiful works of art. Two hundred persons worked unceasingly to save it. Houses near by were blown up with gunpowder, and "the cannon of the Hanoverian artillery," the same writer adds, "were fired against others, but with no useful result. During the night of Friday, the heated wood-work several times burst into flames, and, although as often extinguished, the heat became so intense that about nine in the morning it was necessary to abandon the church to its fate. A scene similar to that of the burning of St. Nicholas was renewed; again the green and yellow flames rose high above the summit, the bells tolled their own departure, and when the steeple broke off from the tower, it buried itself many feet in the earth from the violence of its fall."

Another phenomenon was the burning of the piles in the various canals and in the Alster River. According to a writer in the *London Times*, these piles, used for the mooring of boats, caught fire in such rapid succession that they presented the effect of an intentional illumination of the street with huge flambeaux set up on end.

A third remarkable occurrence was the saving of the New Exchange in the midst of the burnt district, although the copper roof of the building had become so hot as to burn the shoes of the men working there.

An amusing incident was the adjournment of the Senate, for the first time in its history, without the formality of a seconded motion. The Senate, or supreme legislative assembly of Hamburg, had met and voted (in view of the disastrous character the fire had already assumed, and the probable necessity of voting on urgent measures of relief, etc.) not to adjourn until the flames had been finally extinguished. When the church of St. Nicholas fell, it became evident that nothing could save the Senate House; and, as the public treasure was all contained in the vaults underneath, the fire-fighting authorities determined to blow up the building. They hastily sent for the powder, and then gave notice to the Senate of what had been done. The Senators, regardless of their resolution to sit the conflagration out, and without waiting to move, second, and vote an adjournment, hastily threw papers, hats, gowns, and other personal effects together, and scampered from the building, the blasting powder being carried into their chamber by the military engineers just as the last Senator was making his hasty exit.

In a few minutes more the Senate House was a mere heap of stones and dust.

THE LAST OF THE GLADIATORS

The first gladiatorial show which we read of in Roman history was about the year of the city 490 (263 B.C.), given by Marcus and Decius Brutus (called the Bruti) at the funeral of their father. Afterwards these exhibitions were given by the magistrates at regular periods, and at length they became the chief means of obtaining the favor of the people.

The emperors exceeded all others in the extent and magnificence of these cruel spectacles. Julius Caesar gave a show of three hundred and twenty couples. Titus gave a show of gladiators with wild beasts for one hundred days; Trajan, for one hundred and twenty-three days, in which twenty thousand gladiators, chiefly Dacian prisoners, and eleven thousand wild beasts, are said to have been slain for the amusement of seventy thousand Romans, patricians and plebians, the highest ladies and the lowest rabble, assembled in the Coliseum.

The gladiators consisted chiefly of slaves, captives, and condemned malefactors; but sometimes free-born citizens became gladiators for hire. Even persons of high birth were induced to display their skill and courage before the people in these combats.

The gladiators were trained and sworn to fight to the death. If they showed cowardice, they were killed after torture.

When one of the combatants was disarmed or upon the ground, the victor looked to the emperor if present, or to the people, for the signal of death. If they raised their thumbs, his life was spared; if they turned them down, the victor executed the fatal mandate.

A gladiator who conquered was rewarded with a branch of palm or with his freedom. The Emperor Constantine prohibited these contests of gladiators (A.D. 325), but they could not at once be abolished.

In the reign of Honorius, son of Theodosius the Great, the retreat of the Goths from Rome, under their chieftain Alaric, was celebrated with great rejoicing in the city, and with the revival of the gladiatorial contests. In the midst of the games in the Coliseum, Telemachus, a Christian monk, sprang into the arena, and, raising the cross above his head, commanded the gladiators, in the name of their crucified Lord, to cease from their inhuman sport.

The enraged multitude stoned him to death; but a little later, overwhelmed with remorse for the act, they proclaimed him a martyr.

The Emperor Honorius took advantage of this occasion to prohibit gladiatorial combats forever within the amphitheatre at Rome (A.D. 404). They ceased throughout the empire in the year A.D. 500.

THE ADOPTED SON

Guy de Maupassant

The two cottages stood beside each other at the foot of a hill near a little seashore resort. The two peasants labored hard on the unproductive soil to rear their little ones, and each family had four.

Before the adjoining doors a whole troop of urchins played and tumbled about from morning till night. The two eldest were six years old, and the youngest were about fifteen months; the marriages, and afterward the births, having taken place nearly simultaneously in both families.

The two mothers could hardly distinguish their own offspring among the lot, and as for the fathers, they were altogether at sea. The eight names danced in their heads; they were always getting them mixed up; and when they wished to call one child, the men often called three names before getting the right one.

The first of the two cottages, as you came up from the bathing beach, Rolleport, was occupied by the Tuvaches, who had three girls and one boy; the other house sheltered the Vallins, who had one girl and three boys.

They all subsisted frugally on soup, potatoes and fresh air. At seven o'clock in the morning, then at noon, then at six o'clock in the evening, the housewives got their broods together to give them their food, as the gooseherds collect their charges. The children were seated, according to age, before the wooden table, varnished by fifty years of use; the mouths of the youngest hardly reaching the level of the table. Before them was placed a bowl filled with bread, soaked in the water in which the potatoes had been boiled, half a cabbage and three onions; and the whole line ate until their hunger was appeased. The mother herself fed the smallest.

A small pot roast on Sunday was a feast for all; and the father on this day sat longer over the meal, repeating: "I wish we could have this every day."

One afternoon, in the month of August, a phaëton stopped suddenly in front of the cottages, and a young woman, who was driving the horses, said to the gentleman sitting at her side:

"Oh, look at all those children, Henri! How pretty they are, tumbling about in the dust, like that!"

The man did not answer, accustomed to these outbursts of admiration, which were a pain and almost a reproach to him. The young woman continued:

"I must hug them! Oh, how I should like to have one of them—that one there—the little tiny one!"

Springing down from the carriage, she ran toward the children, took one of the youngest—a Tuvache child—and lifting it up in her arms, she kissed him passionately on his dirty cheeks, on his tousled hair daubed with earth, and on his little hands, with which he fought vigorously, to get away from the caresses which displeased him.

Then she got into the carriage again, and drove off at a lively trot. But she returned the following week, and seating herself on the ground, took the youngster in her arms, stuffed him with cakes, gave candies to all the others, and played with them like a young girl, while the husband waited patiently in the carriage.

She returned again; made the acquaintance of the parents, and reappeared every day with her pockets full of dainties and pennies.

Her name was Madame Henri d'Hubières.

One morning, on arriving, her husband alighted with her, and without stopping to talk to the children, who now knew her well, she entered the farmer's cottage.

They were busy chopping wood for the fire. They rose to their feet in surprise, brought forward chairs, and waited expectantly.

Then the woman, in a broken, trembling voice, began:

"My good people, I have come to see you, because I should like—I should like to take—your little boy with me —"

The country people, too bewildered to think, did not answer.

She recovered her breath, and continued: "We are alone, my husband and I. We would keep it. Are you willing?"

The peasant woman began to understand. She asked:

"You want to take Charlot from us? Oh, no, indeed!"

Then M. d'Hubières intervened:

"My wife has not made her meaning clear. We wish to adopt him, but he will come back to see you. If he turns out well, as there is every reason to expect, he will be our heir. If we, perchance, should have children, he will share equally with them; but if he should not reward our care, we should give him, when he comes of age, a sum of twenty thousand francs, which shall be deposited immediately in his name, with a lawyer. As we have thought also of you, we should pay you, until your death, a pension of one hundred francs a month. Do you understand me?"

The woman had arisen, furious.

"You want me to sell you Charlot? Oh, no, that's not the sort of thing to ask of a mother! Oh, no! That would be abomination!"

The man, grave and deliberate, said nothing; but approved of what his wife said by a continued nodding of his head.

Madame d'Hubières, in dismay, began to weep; turning to her husband, with a voice full of tears, the voice of a child used to having all its wishes gratified, she stammered:

"They will not do it, Henri, they will not do it."

Then he made a last attempt: "But, my friends, think of the child's future, of his happiness, of —"

The peasant woman, however, exasperated, cut him short:

"It's all considered! It's all understood! Get out of here, and don't let me see you again—the idea of wanting to take away a child like that!"

Madame d'Hubières remembered that there were two children, quite little, and she asked, through her tears, with the tenacity of a wilful and spoiled woman:

"But is the other little one not yours?"

Father Tuvache answered: "No, it is our neighbors'. You can go to them if you wish." And he went back into his house, whence resounded the indignant voice of his wife.

The Vallins were at table, slowly eating slices of bread which they parsimoniously spread with a little rancid butter on a plate between the two.

M. d'Hubières recommenced his proposals, but with more insinuations, more oratorical precautions, more shrewdness.

The two country people shook their heads, in sign of refusal, but when they learned that they were to have a hundred francs a month, they considered the matter, consulting one another by glances, much disturbed. They kept silent for a long time, tortured, hesitating. At last the woman asked: "What do you say to it, man?" In a weighty tone he said: "I say that it's not to be despised."

Madame d'Hubières, trembling with anguish, spoke of the future of their child, of his happiness, and of the money which he could give them later.

The peasant asked: "This pension of twelve hundred francs, will it be promised before a lawyer?"

M. d'Hubières responded: "Why, certainly, beginning with to-morrow."

The woman, who was thinking it over, continued:

"A hundred francs a month is not enough to pay for depriving us of the child. That child would be working in a few years; we must have a hundred and twenty francs."

Tapping her foot with impatience, Madame d'Hubières granted it at once, and, as she wished to carry off the child with her, she gave a hundred francs extra, as a present, while her husband drew up a paper. And the young woman, radiant, carried off the howling brat, as one carries away a wished-for knick-knack from a shop.

The Tuvaches, from their door, watched her departure, silent, serious, perhaps regretting their refusal.

Nothing more was heard of little Jean Vallin. The parents went to the lawyer every month to collect their hundred and twenty francs. They had quarrelled with their neighbors, because Mother Tuvache grossly insulted them, continually, repeating from door to door that one must be unnatural to sell one's child; that it was horrible, disgusting, bribery. Sometimes she would take her Charlot in her arms, ostentatiously exclaiming, as if he understood:

"I didn't sell *you*, I didn't! I didn't sell *you*, my little one! I'm not rich, but I don't sell my children!"

The Vallins lived comfortably, thanks to the pension. That was the cause of the unappeasable fury of the Tuvaches, who had remained miserably poor. Their eldest went away to serve his time in the army; Charlot alone remained to labor with his old father, to support the mother and two younger sisters.

He had reached twenty-one years when, one morning, a brilliant carriage stopped before the two cottages. A young gentleman, with a gold watch-chain, got out, giving his hand to an aged, white-haired lady. The old lady said to him: "It is there, my child, at the second house." And he entered the house of the Vallins as though at home.

The old mother was washing her aprons; the infirm father slumbered at the chimney-corner. Both raised their heads, and the young man said:

"Good-morning, papa; good-morning, mamma!"

They both stood up, frightened! In a flutter, the peasant woman dropped her soap into the water, and stammered:

"Is it you, my child? Is it you, my child?"

He took her in his arms and hugged her, repeating: "Good-morning, mamma," while the old man, all a-tremble, said, in his calm tone which he never lost: "Here you are, back again, Jean," as if he had just seen him a month ago.

When they had got to know one another again, the parents wished to take their boy out in the neighborhood, and show him. They took him to the mayor, to the deputy, to the *curé*, and to the schoolmaster.

Charlot, standing on the threshold of his cottage, watched him pass.

In the evening, at supper, he said to the old people: "You must have been stupid to let the Vallins' boy be taken."

The mother answered, obstinately: "I wouldn't sell *my* child."

The father remained silent. The son continued:

"It is unfortunate to be sacrificed like that."

Then Father Tuvache, in an angry tone, said:

"Are you going to reproach us for having kept you?" And the young man said, brutally:

"Yes, I reproach you for having been such fools. Parents like you make the misfortune of their children. You deserve that I should leave you."

The old woman wept over her plate. She moaned, as she swallowed the spoonfuls of soup, half of which she spilled: "One may kill one's self to bring up children!"

Then the boy said, roughly: "I'd rather not have been born than be what I am. When I saw the other, my heart stood still. I said to myself: 'See what I should have been now!'" He got up: "See here, I feel that I would do better not to stay here, because I would throw it up to you from morning till night, and I would make your life miserable. I'll never forgive you for that!"

The two old people were silent, downcast, in tears.

He continued: "No, the thought of that would be too much. I'd rather look for a living somewhere else."

He opened the door. A sound of voices came in at the door. The Vallins were celebrating the return of their child.

FAMOUS HOSTS AND GUESTS

QUEEN ELIZABETH I was probably history's least welcome guest. It wasn't that her hosts didn't like her; but the expense was ruinous. The whole court accompanied her on her "progresses" through the kingdom. When the Earl of Bedford was faced with entertaining the queen and her retinue in 1572, we find him writing nervously to Lord Treasurer Burleigh: "I trust Your Lordship will have a remembrance to provide and help that Her Majesty's tarrying will not be above two nights and a daye." His apprehension was well founded. In two days with Lord North of Kertlinge, they romped through the following provisions: 4,800 loaves of bread, eleven steers and oxen, sixty-six sheep, seventeen calves, seven lambs, thirty-four pigs, four stags, sixteen bucks, a total of 2,075 birds (ranging in size from six turkeys and thirty-two swans down to 325 quail), seventy-four hogsheads of beer, 430 pounds of butter, 2,522 eggs, one cartload and two horse-loads of oysters and 400 red herrings.

QUEEN VICTORIA was a total frost as a hostess. Not only did she introduce dry "Drawing Rooms" (afternoon receptions at Buckingham Palace at which, greatly to everyone's distress, no refreshments of any kind were served), but those rash enough to stay with her in the Highlands of Scotland were in for sheer hell. The food was dreadful, the domestic arrangements were (to put it politely) embryonic, and John Brown, her coarse-grained major-domo, was rude to the guests and wouldn't let anyone ride the ponies.

THE WEEKEND, known to the oldest generation as a "Saturday to Monday" and to the French, sensibly enough, as *le weekend,* is a relatively modern invention, and some people never quite got the hang of it. The 8th Duke of Rutland, confronted with a merry throng bustling through his front door on a Friday, would panic completely and demand, ashen-faced, "What train are you taking on Monday?" The dowagers with weekend palaces on San Francisco's fashionable Peninsula were far more poised; faced with lingering weekend guests, they would trundle them into San Francisco on Monday for lunch at the St. Francis Hotel; politely but firmly their baggage would be brought along, too, and that took care of that.

QUEEN OF ENGLAND AND EMPRESS OF INDIA

It is a singular fact that prior to 1877, Germany, Russia, and Austria, amongst the civilized nations, and Turkey, China, Japan, Persia, and other semi-civilized powers, were ruled by potentates nominally of higher rank than the Queen of England; and on one or two occasions, members of the Queen's family, sent to represent her at festivities at other courts, complained of the indignity of being obliged to yield precedence to the representatives of imperial monarchs not nearly so powerful in fact as she.

Primarily, therefore, Queen Victoria assumed the title Empress of India to enhance the dignity of her sovereign office. The English people would not, of course, listen to the idea of her assuming even the appearance of dictatorial power as far as they were concerned; but Disraeli, then Premier, insisted that the chief object of the new title was to impress the distant subjects of the crown, and proposed that Victoria should confine her imperial rank to India. On this basis Parliament consented, in April, 1876, to pass the "titles bill," as it was called. The subject aroused a great deal of excitement, even among the most loyal people, and most influential London journals were very severe in their arraignment of what they considered a specious humbug. The *Bombay Gazette,* speaking for the people of India, declared the scheme uncalled for, as the native Indian subjects would not know the difference between the old title and the new one. But these arguments were met in Parliament and by the strictly conservative press with the statement that the dignitaries of India would certainly understand the mention of their country's name in the sovereign's title, whether they grasped the full significance of the change or not; and that in a conquered oriental country where so many separate chiefs enjoyed a rank nearly, or quite, equivalent to that of a king in Europe, it was necessary to impress upon them the sense that there was a paramount authority to which they must in turn yield the obedience of vassals, and one which was recognized all over the civilized world as of the highest degree.

The proclamation was deferred until New Year's Day, 1877. On that day great state assemblages were convened at Delhi, Calcutta, Bombay and Madras. The Viceroy presided at the one held at Delhi. A dais was erected in a slightly open space, and a throne placed thereon. In front of this, on the south side, were grouped the principal governors and lieutenant-governors, and other state officers, sixty-three of the ruling native chiefs with their suites, and some fifteen thousand troops, white and native. On the north side were drawn up the minor chiefs, with their retainers and troops. The regimental bands were stationed near the dais, and around the entire assemblage was an unbroken circle of elephants in the most gorgeous trappings. At noon the Viceroy ascended the throne, and, after the national anthem had been performed, the Chief Herald read the proclamation. The imperial standard was then raised and honored with a salute of one hundred and one salvos of artillery, of six guns each, and a *feu de joie* from the troops. The Viceroy delivered an address, in which he explained that "the assumption of the title of Empress was intended by their sovereign to be to the princes and people of India a symbol of the union of their interests and a claim upon their loyal allegiance, the imperial power giving them a guaranty of impartial protection." A telegram from the Empress, bearing testimony to what had been said, was then read, and the assembly was dispersed. The next day was one of great festivity, and all civil prisoners who had records for good conduct were set free. There were no formal ceremonies in England. Medals were struck in honor of the occasion and distributed among the leading partakers in the ceremonies. They bore on one side the Queen's head, and on the other, in Arabic and Sanskrit, her new title, KAISERIHIND. Each of the greater native chiefs, also, received a beautiful banner, emblazoned with the arms of his house, and carried on a gilt pole, inscribed, "From Victoria, Empress of India, January 1st, 1877."

It may be recalled, in conclusion, that his skillful procurement of this tribute to his sovereign was promptly followed by Mr. Disraeli's elevation to the peerage, as the Earl of Beaconsfield, at Her Majesty's direct solicitation.

THE MOST CELEBRATED TRIAL

The most celebrated trial in the annals of English jurisprudence is undoubtedly that of Warren Hastings. This case lasted, including preliminary proceedings, nearly ten years—from 1786 to 1795. Hastings (born in 1733) was an Englishman of the middle rank in life, who, at the age of seventeen, went to India as a writer in the employ of the East India Company. After a residence there of fourteen years, he returned to England, having gained such a reputation for clever executive management, that in 1769 he received the appointment as second in the Council at Madras. Three years later he was promoted to the highest office in the gift of the Company, that of President of the Supreme Council of Bengal. The powers of this office were afterward enlarged by an act of Parliament, so that he became Governor-General and supreme head of all the British dependencies in India. By his able management he greatly increased the revenue of the realm, established British authority over the conquered provinces on a firmer basis than it had ever enjoyed before, and made the path of his successors in office comparatively easy. But he called down upon himself the bitter enmity of the native chiefs, and also of many Englishmen of note, who, envious of the increasing power and wealth of Hastings, determined to destroy him. Reports of cruelty and oppression, unjust aggressiveness, lavish and corrupt expenditure, were busily circulated in England. How true or how false the charges were is impossible now to judge; but a split occurred in the management of the East India Company, one party endeavoring to procure his dismissal, and the other and more powerful one standing by him. Thus encouraged, he asked and received constantly more authority, until he became at last practically an irresponsible despot. In February, 1785, either weary of the contention in which he had lived so long, or else feeling that he had exhausted all that was worth having in the office of Governor-General, he resigned and set sail for home. As soon as he reached England, Edumund Burke began preparations to have him impeached by Parliament. The formal proceedings began in 1786, and it was not until the 2nd of June, 1791, that Hastings began his defense. It lasted until the 17th of April, 1795, on which date he was acquitted by a large majority on every article of the indictment. A great nation had been sitting in public judgment upon a great criminal for nearly ten years, and it is said that when his verdict of acquittal was read, the members of Parliament rose as a body and removed their hats—an honor not paid even to royalty. Edmund Burke's opening speech in the trial of Hastings is considered one of the sublimest philippics that ancient or modern oratory has ever produced. The Company in whose service Lord Hastings had won so much glory and suffered such tortures of disgrace granted him a liberal annuity—and justly so, as the protracted trial had completely impoverished his resources. He retired to private life, but shortly before his death (which occurred in August, 1818) he received an appointment to a very important public office, that of Privy Counselor. The bitterness of Burke, the Irishman, during this trial, inspired the following epigram:—

> "Oft 't has been wondered why on Irish ground
> No snake of deadly venom e'er was found.
> Behold the reason of Dame Nature's work.
> She saved her venom, to endow a Burke."

VENETIAN PAGEANT

The safety of Venice depended upon her undisputed sway over the Adriatic. The "Espousal of Venice and the Sea" was the symbol of this supremacy which she arrogated in her title, "Queen of the Adriatic." From the year 997, a national fête had been celebrated annually upon Ascension Day, to commemorate the conquest of Dalmatia, and the victories won over the Marentine pirates during the reign of the Doge Pietro Orsello II. The people of Venice repaired to the sea, beyond the harbor of Lido, and performed certain ceremonies in accordance with the taste of the age. For one hundred and eighty years this custom survived unchanged. But in 1176, after the great naval victory of the Doge Ziani over the imperial fleet of Frederick Barbarossa, Pope Alexander III (who was at that time a refugee in Venice) presented the Doge Ziani with a gold ring, saying, "Take it, my son, as a token of true and perpetual dominion over the sea as your subject; and every year, on this Day of Ascension, shall you and your successors make known to all posterity that the ocean belongs to Venice by the right of conquest, and that she is subservient to Venice, as a spouse is to her husband." Thus was added to the ancient ceremonies of Ascension Day, the "Marriage with the Sea."

The "Bucentaur," a magnificent vessel, was used exclusively for this occasion. It was a galley, one hundred feet in length, consisting of two decks, the lower one occupied by one hundred and sixty rowers, selected from the most skillful sailors of the fleet. The upper deck was divided lengthwise into two parts by an open partition of nine arcades, each seven feet wide, whose pillars were ornamented with gilded figures. Along the sides were arranged ninety seats for the retinue of the Doge. In the stern was a state saloon, where, raised on two steps, glittered the ducal throne. The upper deck was covered through its entire length by an awning; supporting this on either side were pilasters carved in imitation of caryatides. The prow of the boat was armed with two projections, one above the other, both enriched with gigantic allegorical figures of Justice, Peace, the Earth, and the Sea; while numberless ornaments of sphinxes, marine monsters, ocean shells, and scrolls, decorated the broadsides of this magnificent naval edifice. Over all floated the resplendent Banner of St. Mark.

The "Marriage Day" was the greatest festival in Venice. From early dawn bells were ringing, cannon firing, and the whole population, in gayest attire, was hastening toward the Piazzetta of San Marco, where the "Bucentaur" lay. As the great clock struck the hour of noon, the magnificent retinue in attendance upon the Doge slowly and steadily moved to the place of embarkation. This was the signal for a blast of silver trumpets and the shouting of an excited multitude. Thousands of the citizens then embarked in gondolas and boats gaily decorated with ribbons and flags. As the "Bucentaur" weighed anchor, all the bells of the city rang out a jubilant peal, to which the ships of war, the arsenal, and the forts responded with artillery. Mingled with this far-rolling thunder were the strains of joyful music on board the "Bucentaur" and the other vessels which literally covered the sea. Having arrived at the Port of San Nicolas, the ducal vessel crossed the strait amid the thunder of a hundred cannon, and proceeded a short distance out to sea. She then put about; a door behind the sovereign's throne was suddenly thrown open, the Doge stepped into a small gallery in the bow, and from thence cast into the waves a golden ring, accompanying the action with the words: "We wed thee, O Sea, in token of our true and perpetual sovereignty." Then broke again from the assembled thousands a loud cheer of joy and triumph.

The marriage ceremony ended, the gay fleet returned to Venice. The dignitaries repaired to the ducal palace and partook of a sumptuous repast presided over by the Doge himself, while the populace fairly poured into the Piazza di San Marco and abandoned themselves to all kinds of revelry. The "Bucentaur" here described was the one built in 1727 and burned by the French, under Napoleon, in 1797. A model of this famous Ship of State is preserved in the Arsenal of Venice.

TIGERS

Marmaduke Pickthall

The fellâhîn who came to gossip in the winter evenings round our lamp and stove assured us there were tigers in the neighbouring mountain. We, of course, did not accept the statement literally, but our English friend possessed the killing instinct, and held that any feline creatures which could masquerade in popular report as tigers would afford him better sport than he had yet enjoyed in Syria. So when the settled weather came we went to look for them.

For my part I take pleasure in long expeditions with a gun, though nothing in the way of slaughter come of them. My lack of keenness at the proper moment has been the scorn and the despair of native guides and hunters. Once, in Egypt, at the inundation of the Nile, I had been rowed for miles by eager men, and had lain out an hour upon an islet among reeds, only to forget to fire when my adherents whispered as the duck flew over, because the sun was rising and the desert hills were blushing like a rose against a starry sky. I had chased a solitary partridge a whole day among the rocks of En-gedi without the slightest prospect of success; and in the Jordan valley I had endured great hardships in pursuit of wild boar without seeing one. It was the lurking in wild places at unusual hours which pleased me, not the matching of my strength and skill against the might of beasts. I have always been averse to every sort of competition. This I explain that all may know that, though I sallied forth with glee in search of savage creatures, it was not to kill them.

We set out from our village on a fine spring morning, attended by Rashîd, my servant, and a famous hunter of the district named Muhammad, also two mules, which carried all things necessary for our camping out, and were in charge of my friend's cook, Amîn by name. We rode into the mountains, making for the central range of barren heights, which had the hue and something of the contour of a lion's back. At length we reached a village at the foot of this commanding

range, and asked for tigers. We were told that they were farther on. A
man came with us to a point of vantage whence he was able to point
out the very place—a crag in the far distance floating in a haze of heat.
After riding for a day and a half we came right under it, and at a village
near its base renewed inquiry. "Oh," we were told, "the tigers are much
farther on. You see that eminence?" Again a mountain afar off was
indicated. At the next village we encamped, for night drew near. The
people came out to inspect us, and we asked them for the tigers.

"Alas!" they cried. "It is not here that you must seek them. By Allah,
you are going in the wrong direction. Behold that distant peak!"

And they pointed to the place from which we had originally started.

Our English friend was much annoyed, Rashîd and the shikari and
the cook laughed heartily. No one, however, was for going back. Upon
the following day our friend destroyed a jackal and two conies, which
consoled him somewhat in the dearth of tigers, and we rode forward
resolutely, asking our question at each village as we went along. Everywhere we were assured that there were really tigers in the mountain,
and from some of the villages young sportsmen who owned guns insisted
upon joining our excursion, which showed that they themselves believed
such game existed. But their adherence, though it gave us hope, was
tiresome, for they smoked our cigarettes and ate our food.

At last, towards sunset on the seventh evening of our expedition, we
saw a wretched-looking village on the heights with no trees near it, and
only meagre strips of cultivation on little terraces, like ledges, of the slope
below.

Our friend had just been telling me that he was weary of this wild-
goose chase, with all the rascals upon earth adhering to us. He did not
now believe that there were tigers in the mountain, nor did I. And we
had quite agreed to start for home upon the morrow, when the people
of that miserable village galloped down to greet us with delighted shouts,
as if they had been waiting for us all their lives.

"What is your will?" inquired the elders of the place, obsequiously.

"Tigers," was our reply. "Say, O old man, are there any tigers in your
neighbourhood?"

The old man flung up both hands to heaven, and his face became
transfigured as in ecstasy. He shouted: "Is it tigers you desire? This,
then, is the place where you will dwell content. Tigers? I should think so!
Tigers everywhere!"

The elders pointed confidently to the heights, and men and women—
even children—told us: "Aye, by Allah! Hundreds—thousands of them;
not just one or two. As many as the most capacious man could possibly
devour in forty years."

"It looks as if we'd happened right at last," our friend said, smiling for the first time in three days.

We pitched our tent upon the village threshing floor, the only flat place, except roofs of houses, within sight. The village elders dined with us, and stayed till nearly midnight, telling us about the tigers and the way to catch them. Some of the stories they related were incredible, but not much more so than is usual in that kind of narrative. It seemed unnecessary for one old man to warn us gravely on no account take them by their tails.

"For snakes it is the proper way," he said sagaciously, "since snakes can only double half their length. But tigers double their whole length, and they object to it. To every creature its own proper treatment."

But there was no doubt of the sincerity of our instructors, nor of their eagerness to be of use to us in any way. Next morning, when we started out, the headman came with us some distance, on purpose to instruct the guide he had assigned to us, a stupid-looking youth, who seemed afraid. He told him: "Try first over there among the boulders, and when you have exhausted that resort, go down to the ravine, and thence beat upwards to the mountain top. Please God, your Honours will return with half a hundred of those tigers which devour our crops."

Thus sped with hope, we set out in good spirits, expecting not a bag of fifty tigers, to speak truly, but the final settlement of a dispute which had long raged among us, as to what those famous tigers really were. Rashîd would have it they were leopards, I said lynxes, and our English friend, in moments of depression, thought of polecats. But, though we scoured the mountain all that day, advancing with the utmost caution and in open order, as our guide enjoined, we saw no creature of the feline tribe. Lizards, basking motionless upon the rocks, slid off like lightning when aware of our approach. Two splendid eagles from an eyrie on the crags above hovered and wheeled, observing us, their shadows like two moving spots of ink upon the mountain side. A drowsy owl was put up from a cave, and one of our adherents swore he heard a partridge calling. No other living creature larger than a beetle did we come across that day.

Returning to the camp at evening, out of temper, we were met by all the village, headed by the sheykh, who loudly hoped that we had had good sport, and brought home many tigers to provide a feast. When he heard that we had not so much as seen a single one he fell upon the luckless youth who had been told off to conduct us, and would have slain him, I believe, had we not intervened.

"Didst seek in all the haunts whereof I told thee? Well I know thou didst not, since they saw no tiger! Behold our faces blackened through thy sloth and folly, O abandoned beast!"

Restrained by force by two of our adherents, the sheykh spat venomously at the weeping guide, who swore by Allah that he had obeyed instructions to the letter.

Our English friend was much too angry to talk Arabic. He bade me tell the sheykh he was a liar, and that the country was as bare of tigers as his soul of truth. Some of our fellâh adherents seconded my speech. The sheykh appeared amazed and greatly horrified.

"There are tigers," he assured us, "naturally! All that you desire."

"Then go and find them for us!" said our friend, vindictively.

"Upon my head," replied the complaisant old man, laying his right hand on his turban reverently. "To hear is to obey."

We regarded this reply as mere politeness, the affair as ended. What was our surprise next morning to see the sheykh and all the able men, accompanied by many children, set off up the mountain armed with staves and scimitars, and all the antique armament the village boasted! It had been our purpose to depart that day, but we remained to watch the outcome of that wondrous hunting.

The villagers spread out and "beat" the mountain. All day long we heard their shouts far off among the upper heights. If any tiger had been there they must assuredly have roused him. But they returned at evening empty-handed, and as truly crestfallen as if they had indeed expected to bring home a bag of fifty tigers. One man presented me with a dead owl—the same, I think, which we had startled on the day before, as if to show that their display had not been quite in vain.

"No tigers!" sighed the sheykh, as though his heart were broken. "What can have caused them all to go away? Unhappy day!" A lamentable wail went up from the whole crowd. "A grievous disappointment, but the world is thus. But," he added, with a sudden brightening, "if your Honours will but condescend to stay a week or two, no doubt they will return."

THE CARROCCIO

The Carroccio was the great standard car of state and the sacred palladium of the Lombard Republic, and was invented about the year 1035.

It was a strong car on four wheels, painted red, drawn by four pairs of milk-white oxen with splendid trappings of scarlet.

In the centre of the car, raised upon a mast which was crowned with a golden ball, floated the banner of the republic: beneath it was an image of the Saviour extended upon the cross, as if to pour benediction upon the surrounding hosts.

It was the custom whenever they took the field, to conduct the Carroccio into the midst of the army; and its sight was supposed to inspire courage in the hearts of the combatants. Three hundred of the most distinguished soldiers were appointed to guard it in the battle, and the loss of it was considered the most grievous calamity and the greatest disgrace.

In the Lombard Republic, to belong to the gallant Cohort of the Three Hundred was a great honor. Next in point of rank came nine hundred chosen men called the "Cohort of Death."

Feelings of religion and military glory were strangely associated with the Carroccio. It was an imitation of the Jewish ark of the covenant, and from its platform the chaplain of the army administered Christian rites to the people.

The thickest of the battle ever encircled the Carroccio: it guided the advance, and the duty of defending it insured order in a retreat.

The liberty of Lombardy was secured by the battle of Legnano (1176), and the victory was due to the rallying of the "Three Hundred" and the "Cohort of Death" around the Carroccio.

The return of the Carroccio to Milan after this decisive battle (in which the disciplined forces of Germany, commanded by the Emperor Frederick Barbarossa in person, gave way, and were defeated) was celebrated by eight days of festivity.

WAR

Luigi Pirandello

The passengers who had left Rome by the night express had had to stop until dawn at the small station of Fabriano in order to continue their journey by the small old-fashioned local joining the main line with Sulmona.

At dawn, in a stuffy and smoky second-class carriage in which five people had already spent the night, a bulky woman in deep mourning was hoisted in—almost like a shapeless bundle. Behind her—puffing and moaning, followed her husband—a tiny man, thin and weakly, his face death-white, his eyes small and bright and looking shy and uneasy.

Having at last taken a seat he politely thanked the passengers who had helped his wife and who had made room for her; then he turned round to the woman trying to pull down the collar of her coat, and politely inquired:

"Are you all right, dear?"

The wife, instead of answering, pulled up her collar again to her eyes, so as to hide her face.

"Nasty world," muttered the husband with a sad smile.

And he felt it his duty to explain to his traveling companions that the poor woman was to be pitied for the war was taking away from her her only son, a boy of twenty to whom both had devoted their entire life, even breaking up their home at Sulmona to follow him to Rome, where he had to go as a student, then allowing him to volunteer for war with an assurance, however, that at least for six months he would not be sent to the front and now, all of a sudden, receiving a wire saying that he was due to leave in three days' time and asking them to go and see him off.

The woman under the big coat was twisting and wriggling, at times growling like a wild animal, feeling certain that all those explanations would not have aroused even a shadow of sympathy from those people who—most likely—were in the same plight as herself. One of them, who had been listening with particular attention, said:

"You should thank God that your son is only leaving now for the front. Mine has been there since the first day of the war. He has already come back twice wounded and been sent back again to the front."

"What about me? I have two sons and three nephews at the front," said another passenger.

"Maybe, but in our case it is our *only* son," ventured the husband.

"What difference can it make? You may spoil your only son with excessive attentions, but you cannot love him more than you would all your other children if you had any. Paternal love is not like bread that can be broken into pieces and split amongst the children in equal shares. A father gives _all_ his love to each one of his children without discrimination, whether it be one or ten, and if I am suffering now for my two sons, I am not suffering half for each of them but double . . ."

"True . . . true . . ." sighed the embarrassed husband, "but suppose (of course we all hope it will never be your case) a father has two sons at the front and he loses one of them, there is still one left to console him . . . while . . ."

"Yes," answered the other, getting cross, "a son left to console him but also a son left for whom he must survive, while in the case of the father of an only son if the son dies the father can die too and put an end to his distress. Which of the two positions is the worse? Don't you see how my case would be worse than yours?"

"Nonsense," interrupted another traveler, a fat, red-faced man with bloodshot eyes of the palest gray.

He was panting. From his bulging eyes seemed to spurt inner violence of an uncontrolled vitality which his weakened body could hardly contain.

"Nonsense," he repeated, trying to cover his mouth with his hand so as to hide the two missing front teeth. "Nonsense. Do we give life to our children for our own benefit?"

The other travelers stared at him in distress. The one who had had his son at the front since the first day of the war sighed: "You are right. Our children do not belong to us, they belong to the Country...."

"Bosh," retorted the fat traveler. "Do we think of the Country when we give life to our children? Our sons are born because ... well, because they must be born and when they come to life they take our own life with them. This is the truth. We belong to them but they never belong to us. And when they reach twenty they are exactly what we were at their age. We too had a father and mother, but there were so many other things as well ... girls, cigarettes, illusions, new tires ... and the Country, of course, whose call we would have answered—when we were twenty—even if father and mother had said no. Now at our age, the love of our Country is still great, of course, but stronger than it is the love for our children. Is there any one of us here who wouldn't gladly take his son's place at the front if he could?"

There was a silence all round, everybody nodding as to approve.

"Why then," continued the fat man, "shouldn't we consider the feelings of our children when they are twenty? Isn't it natural that at their age they should consider the love for their Country (I am speaking of decent boys, of course) even greater than the love for us? Isn't it natural that it should be so, as after all they must look upon us as upon old boys who cannot move any more and must stay at home? If Country exists, if Country is a natural necessity, like bread, of which each of us must eat in order not to die of hunger, somebody must go to defend it. And our sons go, when they are twenty, and they don't want tears, because if they die, they die inflamed and happy (I am speaking, of course, of decent boys). Now, if one dies young and happy, without having the ugly sides of life, the boredom of it, the pettiness, the bitterness of disillusion ... what more can we ask for him? Everyone should stop crying; everyone should laugh, as I do . . . or at least thank God—as I do—because my son, before dying, sent me a message saying that he was dying satisfied at having ended his life in the best way he could have wished. That is why, as you see, I do not even wear mourning. . . ."

He shook his light fawn coat as to show it; his livid lip over his missing teeth was trembling, his eyes were watery and motionless, and soon after he ended with a shrill laugh which might well have been a sob.

"Quite so . . . quite so . . ." agreed the others.

The woman who, bundled in a corner under her coat, had been sitting and listening had—for the last three months—tried to find in the words of her husband and her friends something to console her in her deep sorrow, something that might show her how a mother should resign herself to send her son not even to death but to a probably dangerous life. Yet not a word had she found amongst the many which had been said . . . and her grief had been greater in seeing that nobody—as she thought— could share her feelings.

But now the words of the traveler amazed and almost stunned her. She suddenly realized that it wasn't the others who were wrong and could not understand her but herself who could not rise up to the same height of those fathers and mothers willing to resign themselves, without crying, not only to the departure of their sons but even to their death.

She lifted her head, she bent over from her corner trying to listen with great attention to the details which the fat man was giving to his companions about the way his son had fallen as a hero, for his King and his Country, happy and without regrets. It seemed to her that she had stumbled into a world she had never dreamt of, a world so far unknown to her and she was so pleased to hear everyone joining in congratulating that brave father who could so stoically speak of his child's death.

Then suddenly, just as if she had heard nothing of what had been said and almost as if waking up from a dream, she turned to the old man, asking him:

"Then . . . is your son really dead?"

Everybody stared at her. The old man, too, turned to look at her, fixing his great, bulging, horribly watery light gray eyes, deep in her face. For some little time he tried to answer, but words failed him. He looked and looked at her, almost as if only then—at that silly, incongruous question —he had suddenly realized at last that his son was really dead—gone for ever—for ever. His face contracted, became horribly distorted, then he snatched in haste a handkerchief from his pocket and, to the amazement of everyone, broke into harrowing, heart-rending, uncontrollable sobs.

THE CANDY PULL

Mark Twain

It was back in those far-distant days that Jim Wolf came to us. He was from Shelbyville, a hamlet thirty or forty miles back in the country, and he brought all his native sweetness and gentlenesses and simplicities with him. He was approaching seventeen, a grave and slender lad, trustful, honest, honorable, a creature to love and cling to. And he was incredibly bashful. He was with us a good while but he could never conquer that peculiarity; he could not be at ease in the presence of any woman, not even in my good and gentle mother's; and as to speaking to any girl, it was wholly impossible.

It is to this kind that untoward things happen. My sister gave a "candy-pull" on a winter's night. I was too young to be of the company and Jim was too diffident. I was sent up to bed early and Jim followed of his own motion. His room was in the new part of the house and his window looked out on the roof of the L annex. That roof was six inches deep in snow and the snow had an ice crust upon it which was as slick as glass. Out of the comb of the roof projected a short chimney, a common resort for sentimental cats on moonlight nights—and this was a moonlight night. Down at the eaves, below the chimney, a canopy of dead vines spread away to some posts, making a cozy shelter, and after an hour or two the rollicking crowd of young ladies and gentlemen grouped themselves in its shade, with their saucers of liquid and piping-hot candy disposed about them on the frozen ground to cool. There was joyous chaffing and joking and laughter—peal upon peal of it.

About this time a couple of old, disreputable tomcats got up on the chimney and started a heated argument about something; also about this time I gave up trying to get to sleep and went visiting to Jim's room. He was awake and fuming about the cats and their intolerable yowling. I asked him, mockingly, why he didn't climb out and drive them away. He was nettled and said overboldly that for two cents he *would*.

It was a rash remark and was probably repented of before it was fairly out of his mouth. But it was too late—he was committed. I knew him; and I knew he would rather break his neck than back down, if I egged him on judiciously.

"Oh, of course you would! Who's doubting it?"

It galled him and he burst out, with sharp irritation, "Maybe *you* doubt it!"

"I? Oh No! I shouldn't think of such a thing. You are always doing wonderful things, with your mouth."

He was in a passion now. He snatched on his yarn socks and began to raise the window, saying in a voice quivering with anger:

"*You* think I dasn't—you do! Think what you blame please. *I* don't care what you think. I'll show you!"

The window made him rage; it wouldn't stay up.

I said, "Never mind, I'll hold it."

Indeed, I would have done anything to help. I was only a boy and was already in a radiant heaven of anticipation. He climbed carefully out, clung to the window sill until his feet were safely placed, then began to pick his perilous way on all fours along the glassy comb a foot and a hand on each side of it. I believe I enjoy it now as much as I did then; yet it is nearly fifty years ago. The frosty breeze flapped his short shirt about his lean legs; the crystal roof shone like polished marble in the intense glory of the moon; the unconscious cats sat erect upon the chimney, alertly watching each other, lashing their tails and pouring out their hollow grievances; and slowly and cautiously Jim crept on, flapping as he went, the gay and frolicsome young creatures under the vine canopy unaware, and outraging these solemnities with their misplaced laughter. Every time Jim slipped I had a hope; but always on he crept and disappointed it. At last he was within reaching distance. He paused, raised himself carefully up, measured his distance deliberately, then made a frantic grab at the nearest cat—and missed it. Of course he lost his balance. His heels flew up, he struck on his back, and like a rocket he darted down the roof feet first, crashed through the dead vines and landed in a sitting position in fourteen saucers of red-hot candy in the midst of all that party—and dressed as *he* was—this lad who could not look a girl in the face with his clothes on. There was a wild scramble and a storm of shrieks and Jim fled up the stairs, dripping broken crockery all the way.

THE SOUTH'S FIRST CROP
OF SUGAR

Indigo had been the principal staple of the colony, but at last a worm which attacked the plant and destroyed it, through consecutive years, was reducing to poverty and to the utmost despair the whole population. Jean Étienne de Boré determined to make a bold experiment to save himself and his fellow-citizens, and convert his indigo plantation into one of sugar-cane.

In these critical circumstances he resolved to renew the attempt which had been made to manufacture sugar. He immediately prepared to go into all the expenses and incur all the obligations consequent on so costly an undertaking. His wife warned him that her father had in former years vainly made a similar attempt; she represented that he was hazarding on the cast of a die all that remained of their means of existence; that if he failed, as was so probable, he would reduce his family to hopeless poverty; that he was of an age—being over fifty years old—when fate was not to be tempted by doubtful experiments, as he could not reasonably entertain the hope of a sufficiently long life to rebuild his fortune if once completely shattered; and that he would not only expose himself to ruin, but also to a risk much more to be dreaded—that of falling into the grasp of creditors. Friends and relatives joined their remonstrances to hers, but could not shake the strong resolve of his energetic mind. He had fully matured his plan, and was determined to sink or swim with it.

Purchasing a quantity of canes from two individuals named Mendez and Solis, who cultivated them only for sale as a dainty in the New Orleans market, and to make coarse syrup, he began to plant in 1794, and to make all the other necessary preparation, and in 1795 he made a crop of sugar which sold for twelve thousand dollars—a large sum at that time. Boré's attempt had excited the keenest interest; many had frequently visited him during the year to witness his preparations; gloomy predictions had been set afloat, and on the day when the grinding of the cane was to begin, a large number of the most respectable inhabitants had gathered in and about the sugar-house to be present at the failure or success of the experiment. Would the syrup granulate? Would it be converted into sugar? The crowd waited with eager impatience for the moment when the man who watches the coction of the juice of the cane determines whether it is ready to granulate. When that moment arrived the stillness of death came among them, each one holding his breath, and feeling that it was a matter of ruin or prosperity for them all. Suddenly the sugar-maker cried out with exultation, "It granulates!" Inside and outside of the building one could have heard the wonderful tidings flying from mouth to mouth and dying in the distance, as if a hundred glad echoes were telling it to one another. Each one of the bystanders pressed forward to ascertain the fact on the evidence of his own senses, and when it could no longer be doubted, there came a shout of joy, and all flocked around Étienne de Boré, overwhelming him with congratulations, and almost hugging the man whom they called their savior—the savior of Louisiana. Many years have elapsed since, and an event which produced so much excitement at the time is very nearly obliterated from the memory of the present generation.

TWO SOLDIERS

William Faulkner

Me and Pete would go down to Old Man Killegrew's and listen to his radio. We would wait until after supper, after dark, and we would stand outside Old Man Killegrew's parlor window, and we could hear it because Old Man Killegrew's wife was deaf, and so he run the radio as loud as it would run, and so me and Pete could hear it plain as Old Man Killegrew's wife could, I reckon, even standing outside with the window closed.

And that night I said, "What? Japanese? What's a pearl harbor? and Pete said, "Hush."

And so we stood there, it was cold, listening to the fellow in the radio talking, only I couldn't make no heads nor tails out of it. Then the fellow said that would be all for a while, and me and Pete walked back up the road to home, and Pete told me what it was. Because he was nigh twenty and he had done finished the Consolidated last June and he knowed a heap: about them Japanese dropping bombs on Pearl Harbor and that Pearl Harbor was across the water.

"Across what water?" I said. "Across that Government reservoy up at Oxford?"

"Naw," Pete said. "Across the big water. The Pacific Ocean."

We went home. Maw and pap was already asleep and me and Pete laid in bed, and I still couldn't understand where it was, and Pete told me again—the Pacific Ocean.

"What's the matter with you?" Pete said. "You're going on nine years old. You been in school now ever since September. Ain't you learned nothing yet?"

"I reckon we ain't got as fer as the Pacific Ocean yet," I said.

We was still sowing the vetch then that ought to been all finished by the fifteenth of November, because pap was still behind, just like he had been ever since me and Pete had knowed him. And we had firewood to git in, too, but every night me and Pete would go down to Old Man Killegrew's and stand outside his parlor window in the cold and listen to his radio; then we would come back home and lay in bed and Pete would tell me what it was. That is, he would tell me for a while. Then he wouldn't tell me. It was like he didn't want to talk about it no more. He would tell me to shut up because he wanted to go to sleep, but he never wanted to go to sleep.

He would lay there, a heap stiller than if he was asleep, and it would be something, I could feel it coming out of him, like he was mad at me, or like he was worried about something, and it wasn't that neither, because he never had nothing to worry about. He never got behind like pap, let alone stayed behind. Pap give him ten acres when he graduated from the Consolidated, and me and Pete both reckoned pap was durn glad to get shut of at least ten acres, less to have to worry about himself; and Pete had them ten acres all sowed to vetch and busted out and bedded for the winter, and so it wasn't that. But it was something. And still we would go down to Old Man Killegrew's every night and listen to his radio, and they was at it in the Philippines now, but General MacArthur was holding um. Then we would come back home and lay in the bed, and Pete wouldn't tell me nothing or talk at all. He would just lay there still as an ambush and when I would touch him, his side or his leg would feel hard and still as iron, until after a while and I would go to sleep.

Then one night—it was the first time he had said nothing to me except to jump on me about not chopping enough wood at the wood tree where he was cutting—he said, "I got to go."

"Go where?" I said.

"To that war," Pete said.

"Before we even finish gettin' in the firewood?"

"Firewood, heck," Pete said.

"All right," I said. "When we going to start?"

But he wasn't even listening. He laid there, hard and still as iron in the dark. "I got to go," he said. "I jest ain't going to put up with no folks treating the Unity States that way."

"Yes," I said. "Firewood or no firewood, I reckon we got to go."

This time he heard me. He laid still again, but it was a different kind of still.

"You?" he said. "To a war?"

"You'll whup the big uns and I'll whup the little uns," I said.

Then he told me I couldn't go. At first I thought he just never wanted me tagging after him, like he wouldn't leave me go with him when he went sparking them girls of Tull's. Then he told me the Army wouldn't leave me go because I was too little, and then I knowed he really meant it and that I couldn't go nohow noways. And somehow I hadn't believed until then that he was going himself, but now I knowed he was and that he wasn't going to leave me go with him a-tall.

"I'll chop the wood and tote the water for you-all then!" I said. "You got to have wood and water!"

Anyway, he was listening to me now. He wasn't like iron now.

He turned onto his side and put his hand on my chest because it was me that was laying straight and hard on my back now.

"No," he said. "You got to stay here and help pap."

"Help him what?" I said. "He ain't never caught up nohow. He can't get no further behind. He can sholy take care of this little shirttail of a farm while me and you are whupping them Japanese. I got to go too. If you got to go, then so have I."

"No," Pete said. "Hush now. Hush." And he meant it, and I knowed he did. Only I made sho from his own mouth. I quit.

"So I just can't go then," I said.

"No," Pete said. "You just can't go. You're too little, in the first place, and in the second place—"

"All right," I said. "Then shut up and leave me to go to sleep."

So he hushed then and laid back. And I laid there like I was already asleep, and pretty soon he was asleep and I knowed it was the wanting to go to the war that had worried him and kept him awake, and now that he had decided to go, he wasn't worried any more.

The next morning he told maw and pap. Maw was all right. She cried.

"No," she said, crying, "I don't want him to go. I would rather go myself in his place, if I could. I don't want to save the country. Them Japanese could take it all and keep it, so long as they left me and my family and my children alone. But I remember my brother Marsh in that other war. He had to go to that one when he wasn't but nineteen and our mother couldn't understand it then any more than I can now. But she told Marsh if he had to go, he had to go. And so, if Pete's got to go to this one, he's got to go to it. Just don't ask me to understand why."

But pap was the one. He was the feller. "To the war?" he said. "Why I don't see a bit of use in that. You ain't old enough for the draft, and the country ain't being invaded. Our President in Washington, D.C., is watching the conditions and he will notify us. Besides, in that other war your maw just mentioned, I was drafted and sent clean to Texas and was held there nigh eight months until they finally quit fighting. It seems to me that that, along with your Uncle Marsh who received a actual wound on the battlefields of France, is enough for me and mine to have to do to protect the country, at least in my lifetime. Besides, what'll I do for help on the farm with you gone? It seems to me I'll get mighty far behind."

"You been behind as long as I can remember," Pete said. "Anyway I'm going. I got to."

"Of course he's got to go," I said. "Them Japanese—"

"You hush your mouth!" maw said, crying. "Nobody's talking to you! Go and get ma a armful of wood! That's what you can do!"

So I got the wood. And all the next day, while me and Pete and pap was getting in as much wood as we could in that time because Pete said how pap's idea of plenty of wood was one more stick laying against the wall that maw ain't put on the fire yet, maw was getting Pete ready to go. She washed and mended his clothes and cooked him a shoe box of vittles. And that night me and Pete laid in the bed and listened to her packing his grip and crying, until after a while Pete got up in his nightshirt and went back there, and I could hear them talking, until at last maw said, "You ought to go, and so I want you to go. But I don't understand it, and I won't never, and so don't expect me to." And Pete come back and got into bed again and laid again still and hard as iron on his back, and then he said, and he wasn't talking to me, he wasn't talking to nobody: "I got to go. I just got to."

"Sho you got to," I said. "Them Japanese —" He turned over hard, he kind of surged over onto his side, looking at me in the dark.

"Anyway, you're all right," he said. "I expected to have more trouble with you than with all the rest of them put together."

"I reckon I can't help it neither," I said. "But maybe it will run a few years longer and I can get there. Maybe someday I will jest walk in on you."

"I hope not," Pete said. "Folks don't go to wars for fun. A man don't leave his maw crying just for fun."

"Then why are you going?" I said.

"I got to," he said. "I just got to. Now you go on to sleep. I got to ketch that early bus in the morning."

"All right," I said, "I hear tell Memphis is a big place. How will you find where the Army's at?"

"I'll ask somebody where to go to join it," Pete said. "Go on to sleep now."

"Is that what you'll ask for? Where to join the Army?" I said.

"Yes," Pete said. He turned onto his back again. "Shut up and go to sleep."

We went to sleep. The next morning we et breakfast by lamplight because the bus would pass at six o'clock. Maw wasn't crying now. She jest looked grim and busy, putting breakfast on the table while we et it. Then she finished packing Pete's grip, except he never wanted to take no grip to the war, but maw said decent folks never went nowhere, not even to a war, without a change of clothes and something to tote them in. She put in the shoe box of fried chicken and biscuits and she put the Bible in, too, and then it was time to go. We didn't know until then that maw wasn't going to the bus. She jest brought Pete's cap and overcoat, and still she didn't cry no more, she jest stood with her hands on Pete's shoulders and she didn't move, but somehow, and just holding Pete's shoulders, she looked as hard and fierce as when Pete had turned toward me in the bed last night and tole me that anyway I was all right.

"They could take the country and keep the country, as long as they never bothered me and mine," she said. Then she said, "Don't never forget who you are. You ain't rich and the rest of the world outside of Frenchman's Bend never heard of you. But your blood is good as any blood anywhere, and don't you never forget it."

Then she kissed him, and then we was out of the house, with pap toting Pete's grip whether Pete wanted him to or not. There wasn't no dawn even yet, not even after we had stood on the highway by the mailbox, awhile. Then we seen the lights of the bus coming and I was watching the bus until it come up and Pete flagged it, and then, sho enough, there was daylight—it had started while I wasn't watching. And now me and Pete expected pap to say something else foolish, like he done before, about how Uncle Marsh getting wounded in France and that trip to Texas pap had taken in 1918 ought to be enough to save the Unity States in 1942, but he never. He done all right too. He jest said, "Good-by, son. Always remember what your ma told you and write her whenever you find the time." Then he shaken Pete's hand, and Pete looked at me for a minute and put his hand on my head and rubbed my head durn nigh hard enough to wring my neck off and jumped into the bus, and the feller wound the door shut and the bus began to hum; then it was moving, humming and grinding and whining louder and louder; it was going fast, with two little red lights behind it that never seemed to get no littler, but jest seemed to be running together until pretty soon they would touch and jest be one light. But they never did, and then the bus was gone, and even like it was, I could have pretty nigh busted out crying, nigh to nine years old and all.

Me and pap went back to the house. All that day we worked at the wood tree, and so I never had no good chance until about middle of the afternoon. Then I taken my slingshot and I would have liked to took all my bird eggs, too, because Pete had give me his collection and he holp me with mine, and he would like to git the box out and look at them as good as I would, even if he was nigh twenty years old. But the box was too big to tote a long ways and have to worry with, so I just taken the shike poke egg, because it was the best un, and wropped it up good into a matchbox and hid it and the slingshot under the corner of the barn. Then we et supper and went to bed, and I thought then how if I would 'a' had to stay in that room and that bed like that even for one more night, I jest couldn't 'a' stood it. Then I could hear pap snoring, but I never heard no sound from maw, whether she was asleep or not, and I don't reckon she was. So I taken my shoes and drapped them out the window, and then I clumb out like I used to watch Pete do when he was still jest seventeen and pap wouldn't leave him out, and I put on my shoes and went to the barn and got the slingshot and the shikepoke egg and went to the highway.

It wasn't cold, it was just durn confounded dark, and that highway stretched on in front of me like, without nobody using it, it had stretched out half again as fer just like a man does when he lays down, so that for a time it looked like full sun was going to ketch me before I had finished them twenty-two miles to Jefferson. But it didn't. Daybreak was jest starting when I walked up the hill into town. I could smell breakfast cooking in the cabins and I wished I had thought to brought me a cold biscuit, but that was too late now. And Pete had told me Memphis was a piece beyond Jefferson, but I never knowed it was no eighty miles. So I stood there on that empty square, with daylight coming and coming and the street lights still burning and that Law looking down at me, and me still eighty miles from Memphis, and it had took me all night to walk jest twenty-two miles, and so, by the time I got to Memphis at that rate, Pete would 'a' done already started for Pearl Harbor.

"Where do you come from?" the Law said. And I told him again. "I got to git to Memphis. My brother's there."

"You mean you ain't got any folks around here?" the Law said. "Nobody but that brother? What are you doing way off down here and your brother in Memphis?"

And I told him again, "I got to git to Memphis. I ain't got no time to waste talking about it and I ain't got time to walk it. I got to git there today."

"Come on here," the Law said.

We went down another street. And there was the bus, jest like when Pete got into it yestiddy morning, except there wasn't no lights on it now and it was empty. There was a regular bus dee-po like a railroad dee-po, with a ticket counter and a feller behind it, and the Law said, "Set down over there," and I set down on the bench, and the Law said, "I want to use your telephone," and he talked into the telephone a minute and put it down and said to the feller behind the ticket counter, "Keep your eye on him. I'll be back as soon as Mrs. Habersham can arrange to get herself up and dressed." He went out. I got up and went to the ticket counter.

"I want to go to Memphis," I said.

"You bet," the feller said. "You set down on the bench now. Mr. Foote will be back in a minute.

"I don't know no Mr. Foote," I said. "I want to ride that bus to Memphis."

"You got some money?" he said. "It'll cost seventy-two cents."

I taken out the matchbox and unwropped the shikepoke egg. "I'll swap you this for a ticket to Memphis," I said.

"What's that?" he said.

"It's a shikepoke egg," I said. "You never seen one before. It's worth a dollar. I'll take seventy-two cents fer it."

"No," he said, "the fellers that own that bus insist on a cash basis. If I started swapping tickets for bird eggs and livestock and such, they would fire me. You go and set down on the bench now, like Mr. Foote—"

I started for the door, but he caught me, he put one hand on the ticket counter and jumped over it and caught up with me and reached his hand out to ketch my shirt. I whupped out my pocketknife and snapped it open.

"You put a hand on me and I'll cut it off." I said.

I tried to dodge him and run at the door, but he could move quicker than any grown man I ever see, quick as Pete almost. He cut me off and stood with his back against the door and one foot raised a little, and there wasn't no other way to get out. "Get back on that bench and stay there," he said.

And there wasn't no other way out. And he stood against the door. So I went back to the bench. And then it seemed like to me that dee-po was full of folks. There was that Law again, and there was two ladies in fur coats and their faces already painted. But they still looked like they had got up in a hurry and they still never liked it, a old one and a young one, looking down at me.

"He hasn't got an overcoat!" the old one said. "How in the world did he ever get down here by himself?"

"I ask you," the Law said. "I couldn't get nothing out of him except his brother is in Memphis and he wants to get back up there."

"That's right," I said. "I got to git to Memphis today."

"Of course you must," the old one said. "Are you sure you can find your brother when you get to Memphis?"

"I reckon I can," I said. "I ain't got but one and I have knowed him all my life. I reckon I will know him again when I see him."

The old one looked at me. "Somehow he doesn't look like he lives in Memphis," she said.

"He probably don't," the Law said. "You can't tell though. He might live anywhere, overhalls or not. This day and time they get scattered overnight from hope to breakfast; boys and girls, too, almost before they can walk good. He might have been in Missouri or Texas either yestiddy, for all we know. But he don't seem to have any doubt his brother is in Memphis. All I know to do is send him up there and leave him look."

"Yes," the old one said.

The young one set down on the bench by me and opened a hand satchel and taken out a artermatic writing pen and some papers.

"Now, honey," the old one said, "we're going to see that you find your brother, but we must have a case history for our files first. We want to know your name and your brother's name and where you were born and when your parents died."

"I don't need no case history neither," I said. "All I want is to git to Memphis. I got to git there today."

"You see?" the Law said. He said it almost like he enjoyed it. "That's what I told you."

"You're lucky, at that, Mrs. Habersham," the bus feller said. "I don't think he's got a gun on him, but he can open that knife fast enough to suit any man."

But the old one just stood there looking at me.

"Well," she said. "Well. I really don't know what to do."

"I do," the bus feller said. "I'm going to give him a ticket out of my own pocket, as a measure of protecting the company against riot and bloodshed. And when Mr. Foote tells the city board about it, it will be a civic matter and they will give me a medal too. Hey, Mr. Foote?"

But nobody paid him no mind. The old one still stood looking down at me. She said, "Well," again. Then she taken a dollar from her purse and give it to the bus feller. "I suppose he will travel on a child's ticket, won't he?"

"Wellum," the bus feller said, "I just don't know what the regulations would be. Likely I will be fired for not crating him and marking the crate Poison. But I'll risk it."

Then they were gone. Then the Law come back with a sandwich and give it to me.

"You're sure you can find that brother?" he said.

"I ain't yet convinced why not," I said. "If I don't see Pete first, he'll see me. He knows me, too."

Then the Law went out for good, too, and I et the sandwich. Then more folks come in and bought tickets, and then the bus feller said it was time to go, and I got into the bus just like Pete done, and we were gone.

I seen all the towns. I seen all of them. When the bus got to going good, I found out I was jest about wore out for sleep. But there was too much I hadn't never saw before. We run out of Jefferson and run past fields and woods, then we would run into another town and out of that un and past fields and woods again, and then into another town with stores and gins and water tanks, and we run along by the railroad for a spell and I seen the signal arm move, and then some more towns, and I was jest about plumb wore out for sleep, but I couldn't resk it. Then Memphis begun. It seemed like, to me, it went on for miles. We would pass a patch of stores and I would think that was sholy it and the bus would even stop. But it wouldn't be Memphis yet and we would go on

again past water tanks and smokestacks on top of the mills, and if they
was gins and sawmills, I never knowed there was that many and I never
seen any that big, and where they got enough cotton and logs to run um
I don't know.

Then I seen Memphis. I knowed I was right this time. It was standing
up into the air. It looked like about a dozen whole towns bigger than
Jefferson was set up on one edge in a field, standing up into the air
higher than ara hill in all Yoknapatawpha County. Then we was in it,
with the bus stopping every few feet, it seemed like to me, and cars
rushing past on both sides of it and the streets crowded with folks from
ever'where in town that day, until I didn't see how there could 'a' been
nobody left in Mis'sippi a-tall to even sell me a bus ticket, let alone write
out no case histories. Then the bus stopped. It was another bus dee-po, a
heap bigger than the one in Jefferson. And I said, "All right. Where do
folks join the Army?"

"What?" the bus feller said.

And I said it again, "Where do folks join the Army?"

"Oh," he said. Then he told me how to get there. I was afraid at first I
wouldn't ketch on how to do in a town as big as Memphis. But I caught
on all right. I never had to ask but twice more. Then I was there, and I
was durn glad to git out of all them rushing cars and shoving folks and
all that racket fer a spell, and I thought, it won't be long now, and I
thought how if there was any kind of a crowd there that had done already
joined the Army, too, Pete would likely see me before I seen him. And
so I walked into the room. And Pete wasn't there.

He wasn't even there. There was a soldier with a big arrerhead on his
sleeve, writing, and two fellers standing in front of him, and there was
some more folks there, I reckon. It seems to me I remember some more
folks there.

I went to the table where the soldier was writing, and I said, "Where's
Pete?" and he looked up and I said, "My brother. Pete Grier. Where is he?"

"What?" the soldier said. "Who?"

And I told him again. "He joined the Army yestiddy. He's going to
Pearl Harbor. So am I. I want to ketch him. Where you-all got him?"
Now they were all looking at me, but I never paid them no mind. "Come
on," I said. "Where is he?"

The soldier had quit writing. He had both hands spraddled out on
the table. "Oh," he said. "You're going, too, hah?"

"Yes," I said. "They got to have wood and water. I can chop it and
tote it. Come on. Where's Pete?"

The soldier stood up. "Who let you in here?" he said. "Go on. Beat it."

"Durn that," I said. "You tell me where Pete —"

I be dog if he couldn't move faster than the bus feller even. He never come over the table, he come around it, he was on me almost before I knowed it, so that I jest had time to jump back and whup out my pocket-knife and snap it open and hit one lick, and he hollered and jumped back and grabbed one hand with the other and stood there cussing and hollering.

One of the other fellers grabbed me from behind, and I hit at him with the knife, but I couldn't reach him.

Then both of the fellers had me from behind, and then another soldier come out of a door at the back. He had on a belt with a britching strop over one shoulder.

"What's this?" he said.

"That little son cut me with a knife!" the first soldier hollered. When he said that I tried to git at him again, but both them fellers was holding me, two against one, and the soldier with the backing strop said, "Here, here. Put your knife up, feller. None of us are armed. A man don't knife-fight folks that are barehanded." I could begin to hear him then. He sounded jest like Pete talked to me. "Let him go," he said. They let me go. "Now what's all the trouble about?" And I told him. "I see," he said. "And you come up to see if he was all right before he left."

"No," I said. "I come to —"

But he had already turned to where the first soldier was wropping a handkerchief around his hand.

"Have you got him?" he said. The first soldier went back to the table and looked at some papers.

"Here he is," he said. "He enlisted yestiddy. He's in a detachment leaving this morning for Little Rock." He had a watch stropped on his arm. He looked at it. "The train leaves in about fifty minutes. If I know country boys, they're probably all down there at the station right now."

"Get him up here," the one with the backing strop said. "Phone the station. Tell the porter to get him a cab. And you come with me," he said.

It was another office behind that un, with jest a table and some chairs. We set there while the soldier smoked, and it wasn't long; I knowed Pete's feet soon as I heard them. Then the first soldier opened the door and Pete come in. He never had no soldier clothes on. He looked jest like he did when he got on the bus yestiddy morning, except it seemed to me like it was at least a week, so much had happened, and I had done had to do so much traveling. He come in and there he was, looking at me like he hadn't never left home, except that here we was in Memphis, on the way to Pearl Harbor.

"What in durnation are you doing here?" he said.

And I told him, "You got to have wood and water to cook with. I can chop it and tote it for you-all."

"No," Pete said. "You're going back home."

"No, Pete," I said. "I got to go too. I got to. It hurts my heart, Pete."

"No," Pete said. He looked at the soldier. "I jest don't know what could have happened to him, lootenant," he said. "He never drawed a knife on anybody before in his life."

He looked at me. "What did you do it for?"

"I don't know," I said. "I jest had to. I jest had to git here. I jest had to find you."

"Well, don't you never do it again, you hear?" Pete said. "You put that knife in your pocket and you keep it there. If I ever again hear of you drawing it on anybody, I'm coming back from wherever I am at and whump the fire out of you. You hear me?"

"I would pure cut a throat if it would bring you back to stay," I said. "Pete," I said. "Pete."

"No," Pete said. Now his voice wasn't hard and quick no more, it was almost quiet, and I knowed now I wouldn't never change him. "You must go home. You must look after maw, and I am depending on you to look after my ten acres. I want you to go back home. Today. Do you hear?"

"I hear," I said.

"Can he get back home by himself?" the soldier said.

"He come up here by himself," Pete said.

"I can get back, I reckon," I said. "I don't live in but one place. I don't reckon it's moved."

Pete taken a dollar out of his pocket and give it to me. "That'll buy your bus ticket right to our mailbox," he said. "I want you to mind the lootenant. He'll send you to the bus. And you go back home and you take care of maw and look after my ten acres and keep that durn knife in your pocket. You hear me?"

"Yes, Pete," I said.

"All right," Pete said. "Now I got to go." He put his hand on my head again. But this time he never wrung my neck. He just laid his hand on my head a minute. And then I be dog if he didn't lean down and kiss me, and I heard his feet and then the door, and I never looked up and that was all, me setting there, rubbing the place where Pete kissed me and the soldier throwed back in his chair, looking out the window and coughing. He reached into his pocket and handed something to me without looking around. It was a piece of chewing gum.

"Much obliged," I said. "Well, I reckon I might as well start back. I got a right fer piece to go."

"Wait," the soldier said. Then he telephoned again and I said again I better start back, and he said again, "Wait. Remember what Pete told you."

So we waited, and then another lady come in, old, too, in a fur coat, too, but she smelled all right, she never had no artermatic writing pen nor no case history neither. She come in and the soldier got up, and she looked around quick until she saw me, and come and put her hand on my shoulder light and quick and easy as maw herself might 'a' done it.

"Come on," she said. "Let's go home to dinner."

"Nome," I said. "I got to ketch the bus to Jefferson."

"I know. There's plenty of time. We'll go home and eat dinner first."

She had a car. And now we was right down in the middle of all them other cars. We was almost under the busses, and all them crowds of people on the street close enough to where I could have talked to them if I had knowed who they was. After a while she stopped the car. "Here we are," she said, and I looked at it, and if all that was her house, she sho had a big family. But all of it wasn't. We crossed a hall with trees growing in it and went into a little room without nothing in it but a Negro dressed up in a uniform a heap shinier than them soldiers had, and the Negro shut the door, and then I hollered, "Look out!" and grabbed, but it was all right; that whole little room jest went right on up and stopped and the door opened and we was in another hall, and the lady unlocked a door and we went in, and there was another soldier, an old feller, with a britching strop, too, and a silver-colored bird on each shoulder.

"Here we are," the lady said. "This is Colonel McKellogg. Now, what would you like for dinner?"

"I reckon I'll jest have some ham and eggs and coffee," I said.

She had done started to pick up the telephone. She stopped. "Coffee?" she said, "When did you start drinking coffee?"

"I don't know," I said. "I reckon it was before I could remember."

"You're about eight, aren't you?" she said.

"Nome," I said. "I'm eight and ten months. Going on eleven months."

She telephoned then. Then we set there and I told them how Pete had jest left that morning for Pearl Harbor and I had aimed to go with him, but I would have to go back home to take care of maw and look after Pete's ten acres, and she said how they had a little boy about my size, too, in a school in the East. Then a Negro, another one, in a short kind of shirttail coat, rolled a kind of wheelbarrer in. It had my ham and eggs and a glass of milk and a piece of pie, too, and I thought I was hungry. But when I taken the first bite I found out I couldn't swallow it, and I got up quick.

"I got to go," I said.

"Wait," she said.

"I got to go," I said.

"Just a minute," she said. "I've already telephoned for the car. It won't be but a minute now. Can't you drink the milk even? Or maybe some of your coffee?"

"Nome," I said. "I ain't hungry. I'll eat when I git home." Then the telephone rung. She never even answered it.

"There," she said. "There's the car." And we went back down in that 'ere little moving room with the dressed-up Negro. This time it was a big car with a soldier driving it. I got into the front with him. She give the soldier a dollar. "He might get hungry," she said. "Try to find a decent place for him."

"O.K., Mrs. McKellogg," the soldier said.

Then we was gone again. And now I could see Memphis good, bright in the sunshine, while we was swinging around it. And the first thing I knowed, we was back on the same highway the bus run on this morning—the patches of stores and them big gins and sawmills, and Memphis running on for miles, it seemed like to me, before it begun to give out. Then we was running again between the fields and woods, running fast now, and except for that soldier, it was like I hadn't never been to Memphis a-tall. We was going fast now. At this rate, before I knowed it we would be home again, and I thought about me riding up to Frenchman's Bend in this here big car with a soldier running it, and all of a sudden I begun to cry. I never knowed I was fixing to, and I couldn't stop it. I set there by that soldier, crying. We was going fast.

DESERT FLOOD

Bill Mauldin

In a way, it's wrong to call our part of Arizona a desert, for "desert" brings to mind Sahara-like expanses of barren sand, endless and flat. Not only was our country broken up by hills, small mountain ranges, and occasional green spots where the water level came near the surface and where clumps of trees and grasses grew, but the colors of the landscape were often breath-taking.

The sunsets would make sentimentalists out of brass monkeys. In fact, I would recommend them to brass monkeys, for those sunsets are really very tiresome after a while, sort of like a Cecil B. DeMille technicolor produc-

tion or a feed-store calendar. They seem contrived. Many artists have
been attracted to that desert, and it's interesting to note that the hacks
always go to work on the sunset, splashing every bit of their color on
their palettes and smearing it on the canvas. They murmur reverent
platitudes about how "Only God could paint that picture. No mortal can
capture it; we can only make poor copies." Disgusting. And it's the same
with the photographers. The hacks use filters and fancy films and come
up with blazes of glory which are forthwith printed on postcards and sent
home by tourists with no imagination.

The good artists and photographers turn to the desert's real colors: the
subtle hues of the land itself, as the sun changes hills and valleys into
rose and gray from deep blue in the early morning, then golden gray,
then a variety of hot colors until noon, when everything becomes glaring
white and black, then deep red at sunset, lavender and purple at dusk,
then the desert turns back to deep blue with silver highlights under the
moon, or simply gray-blue under the stars. Desert colors are mysterious
blends of many things, and that's why good artists consider them a
challenge, and ignore the sunset, which any child could copy by throwing buckets of paint at a wall.

Winters out there are wonderful, for the days are steadily balmy, with
never a chill, and the nights are just cool enough to make one happy, but
never cold enough to require a second helping of blankets. Because of the
dry air, during all seasons you can watch rain clouds pile up thirty or
forty miles away, start dropping their load of water in a slanting gray
mist, then see the rain become absorbed and fade away long before it
hits the ground.

Occasionally, however, the rain clouds get their heads together, grumble
a bit, and gang up on the desert. The first assault wave, made up of
shock-troop clouds, sacrifices itself to dampen the atmosphere, then before
the air can digest it, the reserves come through and turn the dry land into
a soggy mess.

Our first desert flood came about three months after we'd settled on
our homestead. I remember going to sleep one night listening to the
sound, which we'd almost forgotten in that dry climate, of big raindrops
hitting the roof.... Next morning it was pouring so hard I felt as if the
falling water would beat me to my knees when I stepped outside. Just
for a stunt—we really didn't care for baths—[my brother] Sid and I took
soap outside and had a fast shower and shampoo.

Near our house a shallow, sandy-bottomed wash, about two feet deep
and fifty feet wide, had become a terrifying river which roared and
boiled past, slopping over its banks and whipping bits of wood and brush
along so fast we could hardly follow them with our eyes. Fascinated, I

went over to it and stuck in a tentative toe; a crest came along, caught my foot, and almost yanked me in. It was what's called a flash-flood. Several foolish tourists are killed every year by flash-floods in the Southwest. When they see the weather pile up threateningly they camp in sheltered-looking gullies. The water doesn't wet their feet and climb gradually, awakening them and warning them in the middle of the night—it comes in solid wall, bowling over and smashing everything in its way, even automobiles sometimes.

It happened that we were short of groceries that morning, and we decided to drive to the store and stock up, in case the rain should continue and the roads wash out. The four of us piled into the tiny cab of the truck and set out, with Pop having to drive with his head in the rain because even if the windshield wipers had worked, which they didn't, they couldn't have kept the glass clear. It was as if a fire hose were playing on us.

The store was on a little rise straddled by two shallow washes like the one near our house. For some reason they carried only a six-inch deep stream at the moment and we splashed through easily. Four or five other families were at the store, everybody jabbering about the big rain and speculating on how long it would last. The kids all scrambled around playing in the downpour and inventing games like throwing sticks into the fast-moving water and trying to hit them with rocks before they were whisked away. After a while we all hit on the idea of making a raft, and started looking about for planks. The grownups kept gabbling away, and what with one thing and another, by the time somebody thought of looking again at the washes, they were regular rivers. The rain showed no signs of letting up. The whole lot of us were marooned, for both washes joined a mile above and two miles below the store.

Nobody was really unhappy about it; we kids were overjoyed and even the parents considered it something of an adventure. What better place could one ask for a marooning than a grocery store? The day passed very pleasantly. We finished our raft, a big one, but since we knew better than to try to launch it until the stream quieted down, we turned to rough-housing and other games, never once going inside except to eat. We were probably the cleanest-washed kids in the world that day.

We spent the night in the store and in the owner's house. There was some singing and a great deal more talk during the night, with the kids going to sleep sprawled around the floor on blankets and quilts. The rain droned on and the washes rumbled. I remember waking up several times during the night, looking drowsily at the men sitting around the stove (it wasn't lit, but there's something psychologically good about sitting around a stove)....

Late the next day the washes had dropped and slowed enough to allow us all to plow through in our assorted vehicles. We never did have a chance to use the raft. On the way home, the desert looked like a Midwest valley after a dam has broken. There were thousands of lakes of all sizes. And yet, as soon as the rain had stopped completely, they were sucked into the earth even more quickly than they had been formed. Within a day they were nothing but messy puddles of mud. After the second day they were almost dry, and on the third day the mud had hardened and cracked into desolate, ugly, jigsaw patterns.

After the rain we found tiny casualties everywhere—tarantulas and kangaroo mice and bugs that had been drowned and washed up out of their holes. We hoped to find a large portion of the rattlesnake population drowned too, but evidently the heavens look out for the bums. We didn't find a single rattler, and not even a scorpion. Only an old bull snake, who looked more like a case of hardened arteries than a drowning. Sid and I cut off his head and skinned him, peeling him inside-out like taking off a sock. We cleaned the skin, turned it right-side-out again, and nailed it to the house to dry, intending to make a belt or something out of it, but we never got around to it.

A MARRIAGE PROPOSAL

Anton Chekhov

SCENE: *The reception room in* TSCHUBUKOV's *home,* TSCHUBUKOV *(a country farmer) discovered as the curtain rises. Enter* LOMOV *(his neighbor), wearing a dress-suit.*

TSCHUB *(going toward him and greeting him)*: Who is this I see? My dear fellow! Ivan Vassiliyitch! I'm so glad to see you! *(Shakes hands.)* But this is a surprise! How are you?

LOMOV: Thank you! And how are you?

TSCHUB: Oh, so-so, my friend. Please sit down. It isn't right to forget one's neighbor. But tell me, why all this ceremony? Dress clothes, white gloves and all? Are you on your way to some engagement, my good fellow?

LOMOV: No, I have no engagement except with you, Stepan Stepanovitch.

TSCHUB: But why in evening clothes, my friend? This isn't New Year's!

LOMOV: You see, it's simple this, that—(*Composing himself.*) I have come to you, Stepan Stepanovitch, to trouble you with a request. It is not the first time I have had the honor of turning to you for assistance, and you have always, that is—I beg your pardon, I am a bit excited! I'll take a drink of water first, dear Stepan Stepanovitch. (*He drinks.*)

TSCHUB (*aside*): He's come to borrow money! I won't give him any! (*To* LOMOV). What is it, then, dear Lomov?

LOMOV: You see—dear—Stepanovitch, pardon me, Stepan—Stepan—dear-vitch—I mean—I am terribly nervous, as you will be so good as to see—! What I mean to say—you are the only one who can help me, though I don't deserve it, and—and I have no right whatever to make this request of you.

TSCHUB: Oh, don't beat about the bush, my dear fellow. Tell me!

LOMOV: Immediately—in a moment. Here it is, then: I have come to ask for the hand of your daughter, Natalia Stepanovna.

TSCHUB (*joyfully*): Angel! Ivan Vassiliyitch! Say that once again! I didn't quite hear it!

LOMOV: I have the honor to beg—

TSCHUB (*interrupting*): My dear, dear man! I am so happy that everything is so—everything! (*Embraces and kisses him.*) I have wanted this to happen for so long. It has been my dearest wish! (*He represses a tear.*) And I have always loved you, my dear fellow, as my own son! May God give you His blessings and His grace and—I always wanted it to happen. But why am I standing here like a blockhead? I am completely dumb-founded with pleasure, completely dumbfounded. My whole being—! I'll call Natalia—

LOMOV: Dear Stepan Stepanovitch, what do you think? May I hope for Natalia Stepanovna's acceptance?

TSCHUB: Really! A fine boy like you—and you think she won't accept on the minute? Lovesick as a cat and all that—! (*He goes out, right.*)

LOMOV: I'm cold. My whole body is trembling as though I was going to take my examination! But the chief thing is to settle matters! If a person meditates too much, or hesitates, or talks about it, waits for an ideal or for true love, he never gets it. Brrr! It's cold! Natalia is an excellent housekeeper, not at all bad-looking, well educated—what more could I ask? I'm so excited my ears are roaring! *(He drinks water.)* And not to marry, that won't do! In the first place, I'm thirty-five—a critical age, you might say. In the second place, I must live a well-regulated life. I have a weak heart, continual palpitation, and I am very sensitive and always getting excited. My lips begin to tremble and the pulse in my right temple throbs terribly. But the worst of all is sleep! I hardly lie down and begin to doze before something in my left side begins to pull and tug, and something begins to hammer in my left shoulder—and in my head, too! I jump up like a madman, walk about a little, lie down again, but the moment I fall asleep I have a terrible cramp in the side. And so it is all night long! *(Enter* NATALIA STEPANOVNA.*)*

NATALIA: Ah! It's you. Papa said to go in: there was a dealer in there who'd come to buy something. Good afternoon, Ivan Vassiliyitch.

LOMOV: Good day, my dear Natalia Stepanovna.

NATALIA: You must pardon me for wearing my apron and this old dress: we are working to-day. Why haven't you come to see us oftener? You've not been here for so long! Sit down. *(They sit down.)* Won't you have something to eat?

LOMOV: Thank you, I have just had lunch.

NATALIA: Smoke, do, there are the matches. To-day it is beautiful and only yesterday it rained so hard that the workmen couldn't do a stroke of work. How many bricks have you cut? Think of it! I was so anxious that I had the whole field mowed, and now I'm sorry I did it, because I'm afraid the hay will rot. It would have been better if I had waited. But what on earth is this? You are in evening clothes! The latest cut! Are you on your way to a ball? And you seem to be looking better, too, really. Why are you dressed up so gorgeously?

LOMOV *(excited)*: You see, my dear Natalia Stepanovna—it's simply this: I have decided to ask you to listen to me—of course it will be a surprise, and indeed you'll be angry, but—*(Aside.)* How fearfully cold it is!

NATALIA: What is it? *(A pause.)* Well?

LOMOV: I'll try to be brief. My dear Natalia Stepanovna, as you know, for many years, since my childhood, I have had the honor to know your family. My poor aunt and her husband, from whom, as you know, I inherited the estate, always had the greatest respect for your father and your poor mother. The Lomovs and the Tschubukovs have been for decades on the friendliest, indeed the closest, terms with each other, and furthermore my property, as you know, adjoins your own. If you will be so good as to remember, my meadows touch your birch woods.

NATALIA: Pardon the interruption. You said "my meadows"—but are they yours?

LOMOV: Yes, they belong to me.

NATALIA: What nonsense! The meadows belong to us—not to you!

LOMOV: No, to me! Now, my dear Natalia Stepanovna!

NATALIA: Well, that is certainly news to me. How do they belong to you?

LOMOV: How? I am speaking of the meadows lying between your birch woods and my brick-earth.

NATALIA: Yes, exactly. They belong to us.

LOMOV: No, you are mistaken, my dear Natalia Stepanovna, they belong to me.

NATALIA: Try to remember exactly, Ivan Vassiliyitch. Is it so long ago that you inherited them?

LOMOV: Long ago! As far back as I can remember they have always belonged to us.

NATALIA: But that isn't true! You'll pardon my saying so.

LOMOV: It is all a matter of record, my dear Natalia Stepanovna. It is true that at one time the title to the meadows was disputed, but now everyone knows they belong to me. There is no room for discussion. Be so good as to listen: my aunt's grandmother put these meadows, free from all costs, into the hands of your father's grandfather's peasants for a certain time while they were making bricks for my grandmother. These people used the meadows free of cost for about forty years, living there as they would on their own property. Later, however, when —

NATALIA: There's not a word of truth in that! My grandfather, and my great-grandfather, too, knew that their estate reached back to the swamp, so that the meadows belong to us. What further discussion can there be? I can't understand it. It is really most annoying.

LOMOV: I'll show you the papers, Natalia Stepanovna.

NATALIA: No, either you are joking, or trying to lead me into a discussion. That's not at all nice! We have owned this property for nearly three hundred years, and now all at once we hear that it doesn't belong to us. Ivan Vassiliyitch, you will pardon me, but I really can't believe my ears. So far as I am concerned, the meadows are worth very little. In all they don't contain more than five acres and they are worth only a few hundred roubles, say three hundred, but the injustice of the thing is what affects me. Say what you will, I can't bear injustice.

LOMOV: Only listen until I have finished, please! The peasants of your respected father's grandfather, as I have already had the honor to tell you, baked bricks for my grandmother. My aunt's grandmother wished to do them a favor —

NATALIA: Grandfather! Grandmother! Aunt! I know nothing about them. All I know is that the meadows belong to us, and that ends the matter.

LOMOV: No, they belong to me!

NATALIA: And if you keep on explaining it for two days, and put on five suits of evening clothes, the meadows are still ours, ours, ours! I don't want to take your property, but I refuse to give up what belongs to us!

LOMOV: Natalia Stepanovna, I don't need the meadows, I am only concerned with the principle. If you are agreeable, I beg of you, accept them as a gift from me!

NATALIA: But I can give them to you, because they belong to me! That is very peculiar, Ivan Vassiliyitch! Until now we have considered you as a good neighbor and a good friend; only last year we lent you our threshing machine so that we couldn't thresh until November, and now you treat us like thieves! You offer to give me my own land. Excuse me, but neighbors don't treat each other that way. In my opinion, it's a very low trick—to speak frankly —

LOMOV: According to you I'm a usurper, then, am I? My dear lady, I have never appropriated other people's property, and I shall permit no one to accuse me of such a thing! (*He goes quickly to the bottle and drinks water.*) The meadows are mine!

NATALIA: That's not the truth! They are mine!

LOMOV: Mine!

NATALIA: Eh? I'll prove it to you! This afternoon I'll send my reapers into the meadows.

LOMOV: W—h—a—t?

NATALIA: My reapers will be there to-day!

LOMOV: And I'll chase them off!

NATALIA: If you dare!

LOMOV: The meadows are mine, you understand? Mine!

NATALIA: Really, you needn't scream so! If you want to scream and snort and rage you may do it at home, but here please keep yourself within the limits of common decency.

LOMOV: My dear lady, if it weren't that I were suffering from palpitation of the heart and hammering of the arteries in my temples, I would deal with you very differently! (*In a loud voice.*) The meadows belong to me!

NATALIA: Us!

LOMOV: Me! (Enter TSCHUBUKOV, *right.*)

TSCHUB: What's going on here? What is he yelling about?

NATALIA: Papa, please tell this gentleman to whom the meadows belong, to us or to him?

TSCHUB (*to* LOMOV): My dear fellow, the meadows are ours.

LOMOV: But, merciful heavens, Stepan Stepanovitch, how do you make that out? You at least might be reasonable. My aunt's grandmother gave the use of the meadows free of cost to your grandfather's peasants; the peasants lived on the land for forty years and used it as their own, but later when —

TSCHUB: Permit me, my dear friend. You forget that your grandmother's peasants never paid, because there had been a lawsuit over the meadows, and everyone knows that the meadows belong to us. You haven't looked at the map.

LOMOV: I'll prove to you that they belong to me!

TSCHUB: Don't try to prove it, my dear fellow.

LOMOV: I will!

TSCHUB: My good fellow, what are you shrieking about? You can't prove anything by yelling, you know. I don't ask for anything that belongs to you, nor do I intend to give up anything of my own. Why should I? If it has gone so far, my dear man, that you really intend to claim the meadows, I'd rather give them to the peasants than you, and I certainly shall!

LOMOV: I can't believe it! By what right can you give away property that doesn't belong to you?

TSCHUB: Really, you must allow me to decide what I am to do with my own land! I'm not accustomed, young man, to have people address me in that tone of voice. I, young man, am twice your age, and I beg you to address me respectfully.

LOMOV: No! No! You think I'm a fool! You're making fun of me! You call my property yours and then expect me to stand quietly by and talk to you like a human being. That isn't the way a good neighbor behaves, Stepan Stepanovitch! You are no neighbor, you're no better than a land-grabber. That's what you are!

TSCHUB: Wh—at? What did he say?

NATALIA: Papa, send the reapers into the meadows this minute!

TSCHUB (to LOMOV): What was that you said, sir?

NATALIA: The meadows belong to us and I won't give them up! I won't give them up! I won't give them up!

LOMOV: We'll see about that! I'll prove in court that they belong to me.

TSCHUB: In court! You may sue in court, sir, if you like! Oh, I know you, you are only waiting to find an excuse to go to law! You're an intriguer, that's what you are! Your whole family were always looking for quarrels. The whole lot!

LOMOV: Kindly refrain from insulting my family. The entire race of Lomov has always been honorable! And never has one been brought to trial for embezzlement, as your dear uncle was!

TSCHUB: And the whole Lomov family were insane!

NATALIA: Every one of them!

TSCHUB: Your grandmother was a dipsomaniac, and the younger aunt, Nastasia Michailovna, ran off with an architect.

LOMOV: And your mother limped. (He puts his hand over his heart.) Oh, my side pains! My temples are bursting! Lord in Heaven! Water!

TSCHUB: And your dear father was a gambler—and a glutton!

NATALIA: And your aunt was a gossip like few others!

LOMOV: And you are an intriguer. Oh, my heart! And it's an open secret that you cheated at the elections—my eyes are blurred! Where is my hat?

NATALIA: Oh, how low! Liar! Disgusting thing!

LOMOV: Where's the hat—? My heart! Where shall I go? Where is the door—? Oh—it seems—as though I were dying! I can't—my legs won't hold me—(Goes to the door.)

TSCHUB (following him): May you never darken my door again!

NATALIA: Bring your suit to court! We'll see! (LOMOV staggers out, center.)

TSCHUB (angrily): The devil!

NATALIA: Such a good-for-nothing! And then they talk about being good neighbors!

TSCHUB: Loafer! Scarecrow! Monster!

NATALIA: A swindler like that takes over a piece of property that doesn't belong to him and then dares to argue about it!

TSCHUB: And to think that this fool dares to make a proposal of marriage!

NATALIA: What? A proposal of marriage?

TSCHUB: Why, yes! He came here to make you a proposal of marriage.

NATALIA: Why didn't you tell me that before?

TSCHUB: That's why he had on his evening clothes! The poor fool!

NATALIA: Proposal for me? Oh! (Falls into an armchair and groans.) Bring him back! Bring him back!

TSCHUB: Bring whom back?

NATALIA: Faster, faster, I'm sinking! Bring him back! (She becomes hysterical.)

TSCHUB: What is it? What's wrong with you? (His hands to his head.) I'm cursed with bad luck! I'll shoot myself! I'll hang myself!

NATALIA: I'm dying! Bring him back!

TSCHUB: Bah! In a minute! Don't bawl! *(He rushes out, center.)*

NATALIA *(groaning)*: What have they done to me? Bring him back! Bring him back!

TSCHUB *(comes running in)*: He's coming at once! The devil take him! Ugh! Talk to him yourself, I can't.

NATALIA *(groaning)*: Bring him back!

TSCHUB: He's coming, I tell you! "Oh, Lord! What a task it is to be the father of a grown daughter!" I'll cut my throat! I really will cut my throat! We've argued with the fellow, insulted him, and now we've thrown him out!—and you did it all, you!

NATALIA: No, you! You haven't any manners, you are brutal! If it weren't for you, he wouldn't have gone!

TSCHUB: Oh, yes, I'm to blame! If I shoot or hang myself, remember *you'll* be to blame. You forced me to it! You! (LOMOV *appears in the doorway.)* There, talk to him yourself! *(He goes out.)*

LOMOV: Terrible palpitation! — My leg is lamed! My side hurts me —

NATALIA: Pardon us, we were angry, Ivan Vassiliyitch. I remember now —the meadows really belong to you.

LOMOV: My heart is beating terribly! My meadows—my eyelids tremble— *(They sit down.)* We were wrong. It was only the principle of the thing —the property isn't worth much to me, but the principle is worth a great deal.

NATALIA: Exactly, the principle! Let us talk about something else.

LOMOV: Because I have proofs that my aunt's grandmother had, with the peasants of your good father—

NATALIA: Enough, enough. *(Aside.)* I don't know how to begin. *(To* LOMOV.*)* Are you going hunting soon?

LOMOV: Yes, heath-cock shooting, respected Natalia Stepanovna. I expect to begin after the harvest. Oh, did you hear? My dog, Ugadi, you know him—limps!

NATALIA: What a shame! How did that happen?

LOMOV: I don't know. Perhaps it's a dislocation, or maybe he was bitten by some other dog. *(He sighs.)* The best dog I ever had—to say nothing of his price! I paid Mironov a hundred and twenty-five roubles for him.

NATALIA: That was too much to pay, Ivan Vassiliyitch.

LOMOV: In my opinion it was very cheap. A wonderful dog!

NATALIA: Papa paid eighty-five roubles for his Otkatai, and Otkatai is much better than your Ugadi.

LOMOV: Really? Otkatai is better than Ugadi? What an idea! *(He laughs.)* Otkatai better than Ugadi!

NATALIA: Of course he is better. It is true Otkatai is still young; he isn't full-grown yet, but in the pack or on the leash with two or three, there is no better than he, ever —

LOMOV: I really beg your pardon, Natalia Stepanovna, but you quite overlooked the fact that he has a short lower jaw, and a dog with a short lower jaw can't snap.

NATALIA: Short lower jaw? That's the first time I ever heard that!

LOMOV: I assure you, his lower jaw is shorter than the upper.

NATALIA: Have you measured it?

LOMOV: I have measured it. He is good at running, though.

NATALIA: In the first place, our Otkatai is pure-bred, a full-blooded son of Sapragavas and Stameskis, and as for your mongrel, nobody could ever figure out his pedigree; he's old and ugly, and as skinny as an old hag.

LOMOV: Old, certainly! I wouldn't take five of your Otkatais for him! Ugadi is a dog and Otkatai is—it is laughable to argue about it! Dogs like your Otkatai can be found by the dozens at any dog dealer's, a whole pound-full!

NATALIA: Ivan Vassiliyitch, you are very contrary to-day. First our meadows belong to you and then Ugadi is better than Otkatai. I don't like it when a person doesn't say what he really thinks. You know perfectly well that Otkatai is a hundred times better than your silly Ugadi. What makes you keep on saying he isn't?

LOMOV: I can see, Natalia Stepanovna, that you consider me either a blindman or a fool. But at least you may as well admit that Otkatai has a short lower jaw!

NATALIA: It isn't so!

LOMOV: Yes, a short lower jaw!

NATALIA *(loudly)*: It's not so!

LOMOV: What makes you scream, my dear lady?

NATALIA: What makes you talk such nonsense? It's disgusting! It is high time that Ugadi was shot, and yet you compare him with Otkatai!

LOMOV: Pardon me, but I can't carry on this argument any longer. I have palpitation of the heart!

NATALIA: I have always noticed that the hunters who do the most talking know the least about hunting.

LOMOV: My dear lady, I beg of you to be still. My heart is bursting! *(He shouts.)* Be still!

NATALIA: I won't be still until you admit that Otkatai is better! *(Enter Tschubukov.)*

TSCHUB: Well, has it begun again?

NATALIA: Papa, say frankly, on your honor, which dog is better: Otkatai or Ugadi?

LOMOV: Stepan Stepanovitch, I beg of you, just answer this: has your dog a short lower jaw or not? Yes or no?

TSCHUB: And what if he has? Is it of such importance? There is no better dog in the whole country.

LOMOV: My Ugadi is better. Tell the truth, now!

TSCHUB: Don't get so excited, my dear fellow! Permit me. Your Ugadi certainly has his good points. He is from a good breed, has a good stride, strong haunches, and so forth. But the dog, if you really want to know it, has two faults; he is old and he has a short lower jaw.

LOMOV: Pardon me, I have palpitation of the heart!—Let us keep to facts—just remember in Maruskins's meadows, my Ugadi kept ear to ear with the Count Rasvachai and your dog.

TSCHUB: He was behind, because the Count struck him with his whip.

LOMOV: Quite right. All the other dogs were on the fox's scent, but Otkatai found it necessary to bite a sheep.

TSCHUB: That isn't so!—I am sensitive about that and beg you to stop this argument. He struck him because everybody looks on a strange dog of good blood with envy. Even you, sir, aren't free from the sin. No sooner do you find a dog better than Ugadi than you begin to—this, that—his, mine—and so forth! I remember distinctly.

LOMOV: I remember something, too!

TSCHUB *(mimicking him)*: I remember something, too! What do you remember?

LOMOV: Palpitation! My leg is lame—I can't—

NATALIA: Palpitation! What kind of hunter are you? You ought to stay in the kitchen by the stove and wrestle with the potato peelings, and not go fox-hunting! Palpitation!

TSCHUB: And what kind of hunter are you? A man with your diseases ought to stay at home and not jolt around in the saddle. If you were a hunter—! But you only ride around in order to find out about other people's dogs, and make trouble for everyone. I am sensitive! Let's drop the subject. Besides, you're no hunter.

LOMOV: You only ride around to flatter the Count!—My heart! You intriguer! Swindler!

TSCHUB: And what of it? *(Shouting.)* Be still!

LOMOV: Intriguer!

TSCHUB: Baby! Puppy! Walking drug-store!

LOMOV: Old rat! Jesuit! Oh, I know you!

TSCHUB: Be still! Or I'll shoot you—with my worst gun, like a partridge! Fool! Loafer!

LOMOV: Everyone knows that—oh, my heart!—that your poor late wife beat you. My leg—my temples—Heavens—I'm dying—I—

TSCHUB: And your housekeeper wears the trousers in your house!

LOMOV: Here—here—there—there— my heart has burst! My shoulder is torn apart. Where is my shoulder? I'm dying! *(He falls into a chair.)* The doctor! *(Faints.)*

TSCHUB: Baby! Half-baked clam! Fool!

NATALIA: Nice sort of hunter you are! You can't even sit on a horse. *(To* TSCHUB.*)* Papa, what's the matter with him? *(She screams.)* Ivan Vassiliyitch! He is dead!

LOMOV: I'm ill! I can't breathe! Air!

NATALIA: He is dead! *(She shakes* LOMOV *in the chair.)* Ivan Vassiliyitch! What have we done! He is dead! *(She sinks into a chair.)* The doctor—doctor! *(She goes into hysterics.)*

TSCHUB: Ahh! What is it? What's the matter with you?

NATALIA *(groaning)*: He's dead!—Dead!

TSCHUB: Who is dead? Who? *(Looking at* LOMOV.*)* Yes, he is dead! Good God! Water! The doctor! *(Holding the glass to* LOMOV's *lips.)* Drink! No, he won't drink! He's dead! What a terrible situation! Why didn't I shoot myself? Why have I never cut my throat? What am I waiting for now? Only give me a knife! Give me a pistol! (LOMOV *moves.)* He's coming to! Drink some water—there!

LOMOV: Sparks! Mists! Where am I?

TSCHUB: Get married! Quick, and then go to the devil! She's willing! *(He joins the hand of* LOMOV *and* NATALIA.*)* She's agreed! Only leave me in peace!

LOMOV: Wh—what? *(Getting up.)* Whom?

TSCHUB: She's willing! Well? Kiss each other and—the devil take you both!

NATALIA *(groans)*: He lives! Yes, yes, I'm willing!

TSCHUB: Kiss each other!

LOMOV: Eh? Whom? (NATALIA *and* LOMOV *kiss.*) Very nice—! Pardon me, but what is this for? Oh, yes, I understand! My heart—sparks—I am happy, Natalia Stepanovna. *(He kisses her hand.)* My leg is lame!

NATALIA: I'm happy, too!

TSCHUB: Ahh! A load off my shoulders! Ahh!

NATALIA: And now at least you'll admit that Ugadi is worse than Otkatai!

LOMOV: Better!

NATALIA: Worse!

TSCHUB: Now the domestic joys have begun.—Champagne!

LOMOV: Better!

NATALIA: Worse, worse, worse!

TSCHUB *(trying to drown them out)*: Champagne, champagne!

HANDY AMERICAN VANISHES

Sydney J. Harris

The handy man who for many years has taken care of a half-dozen houses in the country, including ours, up and quit this winter. He bought a farm and will have no more time for odd jobs and caretaking.

There aren't any others to be found around in this era of specialization. The old-fashioned handy man is a vanishing species; the fellow who did everything pretty well has been replaced by the expert who does one thing poorly, expensively, and at his own dilatory convenience.

This is progress, I suppose. At least we are told that specialization has given us the glories of modern living, that the precise division of labor permits society to reach an ever-increasing level of abundance.

An ever-increasing level of frustration, too. I spent the holidays some years ago with old friends who had just moved from Manhattan to a sprawling house in Connecticut, where the children "had room to grow up in." The children grew up fine, but the parents rapidly became depleted, in substance and in spirit.

They required, at regular intervals, the services of five different plumbers, none of whom would have anything to do with the others. There was a plumber for the water pump, for the chlorinator, for the septic tank, and for the sump pump. There was also the regular plumbing plumber, who repaired only the ordinary plumbing fixtures, more or less.

In addition, they were (and are) continually beholden to the moods and schedules of the roof and ceiling man, the electric wiring man, the man who cleans the burner, the man who cleans the chimney, the gardener, the pruner, the plowman and the gasoline man.

None of these essential functions can be performed by any but an accredited specialist in the field: the man who handles the sump pump professes profound ignorance of the water pump and the septic tank, while the pruner will not plow in winter, nor will the man who cleans the burner clean the chimney.

Last summer, one of my boys accidentally broke a small pane in a window off the front porch. The handy man was sick, and so I made a few calls. But the carpenter couldn't do it, the glazier had no time for such a small job, and the spray kept sailing through the cardboard I had taped to the window until the handy man recovered a week later.

Now he is gone for good, or for bad. Like the whooping crane, he is fast disappearing from the national scene; a generation from now, handy men may be on exhibit, stuffed, in the museums. "Homo handiensis," the identifying card will inform the children, "once prevalent in the country, now extinct, a companion to the Great Auk and the Dodo. Last seen puttying a window in Northern Wisconsin, circa 1964."

HOW TO TELL GOOD GUYS
FROM BAD GUYS

John Steinbeck

Television has crept upon us so gradually in America that we have not yet become aware of the extent of its impact for good or bad. I myself do not look at it very often except for its coverage of sporting events, news, and politics. Indeed, I get most of my impressions of the medium from my young sons.

Whether for good or bad, television has taken the place of the sugar-tit, soothing syrups, and the mild narcotics parents in other days used to reduce their children to semiconsciousness and consequently to seminoisiness. In the past, a harassed parent would say, "Go sit in a chair" or "Go outside and play!" or "If you don't stop that noise, I'm going to beat your dear little brains out!" The present-day parent suggests, "Why don't you go look at television?" From that moment the screams, shouts, revolver shots, and crashes of motor accidents come from the loudspeaker, not from the child. For some reason, this is presumed to be more relaxing to the parent. The effect on the child has yet to be determined.

I have observed the physical symptoms of television-looking on children as well as on adults. The mouth grows slack and the lips hang open; the eyes take on a hypnotized or doped look; the nose runs rather more than usual; the backbone turns to water and the fingers slowly and methodically pick the designs out of brocade furniture. Such is the appearance of semi-consciousness that one wonders how much of the "message" of television is getting through to the brain. This wonder is further strengthened by the fact that a television-looker will look at anything at all and for hours. Recently I came into a room to find my eight-year-old son Catbird sprawled in a chair, idiot slackness on his face, with the doped eyes of an opium smoker. On the television screen stood a young woman of mammary distinction with ice-cream hair listening to a man in thick glasses and a doctor's smock.

"What's happening?" I asked.

Catbird answered in the monotone of the sleeptalker which is known as television voice, "She is asking if she should dye her hair."

"What is the doctor's reaction?"

"If she uses Trutone it's all right," said Catbird. "But if she uses ordinary or adulterated products, her hair will split and lose its golden natural sheen. The big economy size is two dollars and ninety-eight cents if you act now," said Catbird.

You see, something was getting through to him. He looked punch-drunk, but he was absorbing. I did not feel it fair to interject a fact that I have observed—that natural golden sheen does not exist in nature. But I did think of my friend Elia Kazan's cry of despair, and although it is a digression I shall put it down.

We were having dinner in a lovely little restaurant in California. At the table next to us were six beautiful, young, well-dressed American girls of the age and appearance of magazine advertisements. There was only one difficulty with their perfection. You couldn't tell them apart. Kazan, who is a primitive of a species once known as men, regarded the little beauties with distaste, and finally in more sorrow than anger cried, "It's years since I've seen or smelled a dame! It's all products, Golden Glint, l'Eau d'Eau, Butisan, Elyn's puff-adder cream—I remember I used to like how women smelled. Nowadays it's all products!"

End of digression.

Just when the parent becomes convinced that his child's brain is rotting away from television, he is jerked up in another direction. Catbird has corrected me in the Museum of Natural History when I directed his attention to the mounted skeleton of a tyrannosaur. He said it was a brontosaurus but observed kindly that many people made the same error. He argued with his ten-year-old brother about the relative cleanness of the line in Praxiteles and Phidias. He knows the weight a llama will bear before lying down in protest, and his knowledge of entomology is embarrassing to a parent who likes to impart information to his children. And these things he also got from television. I knew that he was picking up masses of unrelated and probably worthless information from television, incidentally the kind of information I also like best, but I did not know that television was preparing him in criticism and politics, and that is what this piece is really about.

I will have to go back a bit in preparation. When television in America first began to be a threat to the motion-picture industry, that industry fought back by refusing to allow its films to be shown on the home screens. One never saw new pictures, but there were whole blocks of the films called Westerns which were owned by independents, and these were released to the television stations. The result is that at nearly any time of the day or night you can find a Western being shown on some television station. It is not only the children who see them. All of America sees them. They are a typically American conception, the cowboy picture. The story never varies and the conventions are savagely adhered to. The hero never kisses a girl. He loves his horse and he stands for right and justice. Any change in the story or the conventions would be taken as an outrage. Out of these films folk heroes have grown up—Hopalong Cassidy, the Lone Ranger, Roy Rogers, and Gene Autry. These are more than great men. They are symbols of courage, purity, simplicity, honesty, and right. You must understand that nearly every American is drenched in the tradition of the Western, which is, of course, the celebration of a whole pattern of American life that never existed. It is also as set in its form as the *commedia dell'arte*.

End of preparation.

One afternoon, hearing gunfire from the room where our television set is installed, I went in with that losing intention of fraternizing with my son for a little while. There sat Catbird with the cretinous expression I have learned to recognize. A Western was in progress.

"What's going on?" I asked.

He looked at me in wonder. "What do you mean, what's going on? Don't you know?"

"Well, no. Tell me!"

He was kind to me. Explained as though I were the child.

"Well, the Bad Guy is trying to steal Her father's ranch. But the Good Guy won't let him. Bullet figured out the plot."

"Who is Bullet?"

"Why, the Good Guy's horse." He didn't add "You dope," but his tone implied it.

"Now wait," I said, "which one is the Good Guy?"

"The one with the white hat."

"Then the one with the black hat is the Bad Guy?"

"Anybody knows that," said Catbird.

For a time I watched the picture, and I realized that I had been ignoring a part of our life that everybody knows. I was interested in the characterizations. The girl, known as Her or She, was a blonde, very pretty but completely unvoluptuous because these are Family Pictures. Sometimes she wore a simple gingham dress and sometimes a leather skirt and boots, but always had a bit of a bow in her hair and her face was untroubled with emotion or, one might almost say, intelligence. This also is part of the convention. She is a symbol, and any acting would get her thrown out of the picture by popular acclaim.

The Good Guy not only wore a white hat but light-colored clothes, shining boots, tight riding pants, and a shirt embroidered with scrolls and flowers. In my young days I used to work with cattle, and our costume was blue jeans, a leather jacket, and boots with run-over heels. The cleaning bill alone of this gorgeous screen cowboy would have been four times what our pay was in a year.

The Good Guy had very little change of facial expression. He went through his fantastic set of adventures with no show of emotion. This is another convention and proves that he is very brave and very pure. He is also scrubbed and has an immaculate shave.

I turned my attention to the Bad Guy. He wore a black hat and dark clothing, but his clothing was definitely not only unclean but unpressed. He had a stubble of beard but the greatest contrast was in his face. His was not an immobile face. He leered, he sneered, he had a nasty laugh. He bullied and shouted. He looked evil. While he did not swear, because this is a Family Picture, he said things like "Wall dog it" and "You rat" and "I'll cut your ears and eat 'em," which would indicate that his language was not only coarse but might, off screen, be vulgar. He was, in a word, a Bad Guy. I found a certain interest in the Bad Guy which was lacking in the Good Guy.

"Which one do you like best?" I asked.

Catbird removed his anaesthetized eyes from the screen. "What do you mean?"

"Do you like the Good Guy or the Bad Guy?"

He sighed at my ignorance and looked back at the screen. "Are you kidding?" he asked. "The Good Guy, of course."

Now a new character began to emerge. He puzzled me because he wore a gray hat. I felt a little embarrassed about asking my son, the expert, but I gathered my courage. "Catbird," I asked shyly, "what kind of a guy is that, the one in the gray hat?"

He was sweet to me then. I think until that moment he had not understood the abysmal extent of my ignorance. "He's the In-Between Guy," Catbird explained kindly. "If he starts bad he ends good and if he starts good he ends bad."

"What's this one going to do?"

"See how he's sneering and needs a shave?" my son asked.

"Yes."

"Well, the picture's just started, so that guy is going to end good and help the Good Guy get Her father's ranch back."

"How can you be sure?" I asked.

Catbird gave me a cold look. "He's got a gray hat, hasn't he? Now don't talk. It's about time for the chase."

There it was, not only a tight, true criticism of a whole art form but to a certain extent of life itself. I was deeply impressed because this simple explanation seemed to mean something to me more profound than television or Westerns.

WHAT PRICE VERBAL
INCOMPETENCE?

Edwin A. Locke, Jr.

It seems to me that I have never heard so much misuse and abuse of the English language by people occupying responsible positions as in recent years. And my question is: What ought we to do about verbal incompetence—about the carelessness in speaking and writing which is so prevalent among us?

It is not exaggerating to say that America's international position depends in some degree on our ability as a people to use words effectively and grasp their actual meanings. We have entered a period of greatly increased competition from other countries. Our qualifications as leader of the free world are being tested as never before. Our diplomats are constantly in the spotlight. Every word that they utter or write is exposed to hard critical judgment. Our government must compete in propaganda with other nations to influence the world's peoples, and our success or failure in this department can profoundly affect our destiny. If we are to maintain leadership, we will have to show great skill in the arts of communication. Those who do not understand us may well turn against us.

I shall never forget one incident of the days when I was working for our government in a diplomatic capacity. There was a meeting in London where a very high official of our government had to explain our position on a touchy matter to the ministers of several other countries. I think all of the Americans present, including myself, were embarrassed for him and for the United States. He rambled, he stumbled, he used words that distorted his meaning. He not only failed to make his point but he confused the issue. It literally took weeks of patient effort to correct the false impressions that he created at that meeting, and we never did win the agreement that we sought.

I have heard a Congressman shock a group of Asiatic visitors by saying proudly that Americans are an "aggressive" people. I suppose he meant to say that we are a courageous, vigorous people. But his audience understood him to mean that we are a warlike people, and their worst fears were confirmed. I hate to think of how many times in our recent history similar episodes must have occurred—meetings where our spokesmen used the wrong words, or failed to use the right ones that would have made their meaning clear. These are days when, as I read the newspapers, I find myself repeating the closing lines of Kipling's *Recessional*: "For frantic boast and foolish word, / Thy mercy on thy people, Lord!"

We are told, and I think we can all agree, that verbal incompetence is often a symptom of deeper problems of the mind and spirit. But there are surely many instances when it results from loose and undisciplined mental habits, from a lack of respect for words. Unless we take action to correct the trend, verbal incompetence may become a national calamity.

Lately I have come to think that the sector of our society that suffers most seriously from verbal incompetence is business. There, too, the national interest is involved. The misleading use of words is a major source of inefficiency and waste motion in business. It is all the more serious because it is hard to measure. I venture to say that all the thefts and embezzlements that corporations suffer every year do not cost our economy as much as verbal incompetence.

The waste created by misunderstanding is one that America can ill afford. Our industry is now compelled to meet concentrated competition, not only from the Communist countries, but even more important, from nations friendly to us. High prices—and waste means high prices—can keep us out of markets all over the world. And if our foreign trade falls away—or even fails to grow—our political influence and strategic alliances could be jeopardized.

All of us, in whatever walks of life, have a big stake in the efficiency of American business. And for that reason, we must take a serious view of the continuous economic losses due to verbal incompetence.

I have seen more than one business shaken by a single letter or memorandum in which words were used loosely or wildly. A story was recently told to me by the head of an important company. Call him Mr. Brown. He was at the time trying to establish friendly relations with an executive of another company, a Mr. Slade, who was an important potential customer for Brown, and Brown had given a good deal of thought to the best way of cultivating him.

One day, a letter from Slade arrived at Brown's office. Slade said that he was reviewing his requirements for the year ahead, and that if Brown would like to talk with him, he would make himself available.

Now it happened that Brown just then was away on a trip. In his absence, Slade's letter went to one of his young assistants for reply—call him Harvey. This is what Harvey wrote to Slade. "Dear Mr. Slade: In Mr. Brown's absence, I am writing to say that your request for an appointment will be brought to his attention immediately on his return."

When Brown got back a few days later, he telephoned Slade at once. Slade shocked him by saying that he was no longer interested in pursuing the matter. He said that he judged companies by the tone of their correspondence, and after receiving Harvey's note he had got in touch with another company, a competitor of Brown's, and had concluded a deal with them. He added that he had been surprised to find that his letter to Brown was regarded as a request for an appointment.

When Brown hung up the phone, he sent for Harvey. Now the point that interests me most is that Harvey could not see that there was anything wrong with the letter he had written. He said, "But Mr. Brown, that letter from Mr. Slade *did* ask for an appointment."

Brown said, "You don't seem to understand. Slade wrote that if I wanted to see him, he would make himself available. He wasn't requesting an appointment. He was giving *me* a chance to request one."

And then young Harvey said, "But after all, it's practically the same thing, isn't it?"

Business is full of Harveys—young men whose minds have never been trained to pin-point the meaning of the words they use, and whose careers suffer accordingly. That little anecdote is characteristic of what goes on all the time. A man can have many virtues and abilities, but if he does not use language accurately and carefully, he can be a positive menace to a business enterprise.

This is a country where each year hundreds of thousands of young men go into business with their hearts set on executive careers. Yet it is relatively rare to find a young business man who recognizes how much his chances for an executive post depend on his ability to use words effectively. Many companies, including the one with which I am connected, today give increasing weight to the ability to communicate effectively as a test of executive potential.

Of course, there are plenty of young people who have a bright surface and glib tongues—who look at first glance as if they might be of executive caliber. But when they begin to talk seriously, or to express themselves in writing, they too often reveal serious verbal limitations. Sometimes, listening to a hopeful young man, or reading something he has written, I have been reminded of the way a child uses finger paint—a dab here and a smear there. The child hopes that father will recognize his painting and say, "Oh, yes, that's a cat." Many otherwise intelligent people, when they talk or write, similarly seem to feel that they have done all that can be expected of them if the other fellow just gets the general idea. They may not know it, but they are intellectually crippled.

The heads of several other companies have told me that they, too, are deeply concerned over this problem. They have all had experience with young executives who seem almost indifferent to the meaning of words. I have been told of a memorandum written by one such young man, which caused a good deal of trouble. His company specializes in issuing reports on the steel industry. One day the editor of these reports received a memo from one of his assistants. It said, "I talked with Anderson, and he predicts a price rise before April." Anderson was an important steel man.

The report for that week was going to press, the editor was in a hurry, and he did not stop to check with Anderson. In a few days the item appeared in print, and then Anderson telephoned in a state of rage. He demanded an apology and a retraction. He had made no prediction, he said. All he had told the young man was that if certain things happened—which had not yet happened—prices could be expected to rise. Since when was that a prediction? If that was the kind of intelligence the editor was relying on, said Anderson, he could never trust him again.

Now the young assistant who had written that memo knew in general what the word "predict" means. But he did not distinguish between a prediction and a qualified statement of possibilities. He was content to use a word that merely approximated his meaning. As a result, he did serious damage to the reputation of his firm.

If verbal incompetence were confined to the use of the wrong word, it would be bad enough. But equally dangerous is the frequent inability of business men to sense the effect of their words on the persons who will hear them or read them.

I have known a single word, used insensitively, to touch off a costly labor dispute. A large company was negotiating a new contract with a labor union. Both sides had presented their views in writing. The negotiation was progressing in a somewhat tense but reasonable atmosphere. At this point, the union leadership presented a letter raising a new condition. The letter hinted that if the new condition was not accepted by the company a strike might result. This was, of course, a familiar bargaining tactic.

The union's letter was given for reply to a young man in the company. By current standards, he is well educated—a graduate of a great university —with a good academic record, and a lively mind. The letter he composed was for the most part sensible. But at one point he said, "It would be criminal to call a strike for such a reason." None of his superiors who read the letter saw anything wrong with it, and it went out.

Now it was true that a strike under those circumstances would have been illegal. The young man knew the difference between "illegal" and "criminal." To do him justice, he used the word "criminal" only in its figurative sense, to show indignation. Unfortunately, the union leaders took it literally. The word "criminal" was like a slap in the face to them. One of them, in fact, had a jail record. They reacted violently to what they felt was a gratuitous insult. "Who is he calling criminals?" was their reaction. From that point on, they became hostile, the situation deteriorated, and a useless strike followed at great cost both to the union members and to the company.

Another costly aspect of verbal incompetence in business is what might be called the careless cliché. Please understand that I am not objecting too much to clichés as a whole. They may be despised by poets, but as we all know a cliché accurately used can on occasion be a time saver and a boon to the weary mind. The trouble arises when the cliché is wrongly used.

I know about a letter written by the sales manager of a well-known company to a customer. The letter explained why a certain salesman had left the company. The sales manager was angry at the salesman for quitting and in his letter he said, "It's just a case of a rat leaving the ship."

He failed to remember that it is the sinking ship that rats desert. But this thought came to his customer, and he mentioned it to others. Soon people were gossiping that the company was in trouble. It took an investigation to unearth the source of the rumor, and a good deal of effort to undo the damage that had been done. The head of that company told me that he figured the cost of that one little misused cliché at about $10,000.

Then there was a memorandum issued by an officer in another company, with this apparently innocent sentence in it: "Let's apply this new credit policy with discretion right across the board."

The writer of that memo meant that the new policy should be applied in all appropriate cases, but that there would be some cases in which it was not applicable, and care should be taken to handle such cases discreetly. That was not the impression that was created in the minds of the men who received the memo. As they understood the order, the new credit policy was to be applied to all of the company's customers, "right across the board," and the words "with discretion" merely meant that they were to be polite about it.

It took just two days for the earthquake to develop. Then complaints began to come in from outraged customers, demanding to know what the company meant by refusing to extend the usual credit terms. Tempers were lost. Orders were canceled. The company's top management became alarmed. Before the tangle was straightened out, I was told, the company had lost $50,000 worth of business.

To me, one of the most irritating forms of verbal incompetence is wordiness. It is of course hard to be concise. I have a good deal of sympathy with the man who said, "If I'd had more time, I would have written you a shorter letter." We all know what he meant. But a great deal of unnecessary verbiage in business, I am convinced, results not so much from lack of time as from mental laziness or confusion.

More than once I have seen executives spend valuable hours and brain energy trying to grasp the meaning of a ten-page report, when a single page of accurate writing would have served the purpose. I have seen the employees of a plant bewildered and disturbed by a long, incomprehensible instruction from the home office, until it was reduced to a few brief sentences that told them clearly what to do.

Business does not want wordy men, but it urgently needs men who respect words. I hate to suggest that our overburdened schools take on more responsibilities than they already have, yet I cannot help wondering if this is not essentially a problem of education.

People are most responsive to the discipline of language when they are young. In several instances I have tried to get mature business associates to sharpen their use of words, but the results have been a good deal less than spectacular. Once a young man has left school, if he has not already been imbued with respect for words and given the mental training necessary to distinguish shades of meaning, the chances are that he will always be weak in this department.

People who cannot use words accurately are likely to be people who cannot grasp meanings successfully. And much may depend on the ability of the American people to understand the actual meanings of the propagandistic words that are being hurled at them today. Why are so many people everywhere carried away by demagogues and fanatics? In part, I think it is because they have never been exposed to the least semantic discipline. They do not really understand the words that they hear or read. It is only the emotional overtones that reach them. And this unthinking emotionalism can in the long run make them dangerous to their countrymen, to themselves, and to the world.

I would go so far as to say that verbal incompetence is threatening to become a chronic disease of the American intellect. It needs to be dealt with by an all-out effort by the qualified men, dealt with as we deal with polio or muscular dystrophy. The literate people of this country, as I see it, have a responsibility to restore respect for the word, to reduce the proportion of verbal incompetents in the population.

I believe from my heart that if the schools and colleges of this country would boldly decide to meet this problem head-on they would have the support not only of business, but of serious-minded citizens from every walk of life. The American people already stand in heavy debt to the teachers and school administrators of the country, but if education can strengthen the use of language in our time, the next generation will have even more to be grateful for.

EXTRA! EXTRA!

Robert Sherwood

From the street below came that most terrifying of sounds, the full-chested roar of two men shouting, "Extra! Extra!" through the rainy night.

"Extra! Extra!"

Mr. Whidden, reading his evening paper, it was the home edition, published at noon, containing no news whatsoever, wondered what the trouble was. He could gather nothing from the ominous shouts that assailed his ears. The two men might have been lusty-lunged Russians for all of him. But there was an ominous note in their voices—the warning of dark calamity—the grim suggestion of wars, plagues, holocausts.

"Where do they get those men with voices like that and what do they do between extras?" he thought.

Mrs. Whidden emerged from the kitchen, whither she had retired to bathe the supper dishes.

"There's an extra out, Roy," she announced.

"So I hear," said her husband, who was not above an occasional facetious sally.

She walked over to the window, opened it, and thrust her head out into the rain. In the street, five stories below, she could see the two news vendors.

"Extra! Extra!"

Mrs. Whidden turned from the window.

"Something must have happened."

There was an overtone of complaint in her remark that Mr. Whidden recognized only too well. It was a tone that always suggested unwelcome activity on Mr. Whidden's part. He wished that she would come right out and say, "Go downstairs and get the paper," but she never did. She always prefaced her commands with a series of whining insinuations.

"I wonder what it was?" she asked, as though expecting her husband to know.

"Oh, nothing, I guess. Those extras never amount to anything."

Mrs. Whidden turned again to the window.

"Something awful must have happened," she observed, and the counterpoint of complaint was even more pronounced.

Mr. Whidden shifted uneasily in his chair—the one comfortable chair in the flat—the chair which he himself had bought for his own occupancy and about which there had been so much argument. He knew what was coming; he didn't want to move, and walk down and up four flights of stairs for the sake of some information that would not affect his life in the remotest degree.

"Don't you intend to find *out*?" asked Mrs. Whidden, and it was evident that she had reached the snappy stage. Her husband knew that if he didn't go down and buy that damned paper, he would provide fuel for an irritation that would burn well into the night. Nevertheless that chair was so comfortable, and the weather was so disagreeable, and the stairs were such a climb . . . !

"I guess I won't go down, Emmy. Those extras are always fakes, anyway, and, besides, if it is anything important, we'll find out about it in the morning paper."

The roars of the men shouting "Extra! Extra!" reverberated through the street, beating with determined violence against the sheer walls of the walk-up apartment houses, shuddering through the open window of the Whiddens' living room, jarring the fringed shade of the reading lamp, the souvenirs on the bookshelves, the tasseled portieres that led into the little hall.

"You're just lazy, Roy Whidden," said Mrs. Whidden. "You sit there reading your paper—night after night—night after night." She turned as though to an invisible jury, to whom she was addressing a fervent plea for recognition of her prolonged martyrdom. Then, with all the dramatic suddenness of an experienced prosecutor, she snapped at the defendant: "What *do* you read, anyway? Answer me that! What *do* you read?"

Mr. Whidden knew that the question was purely rhetorical. No answer was expected.

"You don't read a *thing*. You just sit there and stare at that fool paper —probably the death notices. When anything important happens, you don't even care enough to step out into the street and see what it is."

"How do *you* know it's important?" Mr. Whidden inquired, being inclined, albeit unwisely, to display a little spirit.

"How do you know it *isn't*?" Mrs. Whidden backfired. "How will you ever know *anything* unless you take the trouble to find out?"

Mr. Whidden uncrossed his legs and then crossed them again.

"I suppose you expect *me* to go down and get that paper," cried Mrs. Whidden, whose voice was now rivaling the news vendors'. "With all I've got to do—the dishes, and the baby's ten o'clock feeding, and . . . all right! I'll *go*! I'll walk down the four flights of stairs and *get* the paper, so that Your Majesty won't have to trouble yourself." There was a fine sarcasm in her tone now.

Mr. Whidden knew that it was the end. For seven years this exact scene had been repeating itself over and over again. If there had only been some slight variation in his wife's technique . . . but there never had. At first he had tried to be frightfully sporting about it, assuming the blame at the first hint of trouble and doing whatever was demanded of him with all possible grace; but that pose, and it had not been long before he admitted that it *was* a pose, was worn away by a process of erosion, a process that had kept up for seven years—seven years of writing things in ledgers in an airless office on Dey Street; seven years of listening to those endless scoldings and complaints at home. Whatever of gallantry had existed in Mr. Whidden's soul had crumbled before the persistent and ever-increasing waves of temper. He knew that now, if he gave in, he did so because of cowardice and not because of any worthily chivalrous motives.

He threw his paper down, stood up, and walked into the bedroom to get his coat. Little Conrad was asleep in there, lying on his stomach, his face pressed against the bars of the crib.

Over the crib hung a colored photograph of the Taj Mahal, a lovely, white building that Mr. Whidden had always wanted to see. He also wanted to see Singapore, and the Straits Settlements, and the west coast of Africa, places that he had read about in books.

He was thinking about these places, and wondering whether little Conrad would ever see them, when his wife's voice rasped at him from the next room.

"Are you going or will I have to go?"

"I'm going, dear," he assured her in the manner of one who is tired.

"Well, hurry! Those men are a block away by now."

Mr. Whidden put on his coat, looked at little Conrad and at the Taj Mahal, and then started down the stairs.

There were four flights of them, and it was raining hard outside.

Twelve years later Mrs. Whidden (now Mrs. Burchall) sat sewing on the front porch of a pleasant house in a respectable suburb. It was a brilliantly sunny day, and the hydrangeas were just starting to burst out into profuse bloom on the bushes at either side of the steps.

"And do you mean to tell me you never *heard* from him?" asked Mrs. Lent, who was also sewing.

"Not a word," replied Mrs. Burchall, without rancor. "Not one word in twelve years. He used to send money sometimes to the bank, but they'd never tell me where it came from."

"I guess you ain't sorry he went. Fred Burchall's a good man."

"You'd think he was a good man all right if you could've seen what I had before. My *goodness*! When I think of the seven years I wasted being Roy Whidden's wife!"

Mrs. Burchall heaved a profound sigh.

"Ain't you ever sort of afraid he might show up?" asked Mrs. Lent.

"Not him. And if he did, what of it? Fred could kick him out with one hand tied behind his back. Fred Burchall's a real *man*."

She sewed in silence for a while.

"Of course, I *am* a little worried about Conrad. He thinks his father's dead. You see, we wanted to spare him from knowing about the divorce and all that. We couldn't have the boy starting out in life with his father's disgrace on his shoulders."

Shortly thereafter Mrs. Lent went on her way and Mrs. Burchall stepped into the house to see whether the maid was doing anything constructive. She found her son Conrad curled up in a chair, reading some book.

"You sitting in the house reading on a fine day like this! Go on out into the fresh air and shake your limbs."

"But, Mother —"

"Go on out, I tell you. Can't you try to be a *real* boy for a change?"

"But this book's exciting."

"I'll bet. Anything in print is better than fresh air and outdoor exercise, I suppose. You're just like your—can't you ever stop reading for one instant? I declare! One of these days you'll turn into a book. . . . Now you set that book down and go out of this house this instant."

Conrad went out to the front yard and started, with no enthusiasm, to bounce an old golf ball up and down upon the concrete walk that led from the front porch to the gate. He was thus engaged when a strange man appeared in the street, stopping before the gate to look for the number which wasn't there.

"Hey, sonny, is this Mrs. Burchall's house?"

"Yes," said the boy, "it is. Want to see her?"

The man was short, slight, and none too formidable-looking; although he was obviously a representative of the lower classes—possibly a tramp— Conrad was not in the least afraid of him. He had a rather friendly expression, a peaceful expression, as though he bore ill will to no one.

"What's your name?" the man inquired.

"My name's Conrad—Conrad Whidden."

Conrad wondered why the man stared at him so.

"I used to know your mother," the man explained, "before I went to sea."

"Oh, you're a sailor!" Conrad was obviously impressed. "Where've you been?"

"Oh, all over. I just came from Marseille."

"Gosh," said Conrad. "I'd like to go there. I've been reading about it in a book—it's a book called *The Arrow of Gold*."

The man smiled.

"You were named after the man who wrote that book," said the sailor.

"I never knew that."

"No, I guess not. Your mother didn't know either."

Just then Mrs. Burchall appeared on the front steps, attracted perhaps by the suspicious cessation of the sharp pops that the golf ball had been making on the concrete walk.

When she saw her former husband leaning on the gate her first thought was this: Well, of all things! And here I was talking about him to Adele

Lent not ten minutes ago. Then she realized with sudden horror, that her son was actually in conversation with his father. She wondered whether that fool Roy had said anything . . .

"Conrad, you come here this instant!"

Conrad ambled up the concrete walk.

"How many times do I have to tell you not to talk to every strange man that comes around?"

"He's a sailor, Mother."

"Oh, a sailor, is he!" Somehow or other, that annoyed Mrs. Burchall. "Well, you just chase yourself around to the back and don't let me catch you talking to any tramps—or sailors either."

Conrad cast one glance toward the man who had come from Marseille, and then disappeared from view behind the house.

Mrs. Burchall walked elegantly down to the front gate and confronted Roy Whidden.

"So you're a sailor, are you?" she said, and surveyed him with deliberate satisfaction. "You look to me like a common bum. I always knew you'd never get anywhere."

"I guess you were right."

He smiled as he said this. Mrs. Burchall was irritated by the easy good humor of his tone, by the calm confidence in his eyes.

"Why did you do it?" she asked.

"I don't know. It was a rainy night, and I heard a foghorn out in the river."

"So you left me for a foghorn!"

"Yes—I knew you'd be all right. Your people had money, and I sent some."

"A lot you sent."

"I guess it wasn't much—but it was all I could scrape together."

"Well, what are you bumming around here for now? What do you want? More money? Well, you won't get it. Not one nickel. I told Fred Burchall if you ever showed up he was to kick you right out. And he'd do it, too! I advise you to make yourself scarce before *he* gets home."

"Don't worry, I'm going. My ship sails at six."

"Oh, your *ship* sails, does it! I'll bet it's a *fine* ship." She laughed harshly at the mental picture of any ship on which Roy Whidden could obtain employment. "How did you ever find out where I live?"

"Oh, I kept track of you through the bank. I knew when you got the divorce and got married again."

"Well then, why didn't you leave me alone? What did you come snoopin' around here for?"

"Just curiosity. I wanted to see what the boy looks like."

"Well—you've seen him."

"Yes, I've seen him. That's all I wanted."

He straightened up and started to move away. "Well—good-by, Em."

"Good-by, and I hope you enjoy yourself on that *ship* of yours."

He was walking away down the street when suddenly she called to him: "Roy!" He stopped abruptly in response to that well-remembered summons.

"Here was something I meant to ask you," she said with an unusual hesitancy, "What—what was that extra about?"

He rubbed his none-too-smooth chin and thought for an instant.

"Let's see," he said. "It was something about...no, that was later. I guess I've forgotten."

"Was it about the world series?" she asked, as though trying desperately hard to prompt him. "The morning papers were full of it. Was it about that?"

He smiled with relief. "Of course—that was it! The Red Sox won."

Suggestions for Study

1. To what extent do some of our modern sports seem to stem from the gladiators?
2. Give an account of a trial about which you know some facts.
3. How are marriage proposals made these days?
4. What are your impressions of Queen Victoria, and how did you come by them?
5. Certain stories of the past are "dated." Cite evidence to show this from any of the stories in the section.
6. Discuss your ideas about adoption.
7. Do you know of any instance in which hospitality meant trouble?
8. Describe a fire you have witnessed.
9. Write about any unusual vehicle.
10. Cardinal Newman thought that the function of education should be to train the mind rather than fill it with facts. Applying this criterion to the courses you are now taking, show how each one does or does not measure up to Newman's standard.

Composition Topics

1. I Was in Bad!
2. Good Hunting as I Know (Don't Know) It
3. A Few Opinions of Our Local Newspaper
4. My Favorite Historical Monument
5. A Beauty Pageant (Parade) I Remember

FROM FANTASY TO FACT

Fantasy means literally the look or the appearance of a thing, a making visible. The Greek phantasia, from which it derives, denotes a recognition that one's imagination influences what he perceives. Thus, reality also becomes a relative term, caught up with subjective illusions and perceptions that are nonetheless genuine.

To a few people fantasy may simply bring to mind the ideas of fairies dancing in the moonlight. To others it connotes a legend that extends so deeply into the past that its truth cannot be accurately traced, or a modern legend that captures men's fancies so that they tell and retell it, even after its truth has been refuted. Sometimes fantasy is a fable or a parable used as a device to teach more effectivly. Always, though, it is creative imagination, and its use in varying degrees provides most of our pleasure in listening, watching, and reading. Through the huge range of fantasy we come to opera, ballet, puppets, and all types of literature, including science fiction.

We may also produce fantasies within ourselves. Daydreams, if controlled, are inexpensive entertainment. If uncontrolled, they may prevent adjustment to reality. Man through his imagination can create a world of escape—a transient world, however, from which he must return, ideally refreshed or enlightened, to a life of experiences the "facts," that are eternally real because he shares them with all other men: birth and death, toil and ease, the smallness and greatness of being human.

The imaginative element is constantly used to lend interest and meaning to the presentation of fact. In this way it can be considered an element of style, as is a writer's ability to bring in figures of speech, skillful comparisons, well-turned *phrases, to lend interest to otherwise prosaic subjects. A clever piece of newspaper reporting presents facts with various devices of stylistic fantasy. As subject matter goes toward the purely academic, fantasy gives way to objective thought. The scientist and the inventor, no less than the artist, trace their accomplishments back to dreams that took great minds into realms unexplored until ideas and ideals became reality. Skill in communication, also, may well depend upon the effectiveness with which we are able to combine fantasy and fact.*

PSYCHE

The face which is considered the loveliest in antique sculpture is that of Psyche at Naples.

The touching story of Psyche and Cupid is an allegory taken from the "Golden Ass" of Apuleius.

It forms the subject of a celebrated wall-painting by Raphael, in the Farnese Palace in Rome.

Psyche, so the story runs, was the daughter of a king, and very beautiful. The fame of her beauty awoke the jealousy of Venus, who charged her son, Cupid, to inspire Psyche with love for some mortal.

Cupid obeyed, so far as to visit Psyche; but being himself struck with her beauty, he carried her off to a fairy palace, where they spent many happy hours together, with only this drawback, that she was never to look with her mortal eyes upon her lover. Her curiosity, however, led her to look upon him as he lay asleep, when a drop of oil from her lamp awoke him, and he immediately took flight.

She wandered about from place to place seeking him, subject to severe persecution at the hands of Venus, and enduring great suffering.

Cupid at last came to her rescue, the anger of Venus was appeased, and the marriage of Cupid and Psyche was celebrated with great rejoicing in the presence of the higher gods.

This allegory is thought by some to indicate that castles in the air are exquisite until we look at them as realities, when they instantly vanish, and leave only disappointment and vexation behind. By others it is thought to illustrate the three stages in the existence of a soul—its pre-existence in a blessed state, its existence on earth with its trials and anguish, and its future state of happy immortality.

THE TWO TURKEYS

An Honest Farmer once led his two Turkeys into his Granary and told them to eat, drink, and be merry. One of these Turkeys was wise and one foolish. The foolish Bird at once indulged excessively in the

Pleasures of the Stable, unsuspicious of the Future, but the wiser Fowl, in order that he might not be fattened and slaughtered, fasted continually, mortified his Flesh, and devoted himself to gloomy Reflections upon the brevity of Life. When Thanksgiving approached, the Honest Farmer killed both Turkeys, and by placing a Rock in the interior of the Prudent Turkey made him weigh more than his plumper Brother.

Moral—As we Travel through Life, let us Live by the Way.

THE WORRIED CLAM

A Clam, while passing through a Carpenter's Shop, encountered a hungry Heron, and (for the Wind was southerly) knowing him from the surrounding Handsaws, modestly withdrew into his Shell. The Heron commented unfavorably upon his conduct for some time and proposed a Mutual Council, but all was of no avail. Finally a Thought struck him, and he denounced the Clam before Heaven as a perjurer and a Horse-Thief. The indignant Clam thereupon imprudently abandoned his Policy of Silence, but alas! he had hardly opened his Mouth when the Heron swallowed him.

Moral—Second Thoughts are not Always Best.

THE PRIEST AND THE MULBERRIES

A certain priest having need to go to market, caused his mare to be saddled and brought to his door. The mare had carried her master for two years, and was high and well nourished, for during these years never had she known thirst nor hunger, but of hay and of oats ever had

she enough and to spare. The priest climbed to the saddle and set out
upon his journey; and well I remember that it was the month of September, for in that season mulberries grow upon the bushes in great plenty
and abundance. The priest rode upon his way, repeating his hours, his
matins and his vigils. As he drew near the gate of the town the path ran
through a certain deep hollow, and raising his eyes from his book the
priest marked a bush thick with mulberries, bigger, blacker, and more ripe
than any he had ever seen. Desire entered his heart, for very covetous
was he of this fair fruit, and gradually checking the pace of his mare, he
presently caused her to stand beside the bush. Yet one thing still was
wanting to his delight. The mulberries near the ground were set about
with spines and thorns, whilst the sweetest of all hung so high upon the
tree that in no wise could he reach them from his seat. This thing the
priest saw, so in a while he climbed up, and stood with his two feet upon
the saddle, whence by leaning over a little he could pluck the fruit. Then
he chose the fairest, the ripest, and the sweetest of all these mulberries,
eating them as swiftly and greedily as he might, whilst the mare beneath
him moved never a whit. Now, when this priest had eaten as many mulberries as he was able, he glanced downwards, and saw that the mare
was standing still and coy, with her head turned toward the bank of that
deep road. Thereat the priest rejoiced very greatly, for his two feet were
yet upon the saddle, and the mare was very tall.

"God!" said he, "if any one should cry 'Gee up!'" He thought and spoke
the words at the same moment, whereat the mare was suddenly frighted,
and springing forward on the instant tumbled the luckless priest into the
bush where the thorns and briars grew sharpest and thickest. There he
lay in that uneasy bed, nor might move from one side to the other, backwards or forwards, for all the money in the mint.

The mare galloped straight to her own stable, but when the priest's
household saw her return in this fashion they were greatly discomforted.
The servants cursed her for an evil and a luckless jade, whilst the cook
maid swooned like any dame, for well she believed that her master was
dead. When they were returned a little to themselves, they ran to and
fro, here and there, about the country searching for the priest, and presently on their way to the market town they drew near to that bush where
their master yet lay in much misease. On hearing their words bewailing
his piteous case, the priest raised a lamentable voice, and cried—

"Diva, Diva, do not pass me by. This bush is an uneasy bed, and here
I lie very hurt and troubled and utterly cast down. Do you not see how
my blood is staining these thorns and briars a vermeil red?"

The servants hurried to the bush, and stared upon the priest.

"Sir," said they, "who has flung you herein?"

"Alas," answered he, " 'tis sin that has undone me. This morning when I rode this way reading in my Book of Hours, I desired greatly to eat of the mulberries growing hereon, and so I fell into the sin of gluttony. Therefore this bush gat hold upon me. But help me forth from this place, for I wish now for no other thing but to have a surgeon for my hurts, and to rest in my own house."

Now by this little story we may learn that the prudent man does not cry aloud all he may think in his heart, since by so doing many a one has suffered loss and shame, as we may see by this fable of the Priest and the Mulberries.

THE ACTRESS AND THE SAILOR

"When I was a poor girl," said the British Duchess of St. Alban's, "working very hard for my thirty shillings a week, I went down to Liverpool during the holidays, where I was always kindly received. I was to perform in a drama and in my character I represented a poor, friendless, orphan girl, reduced to the most wretched poverty. A heartless tradesman prosecutes the sad heroine for a heavy debt, and insists on putting her in prison, unless some one will be bail for her. The girl replies, 'Then I have no hope, I have not a friend in the world.' 'What! will no one be bail for you to save you from prison?' asks the stern creditor. 'I have told you I've not a friend on earth,' was my reply. But just as I was uttering the words, I saw a sailor in the upper gallery springing over the railing, letting himself from one tier to another until he bounded clear over the orchestra and foot-lights, and placed himself beside me in a moment. 'Yes, you shall have one friend, at least, my poor young woman,' said he, with the greatest expression in his honest sunburnt countenance; 'I will go bail for you any moment. And as for you, (turning to the actor), if you don't bear a hand and shift your moorings, you lubber, it will be worse for you when I come athwart your bows.' Every creature in the house rose; the uproar was perfectly indescribable; and amidst the universal din stood the unconscious cause of it, sheltering 'the poor young woman,' and breathing defiance against my mimic persecutor. He was only persuaded to relinquish his care of me by the manager's pretending to arrive to rescue me, with a profusion of bank notes."

ANTIGONE

A large proportion both of the interesting persons and of the exalted acts of legendary Greece belongs to the female sex. Antigone was as bright an example of filial and sisterly fidelity as was Alcestis of connubial devotion. She was the daughter of Oedipus and Jocasta, who, with all their descendants, were the victims of an unrelenting fate, dooming them to destruction. Oedipus, in his madness, had torn out his eyes, and was driven forth from his kingdom Thebes, dreaded and abandoned by all men, as an object of divine vengeance. Antigone, his daughter, alone shared his wanderings and remained with him till he died, and then returned to Thebes.

Her brothers, Eteocles and Polynices, had agreed to share the kingdom between them, and reign alternately year by year. The first year fell to the lot of Eteocles, who, when his time expired, refused to surrender the kingdom to his brother. Polynices fled to Adrastus, king of Argos, who gave him his daughter in marriage, and aided him with an army to enforce his claim to the kingdom. This led to the celebrated expedition of the "Seven against Thebes," which furnished ample materials for the epic and tragic poets of Greece.

Amphiaraus, the brother-in-law of Adrastus, opposed the enterprise, for he was a soothsayer, and knew by his art that no one of the leaders except Adrastus would live to return. But Amphiaraus, on his marriage to Eriphyle, the king's sister, had agreed that whenever he and Adrastus should differ in opinion, the decision should be left to Eriphyle. Polynices, knowing this, gave Eriphyle the collar of Harmonia, and thereby gained her to his interest. This collar or necklace was a present which Vulcan had given to Harmonia on her marriage with Cadmus, and Polynices had taken it with him on his flight from Thebes. Eriphyle could not resist so tempting a bribe, and by her decision the war was resolved on, and Amphiaraus went to his certain fate.

He bore his part bravely in the contest, but could not avert his destiny. Pursued by the enemy he fled along the river, when a thunderbolt launched by Jupiter opened the ground, and he, his chariot and his charioteer were swallowed up.

It would not be in place here to detail all the acts of heroism or atrocity which marked the contest; but we must not omit to record the fidelity of Evadne as an offset to the weakness of Eriphyle. Capaneus, the husband of Evadne, in the ardor of the fight declared that he would force his way into the city in spite of Jove himself. Placing a ladder against the wall, he mounted; but Jupiter, offended at his impious language, struck him with a thunderbolt. When his obsequies were celebrated, Evadne cast herself on his funeral pile and perished.

Early in the contest Eteocles consulted the soothsayer Tiresias as to the cause. Tiresias in his youth had by chance seen Minerva bathing. The goddess in her wrath deprived him of his sight, but afterwards relenting, gave him, in compensation, the knowledge of future events. When consulted by Eteocles, he declared that victory should fall to Thebes if Menoeceus, the son of Creon, gave himself a voluntary victim. The heroic youth, learning the response, threw away his life in the first encounter.

The siege continued long, with varying success. At length both hosts agreed that the brothers should decide their quarrel by single combat. They fought and fell by each other's hands.

The armies then renewed the fight, and at last the invaders were forced to yield, and fled, leaving their dead unburied. Creon, the uncle of the fallen princes, now become king, caused Eteocles to be buried with distinguished honor, but suffered the body of Polynices to lie where it fell, forbidding everyone on pain of death to give it burial.

Antigone, the sister of Polynices, heard with indignation the revolting edict which consigned her brother's body to the dogs and vultures, depriving it of those rights which were considered essential to the repose of the dead. Unmoved by the dissuading counsel of an affectionate but timid sister, and unable to procure assistance, she determined to brave the hazard and to bury the body with her own hands. She was detected in the act, and Creon gave orders that she should be buried alive, as having deliberately set at nought the solemn edict of the city.

HAFIZ THE STONECUTTER

Effie Power

In Japan, there once lived a stonecutter who went each day to the mountainside to cut great blocks of stone for use in building strong bridges. He worked long and hard but he sang at his task because he was contented with his lot in life.

One day he was sent to the home of a very rich man where he became envious. "Oh, that I might sleep on a bed of down, with curtains of silk and tassels of gold," he sighed. When he returned to his hut that night it had disappeared and in its place stood a palace with beds such as he had coveted.

After this the stonecutter could work no more but sat at his ease and watched the passers-by. But he soon became tired of doing nothing.

"Would that I might ride in state," he sighed when he saw a handsome Prince in a carriage drawn by four white horses. Straitway he heard a voice which said, "Thy wish is granted," and looking down he saw that he was clothed in crimson and gold. There was also a carriage drawn by white horses standing near.

When summer came, the Prince was too warm in his satin clothes; besides he noticed that in spite of anything he could do, his flowers drooped in his favorite garden. "The sun is mightier than I," he sighed. "Be thou the sun," answered the voice and he found himself high in the heavens casting his warm rays as he willed.

All was well until a tiny cloud got in his path. It grew larger and larger until it shut the sun's rays from off the earth. And as he watched, it moved nearer and nearer the earth until finally it broke into drops of rain that deluged the world beneath and swept everything away, except the mighty rock by the mountainside.

Would I were that rock, sighed the sun, and immediately he was the rock he envied.

But this mighty rock was one day disturbed by a faint tap-tap, and looking down it saw a workman cutting great blocks from its side. "Can it be that a poor workman is mightier than I?" asked the rock. This time there was no answer from the voice. The rock pondered the question, then sighed for his follies and found himself back by the mountainside, a stonecutter, again happy, and wise as well.

PYGMALION

Pygmalion was a bachelor god. He saw so much to blame in women that he came at last to abhor the sex, and resolved to live unmarried. He was a sculptor, and had made with wonderful skill a statue of ivory, so beautiful that no living woman came anywhere near it. It was indeed the perfect semblance of a maiden that seemed to be alive, and only prevented from moving by modesty. His art was so perfect that it concealed itself, and its product looked like the workmanship of nature. Pygmalion admired his own work, and at last fell in love with the counterfeit creation. Oftentimes he laid his hand upon it as if to assure himself

whether it were living or not, and could not even then believe that it was
only ivory. He caressed it, and gave it presents such as young girls love—
bright shells and polished stones, little birds and flowers of various hues,
beads and amber. He put raiment on its limbs, and jewels on its fingers,
and a necklace about its neck. To the ears he hung ear-rings, and strings
of pearls upon the breast. Her dress became her, and she looked not less
charming than when unattired. He laid her on a couch spread with cloths
of Tyrian dye, and called her his wife, and put her head upon a pillow
of the softest feathers.

The festival of Venus was at hand—a festival celebrated with great
pomp at Cyprus. Victims were offered, the altars smoked, and the odor
of incense filled the air. When Pygmalion had performed his part in the
solemnities, he stood before the altar and timidly said, "Ye gods, who can
do all things, give me, I pray you, for my wife"—he dared not say "my
ivory virgin," but said instead—"one like my ivory virgin." Venus, who was
present at the festival, heard him and knew the thought he would have
uttered; and as an omen of her favor, caused the flame on the altar to
shoot up thrice in a fiery point into the air. When he returned home he
went to see his statue, and leaning over the couch, gave a kiss to the mouth.
It seemed to be warm. He pressed its lips again, he laid his hand upon
the limbs; the ivory felt soft to his touch, and yielded to his fingers like
the wax of Hymettus. While he stands astonished and glad, though doubting, and fears he may be mistaken, again and again with a lover's ardor,
he touches the object of his hopes.

It was indeed alive! The veins when pressed yielded to the finger and
again resumed their roundness. Then at last the votary of Venus found
words to thank the goddess, and pressed his lips upon lips as real as his
own. The virgin felt the kisses and blushed, and opening her timid eyes
to the light, fixed them at the same moment on her lover. Venus blessed
the nuptials she had formed, and from this union Paphos was born, from
whom the city, sacred to Venus, received its name.

THE VANISHING LADY

Alexander Woollcott

Then there was the story—told me some years ago as a true
copy of a leaf from the dread secret archives of the Paris police—of the

woman who disappeared during the World Exposition as suddenly, as completely, and as inexplicably as did Dorothy Arnold ten years later from the sidewalks of New York.

As I first heard the story, it began with the arrival from Marseilles of an Englishwoman and her young, inexperienced daughter, a girl of seventeen or thereabouts. The mother was the frail, pretty widow of an English officer who had been stationed in India, and the two had just come from Bombay, bound for home. In the knowledge that, after reaching there, she would soon have to cross to Paris to sign some papers affecting her husband's estate, she decided at the last minute to shift her passage to a Marseilles steamer, and, by going direct to Paris, look up the lawyers there and finish her business before crossing the Channel to settle forever and a day in the Warwickshire village where she was born.

Paris was so tumultuously crowded for the Exposition that they counted themselves fortunate when the *cocher* deposited them at the Crillon, and they learned that their precautionary telegram from Marseilles had miraculously caught a room on the wing—a double room with a fine, spacious sitting-room looking out on the Place de la Concorde. I could wish that they had wired one of those less magnificent caravansaries, if only that I might revel again in such a name as the Hotel of Jacob and of England, or, better still, the Hotel of the Universe and of Portugal. But, as the story reached me, it was to the Crillon that they went.

The long windows of their sitting-room gave on a narrow, stone-railed balcony and were half-shrouded in heavy curtains of plum-colored velvet. As again and again the girl later on had occasion to describe the look of that room when first she saw it, the walls were papered in old rose. A high-backed sofa, an oval satinwood table, a mantel with an ormolu clock that had run down—these also she recalled.

The girl was the more relieved that there would be no need of a house-to-house search for rooms, for the mother had seemed unendurably exhausted from the long train ride, and was now of such a color that the girl's first idea was to call the house physician, hoping fervently that he spoke English, for neither she nor her mother spoke any French at all.

The doctor, when he came—a dusty, smelly little man with a wrinkled face lost in a thicket of whiskers, and a reassuring Legion of Honor ribbon in the button-hole of his lapel—did speak a little English. After a long, grave look and a few questions put to the tired woman on the bed in the shaded room, he called the girl into the sitting-room and told her frankly that her mother's condition was serious; that it was out of the question for them to think of going on to England next day; that on the morrow she might better be moved to a hospital, etc., etc.

All these things he would attend to. In the meantime he wanted the girl to go at once to his home and fetch him a medicine that his wife would give her. It could not be as quickly prepared in any chemist's. Unfortunately, he lived on the other side of Paris and had no telephone, and with all Paris *en fête* it would be perilous to rely on any messenger. Indeed, it would be a saving of time and worry if she could go, armed with a note to his wife he was even then scribbling in French at a desk in the sitting-room. In the lobby below, the manager of the hotel, after an excited colloquy with the doctor, took charge of her most sympathetically, himself putting her into a *sapin* and, as far as she could judge, volubly directing the driver how to reach a certain house in the Rue Val du Grâce, near the Observatoire.

It was then that the girl's agony began, for the ramshackle victoria crawled through the festive streets and, as she afterwards realized, more often than not crawled in the wrong direction. The house in the Rue Val du Grâce seemed to stand at the other end of the world, when the carriage came at last to a halt in front of it. The girl grew old in the time which passed before any answer came to her ring at the bell. The doctor's wife, when finally she appeared, read his note again and again, then with much muttering and rattling of keys stationed the girl in an airless waiting room and left her there so long that she was weeping for very desperation, before the medicine was found, wrapped, and turned over to her.

A hundred times during that wait she rose and started for the door, determined to stay no longer but to run back empty-handed through the streets to her mother's bedside. A thousand times in the wretched weeks that followed she loathed herself for not having obeyed that impulse. But always there was the feeling that having come so far and having waited so long, she must not leave without the medicine just for the lack of the strength of will to stick it out a little longer—perhaps only a few minutes longer.

Then the snail's pace trip back to the Right Bank was another nightmare, and it ended only when, at the *cocher's* mulish determination to deliver her to some hotel in the Place Vendôme, she leaped to the street and in sheer terror appealed for help to a passing young man whose alien tweeds and boots told her he was a compatriot of hers.

He was still standing guard beside her five minutes later when, at long last, she arrived at the desk of the Crillon and called for her key, only to have the very clerk who had handed her a pen to register with that morning look at her without recognition and blandly ask, "Whom does Mademoiselle wish to see?" At that a cold fear clutched her heart, a sudden surrender to a panic that she had fought back as preposterous when first it visited her as she sat and twisted her handkerchief in the waiting room of the doctor's office on the Left Bank; a panic born when, after the doctor had casually told her he had no telephone, she heard the fretful ringing of its bell on the other side of his walnut door.

This then was the predicament of the young English girl as she stood there at the desk of the hotel in Paris—a stranger in the city and a stranger to its bewildering tongue. She had arrived that morning from India and had left her ailing mother in charge of the house physician while she went out in quest of medicine for her—a quest in which, through a malignant conspiracy between perverse circumstances and apparently motiveless passersby, she had lost four hours.

But now with the bottle of medicine clutched in her hand, she reached the hotel at last, only to be stared down by the clerk at the desk, only to have the very man who had shown them their rooms with such a flourish that morning now gaze at her opaquely as though she were some slightly demented creature demanding admission to someone else's apartment.

But, no, Mam'zelle must be mistaken. Was it not at some other hotel she was descended? Two more clerks came fluttering into the conference. They all eyed her without a flicker of recognition. Did Mam'zelle say her room was No. 342? Ah, but 342 was occupied by M. Quelquechose. Yes, a French client of long standing. He had been occupying it these past two weeks and more. Ah, no, it would be impossible to disturb him. All this while the lobby, full of hurrying, polyglot strangers, reeled around her.

She demanded the registration slips only to find in that day's docket no sign of the one she herself had filled out that morning on their arrival, while her tired mother leaned against the desk and told her how. And even as the clerk now shuffled the papers before her eyes, the stupefying bloodstone which she had noticed on his ring-finger when he handed her the pen five hours before, winked at her in confirmation.

From then on she came only upon closed doors. The same house physician who had hustled her off on her tragic wild-goose chase across Paris protested now with all the shrugs and gestures of his people that he had dispatched her on no such errand, that he had never been summoned to attend her mother, that he had never seen her before in all his life. The same hotel manager who had so sympathetically helped her into the carriage when she set forth on her fruitless mission, denied her now as flatly and somehow managed to do it with the same sympathetic solicitude, suggesting that Mam'zelle must be tired, that she should let them provide another chamber where she might repose herself until such time as she could recollect at what hotel she really belonged or until some inquiries should bring in news of where her mother and her luggage were, if —

For always there was in his ever polite voice the unspoken reservation that the whole mystery might be a thing of her own disordered invention.

Then, and in the destroying days that followed, she was only too keenly aware that these evasive people—the personnel of the hotel, the attachés of the embassy, the reporters of the Paris *Herald,* the officials at the Sûreté —were each and every one behaving as if she had lost her wits. Indeed there were times when she felt that all Paris was rolling its eyes behind her back and significantly tapping its forehead.

Her only aid and comfort was the aforesaid Englishman who, because a lovely lady in distress had come up to him in the street and implored his help, elected thereafter to believe her against all the evidence which so impressed the rest of Paris. He proved a pillar of stubborn strength because he was some sort of wellborn junior secretary at the British Embassy with influence enough to keep her agony from gathering dust in the official pigeon-holes.

His faith in her needed to be unreasoning because there slowly formed in his mind a suspicion that for some unimaginable reason all these people —the hotel attendants and even the police—were part of a plot to conceal the means whereby the missing woman's disappearance had been effected. This suspicion deepened when, after a day's delay, he succeeded in forcing an inspection of Room 342 and found that there was no detail of its furnishing which had not been altered from the one etched into the girl's memory.

It remained for him to prove the mechanism of that plot and to guess at its invisible motive—a motive strong enough to enlist all Paris in the silent obliteration of a woman of no importance, moreover a woman who, as far as her daughter knew, had not an enemy in the world. It was the purchased confession of one of the paper-hangers, who had worked all night in the hurried transformation of Room 342, that started the unraveling of the mystery.

By the time the story reached me, it had lost all its content of grief and become as unemotional as an anagram. Indeed, a few years ago it was a kind of circulating parlor game and one was challenged to guess what had happened to the vanished lady. Perhaps you yourself have already surmised that the doctor had recognized the woman's ailment as a case of the black plague smuggled in from India; that his first instinctive step, designed only to give time for spiriting her out of the threatened hotel, had, when she died that afternoon, widened into a conspiracy on the part of the police to suppress, at all costs to this one girl, an obituary notice which, had it ever leaked out, would have emptied Paris overnight and spread ruin across a city that had gambled heavily on the great Exposition for which its gates were even then thrown wide.

The story of this girl's ordeal long seemed to me one of the great nightmares of real life and I was, therefore, the more taken aback one day to have its historicity faintly impaired by my discovering its essence in a novel called *The End of Her Honeymoon* which the incomparable Mrs. Belloc-Lowndes wrote as long ago as 1913. Then I find myself wondering if she unearthed it in the archives of the Paris police or whether she spun its mystery out of her own macabre fancy, making from whole cloth a tale of such felicitous invention that, like Stockton's *The Lady or the Tiger* or Anatole France's *The Procurator of Judea,* it had moved from land to land with the seven-league-boots of folk-music and so been told and retold at hearths the world around by people who had never read it anywhere.

THE OTHER SIDE OF IT

O. Henry

There is an item going the rounds of the press relative to the well-known curiosity of woman. It states that if a man brings a newspaper home out of which a piece has been clipped his wife will never rest until she has procured another paper to see what it was that had been cut out.

A Houston man was quite impressed with the idea, so he resolved to make the experiment. One night last week he cut out of the day's paper a little two-inch catarrh cure advertisement, and left the mutilated paper on the table where his wife would be sure to read it.

He picked up a book and pretended to be interested, while he watched her glance over the paper. When she struck the place where the piece had been cut, she frowned and seemed to be thinking very seriously.

However, she did not say anything about it and the man was in doubt as to whether her curiosity had been aroused or not.

The next day when he came home to dinner she met him at the door with flashing eyes and an ominous look about her jaw.

"You miserable, deceitful wretch!" she cried. "After living all these years with you to find that you have been basely deceiving me and leading a double life, and bringing shame and sorrow upon your innocent family! I always thought you were a villain and a reprobate, and now I have positive proof of the fact."

"W—wha—what do you mean, Maria?" he gasped. "I haven't been doing anything."

"Of course you are ready to add lying to your catalogue of vices. Since you pretend not to understand me—look at this."

She held up to his gaze a complete paper of the issue of the day before.

"You thought to hide your actions from me by cutting out part of the paper, but I was too sharp for you."

"Why that was just a little joke, Maria. I didn't think you would take it seriously. I—"

"Do you call that a joke, you shameless wretch?" she cried, spreading the paper before him.

The man looked and read in dismay. In cutting out the catarrh advertisement he had never thought to see what was on the other side of it, and this was the item that appeared, to one reading the other side of the page, to have been clipped:

> A gentleman about town, who stands well in business circles, had a high old time last night in a certain restaurant where he entertained at supper a couple of chorus ladies belonging to the comic opera company now in the city. Loud talking and breaking of dishes attracted some attention, but the matter was smoothed over, owing to the prominence of the gentleman referred to.

"You call that a joke, do you, you old reptile," shrieked the excited lady. "I'm going home to mama this evening and to stay there. Thought you'd fool me by cutting it out, did you? You sneaking, dissipated old snake you! I've got my trunk nicely packed and I'm going straight home—don't you come near me!"

"Maria," gasped the bewildered man. "I swear I —"

"Don't add perjury to your crimes, sir!"

The man tried unsuccessfully to speak three of four times, and then grabbed his hat and ran down town. Fifteen minutes later he came back bringing two new silk dress patterns, four pounds of caramels, and his bookkeeper and three clerks to prove that he was at work in the store on the night in question.

The affair was finally settled satisfactorily, but there is one Houston man who has no further curiosity about woman's curiosity.

GARRICK AND PREVILLE

When Garrick was in France, he made a short excursion from the capital with the celebrated Parisian performer Preville. They were on horseback, and Preville took a fancy to act the part of a drunken cavalier. Garrick applauded the imitation, but told him he wanted one thing which was essential to complete the picture; he did not make his legs drunk. "Hold, my friend," said he, "and I shall show you an English blood, who, after having dined at a tavern, and swallowed three or four bottles of Port, mounts his horse in a summer evening to go to his box in the country." He immediately proceeded to exhibit all the gradations of intoxication. He called to his servant that the sun and the fields were turning round him; whipped and spurred his horse until the animal reared and wheeled in every direction. At length he lost his whip, his feet seemed incapable of resting in the stirrups, the bridle dropped from his hand, and he appeared to have lost the use of all his faculties. Finally, he fell from his horse in such a death-like manner, that Preville gave an involuntary cry of horror; and his terror greatly inceased when he found that his friend made no answer to his questions. After wiping the dust from his face, he asked again, with the emotion and anxiety of friendship, whether he was hurt. Garrick, whose eyes were closed, half opened one of them, hic-coughed, and with the most natural tone of intoxication, called for another glass. Preville was astonished; and when Garrick started up and resumed his usual demeanor, the French actor exclaimed, "My friend, allow the scholar to embrace his master, and thank him for the valuable lesson he has given him!"

OLD PROVERBS MADE NEW

Stephen Leacock

It has occurred to me that somebody in one of the English departments of our colleges ought to get busy and re-write our national proverbs. They are all out of date. They don't fit any longer. Indeed, many of them are precisely the converse of existing facts.

Our proverbs have come down to us from the days of long ago; days when the world was very primitive and very simple and very different; when people never moved more than a mile and a half from home and were all afraid of the dark; and when wisdom was handed out by old men with white whiskers called *prophets*, every one of whom would be "retired" nowadays by any first class board of trustees as past the age-limit of common sense.

But in those days all the things that were said by these wise old men, who had never seen a motor car, were gathered up and called proverbs and repeated by all the common people as the last words of wisdom. The result is that even today we still go on repeating them, without realizing how hopelessly they are off the track.

Take as a first sample the proverb that is perhaps the best known in our language: *Birds of a feather flock together*. But they don't. Ask any first-class naturalist. If the wise old men had taken another look they would have seen that the last thing birds ever want to do is to flock together. In ninety-nine cases out of a hundred they keep away from their own species, and only flock when it is absolutely necessary. So much for the birds. But the proverb is really supposed to refer to people and then it is wrong again. People "of a feather" do not flock together. Tall men fall in love with little women. A girl with a beautiful fair skin and red hair marries a man who looks like a reformed orang-outang. A clergyman makes a friend of an auctioneer and a banker would rather spend a day with an Adirondack fishing guide than with a whole vaultful of bankers. Burglars during the daytime go and swim in the Y.M.C.A. pool. Forgers in their off time sing in the choir, and choirmasters when they are not singing shoot craps.

In short, there is nothing in the proverb whatsoever. It ought to be revised under the modern conditions to read: *Birds of any particular feather and a persons of any particular character or occupation show upon the whole a disposition rather to seek out something dissimilar to their own appearance and nature than to consort with something homologous to their own essential entity.*

In that shape one has a neat workable proverb.

EPIGRAMS

Jonathan Swift

We have just religion enough to make us hate, but not enough to make us love one another.

No preacher is listened to but Time, which gives us the same train and turn of thought that elder people have in vain tried to put into our heads before.

When we desire or solicit any thing, our minds run wholly on the good side or circumstances of it; when it is obtained, our minds run wholly on the bad ones.

Whatever the poets pretend, it is plain they give immortality to none but themselves; 'tis Homer and Virgil we reverence and admire, not Achilles or Aeneas. With historians it is quite the contrary; our thoughts are taken up with the actions, persons, and events we read, and we little regard the authors.

Men who possess all the advantages of life are in a state where there are many accidents to disorder and discompose, but few to please them.

I am apt to think that in the day of judgment there will be small allowance given to the wise for their want of morals, and to the ignorant for their want to faith, because both are without excuse. This renders the advantages equal of ignorance and knowledge. But some scruples in the wise, and some vices in the ignorant will perhaps be forgiven, upon the strength of temptation to each.

There are but three ways for a man to revenge himself of the censure of the world: to despise it, to return the like, or to endeavor to live so as to avoid it. The first of these is usually pretended, the last is almost impossible, the universal practice is for the second.

The stoical scheme of supplying our wants by lopping off our desires is like cutting off our feet when we want shoes.

The power of fortune is confessed only by the miserable; for the happy impute all their success to prudence or merit.

Satire is reckoned the easiest of all wit; but I take it to be otherwise in very bad times: for it is as hard to satirize well a man of distinguished vices as to praise well a man of distinguished virtues. It is easy enough to do either to people of moderate characters.

No wise man ever wished to be younger.

Some people take more care to hide their wisdom than their folly.

To be vain is rather a mark of humility than pride. Vain men delight in telling what honors have been done them, what great company they have kept, and the like, by which they plainly confess that these honors were more than their due, and such as their friends would not believe if they had not been told; whereas a man truly proud thinks the greatest honors below his merit and consequently scorns to boast. I therefore deliver it as a maxim, that whoever desires the character of a proud man ought to conceal his vanity.

Most sorts of diversion in men, children, and other animals, are an imitation of fighting.

As universal a practice as lying is, and as easy a one as it seems, I do not remember to have heard three good lies in all my conversation, even from those who were most celebrated in that faculty.

Imaginary evils soon become real ones by indulging our reflections on them; as he who in a melancholy fancy sees something like a face on the wall or the wainscot, can, by two or three touches with a lead pencil, make it look visible, and agreeing with what he fancied.

Men of great parts are often unfortunate in the management of public business, because they are apt to go out of the common road by the quickness of their imagination. This I once said to my Lord Bolingbroke, and desired he would observe that the clerks in his office used a sort of ivory knife with a blunt edge to divide a sheet of paper, which never failed to cut it even, only requiring a steady hand: whereas if they should make use of a sharp pen-knife the sharpness would make it go often out of the crease and disfigure the paper.

I must complain the cards are ill shuffled, till I have a good hand.

Elephants are always drawn smaller than life, but a flea always larger.

DR. HEIDEGGER'S EXPERIMENT

Nathaniel Hawthorne

That very singular man, old Dr. Heidegger, once invited four venerable friends to meet him in his study. There were three white-bearded gentlemen, Mr. Medbourne, Colonel Killigrew, and Mr. Gascoigne, and a withered gentlewoman, whose name was the Widow Wycherly. They were all melancholy old creatures, who had been unfortunate in life, and whose greatest misfortune it was that they were not long ago in their graves. Mr. Medbourne, in the vigor of his age, had been a prosperous merchant, and had lost his all by a frantic speculation, and was now little better than a mendicant. Colonel Killigrew had wasted his best years, and his health and substance, in the pursuit of sinful pleasures, which had given birth to a brood of pains, such as the gout, and diverse other torments of soul and body. Mr. Gascoigne was a ruined politician, a man of evil fame, or at least had been so, till time had buried him from the knowledge of the present generation, and made him obscure instead of infamous. As for the Widow Wycherly, tradition tells us that she was a great beauty in her day; but, for a long while past, she had lived in deep seclusion, on account of certain scandalous stories, which had prejudiced the gentry of the town against her. It is a circumstance worth mentioning that each of these three old gentlemen, Mr. Medbourne, Colonel Killigrew, and Mr. Gascoigne, where early lovers of the Widow Wycherly, and had once been on the point of cutting each other's throats for her sake. And, before proceeding farther, I will merely hint that Dr. Heidegger and all his four guests were sometimes thought to be a little beside themselves; as is not unfrequently the case with old people, when worried either by present troubles or woeful recollections.

"My dear old friends," said Dr. Heidegger, motioning them to be seated, "I am desirous of your assistance in one of those little experiments with which I amuse myself here in my study."

If all stories were true, Dr. Heidegger's study must have been a very curious place. It was a dim, old-fashioned chamber, festooned with cobwebs and besprinkled with antique dust. Around the walls stood several oaken bookcases, the lower shelves of which were filled with rows of gigantic folios and black-letter quartos, and the upper with little parchment-covered duodecimos. Over the central bookcase was a bronze bust of Hippocrates, with which, according to some authorities, Dr. Heidegger was accustomed to hold consultations, in all difficult cases of his practice. In the obscurest corner of the room stood a tall and narrow oaken closet, with its door ajar, within which doubtfully appeared a skeleton. Between two of the bookcases hung a looking-glass, presenting its high and dusty plate within a tarnished gilt frame. Among many wonderful stories related of this mirror, it was fabled that the spirits of all the doctor's deceased patients dwelt within its verge, and would stare him in the face whenever he looked thitherward. The opposite side of the chamber was ornamented with the full-length portrait of a young lady, arrayed in the faded magnificence of silk, satin, and brocade, and with a visage as faded as her dress. Above half a century ago, Dr. Heidegger had been on the point of marriage with this young lady; but, being affected with some slight disorder, she had swallowed one of her lover's prescriptions, and died on the bridal evening. The greatest curiosity of the study remains to be mentioned; it was a ponderous folio volume, bound in black leather, with massive silver clasps. There were no letters on the back, and nobody could tell the title of the book. But it was well known to be a book of magic; and once, when a chambermaid had lifted it, merely to brush away the dust, the skeleton had rattled in its closet, the picture of the young lady had stepped one foot upon the floor, and several ghastly faces had peeped forth from the mirror, while the brazen head of Hippocrates frowned, and said, "Forbear!"

Such was Dr. Heidegger's study. On the summer afternoon of our tale, a small round table, as black as ebony, stood in the center of the room, sustaining a cut-glass vase of beautiful form and elaborate workmanship. The sunshine came through the window, between the heavy festoons of two faded damask curtains, and fell directly across this vase; so that a mild splendor was reflected from it on the ashen visages of the five old people who sat around. Four champagne glasses were also on the table.

"My dear old friends," repeated Dr. Heidegger, "may I reckon on your aid in performing an exceedingly curious experiment?"

Now Dr. Heidegger was a very strange old gentleman, whose eccentricity had become the nucleus for a thousand fantastic stories. Some of these fables, to my shame be it spoken, might possibly be traced back to mine own veracious self; and if any passages of the present tale should startle the reader's faith, I must be content to bear the stigma of a fiction-monger.

When the doctor's four guests heard him talk of his proposed experiment, they anticipated nothing more wonderful than the murder of a mouse in an air-pump, or the examination of a cobweb by the microscope, or some similar nonsense, with which he was constantly in the habit of pestering his intimates. But without waiting for a reply, Dr. Heidegger hobbled across the chamber, and returned with the same ponderous folio, bound in black leather, which common report affirmed to be a book of magic. Undoing the silver clasps, he opened the volume, and took from among its black-letter pages a rose, or what was once a rose, though now the green leaves and crimson petals had assumed one brownish hue, and the ancient flower seemed ready to crumble to dust in the doctor's hands.

"This rose," said Dr. Heidegger, with a sigh, "this same withered and crumbling flower, blossomed five-and-fifty years ago. It was given me by Sylvia Ward, whose portrait hangs yonder; and I meant to wear it in my bosom at our wedding. Five-and-fifty years it has been treasured between the leaves of this old volume. Now, would you deem it possible that this rose of half a century could ever bloom again?"

"Nonsense!" said the Widow Wycherly, with a peevish toss of her head. "You might as well ask whether an old woman's wrinkled face could ever bloom again."

"See!" answered Dr. Heidegger.

He uncovered the vase, and threw the faded rose into the water which it contained. At first, it lay lightly on the surface of the fluid, appearing to imbibe none of its moisture. Soon, however, a singular change began to be visible. The crushed and dried petals stirred, and assumed a deepening tinge of crimson, as if the flower were reviving from a death-like slumber; the slender stalk and twigs of foliage became green; and there was the rose of half a century, looking as fresh as when Sylvia Ward had first given it to her lover. It was scarcely full-blown; for some of its delicate red leaves curled modestly around its moist bosom, within which two or three dew-drops were sparkling.

"That is certainly a very pretty deception," said the doctor's friends; carelessly, however, for they had witnessed greater miracles at a conjuror's show; "pray, how was it effected?"

"Did you never hear of the 'Fountain of Youth,'" asked Dr. Heidegger, "which Ponce de Leon, the Spanish adventurer, went in search of, two or three centuries ago?"

"But did Ponce de Leon ever find it?" said the Widow Wycherly.

"No," answered Dr. Heidegger, "for he never sought it in the right place. The famous Fountain of Youth, if I am rightly informed, is situated in the southern part of the Floridian peninsula, not far from Lake Macaco. Its source is overshadowed by several gigantic magnolias, which, though numberless centuries old, have been kept as fresh as violets, by the virtues of this wonderful water. An acquaintance of mine, knowing my curiosity in such matters, has sent me what you see in the vase."

"Ahem!" said Colonel Killigrew, who believed not a word of the doctor's story; "and what may be the effect of this fluid on the human frame?"

"You shall judge for yourself, my dear Colonel," replied Dr. Heidegger; "and all of you, my respected friends, are welcome to so much of this admirable fluid as may restore to you the bloom of youth. For my own part, having had much trouble in growing old, I am in no hurry to grow young again. With your permission, therefore, I will merely watch the progress of the experiment."

While he spoke, Dr. Heidegger had been filling the four champagne glasses with the water of the Fountain of Youth. It was apparently impregnated with an effervescent gas, for little bubbles were continually ascending from the depths of the glasses, and bursting in silvery spray at the surface. As the liquor diffused a pleasant perfume, the old people doubted not that it possessed cordial and comfortable properties; and, though utter skeptics as to its rejuvenescent power, they were inclined to swallow it at once. But Dr. Heidegger besought them to stay a moment.

"Before you drink, my respectable old friends," said he, "it would be well that, with the experience of a lifetime to direct you, you should draw up a few general rules for your guidance, in passing a second time through the perils of youth. Think what a sin and shame it would be, if, with your peculiar advantages, you should not become patterns of virtue and wisdom to all the young people of the age."

The doctor's four venerable friends made him no answer, except by a feeble and tremulous laugh; so very ridiculous was the idea that, knowing how closely repentance treads behind the steps of error, they should ever go astray again.

"Drink, then," said the doctor, bowing. "I rejoice that I have so well selected the subjects of my experiment."

With palsied hands, they raised the glasses to their lips. The liquor, if it really possessed such virtues as Dr. Heidegger imputed to it, could not have been bestowed on four human beings who needed it more woefully. They looked as if they had never known what youth or pleasure was, but had been the offspring of Nature's dotage, and always the gray, decrepit, sapless, miserable creatures who now sat stooping round the doctor's table, without life enough in their souls or bodies to be animated even by the prospect of growing young again. They drank off the water, and replaced their glasses on the table.

Assuredly there was an almost immediate improvement in the aspect of the party, not unlike what might have been produced by a glass of generous wine, together with a sudden glow of cheerful sunshine, brightening over all their visages at once. There was a healthful suffusion on their cheeks, instead of the ashen hue that had made them look so corpselike. They gazed at one another, and fancied that some magic power had really begun to smooth away the deep and sad inscriptions which Father Time had been so long engraving on their brows. The Widow Wycherly adjusted her cap, for she felt almost like a woman again.

"Give us more of this wondrous water!" cried they, eagerly. "We are younger—but we are still too old! Quick—give us more!"

"Patience, patience!" quoth Dr. Heidegger, who sat watching the experiment, with philosophic coolness. "You have been a long time growing old. Surely, you might be content to grow young in half an hour! But the water is at your service."

Again he filled their glasses with the liquor of youth, enough of which still remained in the vase to turn half the old people in the city to the age of their own grandchildren. While the bubbles were yet sparkling on the brim, the doctor's four guests snatched their glasses from the table, and swallowed the contents at a single gulp. Was it delusion? Even while the draught was passing down their throats, it seemed to have wrought a change on their whole systems. Their eyes grew clear and bright; a dark shade deepened among their silvery locks; they sat around the table, three gentlemen of middle age, and a woman, hardly beyond her buxom prime.

"My dear widow, you are charming!" cried Colonel Killigrew, whose eyes had been fixed upon her face, while the shadows of age were flitting from it like darkness from the crimson daybreak.

The fair widow knew, of old, that Colonel Killigrew's compliments were not always measured by sober truth; so she started up and ran to the mirror, still dreading that the ugly visage of an old woman would meet her gaze. Meanwhile, the three gentlemen behaved in such a manner as proved that the water of the Fountain of Youth possessed some intoxicating qualities; unless, indeed, their exhilaration of spirits were merely a lightsome dizziness, caused by the sudden removal of the weight of years. Mr. Gascoigne's mind seemed to run on political topics, but whether relating to the past, present, or future, could not easily be determined, since the same ideas and phrases have been in vogue these fifty years. Now he rattled forth full-throated sentences about patriotism, national glory, and the people's right; now he muttered some perilous stuff or other, in a sly and doubtful whisper, so cautiously that even his own conscience could scarcely catch the secret; and now, again, he spoke in measured accents, and a deeply deferential tone, as if a royal ear were listening to his well-turned periods. Colonel Killigrew all this time had been trolling forth a jolly bottle-song, and ringing his glass in symphony with the chorus, while his eyes wandered toward the buxom figure of the Widow Wycherly. On the other side of the table, Mr. Medbourne was involved in a calculation of dollars and cents, with which was strangely intermingled a project for supplying the East Indies with ice, by harnessing a team of whales to the polar icebergs.

As for the Widow Wycherly, she stood before the mirror curtsying and simpering to her own image, and greeting it as the friend whom she loved better than all the world beside. She thrust her face close to the glass, to see whether some long-remembered wrinkle or crow's-foot had indeed vanished. She examined whether the snow had so entirely melted from her hair that the venerable cap could be safely thrown aside. At last, turning briskly away, she came with a sort of dancing step to the table.

"My dear old doctor," cried she, "pray favor me with another glass!"

"Certainly, my dear madam, certainly!" replied the complaisant doctor; "see! I have already filled the glasses."

There, in fact, stood the four glasses, brimful of this wonderful water, the delicate spray of which, as it effervesced from the surface, resembled the tremulous glitter of diamonds. It was now so nearly sunset that the chamber had grown duskier than ever; but a mild and moon-like splendor gleamed from within the vase, and rested alike on the four guests, and on the doctor's venerable figure. He sat in a high-backed, elaborately-carved oaken armchair, with a gray dignity of aspect that might have well be-fitted that very Father Time whose power had never been disputed, save by this fortunate company. Even while quaffing the third draught of the Fountain of Youth, they were almost awed by the expression of his mysterious visage.

But, the next moment, the exhilarating gush of young life shot through their veins. They were now in the happy prime of youth. Age, with its miserable train of cares, and sorrows, and diseases, was remembered only as the trouble of a dream, from which they had joyously awoke. The fresh gloss of the soul, so early lost, and without which the world's successive scenes had been but a gallery of faded pictures, again threw its enchant-ment over all their prospects. They felt like new-created beings, in a new-created universe.

"We are young! We are young!" they cried exultingly.

Youth, like the extremity of age, had effaced the strongly marked characteristics of middle life, and mutually assimilated them all. They were a group of merry youngsters, almost maddened with the exuberant frolicsomeness of their years. The most singular effect of their gayety was an impulse to mock the infirmity and decrepitude of which they had so lately been the victims. They laughed loudly at their old-fashioned attire, the wide-skirted coats and flapped waistcoats of the young men, and the ancient cap and gown of the blooming girl. One limped across the floor, like a gouty grandfather; one set a pair of spectacles astride of his nose, and pretended to pore over the black-letter pages of the book of magic; a third seated himself in an armchair, and strove to imitate the venerable dignity of Dr. Heidegger. Then all shouted mirthfully, and leaped about the room. The Widow Wycherly—if so fresh a damsel could be called a widow—tripped up to the doctor's chair, with a mischievous merriment in her rosy face.

"Doctor, you dear old soul," cried she, "get up and dance with me!" And then the four young people laughed louder than ever, to think what a queer figure the poor old doctor would cut.

"Pray excuse me," answered the doctor, quietly. "I am old and rheumatic, and my dancing days were over long ago. But either of these gay young gentlemen will be glad of so pretty a partner."

"Dance with me, Clara!" cried Colonel Killigrew.

"No, no, I will be her partner!" shouted Mr. Gascoigne.

"She promised me her hand fifty years ago!" exclaimed Mr. Medbourne.

They all gathered round her. One caught both her hands in his passionate grasp—another threw his arm about her waist—the third buried his hand among the glossy curls that clustered beneath the widow's cap. Blushing, panting, struggling, chiding, laughing, her warm breath fanning each of their faces by turns, she strove to disengage herself, yet still remained in their triple embrace. Never was there a livelier picture of youthful rivalship, with bewitching beauty for the prize. Yet, by a strange deception, owing to the duskiness of the chamber, and the antique dresses which they still wore, the tall mirror is said to have reflected the figures of the three old, gray, withered grandsires, ridiculously contending for the skinny ugliness of a shriveled grandam.

But they were young; their burning passions proved them so. Inflamed to madness by the coquetry of the girl-widow, who neither granted nor quite withheld her favors, the three rivals began to interchange threatening glances. Still keeping hold of the fair prize, they grappled fiercely at one another's throats. As they struggled to and fro, the table was overturned, and the vase dashed into a thousand fragments. The precious

Water of Youth flowed in a bright stream across the floor, moistening the wings of a butterfly, which, grown old in the decline of summer, had alighted there to die. The insect fluttered lightly through the chamber, and settled on the snowy head of Dr. Heidegger.

"Come, come, gentlemen!—come, Madam Wycherly," exclaimed the doctor, "I really must protest against this riot."

They stood still and shivered; for it seemed as if gray Time were calling them back from their sunny youth, far down into the chill and darksome vale of years. They looked at old Dr. Heidegger, who sat in his carved armchair, holding the rose of half a century, which he had rescued from among the fragments of the shattered vase. At the motion of his hand, the four rioters resumed their seats; the more readily because their violent exertions had wearied them, youthful though they were.

"My poor Sylvia's rose!" ejaculated Dr. Heidegger, holding it in the light of the sunset clouds; "it appears to be fading again."

And so it was. Even while the party were looking at it, the flower continued to shrivel up, till it became as dry and fragile as when the doctor had first thrown it into the vase. He shook off the few drops of moisture which clung to its petals.

"I love it as well thus, as in its dewy freshness," observed he, pressing the withered rose to his withered lips. While he spoke, the butterfly fluttered down from the doctor's snowy head, and fell upon the floor.

His guests shivered again. A strange chillness, whether of the body or spirit they could not tell, was creeping gradually over them all. They gazed at one another, and fancied that each fleeting moment snatched away a charm, and left a deepening furrow where none had been before. Was it an illusion? Had the changes of a lifetime been crowded into so brief a space, and were they now four aged people, sitting with their old friend, Dr. Heidegger?

"Are we grown old again, so soon!" cried they, dolefully.

In truth, they had. The Water of Youth possessed merely a virtue more transient than that of wine. The delirium which it created had effervesced away. Yes! they were old again. With a shuddering impulse, that showed her a woman still, the widow clasped her skinny hands before her face, and wished that the coffin-lid were over it, since it could be no longer beautiful.

"Yes, friends, ye are old again." said Dr. Heidegger; "and lo! the Water of Youth is all lavished on the ground. Well—I bemoan it not; for if the fountain gushed at my very doorstep, I would not stoop to bathe my lips in it—no, though its delirium were for years instead of moments. Such is the lesson ye have taught me!"

But the doctor's four friends had taught no such lesson to themselves.

They resolved forthwith to make a pilgrimage to Florida, and quaff at morning, noon, and night from the Fountain of Youth.

THE CASE AGAINST WOMEN

James Thurber

A bright-eyed woman, whose sparkle was rather more of eagerness than of intelligence, approached me at a party one afternoon and said, "Why do you hate women, Mr. Thurber?" I quickly adjusted my fixed grin and denied that I hated women; I said I did not hate women at all. But the question remained with me, and I discovered when I went to bed that night that I had been subconsciously listing a number of reasons why I do hate women. It might be interesting—at least it will help pass the time—to set down these reasons, just as they came up out of my subconscious.

In the first place, I hate women because they always know where things are. At first blush. you might think that a perverse and merely churlish reason for hating women, but it is not. Naturally, every man enjoys having a woman around the house who knows where his shirt studs and his briefcase are, and things like that, but he detests having a woman around who knows where *everything* is, even things that are of no importance at all, such as, say, the snapshots her husband took three years ago at Elbow Beach. The husband has never known where these snapshots were since the day they were developed and printed; he hopes, in a vague way, if he thinks about them at all, that after three years they have been thrown out. But his wife knows where they are, and so do his mother, his grandmother, his great-grandmother, his daughter, and the maid. They could put their fingers on them in a moment, with that quiet air of superior knowledge which makes a man feel that he is out of touch with all the things that count in life.

A man's interest in old snapshots, unless they are snapshots of himself in action with a gun, a fishing rod, or a tennis racquet, languishes in about two hours. A woman's interest in old snapshots, particularly of groups of people, never languishes; it is always there, as the years roll on, as strong and vivid as it was right at the start. She remembers the snapshots when people come to call, and just as the husband, having mixed drinks for everybody, sits down to sip his own, she will say, "George, I wish you would go and get those snapshots we took at Elbow Beach and show them to the Murphys." The husband, as I have said, doesn't know where the snapshots are; all he knows is that Harry Murphy doesn't want to see them; Harry Murphy wants to talk, just as he himself wants to talk. But Grace Murphy says that she wants to see the pictures; she is crazy to see the pictures; for one thing, the wife, who has brought the subject up, wants Mrs. Murphy to see the photo of a certain costume that the wife wore at Elbow Beach in 1933. The husband finally puts down his drink and snarls, "Well, where are they, then?" The wife, depending on her mood, gives him either the look she reserves for spoiled children or the one she reserves for drunken workmen, and tells him he knows perfectly well where they are. It turns out, after a lot of give and take, the slightly bitter edge of which is covered by forced laughs, that the snapshots are in the upper right-hand drawer of a certain desk, and the husband goes out of the room to get them. He comes back in three minutes with the news that the snapshots are not in the upper right-hand drawer of the certain desk. Without stirring from her chair, the wife favors her husband with a faint smile (the one that annoys him most of all her smiles) and reiterates that the snapshots *are* in the upper right-hand drawer of the desk. He simply didn't look, that's all. The husband knows that he looked; he knows that he prodded and dug and excavated in that drawer and that the snapshots simply are not there. The wife tells him to go look again and he will find them. The husband goes back and looks again—the guests can hear him growling and cursing and rattling papers. Then he shouts out from the next room. "They are *not* in this *drawer*, just as I told you, Ruth!" The wife quietly excuses herself and leaves the guests and goes into the room where her husband stands, hot, miserable, and defiant— and with a certain nameless fear in his heart. He has pulled the desk drawer out so far that it is about to fall on the floor, and he points at the disarray of the drawer with bitter triumph (still mixed with that nameless fear). "Look for yourself!" he snarls. The wife does not look. She says with quiet coldness, "What is that you have in your hand?" What he has in his hand turns out to be an insurance policy and an old bankbook—and the snapshots. The wife gets off the old line about what it would have done if it had been a snake, and the husband is upset for the rest of the evening; in some cases he cannot keep anything on his stomach for twenty-four hours.

Another reason I hate women (and I am speaking, I believe, for the American male generally) is that in almost every case where there is a sign reading "Please have exact change ready," a woman never has anything smaller than a ten-dollar bill. She gives ten-dollar bills to bus conductors and change men in subways and other such persons who deal in nickels and dimes and quarters. Recently, in Bermuda, I saw a woman hand the conductor on the little railway there a bill of such huge denomination that I was utterly unfamiliar with it. I was sitting too far away to see exactly what it was, but I had the feeling that it was a five-hundred-dollar bill. The conductor merely ignored it and stood there waiting—the fare was just one shilling. Eventually, scrabbling around in her handbag, the woman found a shilling. All the men on the train who witnessed the transaction tightened up inside; that's what a woman with a ten-dollar bill or a twenty or a five-hundred does to a man in such situations—she tightens him up inside. The episode gives him the feeling that some monstrous triviality is threatening the whole structure of civilization. It is difficult to analyze this feeling, but there it is.

Another spectacle that depresses the male and makes him fear women, and therefore hate them, is that of a woman looking another woman up and down, to see what she is wearing. The cold, flat look that comes into a woman's eyes when she does this, the swift coarsening of her countenance, and the immediate evaporation from it of all humane quality make the male shudder. He is likely to go to his stateroom or his den or his private office and lock himself in for hours. I know one man who surprised that look in his wife's eyes and never afterward would let her come near him. If she started toward him, he would dodge behind a table or a sofa, as if he were engaging in some unholy game of tag. That look, I believe, is one reason men disappear, and turn up in Tahiti or the Arctic or the United States Navy.

I (to quit hiding behind the generalization of "the male") hate women because they almost never get anything exactly right. They say "I have been faithful to thee, Cynara, after my fashion" instead of "in my fashion." They will bet you that Alfred Smith's middle name is Aloysius, instead of Emanuel. They will tell you to take the 2:57 train, on a day that the 2:57 does not run, or, if it does run, does not stop at the station where you are supposed to get off. Many men, separated from a woman by this particular form of imprecision, have never showed up in her life again. Nothing so embitters a man as to end up in Bridgeport when he was supposed to get off at Westport.

I hate women because they have brought into the currency of our language such expressions as "all righty" and "yes indeedy" and hundreds of others. I hate women because they throw baseballs (or plates or vases) with the wrong foot advanced. I marvel that more of them have not broken their backs. I marvel that women, who coordinate so well in languorous motion, look uglier and sillier than a goose-stepper when they attempt any form of violent activity.

I had a lot of other notes jotted down about why I hate women, but

I seem to have lost them all, except one. That one is to the effect that I hate women because, while they never lose old snapshots or anything of that sort, they invariably lose one glove. I believe that I have never gone anywhere with any woman in my whole life who did not lose one glove. I have searched for single gloves under tables in crowded restaurants and under the feet of people in darkened movie theatres. I have spent some part of every day or night hunting for a woman's glove. If there were no other reason in the world for hating women. that one would be enough. In fact, you can leave all the others out.

GILBERT CLAVEL

Norman Douglas

A deformed young Swiss, with pushful and almost offensive manners, unhealthy complexion, and a horrible, rasping voice. His vulgarity was mitigated, but not redeemed, by a considerable love of natural history, common to many of his nation. There is a caricature of him, if such object can be caricatured, as the "ebullient Belgian hunch-back called Martel" in Compton Mackenzie's *Vestal Fire*.

He came to see me once, and, under the pretext of being wildly enthusiastic about such things, borrowed five or six precious books of mine, zoological monographs, all on the same subject, and almost impossible to replace. Do what I would, by word of mouth or note of hand, I was unable to get them back; each time he discovered a fresh excuse for keeping them a little longer. The months passed; he had plainly made up his mind not to disgorge my property again. And now I was due to leave for England! The thought of surrendering those monographs for ever made me sick; collectors will understand. Luckily I knew his daily habits sufficiently well to be able to run into him just before my departure.

"Hallo, Clavel!"

"Hallo! where are you going?'"

"Off to England tomorrow. Shan't be back for ages. So goodbye. I should have left yesterday, but I simply must see some Japanese mice before I go."

"Japanese mice?"

"They're white, and they dance. Dancing mice; a Japanese specialty. You can read about them in Brehm, I daresay, or in Siebold. They have stuffed ones in museums. But they are very rare, and very delicate. This is the first pair that has reached Europe alive. I wouldn't miss seeing them for worlds."

"Orientals are wonderful. You know they have fishes with two tails, and dogs without hair, and hens that cannot stand on their feet, and fir-trees no bigger than this cigarette, and grasshoppers that fight as if they were gladiators. Now these mice. Who has them?"

"A sea-captain. Friend of mine. He is taking them to Hamburg, if they survive. It's a great secret. They sleep all day long, wrapped in cotton wool. That's why I couldn't see them dance, when I called yesterday morning. Then at sunset they wake up, eat some doves' liver and rice out of a small cloisonné trough, and begin to kick their legs about like Pavlova gone crazy. I wouldn't miss . . ."

"Gott, how curious! How I should love to see them too."

"Would you really? Well, I don't mind taking you, if you care to meet me at the café at half past six. But do be punctual, and keep this between ourselves."

Doubtless he went to the café; doubtless he waited for me there. I was in his house, meanwhile, where I collected all my books together with one or two of his own more valuable ones, which I possess to this day. I never saw him again. He migrated afterwards to Positano, and died there.

THE LUMBER-ROOM

Saki (H. H. Munro)

The children were to be driven, as a special treat, to the sands at Jagborough. Nicholas was not to be of the party; he was in disgrace. Only that morning he had refused to eat his wholesome bread-and-milk on the seemingly frivolous ground that there was a frog in it. Older and wiser and better people had told him that there could not possibly be a frog in his bread-and-milk and that he was not to talk nonsense; he continued, nevertheless, to talk what seemed the veriest nonsense, and described with much detail the colouration and markings of the alleged frog. The dramatic part of the incident was that there really was a frog in Nicholas' basin of bread-and-milk; he had put it there himself, so he felt entitled to know something about it. The sin of taking a frog from the garden and putting it into a bowl of wholesome bread-and-milk was enlarged on at great length, but the fact that stood out clearest in the whole affair, as it presented itself to the mind of Nicholas. was that the older, wiser, and better people had been proved to be profoundly in error in matters about which they had expressed the utmost assurance.

"You said there couldn't possibly be a frog in my bread-and-milk; there *was* a frog in my bread-and-milk," he repeated, with the insistence of a skilled tactician who does not intend to shift from favourable ground.

So his boy-cousin and girl-cousin and his quite uninteresting younger brother were to be taken to Jagborough sands that afternoon and he was to stay home. His cousins' aunt, who insisted, by an unwarranted stretch of imagination, in styling herself his aunt also, had hastily invented the Jagborough expedition in order to impress on Nicholas the delights that he had justly forfeited by his disgraceful conduct at the breakfast-table. It was her habit, whenever one of the children fell from grace, to improvise something of a festival nature from which the offender would be rigorously debarred; if all the children sinned collectively they were suddenly informed of a circus in a neighbouring town, a circus of unrivalled merit and uncounted elephants, to which, but for their depravity, they would have been taken that very day.

A few decent tears were looked for on the part of Nicholas when the moment for the departure of the expedition arrived. As a matter of fact, however, all the crying was done by his girl-cousin, who scraped her knee rather painfully against the step of the carriage as she was scrambling in.

"How she did howl," said Nicholas cheerfully, as the party drove off without any of the elation of high spirits that should have characterized it.

"She'll soon get over that," said the *soi-disant* aunt; "it will be a glorious afternoon for racing about over those beautiful sands. How they will enjoy themselves!"

"Bobby won't enjoy himself much, and he won't race much either," said Nicholas with a grim chuckle; "his boots are hurting him. They're too tight."

"Why didn't he tell me they were hurting?" asked the aunt with some asperity.

"He told you twice, but you weren't listening. You often don't listen when we tell you important things."

"You are not to go into the gooseberry garden," said the aunt, changing the subject.

"Why not?" demanded Nicholas.

"Because you are in disgrace," said the aunt loftily.

Nicholas did not admit the flawlessness of the reasoning; he felt perfectly capable of being in disgrace and in a gooseberry garden at the same moment. His face took on an expression of considerable obstinacy. It was clear to his aunt that he was determined to get into the gooseberry garden, "only," as she remarked to herself, "because I have told him he is not to."

Now the gooseberry garden had two doors by which it might be entered, and once a small person like Nicholas could slip in there he could effectually disappear from view amid the masking growth of artichokes, raspberry canes, and fruit bushes. The aunt had many other things to do that afternoon, but she spent an hour or two in trivial gardening operations among flower beds and shrubberies, whence she could keep a watchful eye on the two doors that led to the forbidden paradise. She was a woman of few ideas with immense powers of concentration.

Nicholas made one or two sorties into the front garden, wriggling his way with obvious stealth of purpose towards one or other of the doors, but never able for a moment to evade the aunt's watchful eye. As a matter of fact, he had no intention of trying to get into the gooseberry garden, but it was extremely convenient for him that his aunt should believe that he had; it was a belief that would keep her on self-imposed sentry-duty for the greater part of the afternoon. Having thoroughly confirmed and fortified her suspicions, Nicholas slipped back into the house and rapidly put into execution a plan of action that had long germinated in his brain. By standing on a chair in the library one could reach a shelf on which reposed a fat, important-looking key. The key was as important as it looked; it was the instrument which kept the mysteries of the lumber-room secure from unauthorized intrusion, which opened a way only for aunts and such-like privileged persons. Nicholas had not had much experience of the art of fitting keys into keyholes and turning locks, but for some days past he had practised with the key of the schoolroom door; he did not believe in trusting too much to luck and accident. The key turned stiffly in the lock, but it turned. The door opened, and Nicholas was in an unknown land, compared with which the gooseberry garden was a stale delight, a mere material pleasure.

Often and often Nicholas had pictured to himself what the lumber-room might be like, that region that was so carefully sealed from youthful eyes and concerning which no questions were ever answered. It came up to his expectations. In the first place it was large and dimly lit, one high window opening on to the forbidden garden being its only source of illumination. In the second place it was a storehouse of unimagined treasures. The aunt-by-assertion was one of those people who think that things spoil by use and consign them to dust and damp by way of preserving them. Such parts of the house as Nicholas knew best were rather bare and cheerless, but here there were wonderful things for the eye to feast on. First and foremost there was a piece of framed tapestry that was evidently meant to be a fire-screen. To Nicholas it was a living, breathing story; he sat down on a roll of Indian hangings, glowing in wonderful colours beneath a layer of dust, and took in all the details of the tapestry picture. A man, dressed in the hunting costume of some remote period, had just transfixed a stag with an arrow; it could not have been a difficult shot because the stag was only one or two paces away from him; in the thickly growing vegetation that the picture suggested it would not have been difficult to creep up to a feeding stag, and the two spotted dogs that were springing forward to join in the chase had evidently been trained to keep to heel till the arrow was discharged. That part of the picture was simple, if interesting, but did the huntsman see, what Nicholas saw, that four galloping wolves were coming in his direction through the wood? There might be more than four of them hidden behind the trees, and in any case would the man and his dogs be able to cope with the four wolves if they made an attack? The man had only two arrows left in his quiver, and he might miss with one or both of them; all one knew about his skill in shooting was that he could hit a large stag at a ridiculously short range. Nicholas sat for many golden minutes revolving the possibilities of the scene; he was inclined to think that there were more than four wolves and that the man and his dogs were in a tight corner.

But there were other objects of delight and interest claiming his instant attention: there were quaint twisted candlesticks in the shape of snakes, and a teapot fashioned like a china duck, out of whose open beak the tea was supposed to come. How dull and shapeless the nursery teapot seemed in comparison! And there was a carved sandal-wood box packed tight with aromatic cotton-wool, and between the layers of cotton-wool were little brass figures, hump-necked bulls, and peacocks and goblins, delightful to see and to handle. Less promising in appearance was a large square book with plain black covers; Nicholas peeped into it, and, behold, it was full of coloured pictures of birds. And such birds! In the garden, and in the lanes when he went for a walk, Nicholas came across a few birds, of which the largest were an occasional magpie or wood pigeon; here were herons and bustards, kites, toucans, tiger-bitterns, brush turkeys, ibises, golden pheasants, a whole portrait gallery of undreamed-of creatures. And as he was admiring the colouring of the mandarin duck and assigning a life-history to it, the voice of his aunt in shrill vociferation of his name came from the gooseberry garden without. She had grown suspicious at his long disappearance, and had leapt to the conclusion that he had climbed over the wall behind the sheltering screen of the lilac bushes; she was now engaged in energetic and rather hopeless search for him among the artichokes and raspberry canes.

"Nicholas, Nicholas!" she screamed, "you are to come out of this at once. It's no use trying to hide there; I can see you all the time."

It was probably the first time for twenty years that anyone had smiled in that lumber-room.

Presently the angry repetitions of Nicholas' name gave way to a shriek, and a cry for somebody to come quickly. Nicholas shut the book, restored it carefully to its place in a corner, and shook some dust from a neighbouring pile of newspapers over it. Then he crept from the room, locked the door, and replaced the key exactly where he had found it. His aunt was still calling his name when he sauntered into the front garden.

"Who's calling?" he asked.

"Me," came the answer from the other side of the wall; "didn't you hear me? I've been looking for you in the gooseberry garden, and I've slipped into the rain-water tank. Luckily there's no water in it, but the sides are slippery and I can't get out. Fetch the little ladder from under the cherry tree—"

"I was told I wasn't to go into the gooseberry garden," said Nicholas promptly.

"I told you not to, and now I tell you that you may," came the voice from the rain-water tank, rather impatiently.

"Your voice doesn't sound like aunt's," objected Nicholas; "you may be the Evil One tempting me to be disobedient. Aunt often tells me that the Evil One tempts me and that I always yield. This time I'm not going to yield."

"Don't talk nonsense," said the prisoner in the tank; "go and fetch the ladder."

"Will there be strawberry jam for tea?" asked Nicholas innocently.

"Certainly there will be," said the aunt, privately resolving that Nicholas should have none of it.

"Now I know that you are the Evil One and not aunt," shouted Nicholas gleefully; "when we asked aunt for strawberry jam yesterday she said there wasn't any. I know there are four jars of it in the store cupboard, because I looked, and of course you know it's there, but *she* doesn't, because she said there wasn't any. Oh, Devil, you *have* sold yourself!"

There was an unusual sense of luxury in being able to talk to an aunt as though one was talking to the Evil One, but Nicholas knew, with childish discernment, that such luxuries were not to be over-indulged in. He walked noisily away, and it was a kitchen-maid, in search of parsley, who eventually rescued the aunt from the rain-water tank.

Tea that evening was partaken of in a fearsome silence. The tide had been at its highest when the children had arrived at Jagborough Cove, so there had been no sands to play on—a circumstance that the aunt had overlooked in the haste of organizing her punitive expedition. The tightness of Bobby's boots had had disastrous effect on his temper the whole of the afternoon, and altogether the children could not have been said to have enjoyed themselves. The aunt maintained the frozen muteness of one who has suffered undignified and unmerited detention in a rain-water tank for thirty-five minutes. As for Nicholas, he, too, was silent, in the absorption of one who has much to think about; it was just possible, he considered, that the huntsman would escape with his hounds while the wolves feasted on the stricken stag.

HANGING A PICTURE

Jerome K. Jerome

You never saw such a commotion up and down a house, in all your life as when my Uncle Podger undertook to do a job. A picture would have come home from the frame maker's, and be standing in the dining room, waiting to be put up; and Aunt Podger would ask what was to be done with it, and Uncle Podger would say:

"Oh, you leave that to *me*. Don't you, any of you, worry yourselves about that. *I'll* do all that."

And then he would take off his coat, and begin. He would send the girl out for sixpen'orth of nails, and then one of the boys after her to tell her what size to get; and, from that, he would gradually work down, and start the whole house.

"Now you go and get me my hammer, Will," he would shout; "and you bring me the rule, Tom; and I shall want the stepladder, and I had better have a kitchen chair, too; and, Jim! you run round to Mr. Goggles, and tell him, 'Pa's kind regards, and hopes his leg's better; and will he lend him his spirit-level?' And don't you go, Maria, because I shall want somebody to hold me the light; and when the girl comes back, she must go out again for a bit of picture cord; and Tom!—where's Tom?—Tom, you come here; I shall want you to hand me up the picture."

And then he would lift up the picture, and drop it, and it would come out of the frame, and he would try to save the glass, and cut himself; and then he would spring round the room, looking for his handkerchief. He could not find his handkerchief, because it was in the pocket of the coat he had taken off, and he did not know where he had put the coat, and all the house had to leave off looking for his tools, and start looking for his coat; while he would dance round and hinder them.

"Doesn't anybody in the whole house know where my coat is? I never came across such a set in all my life—upon my word I didn't. Six of you!— and you can't find a coat that I put down not five minutes ago! Well, of all the—"

Then he'd get up, and find that he had been sitting on it, and would call out: "Oh, you can give it up! I've found it myself now. Might just as well ask the cat to find anything as expect you people to find it."

And, when half an hour had been spent in tying up his finger, and a new glass had been got, and the tools, and the ladder, and the chair, and the candle had been brought, he would have another go, the whole family, including the girl and the charwoman, standing round in a semi-circle, ready to help. Two people would have to hold the chair, and a third would help him up on it, and hold him there, and a fourth would hand him a nail, and a fifth would pass him up the hammer, and he would take hold of the nail, and drop it.

"There!" he would say, in an injured tone, "now the nail's gone."

And we would all have to go down on our knees and grovel for it, while he would stand on the chair, and grunt, and want to know if he was to be kept there all the evening.

The nail would be found at last, but by that time he would have lost the hammer.

"Where's the hammer? What did I do with the hammer? Great heavens! Seven of you, gaping round there, and you don't know what I did with the hammer!"

We would find the hammer for him, and then he would have lost sight of the mark he had made on the wall, where the nail was to go in, and each of us had to get up on the chair, beside him, and see if we could find it; and we would each discover it in a different place, and he would call us all fools, one after another, and tell us to get down. And he would take the rule, and re-measure and find that he wanted half thirty-one and three-eighths inches from the corner, and would try to do it in his head, and go mad.

And we would all try to do it in our heads, and all arrive at different results, and sneer at one another. And in the general row, the original number would be forgotten, and Uncle Podger would have to measure it again.

He would use a bit of string this time, and at the critical moment, when he was leaning over the chair at an angle of forty-five degrees, and trying to reach a point three inches beyond what was possible for him to reach, the string would slip, and down he would slide on to the piano, a really fine musical effect being produced by the suddenness with which his head and body struck all the notes at the same time.

And Aunt Maria would say that she would not allow the children to stand round and hear such language.

At last, Uncle Podger would get the spot fixed again, and put the point of the nail on it with his left hand, and take the hammer in his right hand. And, with the first blow, he would smash his thumb, and drop the hammer, with a yell, on somebody's toes.

Aunt Maria would mildly observe that, next time Uncle Podger was going to hammer a nail into the wall, she hoped he'd let her know in time, so that she could make arrangements to go and spend a week with her mother while it was being done.

"Oh! you women, you make such a fuss over everything." Uncle Podger would reply, picking himself up. "Why, I *like* doing a little job of this sort."

And then he would have another try, and, at the second blow, the nail would go clean through the plaster, and half the hammer after it, and Uncle Podger be precipitated against the wall with force nearly sufficient to flatten his nose.

Then we had to find the rule and the string again, and a new hole was made; and, about midnight, the picture would be up—very crooked and insecure, the wall for yards round looking as if it had been smoothed down with a rake, and everybody dead beat and wretched—except Uncle Podger.

"There you are," he would say, stepping heavily off the chair onto the charwoman's corns, and surveying the mess he had made with evident pride. "Why, some people would have had a man in to do a little thing like that!"

THE MAN-EATING TREE
OF MADAGASCAR

On the island of Madagascar, off the southeast coast of Africa, live a race of people called the Mkodos; they are one of the smallest races in the world, the men seldom exceeding fifty-six inches in height. Their religious consists solely in the awful worship of their sacred tree, the Crinoida Dajeeana. The tree is most peculiar in its appearance and nature; its trunk is somewhat like a pineapple in shape, and when full-grown about eight feet high; from the top (which is at least two feet in diameter) hang down eight leaves, eleven or twelve feet long, two feet through in their thickest part, and tapering from a width of three feet to a sharp point; they are very convex on the under, and concave on the upper side; the concave side is thickly set with strong horny hooks. The top of the trunk is in shape like a smaller plate set within a larger one, and this plate is filled with a sweet liquid, which, when tasted, produces delirium and sleep. From under the rim of the lower plate a series of great green tendrils from seven to eight feet long stretch out stiffly towards the horizon, while above these, six long white palpi (thin as reeds and frail as quills apparently) rear themselves towards the sky, twirling and twisting with incessant motion. The tree and the worship of it were discovered by Karl Leche, who wrote to Dr. Omehus Friedlowsky this description, which was immediately published in the Carlsruhe scientific journal. The mode of sacrifice as witnessed on one occasion was as follows: The natives had been shrieking around the tree and chanting propitiatory hymns to the great tree devil. With still wilder shrieks they now surrounded one of the women and goaded her on with the points of their javelins until she mounted the trunk and drank of the fluid in the plate, rising instantly again with wild frenzy in her face. But she did not jump down as she seemed to intend to do, oh no! The atrocious cannibal tree that had been so inert and dead came to sudden savage life. The slender delicate palpi quivered a moment over her head, then coiled round and round her neck and arms; the green tendrils wrapped her about in fold after fold ever tightening; then the great leaves rose slowly and stiffly, approached one another, and closed about the dead victim with the force of a hydraulic press. As the bases of the leaves pressed more tightly together, from between them there trickled down the trunk of the tree great streams of the fluid mingled with the blood and oozing viscera of the victim. The savages bounded forward, and with cups, leaves, hands, and tongues, got each enough of the liquor to set him mad and frantic. The tree remained unchanged in appearance during ten days, and at the end of that time the leaves, the tendrils and the palpi had all regained their natural position, and nothing but the skull of the victim remained as a proof of the sacrifice which had taken place there. Another witness of a sacrifice to the Crinoida Dajeeana says that when the tree had completely enveloped the woman, the natives set fire to it, and it became her funeral pyre.

If the story of this wonderful tree is even half true, we must be more than ever convinced how little we can as yet read nature's infinite book of secrecy.

ON DOORS

Christopher Morley

The opening and closing of doors are the most significant actions of man's life. What a mystery lies in doors!

No man knows what awaits him when he opens a door. Even the most familiar room, where the clock ticks and the hearth grows red at dusk, may harbor surprises. The plumber may actually have called (while you were out) and fixed that leaking faucet. The cook may have had a fit of the vapors and demanded her passports. The wise man opens his front door with humility and a spirit of acceptance.

Which one of us has not sat in some anteroom and watched the inscrutable panels of a door that was full of meaning? Perhaps you were waiting to apply for a job; perhaps you had some "deal" you were ambitious to put over. You watched the confidential stenographer flit in and out, carelessly turning that mystic portal which, to you, revolved on hinges of fate. And then the young woman said, "Mr. Cranberry will see you now." As you grasped the knob the thought flashed, "When I open this door again, what will have happened?"

There are many kinds of doors. Revolving doors for hotels, shops, and public buildings. These are typical of the brisk, bustling ways of modern life. Can you imagine John Milton or William Penn skipping through a revolving door? Then there are the curious little slatted doors that still swing outside denatured barrooms, and extend only from shoulder to knee. There are trapdoors, sliding doors, double doors, stage doors, prison doors, glass doors. But the symbol and mystery of a door resides in its quality of concealment. A glass door is not a door at all, but a window. The meaning of a door is to hide what lies inside; to keep the heart in suspense.

Also, there are many ways of opening doors. There is the cheery push of elbow with which the waiter shoves open the kitchen door when he bears in your tray of supper. There is the suspicious and tentative withdrawal of a door before the unhappy book agent or peddler. There is the genteel and carefully modulated recession with which footmen swing wide the oaken barriers of the great. There is the sympathetic and awful silence of the dentist's maid who opens the door into the operating room and, without speaking, implies that the doctor is ready for you. There is the brisk cataclysmic opening of a door when the nurse comes in, very early in the morning—"It's a boy!"

Doors are the symbol of privacy, of retreat, of the mind's escape into blissful quietude or sad secret struggle. A room without doors is not a room, but a hallway. No matter where he is, a man can make himself at home behind a closed door. The mind works best behind closed doors. Men are not horses to be herded together. Dogs know the meaning and anguish of doors. Have you ever noticed a puppy yearning at a shut portal? It is a symbol of human life.

The opening of doors is a mystic act: it has in it some flavor of the unknown, scme sense of moving into a new movement, a new pattern of the human rigmarole. It includes the highest glimpses of mortal gladness: reunions, reconciliations, the bliss of lovers long parted. Even in sadness, the opening of a door may bring relief: it changes and redistributes human forces. But the closing of doors is far more terrible. It is a confession of finality. Every door closed brings something to an end. And there are degrees of sadness in the closing of doors. A door slammed is a confession of weakness. A door gently shut is often the most tragic gesture in life. Every one knows the seizure of anguish that comes just after the closing of a door, when the loved one is still near, within sound of voice, and yet already far away.

The opening and closing of doors is a part of the stern fluency of life. Life will not stay still and let us alone. We are continually opening doors with hope, closing them with despair. Life lasts not much longer than a pipe of tobacco, and destiny knocks us out like the ashes.

The closing of a door is irrevocable. It snaps the packthread of the heart. It is no avail to reopen, to go back. Pinero spoke nonsense when he made Paula Tanqueray say, "The future is only the past entered through another gate." Alas, there is no other gate. When the door is shut, it is shut forever. There is no other entrance to that vanished pulse of time. "The moving finger writes, and having writ—"

There is a certain kind of door-shutting that will come to us all. The kind of door-shutting that is done very quietly, with the sharp click of the latch to break the stillness. They will think then, one hopes, of our unfulfilled decencies rather than of our pluperfected misdemeanors. Then they will go out and close the door.

THE SANDBOX

Edward Albee

The Players

The Young Man, 25; a good-looking, well-built boy in a bathing suit.

Mommy, 55; a well-dressed, imposing woman.

Daddy, 60; a small man; gray, thin.

Grandma, 86; a tiny, wizened woman with bright eyes.

The Musician; no particular age, but young would be nice.

Note: When, in the course of the play, Mommy *and* Daddy *call each other by these names, there should be no suggestion of regionalism. These names are of empty affection and point up the pre-senility and vacuity of their characters.*

(The Scene: A bare stage, with only the following: Near the footlights, far stage-right, two simple chairs set side by side, facing the audience; near the footlights, far stage-left, a chair facing stage-right with a music stand before it; farther back, and stage-center, slightly elevated and raked, a large child's sandbox with a toy pail and shovel, the background is the sky, which alters from brightest day to deepest night.

At the beginning, it is brightest day; the Young Man *is alone on stage, to the rear of the sandbox, and to one side. He is doing calisthenics; he does calisthenics until quite at the very end of the play. These calisthenics, employing the arms only, should suggest the beating and fluttering of wings. The* Young Man *is, after all, the Angel of Death.*

Mommy *and* Daddy *enter from stage-left,* Mommy *first.)*

Mommy *(motioning to* Daddy*)*: Well, here we are; this is the beach.

Daddy *(whining)*: I'm cold.

Mommy *(dismissing him with a little laugh)*: Don't be silly; it's as warm as toast. Look at that nice young man over there: *he* doesn't think it's cold. *(Waves to the* Young Man.*)* Hello.

Young Man *(with an endearing smile)*: Hi!

Mommy *(looking about)*: This will do perfectly ... don't you think so, Daddy? There's sand there ... and the water beyond. What do you think, Daddy?

Daddy *(vaguely)*: Whatever you say, Mommy.

Mommy *(with the same little laugh)*: Well, of course ... whatever I say.

Then, it's settled, is it?

DADDY (*shrugs*): She's *your* mother, not mine.

MOMMY: *I* know she's my mother. What do you take me for? (*A pause.*) All right, now; let's get on with it. (*She shouts into the wings, stage-left.*) You! Out there! You can come in now.

    (*The* MUSICIAN *enters, seats himself in the chair, stage-left, places music on the music stand, is ready to play.* MOMMY *nods approvingly.*)

MOMMY: Very nice; very nice. Are you ready, Daddy? Let's go get Grandma.

DADDY: Whatever you say, Mommy.

MOMMY (*leading the way out, stage-left*): Of course, whatever I say. (*To the* MUSICIAN.) You can begin now.

    (*The* MUSICIAN *begins playing;* MOMMY *and* DADDY *exit; the* MUSICIAN, *all the while playing, nods to the* YOUNG MAN.)

YOUNG MAN (*with the same endearing smile*). Hi!

    (*After a moment,* MOMMY *and* DADDY *re-enter, carrying* GRANDMA. *She is borne in by their hands under her armpits; she is quite rigid; her legs are drawn up; her feet do not touch the ground; the expression on her ancient face is that of puzzlement and fear.*)

DADDY: Where do we put her?

MOMMY (*the same little laugh*): Wherever I say, of course. Let me see . . . well . . . all right, over there . . . in the sandbox. (*Pause.*) Well, what are you waiting for, Daddy? . . . The sandbox!

    (*Together they carry* GRANDMA *over to the sandbox and more or less dump her in.*)

GRANDMA (*righting herself to a sitting position; her voice a cross between a baby's laugh and cry*): Ahhhhhh! Graaaaa!

DADDY (*dusting himself*): What do we do now?

MOMMY (*to the* MUSICIAN): You can stop now.

    (*The* MUSICIAN *stops.*)

    (*Back to* DADDY.) What do you mean, what do we do now? We go over there and sit down, of course. (*To the* YOUNG MAN.) Hello there.

YOUNG MAN (*again smiling*): Hi!

    (MOMMY *and* DADDY *move to the chairs, stage-right, and sit down. A pause.*)

GRANDMA (*same as before*): Ahhhhhh! Ah-haaaaaa! Graaaaaaaa!

DADDY: Do you think . . . do you think she's . . . comfortable?

MOMMY (*impatiently*): How would I know?

DADDY (*pause*): What do we do now?

MOMMY (*as if remembering*): We . . . wait. We . . . sit here . . . and we wait . . . that's what we do.

DADDY *(after a pause)*: Shall we talk to each other?

MOMMY *(with that little laugh; picking something off her dress)*: Well. *you* can talk, if you want to ... if you can think of anything to *say* ... if you can think of anything *new*.

DADDY *(thinks)*: No ... I suppose not.

MOMMY *(with a triumphant laugh)*: Of course not!

GRANDMA *(banging the toy shovel against the pail)*: Haaaaaa! Ah-haaaaaa!

MOMMY *(out over the audience)*: Be quiet, Grandma ... just be quiet, and wait.

   (GRANDMA throws a shovelful of sand at MOMMY.)

MOMMY *(still out over the audience)*: She's throwing sand at me! You stop that, Grandma; you stop throwing sand at Mommy! *(To DADDY.)* She's throwing sand at me.

   (DADDY looks around at GRANDMA, who screams at him.)

GRANDMA: GRAAAAAA!

MOMMY: Don't look at her. Just ... sit here ... be very still ... and wait. *(To the MUSICIAN.)* You ... uh ... you go ahead and do whatever it is you do.

   (The MUSICIAN plays. MOMMY and DADDY are fixed, staring out beyond the audience. GRANDMA looks at them, looks at the MUSICIAN, looks at the sandbox, throws down the shovel.)

GRANDMA: Ah-haaaaaa! Graaaaaa! *(Looks for reaction; gets none. Now ... directly to the audience.)* Honestly! What a way to treat an old woman! Drag her out of the house ... stick her in a car ... bring her out here from the city ... dump her in a pile of sand ... and leave her here to set. I'm eighty-six years old! I was married when I was seventeen. To a farmer. He died when I was thirty. *(To the MUSICIAN.)* Will you stop that, please?

   (The MUSICIAN stops playing.)

I'm a feeble old woman ... how do you expect anybody to hear me over that peep! peep! *(To herself.)* There's no respect around here. *(To the YOUNG MAN.)* There's no respect around here!

YOUNG MAN *(same smile)*: Hi!

GRANDMA *(after a pause, a mild double-take, continues, to the audience)*: My husband died when I was thirty *(indicates MOMMY)*, and I had to raise that big cow over there all by my lonesome. You can imagine what *that* was like. Lordy! *(To the YOUNG MAN.)* Where'd they get *you*?

YOUNG MAN: Oh ... I've been around for a while.

GRANDMA: I'll bet you have! Heh, heh, heh. Will you look at you!

YOUNG MAN *(flexing his muscles)*: Isn't that something? *(Continues his calisthenics.)*

GRANDMA: Boy, oh boy; I'll say. Pretty good.

YOUNG MAN (*sweetly*): I'll say.

GRANDMA: Where ya from?

YOUNG MAN: Southern California.

GRANDMA (*nodding*): Figgers; figgers. What's your name, honey?

YOUNG MAN: I don't know . . .

GRANDMA (*to the audience*). Bright, too!

YOUNG MAN: I mean . . . I mean, they haven't given me one yet . . . the studio . . .

GRANDMA (*giving him the once-over*): You don't say . . . you don't say. Well . . . uh, I've got to talk some more . . . don't you go 'way.

YOUNG MAN: Oh, no.

GRANDMA (*turning her attention back to the audience*). Fine; fine. (*Then, once more, back to the* YOUNG MAN.) You're . . . you're an actor, hunh?

YOUNG MAN (*beaming*): Yes. I am.

GRANDMA (*to the audience again, shrugs*): I'm smart that way. *Anyhow*, I had to raise . . . *that* over there all by my lonesome; and what's next to her there . . . that's what she married. Rich? I tell you . . . money, money, money. They took me off the *farm* . . . which was real decent of them . . . and they moved me into the big town house with *them* . . . fixed a nice place for me under the stove . . . gave me an army blanket . . . and my own dish . . . my very own dish! So, what have I got to complain about? Nothing, of course. I'm not complaining. (*She looks up at the sky, shouts to someone off stage.*) Shouldn't it be getting dark now, dear?

    (*The lights dim; night comes on. The* MUSICIAN *begins to play; it becomes deepest night. There are spots on all the players, including the* YOUNG MAN, *who is, of course, continuing his calisthenics.*)

DADDY (stirring): It's nighttime.

MOMMY: Shhhh. Be still . . . wait.

DADDY (*whining*): It's so hot.

MOMMY: Shhhhhh. Be still . . . wait.

GRANDMA (*to herself*): That's better. Night. (*To the* MUSICIAN.) Honey, do you play all through this part? (*The* MUSICIAN *nods.*) Well, keep it nice and soft; that's a good boy. (*The* MUSICIAN *nods again; plays softly.*) That's nice.

    (*There is an off-stage rumble.*)

DADDY (*starting*): What was that?

MOMMY (*beginning to weep*): It was nothing.

DADDY: It was . . . it was . . . thunder . . . or a wave breaking . . . or something.

MOMMY (*whispering, through her tears*): It was an off-stage rumble . . . and you know what *that* means. . . .

DADDY: I forget. . . .

MOMMY *(barely able to talk)*: It means the time has come for poor Grandma . . . and I can't bear it!

DADDY *(vacantly)*: I . . . I suppose you've got to be brave.

GRANDMA *(mocking)*: That's right, kid; be brave. You'll bear up; you'll get over it.

    (Another off-stage rumble . . . louder.)

MOMMY: Ohhhhhhhhhh . . . poor Grandma . . . poor Grandma. . . .

GRANDMA *(to MOMMY)*: I'm fine! I'm all right! It hasn't happened yet!

    (A violent off-stage rumble. All the lights go out, save the spot on the YOUNG MAN; the MUSICIAN stops playing.)

MOMMY: Ohhhhhhhhhh. . . . Ohhhhhhhhhh. . . .

    (Silence.)

GRANDMA: Don't put the lights up yet . . . I'm not ready; I'm not quite ready. *(Silence.)* All right, dear . . . I'm about done.

    (The lights come up again, to brightest day; the MUSICIAN begins to play. GRANDMA is discovered, still in the sandbox, lying on her side, propped upon an elbow, half covered, busily shoveling sand over herself.)

GRANDMA *(muttering)*: I don't know how I'm supposed to do anything with this goddam toy shovel. . . .

DADDY: Mommy! It's daylight!

MOMMY *(brightly)*: So it is! Well! Our long night is over. We must put away our tears, take off our mourning . . . and face the future. It's our duty.

GRANDMA *(still shoveling; mimicking)*: . . . take off our mourning . . . face the future. . . . Lordy!

    (MOMMY and DADDY rise, stretch. MOMMY waves to the YOUNG MAN.)

YOUNG MAN *(with that smile)*: Hi!

    (GRANDMA plays dead. (!) MOMMY and DADDY go over to look at her; she is a little more than half buried in the sand; the toy shovel is in her hands, which are crossed on her breast.)

MOMMY *(before the sandbox; shaking her head)*: Lovely! it's . . . it's hard to be sad . . . she looks . . . so happy. *(With pride and conviction.)* It pays to do things well. *(To the MUSICIAN.)* All right, you can stop now, if you want to. I mean, stay around for a swim, or something; it's all right with us. *(She sighs heavily.)* Well, Daddy . . . off we go.

DADDY: Brave Mommy!

MOMMY: Brave Daddy!

    (They exit, stage-left.)

GRANDMA *(After they leave; lying quite still)*: It pays to do things well. . . . Boy, oh boy! *(She tries to sit up)* . . . well, kids . . . *(but finds she can't.)* . . . I . . . I can't get up. I . . . I can't move. . . .

(The Young Man *stops his calisthenics, nods to the* Musician, *walks over to* Grandma, *kneels down by the sandbox.)*

GRANDMA: I . . . can't move. . . .

YOUNG MAN: Shhhhh . . . be very still. . . .

GRANDMA: I . . . I can't move. . . .

YOUNG MAN: Uh . . . ma'am; I . . . I have a line here.

GRANDMA: Oh, I'm sorry, sweetie; you go right ahead.

YOUNG MAN: I am . . . uh . . .

GRANDMA: Take your time, dear.

YOUNG MAN *(prepares; delivers the line like a real amateur)*: I am the Angel of Death. I am . . . uh . . . I am come for you.

GRANDMA: What . . . wha . . . *(Then, with resignation:)* . . . ohhhh . . . ohhhh, I see.

   (The Young Man *bends over, kisses* Grandma *gently on the forehead.)*

GRANDMA *(her eyes closed, her hands folded on her breast again, the shovel between her hands, a sweet smile on her face)*: Well . . . that was very nice, dear. . . .

YOUNG MAN *(still kneeling)*: Shhhhhh . . . be still. . . .

GRANDMA: What I meant was . . . you did that very well, dear. . . .

YOUNG MAN *(blushing)*: . . . oh . . .

GRANDMA: No; I mean it. You've got that . . . you've got a quality.

YOUNG MAN *(with his endearing smile)*: Oh . . . thank you; thank you very much . . . ma'am.

GRANDMA *(slowly; softly—as the* Young Man *puts his hands on top of* Grandma's*)*: You're . . . you're welcome . . . dear.

   (Tableau. The Musician *continues to play as the curtain slowly comes down.)*

JOHN SMITH –
CONVICTED OF ROBBERY

Though the crimes committed by this man were not particularly atrocious, nor his life sufficiently remarkable for a place in this work, yet the circumstances attending his fate at the place of execution are perhaps more singular than any we may have to record. He was the son of a farmer at Malton, about fifteen miles from the city of York, who bound him apprentice to a packer in London, with whom he served out his time, and afterwards worked as a journeyman. He then went to sea in a merchantman, after which he entered on board a man-of-war, and was at the famous expedition against Vigo; but on the return from that expedition he was discharged.

He had not been long disengaged from the naval service when he enlisted as a soldier in the regiment of guards commanded by Lord Cutts; but in this station he soon made bad connexion, and engaged with some of his dissolute companions as a housebreaker.

On the 5th of December, 1705, he was arraigned on four different indictments, on two of which he was convicted. While he lay under sentence of death, he seemed very little affected with his situation, absolutely depending on a reprieve, through the interest of his friends.

However, an order came for his execution on the 24th day of the same month, in consequence of which he was carried to Tyburn, where he performed his devotions, and was turned off in the usual manner; but when he had hung near fifteen minutes, the people present cried out, "A reprieve!" Hereupon the malefactor was cut down, and, being conveyed to a house in the neighbourhood, he soon recovered, in consequence of bleeding and other proper applications.

When he perfectly recovered his senses, he was asked what were his feelings at the time of execution; to which he repeatedly replied, in substance, as follows: "That when he was turned off, he, for some time, was sensible of very great pain, occasioned by the weight of his body, and felt his spirits in a strange commotion, violently pressing upwards; that having forced their way to his head, he, as it were, saw a great blaze, or glaring light, which seemed to go out at his eyes with a flash, and then he lost all sense of pain. That after he was cut down, and began to come to himself, the blood and spirits, forcing themselves into their former channels, put him, by a sort of pricking or shooting, to such intolerable pain that he could have wished those hanged who had cut him down." From this circumstance he was called "Half-hanged Smith."

After this narrow escape from the grave, Smith pleaded to his pardon on the 20th of February; yet such was his propensity to evil deeds, that he returned to his former practices, and, being apprehended, was tried at the Old Bailey, for house-breaking; but some difficulties arising in the case, the jury brought in a special verdict, in consequence of which the affair was left to the opinion of the twelve judges, who determined in favour of the prisoner.

After this second extraordinary escape, he was a third time indicted;

but the prosecutor happening to die before the day of trial, he once more obtained that liberty which his conduct showed he had not deserved.

We have no account what became of this man after this third remarkable incident in his favour; but Christian charity inclines us to hope that he made a proper use of the singular dispensation of Providence evidenced in his own person.

When once the mind has consented to the commission of sin, it is hard to be reclaimed. The memory of the pangs of an ignominious death could not deter this man from following the evil course he had begun. Thus, by giving way to small propensities, we imperceptibly go on to enormities which lead us to a shameful fate. Let us, therefore, at once resolve never to depart from the path of rectitude.

COLONEL STENTOR

Kazlitt Arvine

Colonel Stentor was at one time a legislator in a certain legislative hall. He had been an Indian agent among the Osages, and whenever he took the floor he was exceedingly famous for making tropes and similes of buffaloes, wolves, panthers, bears, foxes, and all other voracious animals. In this way he got to be quite a *lion* himself, and his opponents all shrank in terror from his roar. But on one occasion, a young lawyer, new upon the floor, but who knew the roaring colonel of old, got up and replied to him as follows:—

"Mr. Speaker, does the gentleman imagine he is going to frighten us down here with a menagerie of wild beasts? Though the gentleman is so anxious to let us know that he was born in the woods, can he assert that he was never scared by an owl? The honorable member may, possibly, recognize a reminiscence which may be related thus:—

"A certain valiant gentleman was once benighted, even in his native woods, and, calling aloud for assistance from his dilemma, he heard a sepulchral voice exclaim in answer, 'Hoo—hoo—hoo—hoo— who are you?' The gentleman instantly replied at the top of his voice, 'I am Colonel David Crockett Julius Caesar Alexander Napoleon Stentor, formerly of Nicholas county, Kentucky, now a candidate to represent Caloway county

in the lower branch of the next General Assembly in Missouri, I am lost.'
"Hoo—hoo—hoo—hoo—who are you?' again demanded the mysterious
voice. 'I tell you,' shouted the colonel, in a still higher key, 'I am Colonel
David Crockett Julius Caesar Alexander Napoleon Stentor, formerly of
Nicholas county, Kentucky, now a candidate to represent Caloway county
in the lower branch of the next General Assembly of Missouri, and I am
lost.' 'Hoo—hoo—ho-ho-ha-ha-ha-hah!' returned the distant stranger; and,
Mr. Speaker, the valiant colonel was left by the owl to find his own way
out of the woods, which I presume he did, as he sits among us at present."

The speech was interrupted throughout with uproarious laughter, which
echoed again and again in violent gusts for some moments after the
juvenile member sat down. At length, to the surprise of everybody,
Colonel Stentor slowly arose with witticism, and replied,—

"Mr. Speaker, the gentleman inquires if it is possible for me to be
scared by an owl! I confess I am!"

PIZARRO IN PERU

John Crosby

The Inca empire which Pizarro invaded with less than 200 men
stretched through modern Peru, Ecuador, Bolivia, and Chile and perhaps
even farther, a land where both riches and poverty were unknown, but
whose capital wealth exceeded that of Rome, Persia, or Jerusalem,
inhabited by 12 million happy, industrious, and magnificently organized
human beings. These people and their sun god, the king, welcomed Pizarro
with nothing but kindness, trust, and friendship, and were repaid with
nothing but avarice, cruelty, betrayal, and total ruin.

One of the conquistadors, named Mancio Sierra de Leguizamo, in a final
penitent message in his will addressed to his King Philip declared: "His
Catholic Majesty must know that we found these countries in such a condition that there were no thieves, no vicious men, no idlers, no adulterers
or evil-living women. I draft this account to unburden my conscience and
to acknowledge my fault. For we have transformed these natives, who
had so much wisdom and committed so few crimes. The realm has fallen
into such disorder that it has passed from one extreme to another. There
was then no evil thing, but today there is no good or almost none."

A CLEPSYDRA

Among the valuable presents sent to the Emperor Charlemagne by Haroun al Raschid, which astonished the Western world by their rarity, and the ingenuity displayed in their construction, was a clepsydra, or water-clock of metal. From the admiration this clock elicited, we are led to presume that the clepsydra—first used by the Romans—was a lost art to the Western people.

The Romans had used the clepsydra to limit time in courts. That of Ctesilaus of Alexandria, 135 B.C., had a little figure which rose with the water, and pointed out the hours. But the more simple ones consisted of a vase filled with water, with a small opening at the bottom, through which the water escaped, drop by drop, into a vessel beneath, which was said by the Romans to steal the water, clepsydra meaning water-stealer. The sides of the vase were divided by lines, and the height of the water marked the time.

But the clepsydra sent to Charlemagne, in its delicate and complicated machinery, showed what great progress mechanical art had made in the East. "It had twelve gates corresponding to the twelve hours. When the hour was striking on the clock, one of the gates opened itself, from which proceeded a regular number of small brass balls; and these, falling in turn on a brazen vessel, marked the hour by the noise which they caused: the eye perceived the hour by the number of opened gates and the ear by the number of falling balls. At the twelfth hour, twelve small horsemen issued out, each through its gate, and closed them all by their momentum in their course round the dial.

The clepsydra, or water-clock, is still used in some countries; but, the flow of water being affected by temperature and barometric pressure, the pendulum has superseded it in modern times.

The invention of pendulum-clocks is, by some, ascribed to Pacificus, Arch-deacon of Verona, in the ninth century; and by others to Boethius, in the early part of the sixth. The Saracens are said to have had clocks moved by weights in the eleventh century; and, as Dante applies the term to a machine which struck the hours, clocks must have been known in Italy at the end of the thirteenth, or beginning of the fourteenth, century. The most ancient clock of which there is any certain record was erected in a tower of the palace of Charles V, King of France, in 1364, by Henry de Wyck, a German artist. A clock was erected at Strasbourg, in 1370, at Courtray, about the same time, and at Speyer in 1395.

The invention of the pendulum was suggested to Galileo by a circumstance somewhat similar to that which started Newton's mind to the discovery of the theory of gravitation.

When Galileo was standing one day in the Metropolitan Church of

Pisa, he observed a lamp, which was suspended from the ceiling, and which had been moved by accident, swing backwards and forwards. Thousands of people might have observed it before; but Galileo, noticing the regularity with which it moved, reflected upon it until he was enabled to perfect the method of measuring time now in use by means of a wheel and pendulum. Watches are said to have been made at Nuremberg as early as 1477, but the watches of that early date bear a very small resemblance to those now in use. Some were immensely large, and some so small that they could be fitted into the top of a walking-stick. As time-keepers, they could have been of very little value until the application of the spiral spring, invented by Hooke, in 1658.

THE TAJ MAHAL

This magnificent mausoleum in Agra (or, as it is sometimes called, Akbarabad), India, was erected by Shah Jehan, to the memory of his favorite queen.

It is octagonal in form; the four sides which face the cardinal points being one hundred and thirty feet long, the others much smaller. It is built of the finest Jeypore marble, finely polished; and all the beautiful tints of the stone are retained.

The roof is seventy feet high, and expands in the centre into a noble dome seventy feet in diameter, and one hundred and twenty feet high; and when to the height of the dome is added the height of the building and terraces, it shows that the gilt crescent at its apex is two hundred and seventy feet from the ground level. This mausoleum is inlaid with jasper, cornelian, turquoise, agate, onyx, amethysts, and sapphires; and it is said that the whole of the Koran is inlaid within its stately walls.

The sarcophagus of the sultana is in a vault directly under the centre of the building, and near it that of the shah.

There is no part of the exterior, except the dome, that is not covered with arabesques and inscriptions in black marble on the polished white of the surface.

The great dome produces an echo that travellers pronounce to be the finest in the world.

Of this echo, Bayard Taylor has said,—

> "A single musical note uttered by the voice floats and soars overhead in long, delicious undulations, fading

> away so slowly, that you hear it after it is silent, as you
> see, or seem to see, a lark you have been watching, after
> it is swallowed up in the blue vault of heaven."

This magnificent edifice was commenced in 1630, and finished in 1647; and, during the seventeen years, twenty thousand workmen were constantly employed upon it. Every province of the empire contributed to its adornment, sending precious stones, of which a list was preserved in the public archives.

Notwithstanding these free gifts and the forced labor of the workmen, the total cost was about twelve millions of dollars.

An English writer has said,—

> "Were there nothing to be seen in India but the Taj, it
> would be, for an artist or an architect, sufficient com-
> pensation for the long voyage; for no pen can do justice
> to its incomparable beauty, and its astonishing grandeur."

A TAHITI FEAST

James Norman Hall

The people of Rutiaro worked, as they had always done, only under the pressure of necessity. Their simple needs being satisfied, their inertia was a thing to marvel at. I have often seen them sitting for hours at a time, moving only with the shadows that sheltered them. There was something awe-inspiring in their immobility, in their attitudes of profound reverie. I felt at times that I was living in a land under a perpetual enchantment of silence and sleep. These periods of calm—or, as some would say, sheer laziness—were usually brought to an end by Puarei. It was fascinating to watch him throwing off the enchantment, so gradual was the process, and so strange the contrast when he was thoroughly awake and had roused the village from its long sleep. Then would follow a period of activity: fishing, copra making, canoe building—whatever there was to do would be accomplished, not speedily, perhaps, but smoothly, with no waste effort. My house was built during such a period. I was wondering whether I was ever to have the promised dwelling. Then, one afternoon when I was absent on a shell-collecting expedition, the village set out en masse for Soul Eaters' Island, cut the timbers, plaited the palm fronds, erected, swept and garnished my dwelling and were at the village island again before I myself had returned. That task finished, here they were back again for the house-warming festival, and the energy spent in preparing for it would have more than loaded a ninety-ton trading schooner with copra. I couldn't flatter myself that all of this was done solely to give me pleasure, and, furthermore, I knew that an unusually long interval of fasting called for compensation in the way of feasting. . . .

Canoes were arriving during this time, one of them loaded with pigs and chickens, the most important part of the feast to come. Some of the chickens, having been insecurely tethered, escaped. Like the dogs of the islands, the chickens are of a wild, strangely mixed breed, and they took to the air with sturdy wings. The chase began at once but it was hopeless. Soul Eaters' Island is five hundred yards long by three hundred broad, and there is another, on the opposite side of the pass leading to the open sea, which is more than a mile long. We made frantic efforts to prevent them from reaching it. It was to no purpose; several hours of captivity had made them wary. The last we saw of them they were in flight over the wide pass separating the two islands.

Knowing the wholesomeness of the Tuamotuan appetite I could understand why the loss of the fowls was regarded seriously. A dozen remained, and there were the pigs; nevertheless there was a gloomy shaking of heads as we returned from our fruitless chase. In this emergency I contributed some one-pound tins of beef and salmon, most of my stock of substantial provisions for the adventure in solitude, but I could see that Puarei as well as the others regarded this as a mere relish, an acceptable but light course of hors d'oeuvres. Fortunately, there was at hand an inexhaustible reservoir of food—the sea, and we prepared to go there for further supplies. I never lost an opportunity to witness those fish-spearing expeditions. The native spears are true sportsman's weapons, provided with a single unbarbed dart, bound with sinnet to a slender shaft from eight to ten feet long. Their water goggles, like their spears, they make for themselves. They are somewhat like an airman's goggles, discs of clear glass fitted in brass rims, with an inner cushion of rubber which cups closely around the eyes, preventing the entrance of water. Thus equipped, with their pareus girded into loin-cloths, half a dozen of the younger men dived into the lagoon passage and swam out to sea. . . .

We returned with the canoe filled with fish: square-nosed tingatingas, silvery tamures, brown-spotted kitos, gnareas—we had more than made good the loss of the chickens. The fish were quickly cleaned, wrapped in green leaves, and placed in the earth ovens with the other food. The table was already set, or, rather, the cloth of green fronds was laid on the sand near the beach. Down the center of it were scattered my tins of corned beef and salmon, and at each place was the half of a coconut shell filled with raw fish in a sauce of miti haari—salted coconut milk—and a green coconut for drinking. When at last the feast was ready I heard Puarei calling, "Haere mai to maa," and went out to join the others. Great piles of baked fish, pork, and chicken, steaming from the ovens, were heaped up along the center of the table, so called, and the mounds of bread were stacked like cannon balls. These were prepared in the native fashion— lumps of boiled dough the size of large grapefruit. One might think that the hardiest stomach would ache at the prospect of receiving it, but the Low Island stomach is of ostrichlike hardihood, and, after fasting, it demands quantity rather than quality in food.

A DAY IN JENNY LIND'S LIFE

Many suppose that Jenny Lind's tour in America is, and is to be, one of uninterrupted pleasure and profit; but we opine they will change their opinion when they read the following report of the experience of a single day in New York—the day previous to her leaving for this city, and after she had given away in charity to thousands of deserving objects no less than thirty thousand dollars. We extract from the Home Journal:—

But while all these sufferers were receiving her bounty, and she was settling with banks and managers for the payments—what else was her life made up of on that day?

It was half past nine in the morning, and three servants of the hotel, and two of her own servants, had been ordered to guard her rooms till she could eat her breakfast. Well-dressed ladies cannot be stopped by servants, in this country, however, and her drawing-room was already half full of visitors, "on particular business," who had crowded past, insisting on entrance. Most of them were applicants for charities, some for autographs, some to offer acquaintance, but none, of course, with the least claim whatever on her pocket or her time. A lady friend, who was admitted by her servant, saw the onslaught of these intruders, as she rose from her breakfast, (fatigued and dispirited as she always is after the effort and nervous excitement of a concert;) and this friend was not a little astonished at her humble and submissive endurance.

First came a person who had sent a musical box for her to look at, and, "as she had kept it," he wanted the money immediately. Jenny knew nothing of it; but the maid was called, who pointed to one, which had been left mysteriously in the room, and the man was at liberty to take it away, but would not do it, of course, without remonstrance and argument. Then advanced the lady beggars, who, in so many instances, have "put the screw to her," in the same way, that without particularizing, we must describe them as a class. To such unexamined and unexpected applications Miss Lind has usually offered twenty or thirty dollars as the shortest way to be left to herself. In almost every instance, she has had this sum returned to her, with some reproachful and disparaging remark, such as, "We did not expect this pittance from *you*." "We have been mistaken in your character, madam, for we had heard you were generous." "This, from Miss Lind, is too little to accept, and not worthy of you." "Excuse us—we came for a donation, not for alms"—these, and similar speeches, of which, we are assured, Jenny Lind has had one or more specimens every day of her visit to New York. With one or two such visitors, on the morning we speak of, were mingled applicants for musical employment; passionate female admirers, who had come to express their raptures to her; a dozen ladies with albums; one or two with things they had worked for her, for which, by unmistakable tokens, they expected diamond rings in return; one who had come indignantly to know why a note containing a poem had not been answered; and constant messages, meantime, from those who had professional and other authorized errands requiring answers. Letters and notes came in at the rate of one every other minute.

This sort of "audience" lasted at Miss Lind's rooms *all day*! To use her own expression, she was "torn in pieces"; and it was by those whom nothing would keep out. A police force would have protected her, but, while she habitually declined the calls and attentions of fashionable society, she was in constant dread of driving more humble claimants from her door. She submitted, *every day*, to the visits of strangers, as far as strength and her professional duties would any way endure; but as her stay in the place drew to a close, the pressure became so pertinacious and overwhelming as to exceed what may be borne by human powers of attention, human spirits and human nerves.

INAUGURAL COLOR

Bert Collier

Only members of Congress heard George Washington's first inaugural address. All rose as he entered the chamber and stood in respect during his entire speech. Washington was so flustered by this esteem that he could scarcely read from his manuscript. "There were tears in many eyes," recalled one eyewitness.

Plain Thomas Jefferson walked to his inauguration from a house near the Capitol where he boarded. After his speech he walked back home and took his regular place at the table. Other boarders had already begun their dinner without him.

John Quincy Adams, inaugurated in Statuary Hall, had Marquis de Lafayette as a spectator.

Four years later President Adams refused to appear with his successor, Andrew Jackson, whose inauguration was more a brawl than a ball. His followers wrecked the White House and drank enough punch to float Old Ironsides.

William Henry Harrison, Old Tippecanoe, took office in a depression and couldn't afford the money to bring his wife and family to Washington for the occasion. He died before they got there.

When word of his passing reached John Tyler at Williamsburg, Va., the Vice President was too broke to pay his own passage to Washington. Some friends passed the hat and got him to the White House to take over the government.

Tragedy marred the inauguration of Franklin Pierce, whose son had died a few days before his term began. Pierce slipped into Washington incognito to avoid the reception committee. Neither his sorrowing First Lady nor his Vice President was beside him at the ceremony. His Vice President died without reaching Washington. The wife of Millard Fillmore, his predecessor, died of exposure to the chill weather of that sad day.

When U. S. Grant became President the thermometer stood at 4 below zero and the bandsmen were too cold to strike up a tune.

Everything that Abraham Lincoln did seemed to make history. When he took office on the eve of a civil war, four future Presidents—Rutherford B. Hayes, James A. Garfield, Chester A. Arthur and Benjamin Harrison, were in the audience.

Lincoln also managed to kiss 34 ladies, representing each state in the soon-to-be-tested union.

One of the most thrilling inaugurations was Franklin D. Roosevelt's first. The American people were frightened. Banks were closing. Bread lines were long.

His head bare in the chill wind, FDR called on the nation to move forward with courage and decision.

"So first of all," he said, "let me assert my firm belief that the only thing we have to fear is fear itself—nameless, unreasoning, unjustified terror which paralyzes needed efforts to convert retreat into advance."

SPIDER SILK – WONDER STUFF OF NATURE

Donald Culross Peattie

The other day I had my first chance to watch a spider spinning in daytime. Her name was Miranda, according to my scientific books, and she was black with yellow bands. This particular specimen was a young female; hence she was still slender, not having lost her figure from egg-bearing, and her long slim legs were still handsomely clad in the black-and-yellow bands that denote youth in this species.

She had already built two sides of her triangular framework, of the heavy tough thread spiders use for that purpose. At the moment she was starting to make the third side. To do this she climbed back up the perpendicular line she had spun, all the time reeling out a new line, anchored at the base of her perpendicular line and held away from the old one with her hind legs. It looked like thread hanging from the needle of a woman sewing, as she laboriously made her way to the top, then walked down the inclined plane of the other completed side of her triangle. She did not walk upright, like a tight-rope walker, but slung herself underneath the wire, like a tree sloth inching along. When she got to the end she stopped, and reefed in her slack that she had been carrying and spinning, until it was taut. Then she fastened it to the twig from which she started, with a little dab of mucilage-like matter from her glands, and so the third side of her triangular loom was complete.

Here she took a rest, and well she might. She had now to solve the problem of making the radial lines, or spokes, of her wheel. To do this she walked out to the middle of the top side of her triangle, made fast there the beginning of a line and let herself down to the lower side, where she fastened the end of the line she carried. Then she crawled back up and located the center, by what capacity to measure distance we can only guess. This was to be the hub of her wheel. Here she fastened a new line, which she carried free as she climbed to the top of her triangle, crawled a way along the top of her frame, took in her slack line, and fastened it. Now she had a radius, or, counting the two halves of her first diametrical lines, she now had three radii. And, going back each time to the center, she laboriously built one radius after the other.

But not in regular succession, Oh, no, our little lady welder is too smart for that. She does not wish to put too many stresses on one side of the frame at once. Instead, she built first on one side, then on another, then to the right of center, then to the left. After that she rested, built a little hub, a sort of damask platform, her future headquarters, and began to fill in more radii, working now on one side, now on the opposite, as a man tightens nuts on an auto wheel.

When she had nineteen radii in place, Miranda stepped slowly around just outside her hub, forefeet on one radius, hindfeet on another, pacing off the angles between them. At first she was satisfied. Then she found one angle that was twice as wide as it should be. Quickly she filled it in with a twentieth radius; that seemed to be the number that pleased her. Perhaps Miranda could count, but even if not she could do something much more wonderful—she could measure angles, about eighteen degrees in this case, far more exactly than I could do it without a graduated scale! She was, indeed, an able engineer.

Miranda now took another rest. Her body, if not her head, was tired. The human head is the seat of thought. But who can say where the instincts (which replace thought in the lower animals) reside? Who can say where they come from, how they are handed down? The art of weaving by spiders descends, primarily, on the distaff side, from mother to daughter. But presumably Miranda never saw her mother weave a net, and she could not have learned by imitation if she had. Her first bit of workmanship was as good as any she will ever make. And Miranda, in her turn, will never see her children as anything but eggs. Yet she will hand on her exquisite craft to them with the very chromosomes of her reproductive cells.

Her rest over, Miranda began to weave outward from the hub a spiral band, in the nature of a scaffolding to brace the radii for the stresses she was about to put on them. She gave the spiral four and a half turns.

Then, walking deliberately out to the end of one of the lower radii, she began for the first time to spin a sticky stuff; I could see it come gushing from her glands, glistening like dew. It is elastic, too, so that it will not snap; indeed, the victim who gets into its toils will merely entangle himself more with every exertion. Miranda lays a few bands of it on the bottom half of the web, a few bands at the top. Then she goes to the bottom again and builds more concentric lines of what is, in essence, so much sticky fly-paper. Thus, working her way to the center, Miranda encounters the spiral scaffolding and begins to tear it out, as a tailor tears out basting threads. She does not want to leave this nice, dry, escape ladder for any fly to use! As fast as she removes it she replaces it with the sticky loops. But she stops well short of the hub, her personal living quarters.

At last the little miracle is finished, the toil of four and a half hours, counting brief rests. It is the most complex structure built by any living creature. A bird's nest is clumsy beside it, and the vaunted comb of the honeybee monotonous and simple in comparison. The spider web is the work of a little engineer without diploma, of a geometrician who never heard of Euclid, of a weaver whose design never falters.

THE MYSTERY OF MIGRATION

Alan Devoe

They are gone now. No robins carol from the fence posts; no medley of catbird tunes issues from the blackberry tangles; no woodcocks rise on whirring wings from our swamplands and marshes. The populace of birds is now meager and tuneless. Once again the annual mystery has come about. Once again the Summer birds have vanished.

It is a phenomenon older than the memory of man. Ages ago Ojibways and Pequots tilted bronze faces to the sun to watch the wild geese go honking southward, and tribal story-tellers invented legends to explain the mystery. White men of science wrote solemn monographs asserting that in Winter the birds retired to hollow trees, to hibernate until Spring like woodchucks, and so erudite a man as Dr. Samuel Johnson supposed that the English swallows spent the Winter sleeping in the river-mud of the Thames. The theories were innumerable and unconfirmed. They still are. We are not now quite so naïve, of course, as to fancy that the birds spend the Winter asleep in caves or river-bottoms, and we know quite well that they migrate to warmer climates. We have checked their routes, and clocked their arrivals and departures, and graphed their journeyings with great accuracy. And, having done this, we can still only stand awed and wondering. What impulse is abroad on Autumn nights, to tell these orioles and phoebes and sandpipers that the time for traveling is at hand? What secret inner knowledge guides these millions of wings on their long intricate courses? It is not known.

The preparations for migration begin long before the coming of the Fall. They begin, in a real sense, with the molt, in latter Summer when the care of the fledglings is over; for it is then that worn, frayed feathers are replaced by new ones and the bird's light-boned body acquires fresh buoyancy. Like many another happening in fields and forests, the molting of the birds is so casual and unspectacular an event that hardly one man in a thousand even remarks its occurrence, but it deserves rank among the minor miracles. Two feathers, and two feathers only, are shed at one time, and they are shed with perfect symmetry. The middle feather of each wing is the first to go. When the new replacement-feathers for these gaps have achieved half their growth, another pair of quills loosens and is shed. With perfect precision the process continues, until a whole new plumage has come into being. So gradual is the process, so nicely contrived, that at no time is more than a single pair of feathers missing; at no time is the bird's flight-mechanism unbalanced or impaired. And in the case of certain of our species the miracle is of an even more arresting kind. There is the metamorphosis, for instance, which the male scarlet tanagers undergo. Before the molting-time their flame-red plumage affords one of the gaudiest colors in our countryside. When the molt has ended, they are arrayed in dingy green. It will hide them, on their southward flight, from the sharp preying eyes of hawks.

There is a second preparation for the great Autumn flight, and it consists of smaller flights in the nature of trials. Ever since July the adult male robins have been leading their fledglings to communal roosting-places, usually deep-hidden in the leafy woods, and the grackles and swallows and starlings have similarly massed together in tremendous hordes. At every daybreak the great flocks issue forth, and all day they wheel and veer together through the Autumn sky, returning at nightfall to the place of their communal sleep. This is the time when wings are trained and strengthened, when flight-patterns are established and co-ordinated, when there is perfected that deep and subtle mass-harmony of motion which no scientist can pretend to understand. Uncountable thousands of gulls, of swifts, of cowbirds are learning one of the most ancient and most unfathomable techniques in nature.

There is a third and final preparation. It is the same preparation which skunks and bears and woodchucks make before their Winter sleep. It is the taking on of surplus nourishment, the building of a reserve of fat. In obedience to a dim behest, the flycatchers now enormously increase their consumption of tree-hoppers and crickets, the tanagers hunt crane-flies more voraciously than ever, and the dried weed-seeds in man's pastures and gardens are stripped by flocks of finches and sparrows. The birds are insuring that they shall have a reservoir of strength on which to draw, should there be a scarcity of food along their flight-line. If the findings of dissectionists are significant, the tiny brains in these small feathered skulls can hardly be capable of shrewd foresighted reasoning, or indeed of any clear prevision of the journey ahead. The urge which moves them must have another source than mind. No man, yet, can give it any name.

In late July the bobolinks vanish. They are among the first to go. The route of their travels has been fully mapped, and it is known that they are on the wing for nearly two months before they reach the small patch of river-watered jungle which for inscrutable reasons they deem the most suitable wintering place. They pass through South Carolina in the latter part of August; at the turn of the month, through Florida; in September they are in Cuba. Sometimes they cover four hundred miles in a single night, and always they press southward ... down the Andes, across the Amazon, over the great Brazilian plains. When at last they halt, it is in the marsh-lands on the upper Paraguay River.

The departure of the bobolinks is followed presently, in latter August and throughout September, by the going of the flycatchers, the vireos, the warblers. Our Autumn woods are thronged then with voyaging companies of birds. By October the last of them has passed and disappeared, and by November there have arrived to take their places such Winter visitants as juncos and tree sparrows, crossbills and pine grosbeaks ... a colorless and relatively songless little band, but hardily equipped for clinging to frozen sumac-stalks in the whipping January wind and foraging in snow-drifted pastures for stray thistle-seeds. They have nested and passed the Summer to the north of us, some of them as far north as Hudson Bay and the Arctic coast, and they will return to those bleak regions before our first hepaticas bloom.

Prodigious as are the travels of the birds—the tiny blackpoll warblers voyaging five thousand miles, the scimitar-winged nighthawks migrating from the Yukon to Argentina—the rate of speed is in most cases not extremely high. The average is usually some thirty or forty miles a day, and on the return-flights in the Spring may be hardly more than twenty. The trek is leisurely and often interrupted, with side-excursions to feeding-grounds en route and sometimes total rests for several days. But sometimes, too, there are flights of five hundred miles without a single pause, as when the ruby-throated hummingbirds cross the Gulf of Mexico to Yucatan, and it is known that the golden plovers which fly from Alaska to Hawaii cover the whole span of two thousand miles without a respite.

Men used to be puzzled by the fact that, although the migrating birds must number many millions, only occasional flocks are seen passing over head. We know now why it is. We know that only the swiftest travelers—those species that need have no fear of hawks—undertake to fly by day. The rest fly only in the night. On a night in Autumn, when the moon is full, it is possible to watch with field-glasses the endless passing, high above the earth, of feathered legions. It is even possible, if the watcher be in a woods or other quiet place, to hear faintly the remote music of the flight . . . the soft whistle of thrushes, the thin fluting of woodcocks. It is not an experience that the listener readily forgets.

Why do the birds migrate at all? We shall have to be very much wiser than at present before we know. Perhaps it began in the glacial era, when the Arctic ice-fields advanced southward; perhaps it is chiefly a physiological problem, subtly allied to periodic changes in the food supply. By what sense, or combination of senses, do thrushes and snipe and meadowlarks find their way unerringly along complex thousand-mile routes which no man could possibly follow without directional instruments, and what inner bidding moves the individual members of the flocks to wheel and turn and dip in unbroken unison?

It has been supposed, in answer to the first question, that perhaps the great mountain-ranges and water-courses are the guides; and on the second question some ornithologists have theorized that perhaps the birds possess—as almost certainly the ant-world does—some sense that is outside our human ken entirely.

This much only can we say with surety: that every Fall and every Spring the woods and sky present us, for the looking and the listening, with a magic pageantry of beating wings, and with a reminder—not unwelcome in a time as bitterly confused as ours—that the ancient unknowable harmonies of the universe still endure.

BARNUM'S AMERICAN MUSEUM

M. R. Werner

Besides his notorious curiosities, Barnum enlarged the lecture room of the museum, and presented regular dramatic performances there. He felt that what he called the "moral drama" would pay better than anything that was attractively immoral; and the "moral drama" was more palatable to his own conscience, for from childhood until his last year he had a sincere religious fear of impropriety in public presentation. The greatest manifestation of Barnum's genius for theatrical management in this country was his instinctive realization that the largest part of the community is eminently respectable in public, and it was what, more than anything else, contributed to his financial success, that Barnum catered to the reputable who still retained vestiges of curiosity. Many persons who would not be seen in a theater visited regularly the museum lecture room—Barnum would never consent to calling it a theater—where the moral dramas of *Joseph and His Brethren, Moses,* and *The Drunkard* were performed. One afternoon a New England lady walked into Barnum's office and sat down on the sofa. She examined Barnum curiously for a minute, and then remarked that he looked "much like other common folks, after all."

"Mr. Barnum," she said, "I never went to any museum before, nor to any place of amusement or public entertainment, except our school exhibitions; and I have sometimes felt that they even may be wicked, because some parts of the dialogue seemed frivolous; but I have heard so much of your 'moral dramas,' and the great good you are doing for the rising generation, that I thought I must come here and see for myself."

At that moment the gong announcing the beginning of the show in the lecture room rang. The lady jumped from the sofa. "Are the services about to commence?" she asked anxiously.

There was the noise of shuffling feet as the crowd hurried to the seats. "Yes," said Barnum, "the congregation is now going up." Barnum wrote concerning his moral performances: "I resolved, as far as possible, to elevate and refine such amusements as I dispensed. Even Shakespeare's dramas were shorn of their objectionable features when placed upon my stage."

E. A. Sothern, Tony Pastor, and Barney Williams received their first stage training on the stage of Barnum's lecture room. On holidays performances were given every hour throughout the afternoon and evening, and Barnum is given credit in histories of the theater for originating the continuous performance, which has since proved so popular in vaudeville.

These continuous programs on holidays were very popular, and on the first Fourth of July of Barnum's management of the museum so many people visited the building that the sale of tickets was stopped. This Barnum described as "exceedingly harrowing to my feelings." He noted sadly that thousands were waiting outside to purchase tickets, and that those inside did not seem in a hurry to leave. Barnum ordered his carpenter to build a temporary flight of stairs at the rear of the building, which opened out in Ann Street. At three o'clock that afternoon this exit was opened, but much money had been lost. When, on the next St. Patrick's Day, Barnum was informed in advance that the Irish population intended to visit the museum in large numbers, he opened the rear exit again. Before noon the museum was crowded, and the sale of tickets had to be stopped. Barnum rushed to the rear exit and asked how many hundreds had passed out that way. He was told that three persons had used it during the whole morning, for the visitors had brought their dinners and intended to remain in the museum all day and night. Barnum hurriedly called his sign painter and ordered a sign in large letters:

To the Egress

This was nailed over the rear door. Some of the Irish visitors spelled out the sign, "To the Aigress," and many remarked, "Sure, that's an animal we haven't seen," and found themselves on Ann Street, with no chance of re-entering the museum.

It was on his first Fourth of July in the museum that Barnum exhibited another instance of his ingenuity in the face of a difficulty. In order to make the most of the holiday by utilizing the publicity value of the American flag, Barnum fastened a string of large flags across Broadway, tying one end to the museum and the other to a tree in St. Paul's churchyard. Several days before Independence Day, Barnum had visited the vestrymen of St. Paul's and requested permission to use the tree in the churchyard, but they called his request insulting and talked of sacrilege. On the Fourth of July he gave orders for the flags to be attached, as he had originally planned. . . . The flags attracted huge crowds, and at half-past nine in the morning two indignant vestrymen entered Barnum's office and demanded that they be detached from their church immediately. Barnum answered pleasantly that he would go into the street with them and see what could be done. He looked at the flags and remarked solemnly that they were a beautiful sight. He argued with the vestrymen that he always had stopped his Free Music for the Million when they held their services, and he merely requested this favor in return. One of the vestrymen lost patience and shouted that unless Barnum took down the flags within ten minutes he would cut them down. The crowd was attracted by the angry gestures. Barnum suddenly took off his coat, rolled up his shirt sleeves, and shouted in his sonorous voice, tinged with anger, loudly enough for all in the crowd to overhear, "I should like to see you dare to cut down the American flag on the Fourth of July; you must be a Britisher to make such a threat, but I'll show you a thousand pairs of

Yankee hands in two minutes, if you dare to take down the stars and stripes on this great birthday of American freedom." In a moment the vestrymen were surrounded by several heavy, angry men, who threatened varied punishment. The poor bewildered vestrymen disappeared quietly from the crowd, and Barnum with obsequious smiles enjoyed his triumph.

Barnum was apparently indefatigable in his personal interest in the museum and in his personal efforts to make it ever more popular. He often appeared before his audiences with stunts or speeches, because he knew he could entertain them, and because he liked to think that they were interested in him. When Peale, of Peale's Museum, presented an actor who pretended to conduct experiments in mesmerism, Barnum personally conducted his own experiments in animal magnetism from the stage of the moral lecture room. A young girl, carefully trained in advance, sat on the stage. Barnum made a few passes with his hand in front of her, and she was then under his control; she raised her hands when he requested her to do so, grimaced when he put tobacco in his mouth, and smiled when he ate candy. Then it was his practice to turn to the audience and offer to forfeit fifty dollars if he could not put any member of the audience in the same state within five minutes. At the end of three minutes the volunteer was, of course, wide awake. Barnum would look at his watch, remark that he had two minutes, which was plenty of time, and offer to demonstrate to the audience that a person mesmerized was a person insensible to pain, by cutting off one of the fingers of the small girl, who was still asleep. He would take out his knife, feel the sharp edge, and turn toward the girl, who had meanwhile fled behind the scenes in a fright that delighted the audience. Barnum would say in an astonished tone of voice, "Then she was wide awake, was she?"

His volunteer from the audience usually answered, "Of course she was, she was wide awake all the time."

"I suppose so," was Barnum's answer, "and, my dear sir, I promised that you should be 'in the same state' at the end of five minutes, and as I believe you are so, I do not forfeit fifty dollars." This type of trick never seemed to anger, rather than to amuse, the audiences.

No such trickery was too much for Barnum, and he carried out a similar deception on a public scale with no harm to his reputation and no qualms of conscience. In June of 1843 he attended the Bunker Hill celebration, where Daniel Webster delivered a stirring oration, but Barnum was just as interested in an old canvas tent near the Bunker Hill Monument as he was in the ceremonies of the day. He found in that tent a herd of fifteen one-year-old calf buffaloes, which he immediately purchased for seven hundred dollars; a scheme by which he could utilize these buffaloes had hatched in his mind almost as soon as he saw them. The animals were docile and tired, for they had been driven east from the Western plains. At Barnum's order they were brought to New York and then transported to a New Jersey barn near Hoboken. Barnum hired their former owner, C. D. French, to take care of the animals for thirty dollars per month, because French understood the lasso. The newspapers shortly afterward announced that a herd of wild buffaloes, captured in the Rocky Mountains, was passing through New York soon on its way to Europe, in charge of the very men who had captured the animals, and during the next few days suggestions appeared in the newspapers that it would be a fine thing for New York if the owners of these buffaloes could be induced to present a buffalo chase on a racecourse near New York, demonstrating to the Eastern population the use of the lasso and the ferocity of the buffalo. One of the correspondents expressed it as his sincere opinion that it would be worth a dollar to see such a sight, and that he for one would be willing to pay that amount. Another estimated that no less than fifty thousand persons would be interested in a buffalo chase without the danger but with the thrills, and other obliging correspondents suggested places for the hunt, including the racecourse at Hoboken, New Jersey. Before long advertisements appeared in all the newspapers, and handbills were circulated throughout New York announcing that there would be a

> Grand Buffalo Hunt, Free of Charge—At Hoboken, on Thursday, August 31, at 3, 4, and 5 o'clock P.M. Mr. C. D. French, one of the most daring and experienced hunters of the West, has arrived thus far on his way to Europe with a herd of buffaloes, captured by himself, near Santa Fe. He will exhibit a method of hunting the wild buffaloes, and throwing the lasso, by which the animals were captured in their most wild and untamed state. This is perhaps one of the most exciting and difficult feats that can be performed, requiring at the same time the most expert horsemanship and greatest skill and dexterity. Every man, woman, and child can here witness the wild sports of the Western prairies, as the exhibition is to be free to all, and will take place on the extensive grounds and racecourse of Messrs. Stevens, within a few rods of the Hoboken ferry.

The public was further assured that "no possible danger need be apprehended, as a double railing has been put around the whole course, to prevent the possibility of the buffaloes approaching the multitude."

These announcements mystified and delighted New York. Who was the city's anonymous benefactor? Who supplied such entertainment free of charge and kept modestly in the background? Barnum meanwhile had purchased the rights to the receipts of all the ferryboats which crossed between New York and Hoboken on August 31, 1843, and extra ferryboats were provided for the day. The weather was clear, and the boats, under the administration of Captain Barnum, were crowded to the railings with adventurers. Twenty-four thousand people went to Hoboken that day. They stood on the railings and clutched the awnings to support themselves, and each paid six and a quarter cents going and the same to return.

When the crowds arrived in Hoboken, they waited in the arena for the wild buffaloes, who finally appeared in reluctant and tame parade of their alleged ferocity. The animals were thin and pale from lack of nourishment during their first master's patronage, and although they had been crammed with extra rations of oats for several days they refused at the outset to be wild. C. D. French, "one of the most daring and experienced hunters of the West," dressed and painted as an Indian, poked his wild buffaloes with a goad, but the most they would do for the twenty-four thousand interested spectators was to trot. There was much laughter and shouting at their recalcitrance, and the noise made by the crowd frightened the nervous buffaloes so much that they galloped from the inclosure in terror and threw the spectators, who believed that they had actually grown wild, into a panic. The buffaloes took refuge from their oppressors in a nearby swamp, and all that C. D. French could do would not persuade them to return to the racecourse. He finally lassoed one of them, and entertained the crowd with this beast, and with exhibitions of lassoing on horses and horsemen. No one suspected the ferryboat arrangement, and no one suspected Barnum. It was after midnight when the last of the crowds succeeded in getting home from Hoboken, but, apparently, a good time was had by all, for there were no riots, and the receipts of the ferryboats turned over to Barnum amounted to $3,500. After the exhibition Barnum sent his buffaloes to Camden, New Jersey, where they attracted Philadelphia crowds in the same manner. Some of the herd then went to England and were sold, while the others were fattened on a farm and sold for buffalo steak in Fulton Market at fifty cents per pound. In order that the museum might profit by the advertisement, Barnum made public his responsibility for the Great Buffalo Hunt.

Sometime after his success with the buffaloes, Barnum presented the first Wild West Show New York had seen. He engaged a band of Indians from Iowa, among whom were impressive men, beautiful squaws, and two or three papooses. The Indians appeared on the stage of the moral lecture room in real war dances, which they performed with all the vigor and realistic interpretation of their savage origin. In fact, it was necessary to rope them in, for fear that in their frenzy toward the end of a dance they might forget that they were merely players, and make for members of the audience; for Barnum's Indians had never before seen a railroad or a steamboat, and scalps were not yet obsolete in their minds. They seemed thoroughly under the impression that they were not acting but living, which in one particular caused the proprietor of the American Museum some expense. After a week of war dances, Barnum suggested a change of program, including an Indian wedding dance. The interpreter explained, and the chief agreed. On Monday afternoon when the first change to the wedding dance was to take place, Barnum was informed by the chief that he must supply a red woolen blanket as a wedding present for the bridegroom to give to the father of the bride, an inviolable Indian custom. After each performance the chief insisted that he must have another new blanket for the next performance, and when Barnum attempted to explain that the wedding was only "make believe," the chief gave forth an ugly "Ugh!" terrifying Barnum into spending $120 for twelve red woolen blankets for the rest of the week.

These special exhibitions were supplemented by flower shows, dog shows, and poultry shows at the museum, and Barnum, soon after he became manager, decided that he must have a baby show. He organized such an exhibition with graduated scales of prizes for triplets, the fattest baby, the most beautiful baby, and the handsomest twins. The main prize of one hundred dollars for the most perfect baby was a source of considerable difficulty. Barnum thought that it would be a fine thing for him to award this prize himself, a fine thing in publicity for himself, and also for the baby, who could say in later years that he had been personally selected as unique by P. T. Barnum. In later years he did meet many men and women who claimed that honor, but at the time of the awards the defeated mothers stormed about Barnum, and their indignation could not be appeased until he announced that he would award a second prize of one hundred dollars to the baby selected by a committee of mothers. Whereupon each mother became the enemy of every other, and Barnum's one hundred dollars was safe. In deciding future baby contests, however, he sent in written reports and was not to be disturbed for the rest of the day.

In November, 1842, Barnum stopped one night at the Franklin Hotel in Bridgeport, Connecticut, which was kept by his brother, Philo F. Barnum. His brother mentioned that there was a dwarf in Bridgeport, who played daily in the streets and was accepted by the rest of the population as a natural curiosity. Barnum asked his brother to bring the child to the Franklin Hotel, and as soon as he saw this dwarf he realized that here was a natural curiosity who could be transformed by instruction and publicity into a unique and profitable one. The child was the smallest Barnum had ever seen, and was in excellent health, without any deformities. He was two feet, one inch in height and weighed fifteen pounds. His hair was flaxen, and his eyes dark; his cheeks were pink and his whole appearance gave the impression of health, symmetry, and whimsical charm on a lovely, diminutive scale. He was very bashful, and Barnum only learned after difficulty that his name was Charles S. Stratton, and that he was five years old. Barnum visited Mr. and Mrs. Sherwood E. Stratton, the child's parents, and after some persuasion they consented to exhibit their son at Barnum's museum for three dollars per week and board for himself and his mother. Barnum hired him for four weeks only, because at the time he was doubtful whether a five-year-old child who was only two feet in height might not grow before long to a normality that would make him mediocre.

The dwarf and his mother arrived in New York on Thanksgiving Day, 1852, and Barnum had something to be thankful for that day. Mrs. Stratton was astonished and somewhat annoyed when she noticed that her son was announced in large handbills as "General Tom Thumb," a dwarf eleven years of age, "just arrived from England." The "just arrived from England" was the first instance of a method Barnum often repeated. He realized early in his career the love of the American mind for an importation, and he never advertised anything as domestic if he could possibly deceive his patrons into believing that he had incurred much trouble and expense by importing it from abroad, where its popularity was always stupendous. He hoped, patriotically, in his autobiography that such deception might check "our disgraceful preference for foreigners."

Barnum made his dwarf eleven years old for fear that public might not believe that a child five years old would not grow beyond his present height. In the various pamphlets concerning the life of General Tom Thumb, which were sold at his exhibitions, it is recorded that when he was born he weighed nine pounds, two ounces, more than the average weight of a newborn baby, and that at five months he had ceased to grow and weighed only fifteen pounds. His weight of fifteen pounds and his height of two feet, one inch, were said to have remained unchanged from the age of five months until the age of five years and for many years thereafter.

The change of name from Charles S. Stratton to General Tom Thumb was a stroke of Barnum's inspiration, and it contributed largely to the General's subsequent success. Tom Thumb is the most appropriate name a dwarf ever had, and, besides, it possessed the advantage of some familiarity from the story of the legendary Tom Thumb, of whom it will be remembered:

> In Arthur's court Tom Thumb did live,
>   A man of mickle might.
> The best of all the table round,
>   And eke a doughty knight;

> His stature but an inch in height,
>   Or quarter of a span;
> Then think you not this little knight
>   Was prov'd a valiant man?

According to nursery lore, the legendary Tom Thumb was swallowed by a cow when he crossed the cow's blade of grass but was soon delivered up again from the cow's stomach, only to meet his death by a bumblebee after a series of valiant adventures. Barnum's addition of "General" to Tom Thumb enriched the name by a pompous mockery that was more valuable because of its incongruity.

General Tom Thumb was soon domesticated to the ways of public exhibition. Barnum taught his pupil day and night new jokes and old roles, which he learned quickly, for the child, according to Barnum, had a love of the ludicrous and a humorous charm. When he was ready to make his debut, Barnum took General Tom Thumb first on a tour of the newspaper offices, and even invaded the home of one newspaper editor, who happened to be eating dinner. Tom Thumb danced between the tumblers and hopped over the roast. James Gordon Bennett wrote in the *Herald* on December 15, 1842: "We were visited yesterday by the comical little gentleman who is at present holding nightly levees at the American Museum. He is certainly the smallest specimen of a man we have ever seen."

The General's popularity was immediate, and after the first four weeks' engagement was finished, Barnum re-engaged him for one year at seven dollars a week, with a bonus of fifty dollars at the end of the engagement. It is clear that neither General Tom Thumb nor his father had any idea of the value of a dwarf, and Barnum took advantage of the age of the boy and the ignorance of his father. Barnum also retained the privilege of sending the General on a tour of the country. Before the end of the year Barnum increased Tom Thumb's salary to twenty-five dollars per week, and he assures us that the General deserved the raise. Besides exhibiting frequently at the museum, where he sang songs, danced, and told stories in the pert and saucy manner of people who are too small to be slapped, General Tom Thumb was sent to other cities, where he made money for Barnum and advertised the American Museum.

At the same time as the exhibition of General Tom Thumb in New York, Barnum presented at the museum two famous giants, M. Bihin, the tall, thin French giant, and Colonel Goshen, a portly Arab. The giants were amiable enough, but jealous of each other's success, and quarreled furiously one day by engaging in a glorious bout of name-calling. They seized clubs and medieval swords on exhibition in cases, and made for each other, until Barnum interfered. He informed them that he had no objection to their fighting, maiming, or killing each other, but they were both under engagement to him, and if there was to be a duel, it must be duly advertised and take place on the stage of the lecture room. "No performance of yours would be a greater attraction, and if you kill each other, our engagement can end with your duel," Barnum assured them. The giants enjoyed the humor of the situation, and lived in peace until the end of their engagement.

After the contract with General Tom Thumb expired, Barnum engaged him for another year at fifty dollars per week and all his expenses, with the right to exhibit him in Europe. The museum was so successful and operating with so little friction after less than three years that Barnum was looking for new worlds to conquer, and he took his General under his arm and went to Europe. Passage was booked on the packet ship *Yorkshire* for Liverpool, and General Tom Thumb, his father and mother, the General's tutor, Professor Guillaudeu, and Barnum made ready to sail on January 18, 1844. Barnum made use of the General at the museum until the last moment before sailing. Advertisements appeared in the newspapers of the day announcing that the opportunity to see General Tom Thumb was rapidly slipping away. When the boat was delayed by adverse winds and tides, the General remained another day at the museum, and thousands of people visited him in a desperate attempt to get a last look. The *Evening Post* announced as an item of news on January 16, 1844:

> A few hours more remain for General Tom Thumb to be seen at the American Museum, as the packet in which he has engaged passage to England does not sail today, in consequence of the easterly winds now prevailing. He may be seen throughout the entire day and evening; and at three and seven o'clock P.M. there will be grand performances; at each of which the General appears on the stage in the same characters which have excited so much admiration and applause of late.

The next day the weather was still bad, and people stormed the museum. On the day of the sailing, January 19, General Tom Thumb was on exhibition until eleven o'clock in the morning; the boat sailed at noon. He was escorted to the dock by the municipal brass band, and more than ten thousands persons saw him off. It was estimated that more than eighty thousand persons had visited General Tom Thumb at the museum.

Suggestions for Study

1. Although this section is entitled "From Fantasy to Fact," no attempt has been made to categorize any selection as either fantasy or fact. Indeed, many of the selections, though factual, seem to be fanciful. Choose two such selections and determine why they seem to be fantasy instead of fact.

2. After reading "Old Proverbs Made New" by Stephen Leacock, find a common proverb such as "Easy does it" or "A penny saved is a penny earned." Then write about it, imitating Leacock's light style.

3. Write a short paper explaining one of Swift's epigrams.

4. Debate the various concepts of "woman" as presented in this section; then write your own essay entitled "Woman—Is She a Paradox?"

5. Some of the selections depict individuals of courage and cowardice. Find a selection that depicts courage and one that depicts cowardice. Be able to analyze the reasons for your choice; then write an essay entitled "A Coward Would Be Brave If He Had the Courage."

6. Decide what the major theme of each selection is. Be able to prove your estimate. Choose two opposing themes and contrast them. Use examples from your own experience.

Composition Topics

1. A Glimpse at My Future
2. Ghosts I Would Like to Meet
3. We Pulled a Bluff
4. A Pet Dog's Observations
5. It Was My Mistake
6. How Not to Cook
7. If My Pencil Could Speak
8. A Ride I Wouldn't Want
9. The Grass Is Greener on the Other Side
10. Marks of a Successful Man
11. Some Notions I Had as a Child
12. I Can Dream, Can't I?

FROM SENSITIVITY   4
TO STATURE

Sensitivity has little if anything to do with the interpretation of a sign that reads "Room for Rent." To all who read English, those words convey virtually the same meaning. If the sign should include the words "modern conveniences," there might be some small variance of opinion about what is offered. But if it includes the phrase "side by side with Old World charm," immediately we are launched into an area where meaning is subject to individual feeling, to sensitivity. The author of the amended sign is deliberately offering for sale a commodity that can command a much higher price than he could hope to get for a mere room. This landlord is promising relief from the commonplace, with a suggestion of romance. However, the really sophisticated and critical reader, although sensitive to the blandishments of the sign, brings another quality to his reading, which perhaps the author did not bargain for. He has learned to read between the lines, to question the writer's purposes, to appraise as well as to appreciate—in other words, to detect propaganda.

"How can we know," a student frequently will ask, "whether this poem or story is intended to have a limited or a universal application?" "What is there that tells us, when the actual words do not, that a writer is satirical or serious?" Sensitivity is that indefinable quality that provides the insight, the mental equipment needed for the reader to enter into the thoughts and feelings of an author. Such sensitivity is acquired: to some, it comes naturally in due time as a result of wide and thoughtful reading; to others, and that is most of us, there must be careful study of technique as the means by which matter and content are presented.

Many factors are involved in the level of reading that includes appreciation of the author's purpose, his ordering of ideas, his verbal facility, and talent in sentence design—in short, his style. Perhaps they could all be summed up in the *term, mental maturity. This includes broad sympathies, growing culture, responsive imagination, and a willing attempt to divest oneself of prejudice. A sense of humor must not be overlooked, for nowhere is sensitivity to words according to their pliancy of meaning more signficant than in the hard-wrought subtleties of humor. When the student realizes that, even for professionals, composition is careful, slow, and often traumatic, he will accept the necessity for frank self-criticism and patient revision of his own papers.*

The selections in this division focus on mood as much as on mind. There are examinations of values and motivations, of human obligations and relationships. By contrasts and comparisons with the wonderings and confused feelings of others, one can be helped to an understanding of himself. Sensitivity takes the reader beyond mere comprehension of what words say to a realization of what they mean. Imagination and reflection on the human condition may arouse him to have something to say for himself. When he is able to take the thoughts of a writer, integrate them with his own experience, and express his own thoughts precisely and clearly, the student will have attained stature.

PAINT FOR PORTUGAL

Leo Rosten

Lisbon is a gleaming city, an Iberian-Moorish gem on the river Tagus, a beautiful toy of a city (just as San Francisco is a toy city) drenched in sunshine and ablaze with flowers. I have never seen such flaming bougainvillea or so *much* painting—house-painting, I mean. You can't take a ten-minute stroll without passing a dozen sun-bleached scaffoldings crawling up the building fronts, and sidewalk after sidewalk are stacked with buckets of fresh paint.

The ubiquitous painting does not express some Portuguese fetishism over linseed oil; it is the consequence of a law. Every house in Lisbon must be freshly painted every five years, I am told, and the choice of colors is specified by government ordinance. They must be pleasant, playful pastels: ominous or depressing hues are *verboten*.

This is certainly one of the strangest laws I ever heard of, but it produces vistas delicious to behold: watercolor pinks and pale blues, soft yellows and mellow rusts. The law has had another effect, perhaps one nobody could have anticipated: in order to escape the cost of repainting every five years, canny builders use tiles instead of plaster on house fronts. Tile can be cleaned simply, cheaply, with a hose, or, if you want to be a perfectionist, with sponge and soapy water.

The tiles are beautifully patterned and tesify to the Moslem, Arabic strains interwoven in Portugal's history. The architecture is anything but elegant or ethereal; it runs to that squatness and strength which derive from battlements and fortresses: ornamented gates, sudden towers, Moorish embrasures.

In the late afternoon, when the sun turns soft and golden, the light flows down the pastel walls and shines off the intricate mosaics, and the streets sing with color.

This is the cleanest city I have ever seen. There just is no dirt, no soot, no trash, no debris. I mentioned this to Manuel D———, who answered, "Clean? But certainly. Lisbon is clean. Why, *senhor*, should not be? Who in Portugal has anything to throw away?"

IN STILLNESS

Richard Henry Dana

One night, while we were in these tropics, I went out to the end of the flying-jib boom upon some duty, and having finished it, turned round, and lay over the boom for a long time, admiring the beauty of the sight before me. Being so far out from the deck, I could look at the ship as at a separate vessel; and there rose up from the water, supported only by the small black hull, a pyramid of canvas, spreading out far beyond the hull, and towering up almost, as it seemed in the indistinct night air, to the clouds. The sea was as still as an inland lake; the light trade-wind was gently and steadily breathing from astern; the dark blue sky was studded with the tropical stars; there was no sound but the rippling of the water under the stem; and the sails were spread out, wide and high— the two lower studding-sails stretching on each side far beyond the deck; the topmast studding-sails like wings to the topsails; the topgallant studding-sails spreading fearlessly out above them; still higher, the two royal studding-sails looking like two kites flying from the same string; and highest of all, the little sky-sail, the apex of the pyramid seeming actually to touch the stars, and to be out of reach of human hand. So quiet, too, was the sea, and so steady the breeze, that if these sails had been sculptured marble they could not have been more motionless. Not a ripple upon the surface of the canvas; not even a quivering of the extreme edges of the sail, so perfectly were they distended by the breeze. I was so lost in the sight that I forgot the presence of the man who came out with me, until he said (for he, too, rough old man-of-war's-man as he was, had been gazing at the show), half to himself, still looking at the marble sails— "How quietly they do their work!"

MY MOTHER AND THE MASTER OF BALLANTRAE

James M. Barrie

That day, when I should have been at my work, she came upon me in the kitchen, *The Master of Ballantrae* beside me, but I was not reading: my head lay heavy on the table and to her anxious eyes, I doubt not, I was the picture of woe. "Not writing!" I echoed no, I was not writing, I saw no use in ever trying to write again. And down, I suppose, went my head once more. She misunderstood, and thought the blow had fallen; I had awakened to the discovery, always dreaded by her, that I had written myself dry; I was no better than an empty ink-bottle. She wrung her hands, but indignation came to her with my explanation, which was that while R. L. S. was at it we others were only 'prentices cutting our fingers on his tools. "I could never thole his books," said my mother immediately, and indeed vindictively.

"You have not read any of them," I reminded her.

"And never will," said she with spirit.

And I have no doubt that she called him a dark character that very day. For weeks too, if not for months, she adhered to her determination not to read him, though I, having come to my senses and seen that there is a place for the 'prentice, was taking a pleasure, almost malicious, in putting The Master of Ballantrae in her way. I would place it on her table so that it said good-morning to her when she rose. She would frown, and carrying it downstairs, as if she had it in the tongs, replaced it on its book-shelf. I would wrap it up in the cover she had made for the latest Carlyle: she would skim it contemptuously and again bring it down. I would hide her spectacles in it, and lay it on top of the clothes-basket and prop it up invitingly open against her tea-pot. And at last I got her, though I forget by which of many contrivances. What I recall vividly is a key-hole view, to which another member of the family invited me. Then I saw my mother wrapped up in The Master of Ballantrae and muttering the music to her-self, nodding her head in approval, and taking a stealthy glance at the foot of each page before she began at the top. Nevertheless she had an ear for the door, for when I bounced in she had been too clever for me; there was no book to be seen, only an apron on her lap, and she was gazing out at the window. Some such conversation as this followed:

"You have been sitting very quietly, mother."

"I always sit quietly, I never do anything, I'm just a finished stocking."

"Have you been reading?"

"Do I ever read at this time of day?"

"What is that in your lap?"

"Just an apron."

"Is that a book beneath the apron?"

"It might be a book."

"Let me see."

"Go away with you to your work."

But I lifted the apron. "Why, it's The Master of Ballantrae!" I exclaimed, shocked.

"So it is!" said my mother, equally surprised. But I looked sternly at her, and perhaps she blushed.

"Well what do you think: not nearly equal to mine?" said I with humor.

"Nothing like them," she said determinedly.

"Not a bit," said I, though whether with a smile or a groan is immaterial; they would have meant the same thing. Should I put the book back on the shelf? I asked, and she replied that I could put it wherever I liked for all she cared, so long as I took it out of her sight (the implication was that it had stolen on her lap while she was looking out at the window). My behaviour may seem small, but I gave her a last chance, for I said that some people found it a book there was no putting down until they reached the last page.

"I'm not that kind," replied my mother.

ROSALINO, CORASMIN, AND THE PARROTS

D. H. Lawrence

The parrots, even when I don't listen to them, have an extraordinary effect on me. They make my diaphragm convulse with little laughs, almost mechanically. They are a quite common-place pair of green birds, with bits of bluey red, and round, disillusioned eyes, and heavy, overhanging noses. But they listen intently. And they reproduce. The pair whistle now like Rosalino, who is sweeping the *patio* with a twig broom; and yet it is so unlike him, to be whistling full vent, when any of us is around, that one looks at him to see. And the moment one sees him, with his black head bent rather drooping and hidden as he sweeps, one laughs.

The parrots whistle exactly like Rosalino, only a little more so. And this little-more-so is extremely, sardonically funny. With their sad old long-jowled faces and their flat disillusioned eyes, they reproduce Rosalino and a little-more-so without moving a muscle. And Rosalino, sweeping the *patio* with his twig broom, scraping the tittering leaves into little heaps, covers himself more and more with the cloud of his own obscurity. He doesn't rebel. He is powerless. Up goes the wild, sliding Indian whistle into the morning, very powerful, with an immense energy seeming to drive behind it. And always, always a little more than lifelike.

Then they break off into a cackling chatter, and one knows they are shifting their clumsy legs, perhaps hanging on with their beaks and clutching with their cold, slow claws, to climb to a higher bough, like rather raggedy green buds climbing to the sun. And suddenly, the penetrating, demonish mocking voices:

"Perro! Oh, Perro! Perr-rro! Oh, Perr-rro! Perro!"

They are imitating somebody calling the dog. *Perro* means dog. But that any creature should be able to pour such a suave, prussic-acid sarcasm over the voice of a human being calling a dog, is incredible. One's diaphragm chuckles involuntarily. And one thinks: *Is it possible?* Is it possible that we are so absolutely, so innocently, so *ab ovo* ridiculous?

And not only is it possible, it is patent. We cover our heads in confusion.

Now they are yapping like a dog: exactly like Corasmin. Corasmin is a little fat, curly white dog who was lying in the sun a minute ago, and has now come into the verandah shade, walking with slow resignation, to lie against the wall near by my chair. "Yap-yap-yap! Wouf! Wouf! Yap-yap-yap-yap!!" go the parrots, exactly like Corasmin when some stranger comes into the *zaguan*. Corasmin and a little-more-so.

With a grin on my face I look down at Corasmin. And with a silent, abashed resignation in his yellow eyes. Corasmin looks up at me, with a touch of reproach. His little white nose is sharp, and under his eyes there are dark marks, as under the eyes of one who has known much trouble. All day he does nothing but walk resignedly out of the sun, when the sun gets too hot, and out of the shade, when the shade gets too cool. And bite ineffectually in the region of his fleas.

Poor old Corasmin: he is only about six, but resigned, unspeakably resigned. Only not humble. He does not kiss the rod. He rises in spirit above it, letting his body lie.

BIRTHDAY PARTY

Katharine Brush

They were a couple in their late thirties, and they looked unmistakably married. They sat on the banquette opposite us in a little narrow restaurant, having dinner. The man had a round self-satisfied face, with glasses on it; the woman was fadingly pretty, in a big hat. There was nothing conspicuous about them, nothing particularly noticeable, until the end of the meal, when it suddenly became obvious that this was an Occasion—in fact, the husband's birthday, and the wife had planned a little surprise for him.

It arrived, in the form of a small but glossy birthday cake, with one pink candle burning in the center. The headwaiter brought it in and placed it before the husband, and meanwhile the violin-and-piano orchestra played "Happy Birthday to You" and the wife beamed with shy pride over her little surprise, and such few people as there were in the restaurant tried to help out with a pattering of applause. It became clear at once that help was needed, because the husband was not pleased. Instead he was hotly embarrassed, and indignant at his wife for embarrassing him.

You looked at him and you saw this and you thought, "Oh, now, don't be like that!" But he was like that, and as soon as the little cake had been deposited on the table, and the orchestra had finished the birthday piece, and the general attention had shifted from the man and woman, I saw him say something to her under his breath—some punishing thing, quick and curt and unkind. I couldn't bear to look at the woman then, so I stared at my plate and waited for quite a long time. Not long enough, though. She was still crying when I finally glanced over there again. Crying quietly and heartbrokenly and hopelessly, all to herself, under the gay big brim of her best hat.

DEFINITION OF A GENTLEMAN

John Henry Newman

It is almost a definition of a gentleman to say he is one who never inflicts pain. This description is both refined and, as far as it goes, accurate. He is mainly occupied in merely removing the obstacles which hinder the free and unembarrassed action of those about him, and he concurs with their movements rather than takes the initiative himself. His benefits may be considered as parallel to what are called comforts or conveniences in arrangements of a personal nature; like an easy chair or a good fire, which do their part in dispelling cold and fatigue, though nature provides both means of rest and animal heat without them. The true gentleman in like manner carefully avoids whatever may cause a jar or a jolt in the minds of those with whom he is cast—all clashing of opinion, or collision of feeling, all restraint, or suspicion, or gloom, or resentment; his great concern being to make everyone at their ease and at home. He has his eyes on all his company; he is tender toward the bashful, gentle toward the distant, and merciful toward the absurd; he can recollect to whom he is speaking; he guards against unreasonable allusions, or topics which may irritate; he is seldom prominent in conversation, and never wearisome. He makes light of favors while he does them, and seems to be receiving when he is conferring. He never speaks of himself except when compelled, never defends himself by a mere retort, he has no ears for slander or gossip, is scrupulous in imputing motives to those who interfere with him, and interprets everything for the best. He is never mean or little in his disputes, never takes unfair advantage, never mistakes personalities or sharp sayings for arguments, or insinuates evil which he dare not say out. From a long-sighted prudence, he observes the maxim of the ancient sage, that we should ever conduct ourselves toward our enemy as if he were one day to be our friend. He has too much good sense to be affronted at insults; he is too well employed to remember injuries, and too indolent to bear malice. He is patient, forbearing, and resigned, on philosophical principles; he submits to pain because it is inevitable, to bereavement because it is irreparable, and to death because it is his destiny. If he engages in controversy of any kind, his disciplined intellect preserves him from the blundering discourtesy of better, perhaps, but less educated minds, who, like blunt weapons, tear and hack, instead of cutting clean, who mistake the point in argument, waste their strength on trifles, misconceive their adversary, and leave the question more involved than they find it. He may be right or wrong in his opinion, but he is too clear-headed to be unjust; he is as simple as he is forcible, and as brief as he is decisive. Nowhere shall we find greater candor, consideration, indulgence; he throws himself into the minds of his opponents; he accounts for their mistakes. He knows the weakness of human reason as well as its strength, its province and its limits. If he be an unbeliever, he will be too profound and large-minded to ridicule religion or to act against it; he is too wise to be a dogmatist or fanatic in his infidelity. He respects piety and devotion; he even supports institutions as venerable, beautiful, or useful, to which he does not assent; he honors the ministers of religion, and it contents him to decline its mysteries without assailing or denouncing them. He is a friend of religious toleration, and that not only because his philosophy has taught him to look on all forms of faith with an impartial eye, but also from the gentleness and effeminacy of feeling which is the attendant on civilization.

Not that he may not hold a religion too, in his own way, even when he is not a Christian. In that case his religion is one of imagination and sentiment; it is the embodiment of those ideas of the sublime, majestic, and beautiful, without which there can be no large philosophy. Sometimes he acknowledges the being of God, sometimes he invests an unknown principle or quality with the attributes of perfection. And this deduction of his reason, or creation of his fancy, he makes the occasion of such excellent thoughts, and the starting-point of so varied and systematic a teaching, that he even seems like a disciple of Christianity itself. From the very accuracy and steadiness of his logical powers he is able to see what sentiments are consistent in those who hold any religious doctrine at all, and he appears to others to feel and to hold a whole circle of theological truths which exist in his mind no otherwise than as a number of deductions.

INLAND AFRICAN SCENERY

Brantz Mayer

In the six hundred miles I traversed, whilst absent from the coast, my memory, after twenty-six, leads me, from beginning to end, through an almost continuous forest-path. We struck a trail when we started, and we left it when we came home. It was rare, indeed, to encounter a cross-road, except when it led to neighboring villages, water, or cultivated fields. So dense was the forest foliage, that we often walked for hours in shade without a glimpse of the sun. The emerald light that penetrated the wood bathed everything it touched with mellow refreshment. But we were repaid for this partial bliss by intense suffering when we came forth from the sanctuary into the bare valleys, the arid *barrancas*, and marshy *savannas* of an open region. There, the red eye of the African sun glared with merciless fervor. Everything reflected its rays. They struck us like lances from above, from below, from the sides, from the rocks, from the fields, from the stunted herbage, from the bushes. All was glare! Our eyes seemed to simmer in their sockets. Whenever the path followed the channel of a brook, whose dried torrents left bare the scorched and broken rocks, our feet fled from the ravine as from heated iron. Frequently we entered extensive prairies, covered with blades of sword-grass, tall as our heads, whose jagged edges tore us like saws, though we protected our faces with masks of wattled willows. And yet, after all these discomforts, how often are my dreams haunted by charming pictures of natural scenery that have fastened themselves forever in my memory!

As the traveller along the coast turns the prow of his canoe through the surf, and crosses the angry bar that guards the mouth of an African river, he suddenly finds himself moving calmly onward between sedgy shores, buried in mangroves. Presently, the scene expands in the unruffled mirror of a deep, majestic stream. Its lofty banks are covered by innumerable varieties of the tallest forest trees, from whose summits a trailing net-work of vines and flowers floats down and sweeps the passing current. A stranger who beholds this scenery for the first time is struck by the immense size, the prolific abundance, and gorgeous verdure of everything. Leaves, large enough for garments, lie piled and motionless in the lazy air. The bamboo and cane shake their slender spears and pennant leaves as the stream ripples among their roots. Beneath the massive trunks of forest trees, the country opens; and, in vistas through the wood, the traveller sees innumerable fields lying fallow in grass, or waving with harvests of rice and *cassava*, broken by golden clusters of Indian corn. Anon, groups of oranges, lemons, coffee-trees, plantains and bananas, are crossed by the tall stems of cocoas, and arched by the broad and drooping coronals of royal palm. Beyond this, capping the summit of a hill, may be seen the conical huts of natives, bordered by fresh pastures dotted with flocks of sheep and goats, or covered by numbers of the sleekest cattle. As you leave the coast, and shoot round the river-curves of this fragrant wilderness teeming with flowers, vocal with birds, and gay with their radiant plumage, you plunge into the interior, where the rising country slowly expands into hills and mountains.

The forest is varied. Sometimes it is a matted pile of tree, vine, and bramble, obscuring everything, and impervious save with knife and hatchet. At others, it is a Gothic temple. The sward spreads openly for miles on every side, while, from its even surface, the trunks of straight and massive trees rise to a prodigious height, clear from every obstruction, till their gigantic limbs, like the capitals of columns, mingle their foliage in a roof of perpetual verdure.

At length the hills are reached, and the lowland heat is tempered by mountain freshness. The scene that may be beheld from almost any elevation is always beautiful, and sometimes grand. Forest, of course, prevails; yet, with a glass, and often by the unaided eye, gentle hills, swelling from the wooded landscape, may be seen covered with native huts, whose neighborhood is checkered with patches of sward and cultivation, and enclosed by massive belts of primeval wildness. Such is commonly the westward view; but north and east, as far as vision extends, noble outlines of hill and mountain may be traced against the sky, lapping each other with their mighty folds, until they fade away in the azure horizon.

When a view like this is beheld at morning, in the neighborhood of rivers, a dense mist will be observed lying beneath the spectator in a solid stratum, refracting the light now breaking from the east. Here and there, in this lake of vapor, the tops of hills peer up like green islands in a golden sea. But, ere you have time to let fancy run riot, the "cloud compelling" orb lifts its disc over the mountains, and the fogs of the valley, like ghosts at cock-crow, flit from the dells they have haunted since nightfall. Presently, the sun is out in his terrible splendor. Africa unveils to her master, and the blue sky and green forest blaze and quiver with his beams.

THE RETURN OF ODYSSEUS

Alexander S. Murray

Turning now to Odysseus, we find him, long after the other heroes of the Trojan expedition had reached their homes, still being tossed about by storms, passing through great perils, encountering strange beings, and ultimately succeeding in many unhopeful adventures. He had left Troy with a well-manned fleet richly laden with spoil, and after several adventures of less moment, in which, however, he lost a number of men, reached the country of the Cyclops—enormous giants with only one eye. In a cave which was the habitation of one of them, Polyphemus by name, a son of the sea-god Poseidon, Odysseus and his fellow-travellers took shelter, while their ships lay anchored beside a neighboring island. Polyphemus, who was absent at the time of their arrival, returned with his sheep to the cave. The first thing he did on entering was to close up the entrance with a great stone, which a hundred men could not have moved. The next thing was, having discovered the strangers, to eat two of them for his supper, after which he slept soundly. The following morning, after driving out his sheep, he replaced the stone at the mouth of the cave, to prevent the escape of his victims and the consequent loss of several suppers. The history of the first day having repeated itself on the two following days, a plan of escape occurred to Odysseus. The giant having had his usual supper, Odysseus offered him some wine, which had the effect of creating a desire for more. His goblet being constantly replenished, Polyphemus at last sank helpless, through sleep and intoxication. Seeing this, Odysseus, with the help of his companions, laid hold of a great pole, and having made the end of it red hot, let it down on the giant's eye, and burned it out. Polyphemus sprang up in great fury, and after groping in vain for his supple enemies, made for the doorway of the cave, removed the stone, and sat down in its place, determined to permit no one to escape. But Odysseus and his companions fastened themselves each under the belly of one of the great sheep within the cave, knowing that the giant would let them pass out unmolested. And so it was; for, feeling the fleece as they passed, he was quite satisfied. Odysseus once outside the cave, and with what remained of his crew safe in the ship, shouted jeeringly back to the Cyclops, telling him also his name. Polyphemus then implored his father, the god Poseidon, to punish Odysseus for what he had just done. It was in answer to this prayer that Odysseus was driven hither and thither, detained here and there, and at last, after ten years' wandering, and the loss of all his men, reached home in a miserable plight. Of the adventures that befell him after leaving the country of the Cyclops, the most important were the following: After leaving Aeolus, the king of the winds, he reached the habitation of the sorceress Circe (a sister of Medea, it was said), whose first act was to transform his companions into swine. For Odysseus himself her charms had no potency. He compelled her to restore his men to their proper human form. Changing her manner, Circe now exhibited a cordial feeling toward Odysseus, entertaining him and his companions very hospitably for a period of a year, on the expiry of which she advised him to make a journey to the lower world, to question the shade of the seer Tiresias as to the fate in store for him. Acting on her advice, Odysseus penetrated to the region of Hades, saw and conversed with the shades of some of his former companions in the siege of Troy, and then returned to Circe, who gave him good counsel in regard to his future journey. On his voyage homeward he passed the Sirens safely, passed Scylla the sea-monster, with loss of six men, and afterward, in spite of the warnings both of Tiresias and Circe, landed on the island of Trinacia, where his companions plundered the sacred flocks of the sun-god. As a punishment for this they were afterward overtaken by a fearful storm at sea, and all perished except Odysseus, who, clinging to a piece of his ship for nine days, was at length driven on shore on the island belonging to the nymph Calypso, who received him kindly, and out of love detained him as her prisoner for seven years.

Despising her love and her offer of immortality, Odysseus sat disconsolate by the seashore, thinking of his home in Ithaca, and yearning to see it again before he died. The gods, taking compassion on him, prevailed on Calypso to let him go. He made a raft, and put to sea; but Poseidon, not yet appeased for the wrong done to his son Polyphemus, raised a storm which shattered the small craft, and would have caused Odysseus to perish but for the timely aid of the sea-nymph Leucothea. Swimming to land, he found himself in the island of the Phaeacians, was discovered on the shore by the king's daughter, Nausicaa, and entertained hospitably by the king, Alcinous, to whom he related his adventures. After receiving many costly presents, he was conveyed home to Ithaca in a well-manned ship. There he found his wife, Penelope, still faithful to him, in spite of the incessant wooing of all the princes of the neighboring islands in the course of her husband's long absence.

His son, Telemachus, whom he left an infant, had now grown to manhood, and, having just arrived from a journey in search of intelligence concerning his missing father, was staying in the house of a shepherd when Odysseus arrived, and heard the story of how suitors of Penelope were vexing her and consuming her husband's possessions. Odysseus and his son appeared among them in disguise, raised a quarrel, and, with the help of Athene, slew them all. Then took place the touching meeting with his wife. After crushing an insurrection raised by the friends of the slain suitors, Odysseus spent the rest of his life reigning peacefully over his island kingdom of Ithaca.

SHAME

Stephen Crane

When he arrived in the outskirts of the grove, he heard a merry clamour, and when he reached the top of the knoll he looked down the slope upon a scene which almost made his little breast burst with joy. They actually had two camp-fires! Two camp-fires! At one of them Mrs. Earl was making something—chocolate, no doubt—and at the other a young lady in white duck and a sailor hat was dropping eggs into boiling water. Other grown-up people had spread a white cloth and were laying upon it things from baskets. In the deep cool shadow of the trees the children scurried, laughing. Jimmie hastened forward to join his friends.

Homer Phelps caught first sight of him. "Ho!" he shouted; "here comes Jimmie Trescott! Come on, Jimmie; you be on our side!" The children had divided themselves into two bands for some purpose of play. The others of Homer Phelps' party loudly endorsed his plan. "Yes, Jimmie, you be on our side." Then arose the usual dispute. "Well, we got the weakest side."

"Tain't any weaker'n ours."

Homer Phelps suddenly started and, looking hard, said, "What you got in the pail, Jim?"

Jimmie answered, somewhat uneasily, "Got m'lunch in it."

Instantly that brat of a Minnie Phelps simply tore down the sky with her shrieks of derision. "Got his lunch in it! In a pail!" She ran screaming to her mother. "Oh, mamma! Oh, mamma! Jimmie Trescott's got his picnic in a pail!"

Now there was nothing in the nature of this fact to particularly move the others—notably the boys, who were not competent to care if he had brought his luncheon in a coal-bin; but such is the instinct of childish society that they all immediately moved away from him. In a moment he had been made a social leper. All old intimacies were flung into the lake, so to speak. They dared not compromise themselves. At a safe distance the boys shouted, scornfully: "Huh! Got his picnic in a pail!" Never again during that picnic did the little girls speak of him as Jimmie Trescott. His name now was Him.

His mind was dark with pain as he stood, the hang-dog, kicking the gravel, and muttering as defiantly as he was able, "Well, I can have it in a pail if I want to." This statement of freedom was of no importance, and he knew it, but it was the only idea in his head.

He had been baited at school for being detected in writing a letter to little Cora, the angel child, and he had known how to defend himself, but this situation was in no way similar. This was a social affair with grown people on all sides. It would be sweet to catch the Margate twins, for instance, and hammer them into a state of bleating respect for his pail; but that was a matter for the jungles of childhood, where grown folks seldom penetrated. He could only glower.

The amiable voice of Mrs. Earl suddenly called: "Come, children! Everything's ready!" They scampered away, glancing back for one last gloat at Jimmie standing there with his pail.

He did not know what to do. He knew that the grown people expected him at the spread, but if he approached he would be greeted by a shameful chorus from the children—more especially from some of those damnable little girls. Still, luxuries beyond all dreaming were heaped on that cloth. One could not forget them. Perhaps if he crept up modestly, and was very gentle and very nice to the little girls, they would allow him peace. Of course it had been dreadful to come with a pail to such a grand picnic, but they might forgive him.

Oh no, they would not! He knew them better. And then suddenly he remembered with what delightful expectations he had raced to this grove, and self-pity overwhelmed him, and he thought he wanted to die and make every one feel sorry.

The young lady in white duck and a sailor hat looked at him, and then spoke to her sister, Mrs. Earl. "Who's that hovering in the distance, Emily?"

Mrs. Earl peered. "Why, it's Jimmy Trescott! Jimmie, come to the picnic! Why don't you come to the picnic, Jimmie?" He began to sidle toward the cloth.

But at Mrs. Earl's call there was another outburst from many of the children. "He's got his picnic in a pail! In a pail! Got it in a pail!"

Minnie Phelps was a shrill fiend. "Oh, mamma. he's got it in that pail! See! Isn't it funny? Isn't it dreadful funny?"

"What ghastly prigs children are, Emily!" said the young lady. "They are spoiling that boy's whole day, breaking his heart, the little cats! I think I'll go over and talk to him."

"Maybe you had better not," answered Mrs. Earl, dubiously. "Somehow these things arrange themselves. If you interfere, you are likely to prolong everything."

"Well, I'll try, at least," said the young lady.

At the second outburst against him Jimmie had crouched down by a tree, half hiding behind it, half pretending that he was not hiding behind it. He turned his sad gaze toward the lake. The bit of water seen through the shadows seemed perpendicular, a slate-coloured wall. He heard a noise near him, and turning he perceived the young lady looking down at him. In her hand she held plates. "May I sit near you?" she asked, coolly.

Jimmie could hardly believe his ears. After disposing herself and the plates upon the pine needles, she made brief explanation. "They're rather crowded, you see, over there. I don't like to be crowded at a picnic, so I thought I'd come here. I hope you don't mind."

Jimmie made haste to find his tongue. "Oh, I don't mind! I like to have you here." The ingenuous emphasis made it appear that the fact of his liking to have her there was in the nature of a law-dispelling phenomenon, but she did not smile.

"How large is that lake?" she asked.

Jimmie falling into the snare, at once began to talk in the manner of a proprietor of the lake. "Oh, it's almost twenty miles long, an' in one place it's almost four miles wide! an' it's deep too—awful deep—an' it's got real steamboats on it, an'—oh—lots of other boats, an'—an'—an'—"

"Do you go out on it sometimes?"

"Oh, lots of times! My father's got a boat," he said, eyeing her to note the effect of his words.

She was correctly pleased and struck with wonder. "Oh, has he?" she cried, as if she never before had heard of a man owning a boat.

Jimmie continued: "Yes, an' it's a grea' big boat, too, with sails, real sails; an' sometimes he takes me out in her too, an' once he took me fishin', an' we had sandwiches, plenty of 'em, and my father he drank beer right out of the bottle—right out of the bottle!"

The young lady was properly overwhelmed by this amazing intelligence. Jimmie saw the impression he had created, and he enthusiastically resumed his narrative: "An' after, he let me throw the bottles in the water, and I throwed 'em 'way, 'way, 'way out. An' they sank, an'—never comed up," he concluded, dramatically.

His face was glorified; he had forgotten all about the pail; he was absorbed in this communion with a beautiful lady who was so interested in what he had to say.

She indicated one of the plates, and said, indifferently: "Perhaps you would like some of those sandwiches. I made them. Do you like olives? And there's a devilled egg. I made that also."

"Did you really?" said Jimmie, politely. His face gloomed for a moment because the pail was recalled to his mind, but he timidly possessed himself of a sandwich.

"Hope you are not going to scorn my devilled egg," said his goddess, "I am very proud of it." He did not; he scorned little that was on the plate.

Their gentle intimacy was ineffable to the boy. He thought he had a friend, a beautiful lady, who liked him more than she did anybody at the picnic, to say the least. This was proved by the fact that she had flung aside the luxuries of the spread cloth to sit with him, the exile. Thus early did he fall a victim to woman's wiles.

"Where do you live?" he asked, suddenly.

"Oh, a long way from here! In New York."

His next question was put very bluntly. "Are you married?"

"Oh no!" she answered, gravely.

Jimmie was silent for a time, during which he glanced shyly and furtively up at her face. It was evident that he was somewhat embarrassed. Finally he said, "When I grow up to be a man—"

"Oh, that is some time yet!" said the beautiful lady.

"But when I do, I—I should like to marry you."

"Well, I will remember it," she answered; "but don't talk of it now, because it's such a long time; and—I wouldn't wish you to consider yourself bound." She smiled at him.

He began to brag. "When I grow up to be a man, I'm goin' to have lots an' lots of money, an' I'm goin' to have a grea' big house, an' a horse an' a shotgun, an' lots an' lots of books 'bout elephants an' tigers, an' lots an' lots of ice-cream an' pie an'—carmels." As before, she was impressed; he could see it. "An' I'm goin' to have lots an' lots of children—'bout three hundred, I guess—an' there won't none of 'em be girls. They'll all be boys—like me."

"Oh, my!" she said.

His garment of shame was gone from him. The pail was dead and well buried. It seemed to him that months elapsed as he dwelt in happiness near the beautiful lady and trumpeted his vanity.

At last there was a shout. "Come on! we're going home." The picnickers trooped out of the grove. The children wished to resume their jeering, for Jimmie still gripped his pail, but they were restrained by the circumstances. He was walking at the side of the beautiful lady.

During the journey he abandoned many of his habits. For instance, he never travelled without skipping gracefully from crack to crack between the stones, or without pretending that he was a train of cars, or without some mumming device of childhood. But now he behaved with dignity. He made no more noise than a little mouse. He escorted the beautiful lady to the gate of the Earl home, where he awkwardly, solemnly, and wistfully shook hands in good-bye. He watched her go up the walk; the door clanged.

On his way home he dreamed. One of these dreams was fascinating. Supposing the beautiful lady was his teacher in school! Oh, my! wouldn't he be a good boy, sitting like a statuette all day long, and knowing every lesson to perfection, and—everything. And then supposing that a boy should sass her. Jimmie painted himself waylaying that boy on the homeward road, and the fate of the boy was a thing to make strong men cover their eyes with their hands. And she would like him more and more—more and more. And he—would be a little god. . . .

THE PLEASURES OF A
FARM VISIT

Mark Twain

I spent some part of every year at the farm until I was twelve or thirteen years old. . . . I can call back the solemn twilight and mystery of the deep woods, the earthy smells, the faint odors of the wild flowers, the sheen of rain-washed foliage, the rattling clatter of drops when the wind shook the trees, the far-off hammering of woodpeckers and the muffled drumming of wood pheasants in the remoteness of the forest; the snapshot glimpses of disturbed wild creatures scurrying through the grass —I can call it all back and make it as real as it ever was, and as blessed. I can call back the prairie, and its loneliness and peace, and a vast hawk hanging motionless in the sky, with his wings spread wide and the blue of the vault showing through the fringe of their end feathers. I can see the woods in their autumn dress, the oaks purple, the hickories washed with gold, the maples and the sumachs luminous with crimson fires, and I can hear the rustle made by the fallen leaves as we plowed through them. I can see the blue clusters of wild grapes hanging among the foliage of the saplings, and I remember the taste of them and the smell. I know how the wild blackberries looked, and how they tasted, and the same with the paw-paws, the hazelnuts, and the persimmons; and I can feel the thumping rain, upon my head, of hickory nuts and walnuts when we were out in the frosty dawn to scramble for them with the pigs, and the gusts of wind loosed them and sent them down. I know the stain of blackberries, and how pretty it is, and I know the stain of walnut hulls, and how little it minds soap and water, also what grudged experience it had of either of them. I know the taste of maple sap, and when to gather it, and how to arrange the troughs and the delivery tubes, and how to boil down the juice, and how to hook the sugar after it is made, also how much better hooked sugar tastes than any that is honestly come by, let bigots say what they will. I know how a prize watermelon looks when it is sunning its fat rotundity among pumpkin vines and "simblins"; I know how to tell when it is ripe without "plugging" it; I know how inviting it looks when it is cooling itself in a tub of water under the bed, waiting; I know how it looks when it lies on the table in the sheltered great floor space between house and kitchen, and the children gathered for the sacrifice and their mouths watering; I know the crackling sound it makes when the carving knife enters its end, and I can see the split fly along in front of the blade as the knife cleaves its way to the other end; I can see its halves fall apart and display the ripe red meat and the black seeds, and the heart standing there luxury fit for the elect; I know how a boy looks behind a yard-long slice of that melon, and I know how he feels, for I have been there. I know the taste of the watermelon which has been honestly come by, and I know the taste of the watermelon which has been acquired by art. Both taste good, but the experienced know which tastes best. I know the look of green apples and peaches and pears on the trees, and I know how entertaining they are when they are inside of a person. I know how ripe ones look when they are piled in pyramids under the trees, and how pretty they are and how vivid their colors. I know how a frozen apple looks, in a barrel down cellar in the wintertime, and how hard it is to bite, and how the frost makes the teeth ache, and yet how good it is, notwithstanding. I know the disposition of elderly people to select the speckled apples for the children, and I once knew ways to beat the game. I know the look of an apple that is roasting and sizzling on a hearth on a winter's evening, and I know the comfort that comes of eating it hot, along with some sugar and a drench of cream. I know the delicate art and mystery of so cracking hickory nuts and walnuts on a flatiron with a hammer that the kernels will be delivered whole, and I know how the nuts, taken in conjunction with winter apples, cider, and doughnuts, make old people's old tales and old jokes sound fresh and crisp and enchanting, and juggle an evening away before you know what went with the time. I know the look of Uncle Dan'l's kitchen as it was on the privileged nights, when I was a child, and I can see the white and black children grouped on the hearth, with the firelight playing on their faces and the shadows flickering upon the walls, clear back toward the cavernous gloom of the rear, and I can hear Uncle Dan'l telling the immortal tales which Uncle Remus Harris was to gather into his books and charm the world with, by and by; and I can feel again the creepy joy which quivered through me when the time for the ghost story of the "Golden Arm" was reached—and the sense of regret, too, which came over me, for it was always the last story of the evening and there was nothing between it and the unwelcome bed.

I can remember the bare wooden stairway in my uncle's house, and the turn to the left above the landing, and the rafters and the slanting roof over my bed, and the squares of moonlight on the floor, and the white cold world of snow outside, seen through the curtainless window. I can remember the howling of the wind and the quaking of the house on stormy nights, and how snug and cozy one felt, under the blankets, listening; and how the powdery snow used to sift in, around the sashes, and lie in little ridges on the floor and make the place look chilly in the morning and curb the wild desire to get up in case there was any. I can remember how very dark that room was, in the dark of the moon, and how packed it was with ghostly stillness when one woke up by accident away in the night, and forgotten sins came flocking out of the secret chambers of the memory and wanted a hearing; and how ill chosen the time seemed for this kind of business; and how dismal was the hoo-hooing of the owl and the wailing of the wolf, sent mourning by on the night wind.

I remember the raging of the rain on the roof, summer nights, and how pleasant it was to lie and listen to it, and enjoy the white splendor of the lightning and the majestic booming and crashing of the thunder. It was a very satisfactory room, and there was a lightning rod which was reachable from the window, an adorable and skittish thing to climb up and down, summer nights, when there were duties on hand of a sort to make privacy desirable.

I remember the 'coon and 'possum hunts, nights, with the Negroes, and the long marches through the black gloom of the woods, and the excitement which fired everybody when the distant bay of an experienced dog announced that the game was treed; then the wild scramblings and stumblings through briers and bushes and over roots to get to the spot; then the lighting of a fire and the felling of the tree, the joyful frenzy of the dogs and the Negroes, and the weird picture it all made in the red glare—I remember it all well, and the delight that everyone got out of it, except the 'coon.

I remember the pigeon seasons, when the birds would come in millions and cover the trees and by their weight break down the branches. They were clubbed to death with sticks; guns were not necessary and were not used. I remember the squirrel hunts, and prairie-chicken hunts, and wild-turkey hunts, and all that; and how we turned out, mornings, while it was still dark, to go on these expeditions, and how chilly and dismal it was, and how often I regretted that I was well enough to go. A toot on a tin horn brought twice as many dogs as were needed, and in their happiness they raced and scampered about, and knocked small people down, and made no end of unnecessary noise. At the word, they vanished away toward the woods, and we drifted silently after them in the melancholy gloom. But presently the gray dawn stole over the world, the birds piped up, then the sun rose and poured light and comfort all around, everything was fresh and dewy and fragrant, and life was a boon again. After three hours of tramping we arrived back wholesomely tired, overladen with game, very hungry, and just in time for breakfast.

GOING OUT FOR A WALK

Max Beerbohm

It is a fact that not once in all my life have I gone out for a walk. I have been taken out for walks; but that is another matter. Even while

I trotted prattling by my nurse's side I regretted the good old days when I had, and wasn't, a perambulator. When I grew up it seemed to me that the one advantage of living in London was that nobody ever wanted me to come out for a walk. London's very drawbacks—its endless noise and hustle, its smoky air, the squalor ambushed everywhere in it—assured this one immunity. Whenever I was with friends in the country, I knew that at any moment, unless rain were actually falling, some man might suddenly say "Come out for a walk!" in that sharp imperative tone which he would not dream of using in any other connection. People seem to think there is something inherently noble and virtuous in the desire to go for a walk. Anyone thus desirous feels that he has a right to impose his will on whomever he sees comfortably settled in an armchair, reading. It is easy to say simply "No" to an old friend. In the case of a mere acquaintance one wants some excuse. "I wish I could, but"—nothing ever occurs to me except "I have some letters to write." This formula is unsatisfactory in three ways. (1) It isn't believed. (2) It compels you to rise from your chair, go to the writing-table. and sit improvising a letter to somebody until the walkmonger (just not daring to call you liar and hypocrite) shall have lumbered out of the room. (3) It won't operate on Sunday mornings. "There's no post out till this evening" clinches the matter; and you may as well go quietly.

Walking for walking's sake may be as highly laudable and exemplary a thing as it is held to be by those who practise it. My objection to it is that it stops the brain. Many a man has professed to me that his brain never works so well as when he is swinging along the high road or over hill and dale. This boast is not confirmed by my memory of anybody who on a Sunday morning has forced me to partake of his adventure. Experience teaches me that whatever a fellow-guest may have of power to instruct or to amuse when he is sitting on a chair, or standing on a hearthrug, quickly leaves him when he takes one out for a walk. The ideas that came so thick and fast to him in any room, where are they now? where that encyclopaedic knowledge which he bore so lightly? where the kindling fancy that played like summer lightning over any topic that was started? The man's face that was so mobile is set now; gone is the light from his fine eyes. He says that A. (our host) is a thoroughly good fellow. Fifty yards further on, he adds that A. is one of the best fellows he has ever met. We tramp another furlong or so, and he says that Mrs. A. is a charming woman. Presently he adds that she is one of the most charming women he has ever known. We pass an inn. He reads rapidly aloud to me: "The King's Arms. Licensed to sell Ales and Spirits." I foresee that during the rest of the walk he will read aloud any inscription that occurs. We pass an "Uxminster. 11 Miles." We turn a sharp corner at the foot of a hill. He points at the wall, and says "Drive Slowly." I see far ahead, on the other side of the hedge bordering the high road, a small notice-board. He sees it too. He keeps his eye on it. And in due course "Trespassers," he says, "Will Be Prosecuted." Poor man!—mentally a wreck.

Luncheon at the A.'s, however, salves him and floats him in full sail. Behold him once more the life and soul of the party. Surely he will never, after the bitter lesson of this morning, go out for another walk. An hour later, I see him striding forth with a new companion. I watch him out of sight. I know what he is saying. He is saying that I am rather a dull man to go a walk with. He will presently add that I am one of the dullest men he ever went a walk with. Then he will devote himself to reading out the inscriptions.

How comes it, this immediate deterioration in those who go walking for walking's sake? Just what happens? I take it that not by his reasoning faculties is a man urged to this enterprise. He is urged, evidently, by something in him that transcends reason; by his soul, I presume. Yes, it must be the soul that raps out the "Quick march!" to the body.—"Halt! Stand at ease!" interposes the brain, and "To what destination," it suavely asks the soul, "and on what errand, are you sending the body?"—"On no errand whatsoever," the soul makes answer, "and to no destination at all. It is just like you to be always on the look-out for some subtle ulterior motive. The body is going out because the mere fact of its doing so is a sure indication of nobility, probity, and rugged grandeur of character." —"Very well, Vagula, have your own wayula! But I," says the brain, "flatly refuse to be mixed up in this tomfoolery. I shall go to sleep till it is over." The brain then wraps itself up in its own convolutions, and falls into a dreamless slumber from which nothing can rouse it till the body has been safely deposited indoors again.

Even if you go to some definite place, for some definite purpose, the brain would rather you took a vehicle; but it does not make a point of this; it will serve you well enough unless you are going for a walk. It won't, while your legs are vying with each other, do any deep thinking for you, nor even any close thinking; but it will do any number of small odd jobs for you willingly—provided that your legs, also, are making themselves useful, not merely bandying you about to gratify the pride of the soul. Such as it is, this essay was composed in the course of a walk, this morning. I am not one of those extremists who must have a vehicle to every destination. I never go out of my way, as it were, to avoid exercise. I take it as it comes, and take it in good part. That valetudinarians are always chattering about it, and indulging in it to excess, is no reason for despising it. I am inclined to think that in moderation it is rather good for one, physically. But, pending a time when no people wish me to go and see them, and I have no wish to go and see anyone, and there is nothing whatever for me to do off my own premises, I never will go out for a walk.

THE MIGHTY I AM

Leo Rosten

The Temple of the I AM is a gleaming white mosque on Lake Street, just north of Beverly, in the City of the Angels. It is a big, clean, airy tabernacle, with nary a speck of red or black on the premises. That's because red and black are taboo to I AM-ers, who are also sternly opposed to liquor, tobacco, meat, onions, garlic, and sex. It's all part of the I AM creed, which is pretty complicated.

The I AM flock devotes itself to the teachings of the Ninety-Nine Ascended Masters of Saint Germain. These wonderful precepts have been transcribed for humanity by a Mr. and Mrs. G. W. Ballard, the celebrated leaders of the movement. They are referred to lovingly as "Our Messengers of Light," or simply as Papa and Mama Ballard. The head of this immortal household will go down in history as the man who started the I AM single-handed. It seems that he was on a camping trip on Mount Shasta, in sunny California, when suddenly Saint Germain materialized before him and gave him all the dope on the Great I AM Presence, the All-Consuming Flame, the Coming of the Seventh Ray, the Blue Tube of Light, the illusion of "so-called death," and how to stop war, earthquakes, dandruff, and traffic accidents, just by decreeing against them in a loud, firm voice. Saint Germain also told Mr. Ballard about liquor, tobacco, meat, onions, garlic, and sex. Mr. G. W. Ballard promptly rushed down the mountain to Mrs. G. W. Ballard, blurted out the revelation, and mankind passed another milestone on the road to final wisdom. Today the fearless Ballards publish a monthly magazine in violet type (they won't budge an inch on red and black), broadcast Delphic tips several times a week, manufacture I AM books in Braille for those who have lost their so-called sight, and fly all over the land spreading the gospel to thousands of enraptured disciples.

I went to an I AM meeting in the temple in Los Angeles on a Sunday night—a balmy Sunday night. An elderly gentleman—spare and tall and pale, and dressed in white from head to foot—led me down the aisle. There were some five hundred happy converts in the auditorium. Most of them were elderly folk with gray hair and the look of the uplifted. None wore red or black. The whole flock was on its feet singing a hymn. It was a nice, lilting hymn—entitled "Arcturus, We Greet Thee!" They sang it quite loudly. (Arcturus is 29,835,863,103,751 miles from the earth.) When the greeting to Arcturus was completed, everyone sat down and I found a seat....

OLD-FASHIONED TALK ON THE WOMAN QUESTION

John Todd

Nobody pretends that the sexes are equal in weight, in height, or in bodily strength. The bodies of the two sexes seem to have been planned for different ends. As to the mind, I have no difficulty in admitting that the mind of a woman is equal to ours,—nay, if you please, superior. It is quicker, more flexible, more elastic. I certainly have never seen boys learn languages or mathematics, up to a certain point, as fast or as easy as some girls. Woman's intuitions also are far better than ours. She reads character quicker, comes to conclusions quicker, and if I must make a decision on the moment, I had much rather have the woman's decision than man's. She has intuitions given her for her own protection which we have not. She has a delicacy of taste to which we can lay no claim. "Why, then," my lady reader will say, "why can't we be independent of man?" for this is the gist of the whole subject. I reply, you can't, for two reasons; first, God never designed you should, and secondly, your own deep instincts are in the way. God never designed that woman should occupy the same sphere as man, because he has given her a physical organization so refined and delicate that it can never bear the strain which comes upon the rougher nature of man. He has hedged her in by laws which no efforts can alter. We, sons of dust, move slower; we creep, where you bound to the head of the stairs at a single leap. And now bear with me, and keep good-natured, while I show you, what you, dear ladies, cannot do, and God does not ask you to do.

1. You cannot invent. There are all manner of inventions in our age, steam, railroads, telegraphing, machinery of all kinds, often five hundred and fifty weekly applications for patents at the Patent Office, but among

them all no female applicants. You have sewing machines almost numberless, knitting machines, washing, ironing, and churning machines—but I never heard of one that was the emanation of the female mind. Did you? Why sew, or wash, or card off your fingers, rather than to invent, if this was your gift? The old spinning-wheel and the old carding apparatus have gone by, but not by woman's invention. I suppose this power was denied you, lest it should take you out of your most important sphere—as I shall show.

2. You cannot compete with men in a long course of mental labor. Your delicate organization never has and never can bear the study by which you can become Newtons, La Places, or Bowditches in mathematics or astronomy. The world never has seen, and never expects to see, woman excelling in architecture. Neither in ancient or modern times has she one monument of this kind, showing mastership. You do not find them in ancient Corinth, old Athens, great Rome, or in any city of the old or new world.

So of painting and sculpture. You need not tell us what you are hereafter to do; but you have never yet shown a Phidias, a Raphael, a Michael Angelo, or a Canova. You cannot point to a woman who can pretend to stand by the side of Homer, Virgil, Shakespeare, or Milton. The world has never seen a female historian who came near the first rank. And even in cooking and in millinery, as is well known, men must and do stand at the head of these occupations.

But, you will perhaps say, "We have never had a fair chance—a fair fight in the field. We have been held down by prejudice, and tyranny, and public opinion against us, and all that." Suppose it be so, fair one, there is *one* field you have had to yourself, and nobody has lifted against you one finger. I mean that, for the last half century, we, cruel men, have invented, manufactured, and bought, and brought home, the *piano*, and you have had it all to yourselves. What is the result? It is, that the master performers, and teachers, and musicians, are men,—is it not? Nay, have you never seen the girl thumping and drumming her piano for years, under the best teachers, and yet her brother come along and take it up, and without any teaching, soon go in advance of the sister? I have seen it often. In none of these departments can woman compete with man. Not because her immortal mind is inferior,—far from it,—but because her bodily organization cannot endure the pressure of continued and long labor as we can. We may deny this, and declare it is not so; but the history of our race, and the state of the world now, show that it is so. I don't say that here and there a woman can't endure much and long; but they are rare exceptions. Did you ever know a woman who could endure being a teacher till seventy-five, as men often do? The fact that in medical colleges, in medical books, in medical practice, woman is recognized as having a peculiar organization, requiring the most careful and gentle treatment, and the consent of the world, all go to show that her bodily powers are not able to endure like those of the other sex. The wheels and workmanship are too delicate to be driven with the mainspring of the old-fashioned bull's-eye.

The design of God in creating woman was to complete man—a one-sided being without her. Together they make a complete, perfect unit. She has a mission—no higher one could be given her—to be the mother, and *the former of all the character of the human race*. For the first, most important, earthly period of life, the race is committed to her, for about twelve years, almost entirely. The human family is what she makes them. She is the queen of the home, its centre, its light and glory. The home, the home is the fountain of all that is good on earth. If she desires a higher, loftier, nobler trust than this, I know not where she can find it. Mother, wife, daughter, sister, are the tenderest, most endearing words in language. Our mothers train us, and we owe everything to them. Our wives perfect all that is good in us, and no man is ashamed to say he is indebted to his wife for his happiness, his influence, and his character, if there is anything noble about him. Woman is the highest, holiest, most precious gift to man. Her mission and throne is the family, and if anything is withheld that would make her more efficient, useful, or happy in that sphere, she is wronged, and has not her "rights."

THAT STRANGER IS YOURSELF

Sydney J. Harris

Some months ago I mentioned, in one of my goulash columns, that a person wouldn't recognize himself if he met himself walking down the street. The self-image we have is always a gross distortion of reality.

"I thought you were exaggerating for literary effect," said a friend of mine the other night, "but I found out last week that you were absolutely right."

It seems that, while visiting San Francisco, he walked into a bank to cash a check and observed a large television screen inside the door. He paused to look at the scurrying throng, and as he walked forward, he was amazed that a man on the screen did exactly what he did—and, of course, it turned out to be him, on a closed-circuit screen.

"I can't tell you how shocked I was," he said. "I looked at that man and passed over him like a perfect stranger, even though he was wearing the very clothes I put on that morning."

What is important about this shock of recognition is the humility it should give us about the more hidden aspects of our self-image as compared with reality. If we don't even know our own clothes and face and body-build and gait, why do we assume that we know the secret springs of our behavior?

Our drives, our motivations, are usually concealed from ourselves, even though they may be manifest to others who scarcely know us. It is deplorably and distressingly true that someone may meet us and in a half-hour have a more accurate picture of our inner topography than we have gained in a lifetime of living with ourselves.

It is not simply that we cannot "see ourselves as others see us." It is that we cannot see ourselves as we really are, in the total patterning of the personality. I am not suggesting that such insight is always necessary or desirable; merely that it is the most perilous arrogance to presume that we have it, and to act upon the presumption that the motives we are aware of are the "real" or the basic motives.

Everyone is a stranger to himself, in some important areas of behavior. When we speak of "humility" in the common sense, we usually mean a modesty about our talents and accomplishments; but genuine humility should also mean the acceptance of self-ignorance, the frank acknowledgment that even when we "do good," we cannot be sure of virtue.

This is the whole meaning of Jesus' saying, "Judge not, that ye be not judged." We tend to place the worst interpretation on the actions or words of others, while placing the best on our own. Yet if we cannot even recognize our physical selves walking down the street, how can we know the shape or substance of the self we cannot see?

THE BET

Anton Chekhov

It was a dark autumn night. The old banker was pacing from corner to corner of his study, recalling to his mind the party he gave in the autumn fifteen years before. There were many clever people at the party and much interesting conversation. They talked among other things of capital punishment. The guests, among them not a few scholars and journalists, for the most part disapproved of capital punishment. They found it obsolete as a means of punishment, unfitted to the Christan State, and immoral. Some of them thought that capital punishment should be replaced universally by life imprisonment.

"I don't agree with you," said the host. "I myself have experienced neither capital punishment nor life imprisonment, but if one may judge *a priori*, then in my opinion capital punishment is more moral and more humane than imprisonment. Execution kills instantly, life-imprisonment kills by degrees. Who is the more humane executioner, one who kills you in a few seconds or one who draws the life out of you incessantly, for years?"

"They're both equally immoral," remarked one of the guests, "because their purpose is the same, to take away life. The State is not God. It has no right to take away that which it cannot give back, if it should so desire."

Among the company was a lawyer, a young man of about twenty-five. On being asked his opinion, he said:

"Capital punishment and life imprisonment are equally immoral but if I were offered the choice between them, I would certainly choose the second. It's better to live somehow than not to live at all."

There ensued a lively discussion. The banker, who was then younger and more nervous, suddenly lost his temper, banged his fist on the table and turning to the young lawyer, cried out,

"It's a lie. I bet you two millions you wouldn't stick in a cell even for five years."

"If you mean it seriously," replied the lawyer, "then I bet I'll stay not five but fifteen."

"Fifteen! Done!" cried the banker, "Gentlemen, I stake two millions."

"Agreed. You stake two millions, I, my freedom," said the lawyer.

So this wild ridiculous bet came to pass. The banker who, at that time, had too many millions to count, spoiled and capricious, was beside himself with rapture. During supper, he said to the lawyer jokingly:

"Come to your senses young man, before it's too late. Two millions are nothing to me, but you stand to lose three or four of the best years of your life. I say three or four, because you'll never stick it out any longer. Don't forget either, you unhappy man, that voluntary is much heavier than enforced imprisonment. The idea that you have the right to free yourself at any moment will poison the whole of your life in the cell. I pity you."

And now the banker, pacing from corner to corner, recalled all this and asked himself,

"Why did I make this bet? What's the good? The lawyer loses fifteen years of his life and I throw away two millions. Will it convince people that capital punishment is worse or better than imprisonment for life? No, no! All stuff and rubbish. On my part, it was the caprice of a well fed man; on the lawyer's, pure greed of gold."

He recollected further what happened after the evening party. It was decided that the lawyer must undergo his imprisonment under the strictest observation in a garden wing of the banker's house. It was agreed that during the period he would be deprived of the right to cross the threshold, to see living people, to hear human voices, and to receive letters and newspapers. He was permitted to have a musical instrument, to read books, to write letters, to drink wine and smoke tobacco. By the agreement he could communicate, but only in silence, with the outside world through a little window specially constructed for this purpose. Everything necessary, books, music, wine, he could receive in any quantity by sending a note through the window. The agreement provided for all the minutest details, which made the confinement strictly solitary, and it obliged the lawyer to remain exactly fifteen years from 12 o'clock of November 14th, 1870, to 12 o'clock of November 14th, 1885. The least attempt on his part to violate the conditions, to escape if only for two minutes before the time, freed the banker from the obligation to pay him the two millions.

During the first year of imprisonment the lawyer, as far as it was possible to judge from his short note, suffered terribly from loneliness and boredom. From his wing day and night came the sound of the piano. He rejected wine and tobacco. "Wine," he wrote, "excites desires, and desires are the chief foes of a prisoner; besides, nothing is more boring than to drink good wine alone," and tobacco spoiled the air in his room. During the first year the lawyer was sent books of a light character; novels with a complicated love interest, stories of crime and fantasy, comedies, and so on.

In the second year the piano was heard no longer and the lawyer asked only for classics. In the fifth year, music was heard again, and the prisoner asked for wine. Those who watched him said that during the whole of that year he was only eating, drinking, and lying on his bed. He yawned often and talked angrily to himself. Books he did not read. Sometimes at nights he would sit down to write. He would write for a long time and tear it all up in the morning. More than once he was heard to weep.

In the second half of the sixth year, the prisoner began zealously to study languages, philosophy and history. He fell on these subjects so hungrily that the banker hardly had time to get books enough for him.

In the space of four years about six hundred volumes were bought at his request. It was while that passion lasted that the banker received the following letter from the prisoner: "My dear jailer, I am writing these lines in six languages. Show them to experts. Let them read them. If they do not find one single mistake, I beg you to give orders to have a gun fired off in the garden. By the noise, I shall know that my efforts have not been in vain. The geniuses of all ages and countries speak in different languages; but in them all burns the same flame. Oh, if you knew my heavenly happiness now that I can understand them!" The prisoner's desire was fulfilled. Two shots were fired in the garden by the banker's order.

Later on, after the tenth year, the lawyer sat immovable before his table and read only the New Testament. The banker found it strange that a man who in four years had mastered six hundred erudite volumes, should have spent nearly a year in reading one book, easy to understand and by no means thick. The New Testament was then replaced by the history of religions and theology.

During the last two years of his confinement the prisoner read an extra-ordinary amount, quite haphazard. Now he would apply himself to the natural sciences, then he would read Byron or Shakespeare. Notes used to come from him in which he asked to be sent at the same time a book on chemistry, a textbook of medicine, novel, and some treatise on philosophy or theology. He read as though he were swimming in the sea among broken pieces of wreckage, and in his desire to save his life was eagerly grasping one piece after another.

The banker recalled all this, and thought:

"Tomorrow at twelve o'clock he receives his freedom. Under the agreement, I shall have to pay him two millions. If I pay, it's all over with me. I am ruined forever...."

Fifteen years before he had too many millions to count, but now he was afraid to ask himself which he had more of, money or debts. Gambling on the Stock Exchange, risky speculation, and the recklessness of which he could not rid himself even in old age, had gradually brought his business to decay; and the fearful, self-confident, proud man of business had become an ordinary banker, trembling at every rise and fall in the market.

"That cursed bet," murmured the old man, clutching his head in despair. . . . "Why didn't the man die? He's only forty years old. He will take away my last farthing, marry, enjoy life, gamble on the Exchange, and I will look on like an envious beggar and hear the same words from him every day: 'I'm obliged to you for the happiness of my life. Let me help you.' No, it's too much! The only escape from bankruptcy and disgrace—is that the man should die."

The clock had just struck three. The banker was listening. In the house every one was asleep, and one could hear only the frozen trees whining outside the windows. Trying to make no sound, he took out of his safe the key to the door which had not been opened for fifteen years, put on his overcoat and went out of the house. The garden was dark and cold. It was raining. A damp, penetrating wind howled in the garden and gave the trees no rest. Though he strained his eyes, the banker could see neither the ground, nor the white statues, nor the garden wing, nor the trees. Approaching the garden wing, he called the watchman twice. There was no answer. Evidently the watchman had taken shelter from the bad weather and was now asleep somewhere in the kitchen or the greenhouse.

"If I have the courage to fulfill my intention," thought the old man, "the suspicion will fall on the watchman first of all."

In the darkness he groped for the steps and the door and entered the hall of the garden-wing, then poked his way into a narrow passage and struck a match. Not a soul was there. Someone's bed, with no bedclothes on it, stood there, and an iron stove loomed dark in the corner. The seals on the door that led into the prisoner's room were unbroken.

When the match went out, the old man, trembling from agitation, peered into the little window.

In the prisoner's room a candle was burning dimly. The prisoner himself sat by the table. Only his back, the hair on his head and his hands were visible. Open books were strewn about on the table, two chairs, and on the carpet near the table.

Five minutes passed and the prisoner never once stirred. The banker tapped on the window with his finger, but the prisoner made no movement in reply. Then the banker cautiously tore the seals from the door and put the key into the lock. The rusty lock gave a hoarse groan and the door creaked. The banker expected instantly to hear a cry of surprise and the sound of steps. Three minutes passed and it was as quiet inside as it had been before. He made up his mind to enter.

Before the table sat a man, unlike an ordinary human being. It was a skeleton, with tight-drawn skin, with long curly hair like a woman's and the cheeks were sunken, the back long and narrow and the hand upon which he leaned his hairy head was so lean and skinny that it was painful to look upon. His hair was already silvering with gray, and no one who glanced at the senile emaciation of the face would have believed that he was only forty years old. On the table, before his bended head, lay a sheet of paper on which something was written in a tiny hand.

"Poor devil," thought the banker, "he's asleep and probably seeing millions in his dreams. I have only to try and throw this half-dead thing on the bed, smother him a moment with the pillow, and the most careful examination will find no trace of unnatural death. But first, let us read what he has written here."

The banker took the sheet from the table and read:

"Tomorrow at 12 o'clock midnight, I shall obtain my freedom and the right to mix with people. But before I leave this room and see the sun, I think it necessary to say a few words to you. On my own clear conscience and before God who sees me, I declare to you that I despise freedom, life, health and all that your books call the blessings of the world.

"For fifteen years I have diligently studied earthly life. True, I saw neither the earth nor the people, but in your books I drank fragrant wine, sang songs, hunted deer and wild boar in the forest, loved women.... And beautiful women, like clouds ethereal, created by the magic of your poets' genius, visited me by night and whispered to me wonderful tales which made my head drunken. In your books I climbed the summits of Elburz and Mount Blanc, and saw how the sun rose in the morning, and in the evening suffused the sky, the ocean and the mountain ridge with a purple gold. I saw from there how above me lightnings glimmered, cleaving the clouds; I saw green forests, fields, rivers, lakes, cities, heard sirens singing and the playing of the pipes of Pan; I touched the wings of beautiful devils who came flying to me to speak of God.... In your books I cast myself into bottomless abysses, worked miracles, burned cities to the ground, preached new religions.

"Your books gave me wisdom. All that unwearying human thought created in the centuries is compressed to a little lump in my skull. I know that I am cleverer than you all.

"And I despise your books, despise all worldly blessings and wisdom. Everything is void, frail, visionary and delusive as a mirage. Though you be proud and wise and beautiful, yet will death wipe you from the face of the earth like the mice underground; and your posterity, your history and the immortality of your men of genius will be as frozen slag, burnt down together with the terrestrial globe.

"You are mad, and gone the wrong way. You take falsehood for truth and ugliness for beauty. You would marvel if suddenly apple and orange trees should bear frogs and lizards instead of fruit, and if roses should begin to breathe the odor of a sweating horse. So do I marvel at you, who have bartered heaven for earth. I do not want to understand you.

"That I may show you in deed my contempt for that by which you live, I waive the two millions of which I once dreamed as of paradise, and which I now despise. That I may deprive myself of my right to them,

I shall come out from here five minutes before the stipulated term, and thus shall violate the agreement."

When he had read, the banker put the sheet on the table, kissed the head of the strange man and began to weep. He went out of the wing. Never at any other time, not even after his terrible losses on the Exchange, had he felt such contempt for himself as now. Coming home, he lay down on his bed, but agitation and tears kept him from sleeping....

The next morning the poor watchman came running to him and told him that they had seen the man who lived in the wing climb through the window into the garden. He had gone to the gate and disappeared. The banker instantly went with his servants to the wing and established the escape of his prisoner. To avoid unnecessary rumors he took the paper with the renunciation from the table and, on his return, locked it in his safe.

WHY WE SUCCEED OR FAIL

Charles H. Brower

After a good many years of observing human nature in action, I have firmly concluded that two qualities make the difference between leaders and men of average performance. They are curiosity and discontent. These deep human urges work together, I believe, to motivate all human discovery and achievement.

I have never known an outstanding man who lacked either curiosity or discontent. And I have never known a man of small achievement who had both. The two belong together. Without discontent, curiosity is merely idle. Without curiosity, discontent is only useless hand-wringing.

Together, curiosity and discontent count for much more then mere ambition. Galileo was not ambitious when he dropped objects of varying weights from the Leaning Tower at Pisa and timed their fall to the ground. Nor was Jean Henri Fabre when he sat day after day beside anthills, studying the difference between instinct and reason. These men, and all men whose names are large in history, were curious and asked "Why? Why? Why?" And they were discontented because there were no acceptable answers.

My friend Frank has been filled with curiosity and discontent since the day, at the age of three, when his father hauled him from under a trolley car where he had crawled to see "what makes the ding-dong run." In the depression he and his wife found their clothes wearing thin and their income reduced to $50 a month. To get a new suit for herself, Eleanor offered to make a suit for a neighbor if the neighbor would buy cloth for two suits. The suits looked fine except for one thing. "A tweed suit should really have some of those lovely wooden buttons," she said. "But who can afford them?"

"Maybe we can't afford them, but I'll bet I can make them," Frank said. He took a sample of the material and rode his bike across town to a friend's basement workshop.

"I found a piece of mahogany that was a nice deep red like the dark tones of the tweed," he told me recently, "and a piece of silver birch that matched the light tones. I glued the two pieces together and sawed them into button-size squares. Then I slanted them from the edges toward the center like little roofs, so that both colors showed. I made big buttons for the coat front, smaller ones for the pockets, and tiny ones for the sleeves."

Among those who admired the buttons on Eleanor's new suit was the proprietor of a dress shop in Frank's town. At her suggestion, Frank called on several dress manufacturers. In one afternoon he got $87 worth of orders. Today his woodturning company makes what are known as "variety turnings"—wheels, buttons, beads, handles, bottle tops, toy parts —and is valued at more than a quarter of a million dollars.

Fortunately you and I don't have to learn curiosity and discontent. We need only to recapture them. Any healthy baby is a squirming vocal bundle of these two deep human urges. And as he grows, the urges deepen. He wants up. He wants down. He wants out. He pulls things off tables and shelves, and drags the pots and pans out of the cupboards. Later he floods his parents with a tide of unanswerable questions.

"The great man," said Mencius, the Chinese sage, "is he who does not lose his child's heart." Yet that is exactly what most of us seem to do. Somewhere along the line we allow our curiosity and discontent to wither away. We stop asking questions. We stop challenging custom. We stop demanding proof. We drift into step with the crowd.

And the crowd desires only the calm and restful average. It encourages us to brighten our own little corner, to count our blessings, to avoid foolish leaps into the dark, to seek peace of mind—in other words, to budget our desires to what our small achievement can afford. It ignores the fact that peace never comes to the unachieving mind, that the days of contentment are never the golden days of any nation.

If you will strike out on your own, you may miss a few parties with "the crowd" but you will not be lonely. There are a lot of new friends waiting to talk with you, no farther away than your local library: Leonardo da Vinci—probably the most curious and discontented man who ever lived; Shakespeare, Newton and Pasteur. Lincoln will tell you how it felt to see the Union split apart. Dickens will introduce you to an England you may have missed.

All the truly great who ever lived will help arouse your curiosity and discontent anew, so that never again in your life will you think that the world is good enough, never again will you sit idly by while a question remains unanswered that you might find the answer to.

Oh, yes, you can ask these great men questions. Ask stout Samuel Johnson about curiosity: "Curiosity is one of the most permanent and certain characteristics of a vigorous mind." Ask the newspaper editor Frederick Bonfils: "There is no hope for the satisfied man." Then while you are at it, ask Dr. Joseph Leidy, the naturalist, if he didn't sometimes get a little tired of it all: "Tired? Not so long as there is an undescribed intestinal worm, or the riddle of a fossil bone, or a rhizopod new to me."

You will need, of course, more than the friendship of the great. They can only help you, they cannot lead your life for you. You will need a new inventory of your hours, a sharper classification of what is worth doing and what is merely time-killing. You will need to understand that it is often as important to break a good habit as to break a bad one. All habit is suspect. If going to church is nothing more than habit, it may do more to put your soul to sleep than to save it. But don't stop going to church! Rather, re-examine your motives, look around for some activity, some responsibility that breaks the routine.

Most of us meet new people, and new ideas, reluctantly. But once having met and liked them, we think how terrible it would have been had we missed the chance. You will probably have to force yourself to waken your curiosity and discontent and keep them awake. It may seem like work for a while. But Sir James Barrie will tell you, "Nothing is work unless there is something else you'd rather be doing." And what else could one rather be doing than becoming alive once more?

How should you start? Modestly, so as not to become discouraged. Besides, most worth-while things started modestly. I think of one friend who started making puppets to amuse her children and to test her own skill. She and her husband now make puppets for television, and their book on puppetry is a recognized authority. Or I think of another who wanted to increase his reading speed, and now reads—and reviews—three novels a day. Or still another who couldn't arrange flowers to satisfy herself. She was curious about how the experts did it. Now she is one of the experts lecturing and writing books on flower arrangement.

One way to begin is to answer your own excuses.

You haven't any special ability? Most people don't—there are only a few geniuses.

You haven't any time? That's good, because it's always the people with no time who get things done. Harriet Beecher Stowe, mother of six, did not have much time. She wrote parts of *Uncle Tom's Cabin* on sheets of butchers' paper while the roast cooked.

You're too old? You had better not let Winston Churchill, Konrad Adenauer, Bernard Baruch, Robert Frost or Carl Sandburg hear you say that. And if you answer that these people are only continuing what they learned in younger days, remember that Thomas Costain was fifty-seven when he published his first novel, and that Grandma Moses showed her first pictures when she was seventy-eight.

The important thing, as Alexander Graham Bell would tell you, is, "Don't keep forever on the public road, going only where others have gone. Leave the beaten track occasionally and dive into the woods. You will be certain to find something that you've never seen before. It will be a little thing, but do not ignore it. Follow it up, explore all around it; one discovery will lead to another and before you know it you will have something really worth thinking about to occupy your mind."

However you start, remember that curiosity and discontent are continuing operations. You don't turn them on and off whenever you feel like it. You live them, day by day. There is no better time to start than right now for you'll never be more alive than you are at this moment. Treat yourself to a new thought, today. Don't lock yourself up, in a room or in your mind —life is not a spectator sport. Find something to be enthusiastic about, and support it publicly. Find something to be sore about, and fight it openly.

As Oliver Wendell Holmes said: "Man's mind, stretched to a new idea, never goes back to its original dimensions."

ECCLESIASTES III

To every *thing there is* a season, and a time to every purpose under the heaven:

2 A time to be born, and a time to die; a time to plant, and a time to pluck up *that which is* planted;

3 A time to kill, and a time to heal; a time to break down, and a time to build up;

4 A time to weep, and a time to laugh; a time to mourn, and a time to dance;

5 A time to cast away stones, and a time to gather stones together; a time to embrace, and a time to refrain from embracing;

6 A time to get, and a time to lose; a time to keep, and a time to cast away;

7 A time to rend, and a time to sew; a time to keep silence, and a time to speak;

8 A time to love, and a time to hate; a time of war, and a time of peace.

9 What profit hath he that worketh in that wherein he laboureth?

10 I have seen the travail, which God hath given to the sons of men to be exercised in it.

11 He hath made every *thing* beautiful in his time: also he hath set the world in their heart, so that no man can find out the work that God maketh from the beginning to the end.

12 I know that *there is* no good in them, but a man to rejoice, and to do good in his life.

13 And also that every man should eat and drink, and enjoy the good of all his labour, it is the gift of God.

14 I know that, whatsoever God doeth, it shall be for ever: nothing can be put to it, nor any thing taken from it: and God doeth *it*, that *men* should fear before him.

15 That which hath been is now; and that which is to be hath already been; and God requireth that which is past.

16 And moreover I saw under the sun the place of judgment, *that* wickedness *was* there; and the place of righteousness, *that* iniquity *was* there.

17 I said in mine heart, God shall judge the righteous and the wicked: for *there is* a time there for every purpose and for every work.

18 I said in mine heart concerning the estate of the sons of men, that God might manifest them, and that they might see that they themselves are beasts.

19 For that which befalleth the sons of men befalleth beasts; even one thing befalleth them: as the one dieth, so dieth the other; yea, they have all one breath; so that a man hath no preeminence above a beast: for all *is* vanity.

20 All go unto one place; all are of the dust, and all turn to dust again.

21 Who knoweth the spirit of man that goeth upward, and the spirit of the beast that goeth downward to the earth?

22 Wherefore I perceive that *there is* nothing better, than that a man

should rejoice in his own works; for that *is* his portion: for who shall bring him to see what shall be after him?

SPREADING THE NEWS

Lady Gregory

PERSONS

BARTLEY FALLON	MRS. TARPEY
MRS. FALLON	MRS. TULLEY
JACK SMITH	A POLICEMAN
SHAWN EARLY	(JO MULDOON)
TIM CASEY	A REMOVABLE
JAMES RYAN	MAGISTRATE

SCENE: *The outskirts of a fair. An apple stall.* MRS. TARPEY *sitting at it.* MAGISTRATE *and* POLICEMAN *enter.*

MAGISTRATE: So that is the Fair Green. Cattle and sheep and mud. No system. What a repulsive sight!

POLICEMAN: That is so, indeed.

MAGISTRATE: I suppose there is a good deal of disorder in this place?

POLICEMAN: There is.

MAGISTRATE: Common assault?

POLICEMAN: It's common enough.

MAGISTRATE: Agrarian crime, no doubt?

POLICEMAN: That is so.

MAGISTRATE: Boycotting? Maiming of cattle? Firing into houses?

POLICEMAN: There was one time, and there might be again.

MAGISTRATE: That is bad. Does it go any farther than that?

POLICEMAN: Far enough, indeed.

MAGISTRATE: Homicide, then! This district has been shamefully neglected! I will change all that. When I was in the Andaman Islands, my system never failed. Yes, yes, I will change all that. What has that women on her stall?

POLICEMAN: Apples mostly—and sweets.

MAGISTRATE: Just see if there are any unlicensed goods underneath— spirits or the like. We had evasions of the salt tax in the Andaman Islands.

POLICEMAN (*sniffing cautiously and upsetting a heap of apples*): I see no spirits here—or salt.

MAGISTRATE (*to* MRS. TARPEY): Do you know this town well, my good woman?

MRS. TARPEY (*holding out some apples*): A penny the half-dozen, your honor?

POLICEMAN (*shouting*): The gentleman is asking do you know the town! He's the new magistrate!

MRS. TARPEY (*rising and ducking*): Do I know the town? I do, to be sure.

MAGISTRATE (*shouting*): What is its chief business?

MRS. TARPEY: Business, is it? What business would the people here have but to be minding one another's business?

MAGISTRATE: I mean what trade have they?

MRS. TARPEY: Not a trade. No trade at all but to be talking.

MAGISTRATE: I shall learn nothing here.

> (JAMES RYAN *comes in, pipe in mouth. Seeing* MAGISTRATE, *he retreats quickly, taking pipe from mouth.*)

MAGISTRATE: The smoke from that man's pipe has a greenish look; he may be growing unlicensed tobacco at home. I wish I had brought my telescope to this district. Come to the post office; I will telegraph for it. I found it very useful in the Andaman Islands.

> (MAGISTRATE *and* POLICEMAN *go out left.*)

MRS. TARPEY: Bad luck to Jo Muldoon, knocking my apples this way and that way. (*Begins arranging them.*) Showing off he was to the new magistrate.

> (*Enter* BARTLEY FALLON *and* MRS. FALLON.)

BARTLEY: Indeed it's a poor country and a scarce country to be living in. But I'm thinking if I went to America it's long ago the day I'd be dead!

MRS. FALLON: So you might, indeed. (*She puts her basket on a barrel and begins putting parcels in it, taking them from under her cloak.*)

BARTLEY: And it's a great expense for a poor man to be buried in America.

MRS. FALLON: Never fear, Bartley Fallon, but I'll give you a good burying the day you'll die.

BARTLEY: Maybe it's yourself will be buried in the graveyard of Cloonmara before me, Mary Fallon, and I myself that will be dying unbeknownst some night, and no one a-near me. And the cat itself may be gone straying through the country, and the mice squealing over the quilt.

MRS. FALLON: Leave off talking of dying. It might be twenty years you'll be living yet.

BARTLEY (*with a deep sigh*): I'm thinking if I'll be living at the end of twenty years, it's a very old man I'll be then!

MRS. TARPEY (*turns and sees them*): Good morrow, Bartley Fallon; good morrow, Mrs. Fallon. Well, Bartley, you'll find no cause for complaining today; they are all saying it was a good fair.

BARTLEY *(raising his voice)*: It was not a good fair, Mrs. Tarpey. It was a scattered sort of a fair. If we didn't expect more, we got less. That's the way with me always; whatever I have to sell goes down and whatever I have to buy goes up. If there's ever any misfortune coming to this world, it's on myself it pitches, like a flock of crows on seed potatoes.

MRS. FALLON: Leave off talking of misfortunes, and listen to Jack Smith that is coming the way, and he singing.

(Voice of JACK SMITH *heard singing)*:
    "I thought, my first love,
        There'd be but one house between you and me,
    And I thought I would find
        Yourself coaxing my child on your knee.
    Over the tide
        I would leap with the leap of a swan,
    Till I came to the side
        Of the wife of the red-haired man!"

*(*JACK SMITH *comes in; he is a red-haired man, and is carrying a hayfork.)*

MRS. TARPEY: That should be a good song if I had my hearing.

MRS. FALLON *(shouting)*: It's "The Red-haired Man's Wife."

MRS. TARPEY: I know it well. That's the song that has a skin on it! *(She turns her back to them and goes on arranging her apples.)*

MRS. FALLON: Where's herself, Jack Smith?

JACK SMITH: She was delayed with her washing; bleaching the clothes on the hedge she is, and she daren't leave them, with all the tinkers that do be passing to the fair. It isn't to the fair I came myself, but up to the Five Acre Meadow I'm going, where I have a contract for the hay. We'll get a share of it into tramps today. *(He lays down the hayfork and lights his pipe.)*

BARTLEY: You will not get it into tramps today. The rain will be down on it by evening, and on myself, too. It's seldom I ever started on a journey but the rain would come down on me before I'd find any place of shelter.

JACK SMITH: If it didn't itself, Bartley, it is my belief you would carry a leaky pail on your head in place of a hat, the way you'd not be without some cause of complaining.

(A voice heard, "Go on, now, go on out o' that. Go on I say.")

JACK SMITH: Look at that young mare of Pat Ryan's that is backing into Shaughnessy's bullocks with the dint of the crowd! Don't be daunted, Pat; I'll give you a hand with her. *(He goes out, leaving his hayfork.)*

MRS. FALLON: It's time for ourselves to be going home. I have all I bought put in the basket. Look at there, Jack Smith's hayfork he left after him. He'll be wanting it. (*Calls.*) Jack Smith! Jack Smith—He's gone through the crowd—hurry after him, Bartley; he'll be wanting it.

BARTLEY: I'll do that. This is no safe place to be leaving it. (*He takes up fork awkwardly and upsets the basket.*) Look at that now! If there is any basket in the fair upset, it must be our own basket! (*He goes out to the right.*)

MRS. FALLON: Get out of that! It is your own fault, it is. Talk of misfortunes, and misfortunes will come. Glory be! Look at my new eggcups rolling in every part—and my two pound of sugar with the paper broke—

MRS. TARPEY (*turning from stall*): God help us, Mrs. Fallon, what happened your basket?

MRS. FALLON: It's himself that knocked it down, bad manners to him. (*Putting things up.*) My grand sugar that's destroyed, and he'll not drink his tea without it. I had best go back to the shop for more; much good may it do him!

(*Enter* TIM CASEY.)

TIM CASEY: Where is Bartley Fallon, Mrs. Fallon? I want a word with him before he'll leave the fair. I was afraid he might have gone home by this, for he's a temperate man.

MRS. FALLON: I wish he did go home! It'd be best for me if he went home straight from the fair green, or if he never came with me at all! Where is he, is it? He's gone up the road (*jerks elbow*) following Jack Smith with a hayfork. (*She goes out to left.*)

TIM CASEY: Following Jack Smith with a hayfork! Did ever any one hear the like of that? (*Shouts.*) Did you hear that news, Mrs. Tarpey?

MRS. TARPEY: I heard no news at all.

TIM CASEY: Some dispute I suppose it was that rose between Jack Smith and Bartley Fallon, and it seems Jack made off, and Bartley is following him with a hayfork!

MRS. TARPEY: Is he now? Well, that was quick work! It's not ten minutes since the two of them were here, Bartley going home and Jack going to the Five Acre Meadow; and I had my apples to settle up, that Jo Muldoon of the police had scattered, and when I looked round again, Jack Smith was gone, and Bartley Fallon was gone, and Mrs. Fallon's basket upset, and all in it strewed upon the ground—the tea here—the two pound of sugar there—the egg-cups there—Look, now, what a great hardship the deafness puts upon me, that I didn't hear the commincement of the fight! Wait till I tell James Ryan that I see below. He is a neighbor of Bartley's; it would be a pity if he wouldn't hear the news!

(*She goes out. Enter* SHAWN EARLY *and* MRS. TULLY.)

TIM CASEY: Listen, Shawn Early! Listen, Mrs. Tully, to the news! Jack Smith and Bartley Fallon had a falling out, and Jack knocked Mrs.

Fallon's basket into the road, and Bartley made an attack on him with a hayfork, and away with Jack, and Bartley after him. Look at the sugar here yet on the road!

SHAWN EARLY: Do you tell me so? Well, that's a queer thing, and Bartley Fallon so quiet a man!

MRS. TULLY: I wouldn't wonder at all. I would never think well of a man that would have that sort of a moldering look. It's likely he has overtaken Jack by this.

(*Enter* JAMES RYAN *and* MRS. TARPEY.)

JAMES RYAN: That is great news Mrs. Tarpey was telling me! I suppose that's what brought the police and the magistrate up this way. I was wondering to see them in it a while ago.

SHAWN EARLY: The police after them? Bartley Fallon must have injured Jack so. They wouldn't meddle in a fight that was only for show!

MRS. TULLY: Why wouldn't he injure him? There was many a man killed with no more of a weapon than a hayfork.

JAMES RYAN: Wait till I run north as far as Kelly's bar to spread the news! (*He goes out.*)

TIM CASEY: I'll go tell Jack Smith's first cousin that is standing there south of the church after selling his lambs. (*Goes out.*)

MRS. TULLY: I'll go telling a few of the neighbors I see beyond to the west. (*Goes out.*)

SHAWN EARLY: I'll give word of it beyond at the east of the green. (*Is going out when* MRS. TARPEY *seizes hold of him.*)

MRS. TARPEY: Stop a minute, Shawn Early, and tell me did you see red Jack Smith's wife, Kitty Keary, in any place?

SHAWN EARLY: I did. At her own house she was, drying clothes on the hedge as I passed.

MRS. TARPEY: What did you say she was doing?

SHAWN EARLY (*breaking away*): Laying out a sheet on the hedge. (*He goes.*)

MRS. TARPEY: Laying out a sheet for the dead! The Lord have mercy on us! Jack Smith dead, and his wife laying out a sheet for his burying! (*Calls out.*) Why didn't you tell me that before, Shawn Early? Isn't the deafness the great hardship? Half the world might be dead without me knowing of it or getting word of it at all! (*She sits down and rocks herself.*) O my poor Jack Smith! To be going to his work so nice and so hearty, and to be left stretched on the ground in the full light of the day!

(*Enter* TIM CASEY.)

TIM CASEY: What is it, Mrs. Tarpey? What happened since?

MRS. TARPEY: O my poor Jack Smith!

TIM CASEY: Did Bartley overtake him?

MRS. TARPEY: O the poor man!

TIM CASEY: Is it killed he is?

MRS. TARPEY: Stretched in the Five Acre Meadow!

TIM CASEY: The Lord have mercy on us! Is that a fact?

MRS. TARPEY: Without the rites of the Church or a ha'porth!

TIM CASEY: Who was telling you?

MRS. TARPEY: And the wife laying out a sheet for his corpse. (*Sits up and wipes her eyes.*) I suppose they'll wake him the same as another?

    (*Enter* MRS. TULLY, SHAWN EARLY, *and* JAMES RYAN.)

MRS. TULLY: There is great talk about this work in every quarter of the fair.

MRS. TARPEY: Ochone! cold and dead. And myself maybe the last he was speaking to!

JAMES RYAN: The Lord save us! Is it dead he is?

TIM CASEY: Dead surely, and the wife getting provision for the wake.

SHAWN EARLY: Well, now, hadn't Bartley Fallon great venom in him?

MRS. TULLY: You may be sure he had some cause. Why would he have made an end of him if he had not? (*To Mrs. Tarpey, raising her voice.*) What was it rose the dispute at all, Mrs. Tarpey?

MRS. TARPEY: Not a one of me knows. The last I saw of them, Jack Smith was standing there, and Bartley Fallon was standing there, quiet and easy, and he listening to "The Red-haired Man's Wife."

MRS. TULLY: Do you hear that, Tim Casey? Do you hear that, Shawn Early and James Ryan? Bartley Fallon was here this morning listening to red Jack Smith's wife, Kitty Keary that was! Listening to her and whispering with her! It was she started the fight so!

SHAWN EARLY: She must have followed him from her own house. It is likely some person roused him.

TIM CASEY: I never knew, before, Bartley Fallon was great with Jack Smith's wife.

MRS. TULLY: How would you know it? Sure it's not in the streets they would be calling it. If Mrs. Fallon didn't know of it, and if I that have the next house to them didn't know of it, and if Jack Smith himself didn't know of it, it is not likely you would know of it, Tim Casey.

SHAWN EARLY: Let Bartley Fallon take charge of her from this out so, and let him provide for her. It is little pity she will get from any person in this parish.

TIM CASEY: How can he take charge of her? Sure he has a wife of his own. Sure you don't think he'd turn souper and marry her in a Protestant church?

JAMES RYAN: It would be easy for him to marry her if he brought her to America.

SHAWN EARLY: With or without Kitty Keary, believe me it is for America he's making at this minute. I saw the new magistrate and Jo Muldoon of the police going into the post office as I came up—there was hurry on them—you may be sure it was to telegraph they went, the way he'll be stopped in the docks at Queenstown!

MRS. TULLY: It's likely Kitty Keary is gone with him, and not minding a sheet or a wake at all. The poor man, to be deserted by his own wife, and the breath hardly gone out yet from his body that is lying bloody in the field!

(Enter MRS. FALLON.)

MRS. FALLON: What is it the whole of the town is talking about? And what is it you yourselves are talking about? Is it about my man Bartley Fallon you are talking? Is it lies about him you are telling, saying that he went killing Jack Smith? My grief that ever he came into the place at all!

JAMES RYAN: Be easy now, Mrs. Fallon. Sure there is no one at all in the whole fair but is sorry for you!

MRS. FALLON: Sorry for me, is it? Why would anyone be sorry for me? Let you be sorry for yourselves, and that there may be shame on you forever and at the day of judgment, for the words you are saying and the lies you are telling to take away the character of my poor man, and to take the good name off of him, and to drive him to destruction! That is what you are doing!

SHAWN EARLY: Take comfort now, Mrs. Fallon. The police are not so smart as they think. Sure he might give them the slip yet, the same as Lynchehaun.

MRS. TULLY: If they do get him, and if they do put a rope around his neck, there is no one can say he does not deserve it!

MRS. FALLON: Is that what you are saying, Bridget Tully, and is that what you think? I tell you it's too much talk you have, making yourself out to be such a great one, and to be running down every respectable person! A rope, is it? It isn't much of a rope was needed to tie up your own furniture the day you came into Martin Tully's house, and you never bringing as much as a blanket, or a penny, or a suit of clothes with you, and I myself bringing seventy pounds and two feather beds. And now you are stiffer than a woman would have a hundred pounds! It is too much talk the whole of you have. A rope, is it? I tell you the whole of this town is full of liars and schemers that would hang you up for half a glass of whisky. *(Turning to go.)* People they are you wouldn't believe as much as daylight from without you'd get up to have a look at it yourself. Killing Jack Smith, indeed! Where are you at all, Bartley, till I bring you out of this? My nice, quiet little man! My decent comrade! He that is as kind and as harmless as an innocent beast of the field! He'll be doing no harm at all if he'll shed the blood of some of you after this day's work! That much would be no harm at all. *(Calls out.)* Bartley! Bartley Fallon! Where are you? *(Going out.)* Did anyone see Bartley

Fallon? *(All turn to look after her.)*

JAMES RYAN: It is hard for her to believe any such a thing, God help her!

(Enter BARTLEY FALLON from right, carrying hayfork.)

BARTLEY: It is what I often said to myself, if there is ever any misfortune coming to this world, it is on myself it is sure to come!

(All turn round and face him.)

BARTLEY: To be going about with this fork, and to find no one to take it, and no place to leave it down, and I wanting to be gone out of this— Is that you, Shawn Early? *(Holds out fork.)* It's well I met you. You have no call to be leaving the fair for a while the way I have, and how can I go till I'm rid of this fork? Will you take it and keep it until such time as Jack Smith—

SHAWN EARLY *(backing)*: I will not take it, Bartley Fallon, I'm very thankful to you!

BARTLEY *(turning to apple stall)*: Look at it now, Mrs. Tarpey; it was here I got it; let me thrust it in under the stall. It will lie there safe enough, and no one will take notice of it until such time as Jack Smith—

MRS. TARPEY: Take your fork out of that! Is it to put trouble on me and to destroy me you want? Putting it there for the police to be rooting out maybe. *(Thrusts him back.)*

BARTLEY: That is a very unneighborly thing for you to do, Mrs. Tarpey. Hadn't I enough care on me with that fork before this, running up and down with it like the swinging of a clock, and afeard to lay it down in any place. I wish I never touched it or meddled with it at all!

JAMES RYAN: It is a pity, indeed, you ever did.

BARTLEY: Will you yourself take it, James Ryan? You were always a neighborly man.

JAMES RYAN *(backing)*: There is many a thing I would do for you, Bartley Fallon, but I won't do that!

SHAWN EARLY: I tell you there is no man will give you any help or any encouragement for this day's work. If it was something agrarian now—

BARTLEY: If no one at all will take it, maybe it's best to give it up to the police.

TIM CASEY: There'd be a welcome for it with them, surely! *(Laughter.)*

MRS. TULLY: And it is to the police Kitty Keary herself will be brought.

MRS. TARPEY *(rocking to and fro)*: I wonder now who will take the expense of the wake for poor Jack Smith?

BARTLEY: The wake for Jack Smith!

TIM CASEY: Why wouldn't he get a wake as well as another? Would you begrudge him that much?

BARTLEY: Red Jack Smith dead! Who was telling you?

SHAWN EARLY: The whole town knows of it by this.

BARTLEY: Do they say what way did he die?

JAMES RYAN: You don't know that yourself, I suppose, Bartley Fallon? You don't know he was followed and that he was laid dead with the stab of a hayfork?

BARTLEY: The stab of a hayfork!

SHAWN EARLY: You don't know, I suppose, that the body was found in the Five Acre Meadow?

BARTLEY: The Five Acre Meadow!

TIM CASEY: It is likely you don't know the police are after the man that did it?

BARTLEY: The man that did it!

MRS. TULLY: You don't know, maybe, that he was made away with for the sake of Kitty Keary, his wife?

BARTLEY: Kitty Keary, his wife! (Sits down bewildered.)

MRS. TULLY: And what have you to say now, Bartley Fallon?

BARTLEY (crossing himself): I to bring that fork here, and to find that news before me! It is much if I can ever stir from this place at all, or reach as far as the road!

TIM CASEY: Look, boys, at the new magistrate, and Jo Muldoon along with him! It's best for us to quit this.

SHAWN EARLY: That is so. It is best not to be mixed in this business at all.

JAMES RYAN: Bad as he is, I wouldn't like to be an informer against any man.

(All hurry away except MRS. TARPEY, who remains behind her stall. Enter MAGISTRATE and POLICEMAN.)

MAGISTRATE: I knew the district was in a bad state, but I did not expect to be confronted with a murder at the first fair I came to.

POLICEMAN: I am sure you did not, indeed.

MAGISTRATE: It was well I had not gone home. I caught a few words here and there that roused my suspicions.

POLICEMAN: So they would, too.

MAGISTRATE: You heard the same story from everyone you asked?

POLICEMAN: The same story—or if it was not altogether the same, anyway it was no less than the first story.

MAGISTRATE: What is that man doing? He is sitting alone with a hayfork. He has a guilty look. The murder was done with a hayfork!

POLICEMAN (in a whisper): That's the very man they say did the act; Bartley Fallon himself!

MAGISTRATE: He must have found escape difficult—he is trying to brazen it out. A convict in the Andaman Islands tired the same game, but he could not escape my system! Stand aside—Don't go far—Have the hand-cuffs ready. (He walks up to BARTLEY, folds his arms, and stands before him.) Here, my man, do you know anything of John Smith?

BARTLEY: Of John Smith! Who is he, now?

POLICEMAN: Jack Smith, sir, Red Jack Smith!

MAGISTRATE (*coming a step nearer and tapping him on the shoulder*): Where is Jack Smith?

BARTLEY (*with a deep sigh, and shaking his head slowly*): Where is he, indeed?

MAGISTRATE: What have you to tell?

BARTLEY: It is where he was this morning, standing in this spot, singing his share of songs—no, but lighting his pipe—scraping a match on the sole of his shoe—

MAGISTRATE: I ask you, for the third time, where is he?

BARTLEY: I wouldn't like to say that. It is a great mystery, and it is hard to say of any man, did he earn hatred or love.

MAGISTRATE: Tell me all you know.

BARTLEY: All that I know—Well, there are the three estates; there is Limbo, and there is Purgatory, and there is—

MAGISTRATE: Nonsense! This is trifling! Get to the point.

BARTLEY: Maybe you don't hold with the clergy so? That is the teaching of the clergy. Maybe you hold with the old people. It is what they do be saying, that the shadow goes wandering, and the soul is tired, and the body is taking a rest—The shadow! (*Starts up.*) I was nearly sure I saw Jack Smith not ten minutes ago at the corner of the forge, and I lost him again. Was it his ghost I saw, do you think?

MAGISTRATE (*to policeman*): Conscience-struck! He will confess all now!

BARTLEY: His ghost to come before me! It is likely it was on account of the fork! I to have it, and he to have no way to defend himself the time he met with his death!

MAGISTRATE (*to policeman*): I must note down his words. (*Takes out notebook.*) (*To* BARTLEY.) I warn you that your words are being noted.

BARTLEY: If I had ha' run faster in the beginning, this terror would not be on me at the latter end! Maybe he will cast it up against me at the day of judgment—I wouldn't wonder at all at that.

MAGISTRATE (*writing*): At the day of judgment—

BARTLEY: It was soon for his ghost to appear to me—is it coming after me always by day it will be, and stripping the clothes off in the night time?—I wouldn't wonder at all at that, being as I am an unfortunate man!

MAGISTRATE (*sternly*): Tell me this truly. What was the motive of this crime?

BARTLEY: The motive, is it?

MAGISTRATE: Yes; the motive; the cause.

BARTLEY: I'd sooner not say that.

MAGISTRATE: You had better tell me truly. Was it money?

BARTLEY: Not at all! What did poor Jack Smith ever have in his pockets unless it might be his hands that would be in them?

MAGISTRATE: Any dispute about land?

BARTLEY (*indignantly*): Not at all! He never was a grabber or grabbed from anyone!

MAGISTRATE: You will find it better for you if you tell me at once.

BARTLEY: I tell you I wouldn't for the whole world wish to say what it was—it is a thing I would not like to be talking about.

MAGISTRATE: There is no use in hiding it. It will be discovered in the end.

BARTLEY: Well, I suppose it will, seeing that mostly everybody knows it before. Whisper here now. I will tell no lie; where would be the use? (*Puts his hand to his mouth, and* MAGISTRATE *stoops.*) Don't be putting the blame on the parish, for such a thing was never done in the parish before—it was done for the sake of Kitty Keary, Jack Smith's wife.

MAGISTRATE (*to policeman*): Put on the handcuffs. We have been saved some trouble. I knew he would confess if taken in the right way. (*Policeman puts on handcuffs.*)

BARTLEY: Handcuffs now! Glory be! I always said if there was ever any misfortune coming to this place it was on myself it would fall. I to be in handcuffs! There's no wonder at all in that.

(*Enter* MRS. FALLON, *followed by the rest. She is looking back at them as she speaks.*)

MRS. FALLON: Telling lies the whole of the people of this town are; telling lies, telling lies as fast as a dog will trot! Speaking against my poor respectable man! Saying he made an end of Jack Smith! My decent comrade! There is no better man and no kinder man in the whole of the five parishes! It's little annoyance he ever gave to anyone! (*Turns and sees him.*) What in the earthly world do I see before me? Bartley Fallon in charge of the police! Handcuffs on him! O Bartley, what did you do at all at all?

BARTLEY: O Mary, there has a great misfortune come upon me! It is what I always said, that if there is ever any misfortune—

MRS. FALLON: What did he do at all, or is it bewitched I am?

MAGISTRATE: This man has been arrested on a charge of murder.

MRS. FALLON: Whose charge is that? Don't believe them! They are all liars in this place! Give me back my man!

MAGISTRATE: It is natural you should take his part, but you have no cause of complaint against your neighbors. He has been arrested for the murder of John Smith, on his own confession.

MRS. FALLON: The saints of heaven protect us! And what did he want killing Jack Smith?

MAGISTRATE: It is best you should know all. He did it on account of a love affair with the murdered man's wife.

MRS. FALLON (*sitting down*): With Jack Smith's wife! With Kitty Keary! —Ochone, the traitor!

THE CROWD: A great shame, indeed. He is a traitor, indeed.

MRS. TULLY: To America he was bringing her, Mrs. Fallon.

BARTLEY: What are you saying, Mary? I tell you—

MRS. FALLON: Don't say a word! I won't listen to any word you'll say!
(Stops her ears.) Oh, isn't he the treacherous villain? Ohone go deo!

BARTLEY: Be quiet till I speak! Listen to what I say!

MRS. FALLON: Sitting beside me on the ass car coming to the town, so
quiet and so respectable, and treachery like that in his heart!

BARTLEY: Is it your wits you have lost, or is it I myself that have lost my
wits?

MRS. FALLON: And it's hard I earned you, slaving, slaving—and you
grumbling, and sighing, and coughing, and discontented, and the
priest wore out anointing you, with all the times you threatened to die!

BARTLEY: Let you be quiet till I tell you!

MRS. FALLON: You to bring such a disgrace into the parish! A thing that
was never heard of before!

BARTLEY: Will you shut your mouth and hear me speaking?

MRS. FALLON: And if it was for any sort of a fine handsome woman,
but for a little fistful of a woman like Kitty Keary, that's not four feet
high hardly, and not three teeth in her head unless she got new ones!
May God reward you, Bartley Fallon, for the black treachery in your
heart and the wickedness in your mind, and the red blood of poor Jack
Smith that is wet upon your hand!

(Voice of JACK SMITH heard singing):

> "The sea shall be dry,
> The earth under mournings and ban!
> Then loud shall he cry
> For the wife of the red-haired man!"

BARTLEY: It's Jack Smith's voice—I never knew a ghost to sing before—.
It is after myself and the fork he is coming! (Goes back. Enter JACK
SMITH.) Let one of you give him the fork, and I will be clear of him now
and for eternity!

MRS. TARPEY: The Lord have mercy on us! Red Jack Smith; the man
that was going to be waked!

JAMES RYAN: Is it back from the grave you are come?

SHAWN EARLY: Is it alive you are, or is it dead you are?

TIM CASEY: Is it yourself at all that's in it?

MRS. TULLY: Is it letting on you were to be dead?

MRS. FALLON: Dead or alive, let you stop Kitty Keary, your wife, from
bringing my man away with her to America!

JACK SMITH: It is what I think—the wits are gone astray on the whole of
you. What would my wife want bringing Bartley Fallon to America?

MRS. FALLON: To leave yourself, and to get quit of you she wants, Jack

Smith, and to bring him away from myself. That's what the two of them had settled together.

JACK SMITH: I'll break the head of any man that says that! Who is it says it? (*To* TIM CASEY.) Was it you said it? (*To* SHAWN EARLY.) Was it you?

ALL TOGETHER (*backing and shaking their heads*): It wasn't I said it!

JACK SMITH: Tell me the name of any man that said it!

ALL TOGETHER (*pointing to* BARTLEY). It was *him* that said it!

JACK SMITH: Let me at him till I break his head!

(BARTLEY *backs in terror. Neighbors hold* JACK SMITH *back.*)

JACK SMITH (*trying to free himself*): Let me at him! Isn't he the pleasant sort of scarecrow for any woman to be crossing the ocean with! It's back from the docks of New York he'd be turned (*trying to rush at him again*), with a lie in his mouth and treachery in his heart, and another man's wife by his side, and he passing her off as his own! Let me at him, can't you. (*Makes another rush, but is held back.*)

MAGISTRATE (*pointing to* JACK SMITH). Policeman, put the handcuffs on this man. I see it all now. A case of false impersonation, a conspiracy to defeat the ends of justice. There was a case in the Andaman Islands, a murderer of the Mopsa tribe, a religious enthusiast—

POLICEMAN: So he might be, too.

MAGISTRATE: We must take both these men to the scene of the murder. We must confront them with the body of the real Jack Smith.

JACK SMITH: I'll break the head of any man that will find my dead body!

MAGISTRATE: I'll call more help from the barracks. (*Blows policeman's whistle.*)

BARTLEY: It is what I am thinking, if myself and Jack Smith are put together in the one cell for the night, the handcuffs will be taken off him, and his hands will be free, and murder will be done that time surely!

MAGISTRATE: Come on! (*They turn to the right.*)

BORROWING IN A NEW SETTLEMENT

Caroline Kirkland

"Mother wants your sifter," said Miss Ianthe Howard, a young lady of six years' standing, attired in a tattered calico, thickened with dirt; her unkempt locks straggling from under that hideous substitute for a bonnet, so universal in the western country, a dirty cotton handkerchief, which is used, *ad nauseam,* for all sorts of purposes.

"Mother wants your sifter, and she says she guesses you can let her have some sugar and tea, 'cause you've got plenty."

This excellent reason, "'cause you've got plenty," is conclusive as to sharing with your neighbors. Whoever comes into Michigan with nothing will be sure to better his condition; but woe to him that brings with him anything like an appearance of abundance, whether of money or mere household conveniences. To have them, and not be willing to share them in some sort with the whole community is an unpardonable crime. You must lend your best horse to *qui que ce soit,* to go ten miles over hill and marsh, in the darkest night, for a doctor; or your team to travel twenty after a "gal"; your wheelbarrows, your shovels, your utensils of all sorts, belong, not to yourself, but to the public, who do not think it necessary even to ask a loan, but take it for granted. The two saddles and bridles of Montacute spend most of their time travelling from house to house a-manback; and I have actually known a stray martingale to be traced to four dwellings two miles apart, having been lent from one to another, without a word to the original proprietor, who sat waiting, not very patiently, to commence a journey.

Then within doors, an inventory of your plenishing of all sorts would scarcely more than include the articles which you are solicited to lend. Not only are all kitchen utensils as much your neighbor's as your own, but bedsteads, beds, blankets, sheets, travel from house to house, a pleasant and effectual mode of securing the perpetuity of certain efflorescent peculiarities of the skin, for which Michigan is becoming almost as famous as the land "'twixt Maidenkirk and John o' Groat's." Sieves, smoothing-irons, and churns run about as if they had legs; one brass kettle is enough for a whole neighborhood; and I could point to a cradle which has rocked half the babies in Montacute. For my own part, I have lent my broom, my thread, my tape, my spoons, my cat, my thimble, my scissors, my shawl, my shoes; and I have been asked for my combs and brushes; and my husband, for his shaving apparatus and his pantaloons.

But the cream of the joke lies in the manner of the thing. It is so straightforward and honest, none of your hypocritical civility and servile gratitude! Your true republican, when he finds that you possess anything which would contribute to his convenience, walks in with, "Are you going to use your horses today?" if horses happen to be the thing he needs.

"Yes, I shall probably want them."

"Oh, well; if you want them—I was thinking to get 'em to go up north a piece."

Or perhaps the desired article comes within the female department.

"Mother wants to get some butter; that 'ere butter you bought of Miss Barton this mornin'."

And away goes your golden store, to be repaid perhaps with some cheesy, greasy stuff, brought in a dirty pail, with, "Here's your butter!"

A girl came in to borrow a "wash-dish," "because we've got company." Presently she came back: "Mother says you've forgot to send a towel."

"The pen and ink and a sheet o' paper and a wafer," is no unusual request; and when the pen is returned, you are generally informed that you sent "an awful bad pen."

I have been frequently reminded of one of Johnson's humorous sketches. A man returning a broken wheelbarrow to a Quaker, with, "Here I've broke your rotten wheelbarrow usin' on't. I wish you'd get it mended right off, 'cause I want to borrow it again this afternoon." The Quaker is made to reply, "Friend, it shall be done"; and I wish I possessed more of his spirit.

But I did not intend to write a chapter on involuntary loans; I have a story to tell.

One of my best neighbors is Mr. Philo Doubleday, a long, awkward, honest, hard-working Maine man, or Mainote I suppose one might say; so good-natured that he might be mistaken for a simpleton; but that must be by those that do not know him. He is quite an old settler, came in four years ago, bringing with him a wife, who is to him as vinegar-bottle to oil-cruet, or as mustard to the sugar which is used to soften its biting qualities. Mrs. Doubleday has the sharpest eyes, the sharpest nose, the sharpest tongue, the sharpest elbows, and above all, the sharpest voice that ever "penetrated the interior" of Michigan. She has a tall, straight, bony figure, in contour somewhat resembling two hard-oak planks fastened together and stood on end; and, strange to say! she was full five-and-thirty when her mature graces attracted the eye and won the affections of the worthy Philo. What eclipse had come over Mr. Doubleday's usual sagacity when he made choice of his Polly, I am sure I never could guess; but he is certainly the only man in the wide world who could possibly have lived with her; and he makes her a most excellent husband.

She is possessed with a neat devil; I have known many such cases; her floor is scoured every night, after all are in bed but the unlucky scrubber, Betsey, the maid of all work; and woe to the unfortunate "indiffidle," as neighbor Jenkins says, who first sets dirty boot on it in the morning. If men come in to talk over road-business, for Philo is much sought when "the public" has any work to do, or school-business, for that being very troublesome, and quite devoid of profit, is often conferred upon Philo, Mrs. Doubleday makes twenty errands into the room, expressing in her visage all the force of Mrs. Raddle's inquiry, "*Is* them wretches going?" And when at length their backs are turned, out comes the bottled vengeance. The sharp eyes, tongue, elbow, and voice are all in instant requisition.

"Fetch the broom, Betsey! and the scrub-broom, Betsey! and the mop, and that 'ere dish of soap, Betsey; and why on earth didn't you bring some ashes? You didn't expect to clean such a floor as this without ashes, did you?"—"What time are you going to have dinner, my dear?" says the imperturbable Philo, who is getting ready to go out.

"Dinner! I'm sure I don't know! there's no time to cook dinner in this house! nothing but slave, slave, slave, from morning till night, cleaning up after a set of nasty, dirty," etc., etc. "Phew!" says Mr. Doubleday, looking at his fuming helpmate with a calm smile, "It'll all rub out when it's dry, if you'll only let it alone."

"Yes, yes; and it would be plenty clean enough for you if there had been forty horses in here."

Philo on some such occasion waited till his Polly had stepped out of the room, and then with a bit of chalk wrote on the broad black-walnut mantel-piece:

> Bolt and bar hold gate of wood,
> Gate of iron springs make good,
> Bolt nor spring can bind the flame,
> Woman's tongue can no man tame.

and then took his hat and walked off.

This is his favorite mode of vengeance—"poetical justice," he calls it; and as he is never at a loss for a rhyme of his own or other people's, Mrs. Doubleday stands in no small dread of these efforts of genius. Once, when Philo's crony, James Porter, the blacksmith, had left the print of his blackened knuckles on the outside of the oft-scrubbed door, and was the subject of some rather severe remarks from the gentle Polly, Philo, as he left the house with his friend, turned and wrote over the offended spot:

> Knock not here!
> Or dread my dear.
>   P. D.

and the very next person that came was Mrs. Skinner, the merchant's wife, all drest in her red merino, to make a visit. Mrs. Skinner, who did not possess an unusual share of tact, walked gravely round to the back door, and there was Mrs. Doubleday up to the eyes in soap-making. Dire was the mortification, and point-blank were the questions as to how the visitor came to go round that way, and when the warning couplet was produced in justification, we must draw a veil over what followed—as the novelists say.

Sometimes these poeticals came in aid of poor Betsey; as once, when on hearing a crash in the little shanty kitchen, Mrs. Doubleday called in her shrillest tones, "Betsey! what on earth's the matter?" Poor Betsey, knowing what was coming, answered in a deprecatory whine, "The cow's kicked over the buckwheat batter!"

When the clear, hilarious voice of Philo from the yard, where he was chopping, instantly completed the triplet—

"Take up the pieces and throw 'em at her!" for once the grim features of his spouse relaxed into a smile, and Betsey escaped her scolding.

Yet, Mrs. Doubleday is not without her excellent qualities as a wife, a friend, and a neighbor. She keeps her husband's house and stockings in unexceptionable trim. Her "emptin's" are the envy of the neighborhood. Her vinegar is, as how could it fail? the *ne plus ultra* of sharpness; and her pickles are greener than the grass of the field. She will watch night after night with the sick, perform the last sad offices for the dead, or take to her home and heart the little ones whose mother is removed forever from her place at the fireside. All this she can do cheerfully, and she will not repay herself as many good people do by recounting every word of the querulous sick man or the desolate mourner with added hints of tumbled drawers, closets all in heaps, or awful dirty kitchens.

I was sitting one morning with my neighbor Mrs. Jenkins, who is a sister of Mr. Doubleday, when Betsey, Mrs. Doubleday's "hired girl," came in with one of the shingles of Philo's handiwork in her hand, which bore in Mr. Doubleday's well-known chalk-marks—

> Come quick, Fanny!
> And bring the granny,
> For Mrs. Double-
> day's in trouble.

And the next intelligence was of a fine new pair of lungs at that hitherto silent mansion. I called very soon after to take a peep at the "latest found"; and if the suppressed delight of the new papa was a treat, how much more was the softened aspect, the womanized tone of the proud and happy mother. I never saw a being so completely transformed. She would almost forget to answer me in her absorbed watching of the breath of the little sleeper. Even when trying to be polite, and to say what the occasion demanded, her eyes would not be withdrawn from the tiny face. Conversation on any subject but the ever-new theme of "babies" was out of the question. Whatever we began upon whirled round sooner or later to the one point. The needle may tremble, but it turns not with the less constancy to the pole.

As I pass for an oracle in the matter of paps and possets, I had frequent communication with my now happy neighbor who had forgotten to scold her husband, learned to let Betsey have time to eat, and omitted the nightly scouring of the floor, lest so much dampness might be bad for the baby. We were in deep consultation one morning on some important point touching the well-being of this sole object of Mrs. Doubleday's thoughts and dreams, when the very same little Ianthe Howard, dirty as ever, presented herself. She sat down and stared awhile without speaking, *à l'ordinaire;* and then informed us that her mother "wanted Miss Doubleday to let her have her baby for a little while, 'cause Benny's mouth's so sore that"—but she had no time to finish the sentence.

"LEND MY BABY!!!"—and her utterance failed. The new mother's feelings were fortunately too big for speech, and Ianthe wisely disappeared before Mrs. Doubleday found her tongue. Philo, who entered on the instant, burst into one of his electrifying laughs with—

> "Ask my Polly,
> To lend her dolly!"

—and I could not help thinking that one must come "west" in order to learn a little of everything.

DIG WE MUST

Lawrence Levine

My wife, Marguerite, was born in Caen, France; I was born in Fargo, North Dakota. Though separated by 5,000 miles of prairie, ocean, moderately low mountains, rivers, and disparate cultures, our childhoods were similar in one respect: we both dug holes in the family gardens. The holes themselves were largely incidental; it was what we found at the other end that counted. What I mean is that we diggers never lost an opportunity to announce to anybody who would care to listen that if we dug down far enough we'd soon come out on the other side of the world, in the exotic land of China.

No hole ever dug exceeded eighteen inches in depth, but it is safe to say that until the age of twelve or thereabouts, our absolute confidence in the outlandish wonders we would encounter if, by magic or muscle, we ever succeeded in piercing the remaining 7,927 miles of granite, balsite, and molten core, never diminished a single iota.

Some thirty-five years later we inhabit the somewhat less exotic precincts of Forest Hills, New York. The other day we noticed one of the neighborhood kids spading out some kind of hole in his back yard, and as he puffed, sweated, and belabored the dirt, he declaimed to several nearby pals the ancient childhood fiction of the hole direct to China.

Fiction? I could hardly wait to get home and haul down the atlas. What part of China, I wanted to know, would this underaged excavator of New York bang into as soon as he dug through the mucko and the Moho, and emerged on the other side? I got my answer in about three minutes flat. He'd end up in the South Indian Ocean, about 700 miles off the southwest coast of Australia, missing the nearest Chinese land by about 4,200 miles. I dug down from Caen and found myself in the South Pacific, about 400 miles southeast of New Zealand. A perpendicular hole from Fargo, North Dakota, dumped me again into the South Indian Ocean, about 1,500 miles from the nearest substantial land—Australia or Antarctica, take your choice.

The fever mounted, I did a number of further calculations. I dug down from Montreal, Rome, Jerusalem, Addis Ababa, Accra, and the Cape of Good Hope, and came up for air in such unlikely spots as the Tasman Sea, the south coast of Papua, and the Pacific Ocean somewhere north of Hawaii.

At last I halted. If there was a snip of dry land anywhere on this whirling mudball where a kid could dig his hole and reach China, I was going to find it—by the numbers.

The answer came some six sheets later—sheets of messy, but undeniably high-class calculations.

Kids of the world, I can here and now report that from parts of only five countries on this globe can you dig straight down to China: Argentina, Chile, Paraguay, a minuscule unpopulated bump of southern Bolivia, and the Falkland Islands. And here, for your next spading expedition, I present a few of my select digging spots in the Southern Hemisphere:

Los Angeles, Chile: Dig down here and end up on the Great Wall of China, a hop and a skip from the town of Tingpien, Kansu Province.

Falkland Islands: Dig here and end up in Northern Manchuria, smack dab in the Great Khingan Mountains, a couple of hundred miles from absolutely nowhere.

Villa Federal, Argentina: Dig down here and end up, feet first, in little old Shanghai.

Mount Lipez, Bolivia (17,398 feet): Dig down here and come right out into the cellars of Macao, the Portuguese gambling colony on the South China coast where, with a little bit of luck, you can cover digging expenses, and maybe even have a yuan or two left over for a chow mein dinner.

Confuso River, Paraguay: Dig along the banks of this waterway northwest of Asunción, end up in Taipei, Formosa, right in Chiang Kai-shek's lap.

We live in an age of deviousness, an age of overskills, and I know that any American kid with an ounce of inventiveness ought to be able to dig his hole slantwise (like those oil-well bimbos in Texas) and get to China from any old spot on this crust. It wouldn't count, though. In the China-digging game no cheating is permitted. You gotta be a straight digger. Any kid can tell you that.

A BOOK WAS A BOOK

Leo Rosten

A good book makes my nostrils quiver. In all other respects, I like to think, I am a clean, wholesome American boy. The memory of Lou Gehrig brings a lump to my throat; a well-shaped limb brings a gleam to my eye; but a good book makes my nostrils quiver.

It is not that my nostrils are especially quiverable. They quiver because, for reasons you soon shall hear, a book triggers the most delicious associations in my mind between reading and (of all things) pickles. Dill pickles.

"*Dill* pickles?" you echo. "What on earth do books have to do with pickles?"

I'm glad you asked that.

In my youth, I lived on the west side of Chicago. It offered all who inhabited that rough-and-tumble section of the city the vitality of life: crowds, noise, challenge, conflict, camaraderie, sidewalk poets, alley crooks, front-step seminars—plus the priceless dream of someday moving to a nicer neighborhood. This is a life and a dream that my children, raised in antiseptic California and genteel Connecticut, have been cruelly deprived of.

In those days, the Chicago public library used to establish outposts of civilization in depositary branches scattered around the city. The closest depot from which I could get free books was located at the rear of a seedy stationery store near Kedzie Avenue on Twelfth Street, which no campaigns by civic improvementeers could get us to call "Roosevelt Road." The man who ran the stationery store received a fee, I suppose, for the use of the dreariest twenty square feet of his premises.

To the golden, magical promise of that stationery store I would race in breathless excitement from George Howland school several afternoons a week. Neither hail nor fire nor pestilence, nor even Chicago's weather, could slow me down. I ran to my Eldorado in order to pick up such books as might have been deposited there, ear-marked for me, by a truck from the central library in that far-off sector of wealth and lake-front we called Downtown.

To order a book, under the neighborhood depositary system, you first consulted a card catalogue at the rear of the stationery (or dry goods, candy, novelty) store. On a slip of coarse brown paper, with the majestic words CHICAGO PUBLIC LIBRARY printed on top, you wrote your name and address, and then, in the columns provided, listed the call numbers of the books you wanted to get.

All the brown slips from all the depositary branches went to the central library, where the slaves who toiled in the stacks would go down the lists of numbers. If the first number on your list was not on the shelves of the stacks, the cellar gnomes would draw a contemptuous line through that number and proceed to the next. Since I could never be sure that the books I most yearned for would be available, I soon learned to list ten, twenty, even thirty numbers. The faceless lackeys at Michigan and Randolph never would send thirty books, of course, or even twenty, or even ten. They usually meted out no more than two to a customer. In any case, several days after listing my numbers on those library slips, I would race back to the stationery store for the treasures I might have drawn in this strange lottery.

Now the Lord, as we all know, doth move in mysterious ways. In my case, I think He received a special celestial pleasure in afflicting the guys in the stacks with astigmatism or hallucinations whenever they got to the brown slip on which I had so carefully, so legibly, so lovingly printed the numbers of the books I most coveted.

For instead of receiving, say, number 712.8T, a piece of glory I could rattle off in my sleep as *Dave Porter in the Philippines,* I would get instead, say number 912.8T, which is *The Prickle-Edged Flora of the Lower Sudan,* or 782.8R, a racy gem entitled *Aunt Polly's System for Tatting Antimacassars,* or even 742.5B, a dandy little thriller about the drainage problems of the Mosquito Coast. (The Mosquito Coast is that strip of Honduras and Nicaragua I hope to hell I never see.)

Well, a man going mad from thirst is not likely to reject a bottle of wine because of its vintage; I, a book-starved lunatic of no discrimination whatsoever, read any book that fell into my hot little hands. I would be bitterly disappointed, of course, to discover that I had been gulled once more, that the malevolent cabal downtown had not sent me a single book out of the thirty immortal numbers I had listed—books by the great Burt L. Standish, the peerless Frank Packard, the masterly Sax Rohmer, the incomparable Joseph Altsheler. But if I was to be denied the joy of chortling over the antics of *The Red-Headed Outfield*, or cliff-hanging on the exploits of Dr. Fu Manchu, or cheering that matchless modern Robin Hood, Jimmy Dale— then, by heaven, *The Prickle-Edged Flora of the Lower Sudan* it would be. And it was.

Between my passion to read anything and the statistical aberrations of the pixies in the library's nether regions, I managed to stuff my mind with information about as odd, exotic, pointless and useless as you are likely to find in the brain-pan of any bibliophile of my generation. It is not that I have a particularly retentive memory: I am not even blessed with the kind of mentality that latches on to simple facts like my bank balance, or the name of my daughter's latest suitor, or when it was my wife told me to be sure and turn off the oven. It is just that through some perverse arrangement of cells my brain seizes with joy upon such bits and pieces of culture as these:

Nicolas Lancret left 780 paintings.

Sirutel is a river in Rumania. (I'll bet you thought it was a syrup that provides "stomach regularity"— Leturis spelled backward.)

In Borneo, they call 1.36 pounds of anything a Catty.

The sawfly often is wingless.

The Esopus Creek Dam is 252 feet high.

In 1905, our Secretary of the Navy was a man named Bonaparte— Charles J. Bonaparte, to be exact.

I have spent my life walking around with junk like that in my head, hoping that one of these days someone will come right out and ask me how many gametes are in a zygote, or in what year the Diet of Worms convened, or who played third base for the infamous Black Sox. I sometimes dream of dazzling beautiful duchesses in Mayfair with just such nuggets of knowledge—tossed off, need I say, with the most casual of airs and the most memorable aplomb. At dinner parties on Park Avenue I sometimes smile inscrutably as I drop the name of Ethelred the Unready into the table talk, or the diameter of the rose window at Chartres, or the great, undying name of Bonehead Merkle—but no one seems to care about erudition any more. In fact, people tend to draw away from me when I ruminate aloud about Philander Smith College, which you probably didn't know is in Little Rock.

I have learned to enjoy these things just for themselves. It enlivens many a solitary walk for me to chuckle to myself over the sudden recollection that it was in 1811 that Tecumseh, that noble Shawnee, decided to make a stand against the white man, or that "monoecious" denotes the presence of *both male and female flowers on the same plant.*

My experiences at that stationer's shop, so many years ago, taught me (apart from such nonsense) that there are rare and wonderful surprises to be found in the random. The book picked up to browse in, the side street taken just because you feel like it, the bus ride to no place in particular, the pedestrian stopped with a question to which you already know the answer ("How do I get to Fort Knox?")—in these random encounters with the unknown I have often found unexpected and delightful rewards.

I sometimes think that in exchange for the priceless treasures it supplies, every library ought to set aside one day a year for Random Reading. Everyone who comes into the library on Random Day would be invited to reach into a huge barrel filled with books, pull out a volume at random —and read it. I should like to be on the committee that chooses the masterpieces, neglected by passing fads and debased tastes, that would go into those barrels.

Barrels. That brings me back to pickles, from which I have strayed. Why does a good book make my nostrils quiver? Because whenever I left the stationery store, my eyes and mind glued to whatever book I had not ordered, there would be wafted into my nostrils a most pungent and provocative smell—a whiff of garlic and dill. I can't be sure whether the pickle barrel from which it came was concealed behind the stationer's counter, to satisfy some secret, shameless appetite of his, or whether that ambrosian scent came from the grocery store next door. But what does it matter? Just give me a good book and a pickle, or an olfactory facsimile of same, and I am in heaven. Even the gross deadweight tonnage of Liberia's tankers cannot intrude on my ecstasy.

THE USE OF FORCE

William Carlos Williams

They were new patients to me, all I had was the name, Olson. Please come down as soon as you can, my daughter is very sick.

When I arrived I was met by the mother, a big startled-looking woman, very clean and apologetic who merely said, Is this the doctor? and let me in. In the back, she added. You must excuse us, doctor, we have her in the kitchen where it is warm. It is very damp here sometimes.

The child was fully dressed and sitting on her father's lap near the kitchen table. He tried to get up, but I motioned for him not to bother, took off my overcoat and started to look things over. I could see that they were all very nervous, eyeing me up and down distrustfully. As often, in such cases, they weren't telling me more than they had to, it was up to me to tell them; that's why they were spending three dollars on me.

The child was fairly eating me up with her cold, steady eyes, and no expression to her face whatever. She did not move and seemed, inwardly, quiet; an unusually attractive little thing, and as strong as a heifer in appearance. But her face was flushed, she was breathing rapidly, and I realized that she had a high fever. She had magnificent blonde hair, in profusion. One of those picture children often reproduced in advertising leaflets and the photogravure sections of the Sunday papers.

She's had a fever for three days, began the father and we don't know what it comes from. My wife has given her things, you know, like people do, but it don't do no good. And there's been a lot of sickness around. So we tho't you'd better look her over and tell us what is the matter.

As doctors often do I took a trial shot at it as a point of departure. Has she had a sore throat?

Both parents answered me together, No . . . No, she says her throat don't hurt her.

Does your throat hurt you? added the mother of the child. But the little girl's expression didn't change nor did she move her eyes from my face.

Have you looked?

I tried to, said the mother, but I couldn't see.

As it happens we had been having a number of cases of diphtheria in the school to which this child went during that month and we were all, quite apparently, thinking of that, though no one had as yet spoken of the thing.

Well, I said, suppose we take a look at the throat first. I smiled in my best professional manner and asking for the child's first name I said, come on, Mathilda, open your mouth and let's take a look at your throat.

Nothing doing.

Aw, come on, I coaxed, just open your mouth wide and let me take a look. Look, I said opening both hands wide, I haven't anything in my hands. Just open up and let me see.

Such a nice man, put in the mother. Look how kind he is to you. Come on, do what he tells you to. He won't hurt you.

At that I ground my teeth in disgust. If only they wouldn't use the word "hurt" I might be able to get somewhere. But I did not allow myself to be hurried or disturbed but speaking quietly and slowly I approached the child again.

As I moved my chair a little nearer suddenly with one cat-like movement both her hands clawed instinctively for my eyes and she almost reached them too. In fact she knocked my glasses flying and they fell, though unbroken, several feet away from me on the kitchen floor.

Both the mother and father almost turned themselves inside out in embarrassment and apology. You bad girl, said the mother, taking her and shaking her by one arm. Look what you've done. The nice man . . .

For heaven's sake, I broke in. Don't call me a nice man to her. I'm here to look at her throat on the chance that she might have diphtheria and possibly die of it. But that's nothing to her. Look here, I said to the child, we're going to look at your throat. You're old enough to understand what I'm saying. Will you open it now by yourself or shall we have to open it for you?

Not a move. Even her expression hadn't changed. Her breaths however were coming faster and faster. Then the battle began. I had to do it. I had to have a throat culture for her own protection. But first I told the parents that it was entirely up to them. I explained the danger but said that I would not insist on a throat examination so long as they would take the responsibility.

If you don't do what the doctor says you'll have to go to the hospital, the mother admonished her severely.

Oh yeah? I had to smile to myself. After all, I had already fallen in love with the savage brat, the parents were contemptible to me. In the ensuing struggle they grew more and more abject, crushed, exhausted while she surely rose to magnificent heights of insane fury of effort bred of her terror of me.

The father tried his best, and he was a big man but the fact that she was his daughter, his shame at her behavior and his dread of hurting her made him release her just at the critical times when I had almost achieved success, till I wanted to kill him. But his dread also that she might have diphtheria made him tell me to go on, go on though he himself was almost fainting, while the mother moved back and forth behind us raising and lowering her hands in an agony of apprehension.

Put her in front of you on your lap, I ordered, and hold both her wrists.

But as soon as he did the child let out a scream. Don't, you're hurting me. Let go of my hands. Let them go I tell you. Then she shrieked terrifyingly, hysterically. Stop it! Stop it! You're killing me!

Do you think she can stand it, doctor! said the mother.

You get out, said the husband to his wife. Do you want her to die of diphtheria?

Come on now, hold her, I said.

Then I grasped the child's head with my left hand and tried to get the wooden tongue depressor between her teeth. She fought, with clenched teeth, desperately! But now I also had grown furious—at a child. I tried to hold myself down but I couldn't. I know how to expose a throat for inspection. And I did my best. When finally I got the wooden spatula behind the last teeth and just the point of it into the mouth cavity, she opened up for an instant but before I could see anything she came down again and gripping the wooden blade between her molars she reduced it to splinters before I could get it out again.

Aren't you ashamed, the mother yelled at her. Aren't you ashamed to act like that in front of the doctor?

Get me a smooth-handled spoon of some sort, I told the mother. We're going through with this. The child's mouth was already bleeding. Her tongue was cut and she was screaming in wild hysterical shrieks. Perhaps I should have desisted and come back in an hour or more. No doubt it would have been better. But I have seen at least two children lying dead in bed of neglect in such cases, and feeling that I must get a diagnosis now or never I went at it again. But the worst of it was that I too had got beyond reason. I could have torn the child apart in my own fury and enjoyed it. It was a pleasure to attack her. My face was burning with it.

The damned little brat must be protected against her own idiocy, one says to one's self at such times. Others must be protected against her. It is a social necessity. And all these things are true. But a blind fury, a feeling of adult shame, bred of a longing for muscular release are the operatives. One goes on to the end.

In a final unreasoning assault I overpowered the child's neck and jaws. I forced the heavy silver spoon back of her teeth and down her throat till she gagged. And there it was—both tonsils covered with membrane. She had fought valiantly to keep me from knowing her secret. She had been hiding that sore throat for three days at least and lying to her parents in order to escape just such an outcome as this.

Now truly she was furious. She had been on the defensive before but now she attacked. Tried to get off her father's lap and fly at me while tears of defeat blinded her eyes.

GULLIVER'S SECRET

E. B. White

Gulliver, that traveler, offered the King of Brobdingnag the secret of an amazing powder that "would not only destroy whole ranks of an army at once but batter the strongest walls to the ground, sink down ships, with a thousand men in each . . . rip up the pavements, tear the houses to pieces . . . dashing out the brains of all who came near . . . destroy the whole metropolis." The King, struck with horror that anyone could entertain such inhuman ideas, said that some evil genius, enemy to mankind, must have been the first contriver. "As for himself, he protested that although few things delighted him so much as new discoveries in art or in nature, yet he would rather lose half his kingdom than be privy to such a secret, which he commanded me, as I valued my life, never to mention any more."

THE BATTLE OF THE ANTS

Henry D. Thoreau

One day when I went out to my woodpile, or rather my pile of stumps, I observed two large ants, the one red, the other much larger, nearly half an inch long, and black, fiercely contending with one another. Having once got hold, they never let go, but struggled and wrestled and rolled on the chips incessantly. Looking further, I was surprised to find that the chips were covered with such combatants, that it was not a *duellum,* but a *bellum,* a war between two races of ants, the red always pitted against the black, and frequently two red ones to one black. The legions of these Myrmidons covered all the hills and vales in my woodyard, and the ground was already strewn with the dead and dying, both red and black. It was the only battle which I have ever witnessed, the only battlefield I ever trod while the battle was raging; internecine war; the red republicans on the one hand, and the black imperialists on the other. On every side they were engaged in deadly combat, yet without any noise that I could hear, and human soldiers never fought so resolutely. I watched a couple that were fast locked in each other's embraces, in a little sunny valley amid the chips, now at noonday prepared to fight till the sun went down, or life went out. The smaller red champion had fastened himself like a vise to his adversary's front, and through all the tumblings on that field never for an instant ceased to gnaw at one of his feelers near the root, having already caused the other to go by the board; while the stronger black one dashed him from side to side, and, as I saw on looking nearer, had already divested him of several of his members. They fought with more pertinacity than bulldogs. Neither manifested the least disposition to retreat. It was evident that their battle-cry was Conquer or Die. In the meanwhile there came along a single red ant on the hill side of this valley, evidently full of excitement, who either had dispatched his foe, or had not yet taken part in the battle; probably the latter, for he had lost none of his limbs; whose mother had charged him to return with his shield or upon it. Or perchance he was some Achilles, who had nourished his wrath apart, and had now come to avenge or rescue his Patroclus. He saw this unequal combat from afar—for the blacks were nearly twice the size of the reds—he drew near with rapid pace till he stood on his guard within half an inch of the combatants; then, watching his opportunity, he sprang upon the black warrior, and commenced his operations near the root of his right fore-leg, leaving the foe to select among his own members; and so there were three united for life, as if a new kind of attraction had been invented which put all other locks and cements to shame. I should not have wondered by this time to find that they had their respective musical bands stationed on some eminent chip, and playing their national airs the while, to excite the slow and cheer the dying combatants. I was myself excited somewhat even as if they had been men. The more you think of it, the less the difference. And certainly there is not the fight recorded in Concord history, at least, if in the history of America, that will bear a moment's comparison with this, whether for the numbers engaged in it, or for the patriotism and heroism displayed. For numbers and for carnage it was an Austerlitz or Dresden. Concord Fight! Two killed on the patriots' side, and Luther Blanchard wounded! Why, here every ant was a Buttrick— "Fire! for God's sake, fire!"—and thousands shared the fate of Davis and Hosmer. There was not one hireling there. I have no doubt that it was a principle they fought for, as much as our ancestors, and not to avoid a three-penny tax on their tea; and the results of this battle will be as important and memorable to those whom it concerns as those of the battle of Bunker Hill, at least.

THE PARABLE OF THE CAVE

Plato

Imagine the condition of men living in a sort of cavernous chamber underground, with an entrance open to the light and a long passage all down the cave. Here they have been from childhood, chained by the leg and also by the neck, so that they cannot move and can see only what is in front of them, because the chains will not let them turn their heads. At some distance higher up is the light of a fire burning behind them; and between the prisoners and the fire is a track with a parapet built along it, like the screen at a puppet-show, which hides the performers while they show their puppets over the top.

Now behind this parapet imagine persons carrying along various artificial objects, including figures of men and animals in wood or stone or other materials, which project above the parapet. Naturally, some of these persons will be talking, others silent.

For in the first place prisoners so confined would have seen nothing of themselves or of one another, except the shadows thrown by the fire-light on the wall of the Cave facing them.

Not if all their lives they had been prevented from moving their heads.

Now, if they could talk to one another, would they not suppose that their words referred only to those passing shadows which they saw?

And suppose their prison had an echo from the wall facing them? When one of the people crossing behind them spoke, they could only suppose that the sound came from the shadow passing before their eyes.

In every way, then, such prisoners would recognize as reality nothing but the shadows of those artificial objects.

Now consider what would happen if their release from the chains and the healing of their unwisdom should come about in this way. Suppose one of them set free and forced suddenly to stand up, turn his head, and walk with eyes lifted to the light; all these movements would be painful, and he would be too dazzled to make out the objects whose shadows he had been used to see. What do you think he would say, if someone told him that what he had formerly seen was meaningless illusion, but now, being somewhat nearer to reality and turned towards more real objects, he was getting a truer view? Suppose further that he were shown the various objects being carried by and were made to say, in reply to questions, what each of them was. Would he not be perplexed and believe the objects now shown him to be not so real as what he formerly saw?

And if he were forced to look at the fire-light itself, would not his eyes ache, so that he would try to escape and turn back to the things which he could see distinctly, convinced that they really were clearer than these other objects now being shown to him?

And suppose someone were to drag him away forcibly up the steep and rugged ascent and not let him go until he had hauled him out into the sunlight, would he not suffer pain and vexation at such treatment, and, when he had come out into the light, find his eyes so full of its radiance that he could not see a single one of the things that he was now told were real?

He would need, then, to grow accustomed before he could see things in that upper world. At first it would be easiest to make out shadows, and then the images of men and things reflected in water, and later on the things themselves. After that, it would be easier to watch the heavenly bodies and the sky itself by night, looking at the light of the moon and stars rather than the Sun and the Sun's light in the day-time.

Last of all, he would be able to look at the Sun and contemplate its nature, not as it appears when reflected in water or any alien medium, but as it is in itself in its own domain.

And now he would begin to draw the conclusion that it is the Sun that produces the seasons and the courses of the year and controls everything in the visible world, and moreover is in a way the cause of all that he and his companions used to see.

Then if he called to mind his fellow prisoners and what passed for wisdom in his former dwelling-place, he would surely think himself happy in the change and be sorry for them. They may have had a practice of honouring and commending one another, with prizes for the man who had the keenest eye for the passing shadows and the best memory for the order in which they followed or accompanied one another, so that he could make a good guess as to which was going to come next. Would our released prisoner be likely to covet those prizes or to envy the men exalted to honour and power in the Cave? Would he not feel like Homer's Achilles, that he would far sooner be on earth as a hired servant in the house of a landless man or endure anything rather than go back to his old beliefs and live in the old way?

Now imagine what would happen if he went down again to take his former seat in the Cave. Coming suddenly out of the sunlight, his eyes would be filled with darkness. He might be required once more to deliver his opinion on those shadows, in competition with the prisoners who had never been released, while his eyesight was still dim and unsteady; and it might take some time to become used to the darkness. They would laugh at him and say that he had gone up only to come back with his sight ruined; it was worth no one's while even to attempt the ascent. If they could lay hands on the man who was trying to set them free and lead them up, they would kill him.

THE NEW PARTIES

Norman Cousins

Of the classifications of human-kind, there is no end. Man is divided and subdivided, grouped and regrouped, crossed and crisscrossed.

His categories are racial, hemispheric, continental, national, regional, spiritual, vocational, political, psychological, social, economic, cultural. Each category has its own wide spectrum. Stick a pin on a map. It is not just a place; it is a stage for an infinite variety of humans. Touch an individual. He is not just a person; he is a flock of identifications and allegiances. If he is an American, he will be Republican or Democrat, northerner or southerner, easterner or westerner, Negro or white, religionist or nonbeliever, employer or laborer, urbanite or countryman, clubber or loner. In the more personal octaves, the registrations show music lovers and non-music lovers, coffee drinkers and tea drinkers, smokers and non-smokers, sportsmen and sedentaries, meat eaters and vegetarians, Yankee baseball worshippers and Yankee haters.

The significant thing about each category is that it yields to a larger one, where the loyalties are even more acute. Southern Methodists and Northern Methodists may each possess a severe sense of separate identification, but both come together in confrontation with Presbyterians or Episcopalians, each of which has its own subdivisions. But all these groupings take on the unifying identification of Protestantism in confrontation with Catholicism or Judaism. And all these assert the Judaeo-Christian tradition in confrontation with Oriental religions. Finally, it is religionist vs. atheist. Factions within the political parties in the United States consolidate when the choice is between Republican or Democrat. And both parties combine when the juxtaposition is between the United States or another nation. The nations band together in coalitions against other nations.

On less consequential grounds: there are at least a dozen stout divisions of jazz enthusiasts, all of whom will turn as one man on the sweet literalists of the Thirties. Met lovers and Dodger lovers despise one another, but on All Star Day they are brother National Leaguers against the alien rabble from the American League. Nothing is more natural than the escalation of human combinations. Unlike the second law of thermodynamics in science, where things have a way of becoming more random, human evolution bears witness to the development of larger and more encompassing units.

All this is by way of calling attention to the imminent emergence today of a new grouping in the world political arena. Next to the classification of man according to sex, this new grouping may well represent the outermost circle of human divisions. For the situation that gives rise to the new grouping is concerned with the largest question yet to face the human race: how to keep the species from decimating itself. The new grouping, therefore, consists of those who understand the full implications of the nuclear age and those who do not. On one side are those who recognize that the advent of nuclear weapons renders obsolete all the old notions about war and measures leading to war. On the other side are those who find it necessary to scoff at the nuclear horror, or at least to view it as an evil that can be sustained if need be.

This development has been in the making ever since Hiroshima. In the past year, however, it has been pointing to a genuine and visible form. Pope John XXIII's historic encyclical, *Pacem in Terris,* put peace at the top of the human agenda. He made it clear that the Church's historic conflict with Communism must not be allowed to obstruct a view of the new imperatives. He believed that all men, whatever their religious or political affiliations, now had to come together against the threat of human incineration in a nuclear war. Pope Paul VI has identified himself with the party of peace. The two giant branches of Communism have split on the issue of nuclear war. The Soviet branch has asserted that nuclear weapons rule out national or ideological victory through war. The Chinese branch believes that nuclear war would be horrible but that it may have to be sustained.

Echoing the line of the Chinese Communists are those in the United States and the Western world who still think in terms of military solutions. Like the Chinese, they believe that war may be inevitable under the present circumstances of world ideological division. The language used by both groups is almost identical. Each asserts the primacy of its objectives, to which nuclear war is made subordinate.

The new world division, therefore, is between the Thinkables and the Unthinkables—between those who believe that nuclear war is thinkable and those who do not. In short, it is between those who put national and ideological objectives first and those who see a prior obligation to keep this planet from becoming a nuclear furnace. None of the old questions is resolved by the present division; freedom vs. Communism, West vs. East, etc. But at least there is a party consisting of people in both camps who insist that the resolution must not take a nuclear form. This party has made possible a small but vital beginning in the form of a partial ban on nuclear tests. It has far to go before it eliminates all the other dangers. But it has proved that it can act. With encouragement, it will act further.

THE PRICE OF THE HEAD

John Russell

The possessions of Christopher Alexander Pellett were these: his name, which he was always careful to retain intact; a suit of ducks, no longer intact, in which he lived and slept; a continuous thirst for liquor, and a set of red whiskers. Also he had a friend. Now no man can gain friendship, even among the gentle islands of Polynesia, except by virtue of some quality attaching to him. Strength, humor, villainy: he must show some trait by which the friend can catch and hold. How, then, explain the loving devotion lavished upon Christopher Alexander Pellett by Karaki, the company boy? This was the mystery at Fufuti.

There was no harm in Pellett. He never quarreled. He never raised his fist. Apparently he had never learned that a white man's foot, though it wobble ever so, is given him wherewith to kick natives out of the road. He never even cursed anyone except himself and the Chinese half-caste who sold him brandy: which was certainly allowable because the brandy was very bad.

On the other hand, there was no perceptible good in him. He had long lost the will to toil, and latterly even the skill to beg. He did not smile, nor dance, nor exhibit any of the amiable eccentricities that sometimes recommend the drunken to a certain toleration. In any other part of the world he must have passed without a struggle. But some chance had drifted him to the beaches where life is as easy as a song and his particular fate had given him a friend. And so he persisted. That was all. He persisted, a sodden lump of flesh preserved in alcohol. . . .

Karaki, his friend, was a heathen from Bougainville, where some people are smoked and others eaten. Being a black, a Melanesian, he was as much an alien in brown Fufuti as any white. He was a serious, efficient little man with deeply sunken eyes, a great mop of kinky hair, and a complete absence of expression. His tastes were simple. He wore a red cotton kerchief belted around his waist and a brass curtain ring suspended from his nose.

Some powerful chief in his home island had sold Karaki into the service of the trading company for three years, annexing his salary of tobacco and beads in advance. When the time should be accomplished, Karaki would be shipped back to Bougainville, a matter of some eight hundred miles, where he would land no richer than before except in experience. This was the custom. Karaki may have had plans of his own.

It is seldom that one of the black races of the Pacific shows any of the virtues for which subject populations are admired. Fidelity and humility can be exacted from other colors between tan and chocolate. But the black remains the inscrutable savage. His secret heart is his own. Hence the astonishment of Fufuti, which knew the ways of black recruits, when Karaki took the worthless beachcomber to his bosom.

"Hy, you, Johnny," called Moy Jack, the Chinese half-caste. "Better you come catch this fella mahster b'long you. He fella plenty too much drunk, galow."

Karaki left the shade of the copra shed where he had been waiting an hour or more and came forward to receive the sagging bulk that was thrust out-of-doors. He took it scientifically by wrist and armpit and swung toward the beach. Moy Jack stood on his threshold, watching with cynic interest.

"Hy, you," he said; "what name you make so much bobeley 'long that fella mahster? S'pose you bling me all them fella pearl; me pay you one dam' fella good trade—my word!"

It annoyed Moy Jack that he had to provide the white man with a daily drunk in exchange for the little seed pearls with which Pellett was always flush. He knew where those pearls came from. Karaki did forbidden diving in the lagoon to get them. Moy Jack made a good thing of the traffic, but he could have made a much better thing by trading directly with Karaki for a few sticks of tobacco.

"What name you give that fella mahster all them fella pearl?" demanded Moy Jack offensively. "He plenty too much no good, galow. Close up he die altogether."

Karaki did not reply. He looked at Moy Jack once, and the half-caste trailed off into mutterings. For an instant there showed a strange light in Karaki's dull eyes, like the flat, green flicker of a turning shark glimpsed ten fathoms down. . . .

Karaki bore his charge down the beach to the little thatched shelter of pandanus leaves that was all his home. Tenderly he eased Pellett to a mat, pillowed his head, bathed him with cool water, brushed the filth from his hair and whiskers. Pellett's whiskers were true whiskers, the kind that sprout like the barbels of a catfish, and they were a glorious coppery, sun-gilt red. Karaki combed them out with a sandalwood comb. Later he sat by with a fan and kept the flies from the bloated face of the drunkard.

It was a little past midday when something brought him scurrying into the open. For weeks he had been studying every weather sign. He knew that the change was due when the southeast trade begins to harden through this flawed belt of calms and cross winds. And now, as he watched, the sharp shadows began to blur along the sands and a film crept over the face of the sun.

All Fufuti was asleep. The houseboys snored in the back veranda. Under his netting the agent dreamed happily of big copra shipments and bonuses. Moy Jack dozed among his bottles. Nobody would have been mad enough to stir abroad in the noon hour of repose: nobody but Karaki, the untamed black, who cared nothing for customs nor yet for dreams. The light pad of his steps was lost in the surf drone on the barrier reefs. He flitted to and fro like a wraith. And while Fufuti slept he applied himself to a job for which he had never been hired. . . .

Karaki had long ago ascertained two vital facts: where the key to the trade room was kept and where the rifles and ammunition were hidden. He opened the trade room and selected three bolts of turkey-red cloth, a few knives, two cases of tobacco, and a fine small ax. There was much else he might have taken as well. But Karaki was a man of simple tastes, and efficient.

With the ax he next forced the rifle chest and removed therefrom one Winchester and a big box of cartridges. With the ax again he broke into the boat sheds. Finally with the ax he smashed the bottoms out of the whaleboat and the two cutters so they would be of no use to anyone for many days to come. It was really a very handy little ax, a true tomahawk, ground to a shaving edge. Karaki took a workman's pleasure in its keen, deep strokes. It was almost his chief prize.

On the beach lay a big proa, a stout outrigger canoe of the kind Karaki's own people used at Bougainville, so high of prow and stern as to be nearly crescent-shaped. The northwest monsoon of last season had washed it ashore at Fufuti and Karaki had repaired it, by the agent's own order. This proa he now launched in the lagoon, and aboard it he stored his loot.

Of supplies he had to make a hasty selection. He took a bag of rice and another of sweet potatoes. He took as many coconuts as he could carry in a net in three trips. He took a cask of water and a box of biscuit. And here happened an odd thing.

In his search for the biscuit he came upon the agent's private store of liquor, a dozen bottles of rare irish whisky. He glanced at them and passed them by. He knew what the stuff was, and he was a savage, a black man. But he passed it by. When Moy Jack heard of that later he remembered what he had seen in Karaki's eyes and ventured the surprising prediction that Karaki would never be taken alive.

When all was ready Karaki went back to his thatch and aroused Christopher Alexander Pellett.

"Hy, mahster, you come 'long me."

Mr. Pellett sat up and looked at him. That is to say, he looked. Whether he saw anything or not belongs among the obscurer questions of psychopathy.

"Too late," said Mr. Pellett profoundly. "This shop is closed. Copy boy! Give all those damned loafers good night. I'm—I'm goin'—bed!"

Whereupon he fell flat on his back.

"Wake up, mahster," insisted Karaki, shaking him. "You too much strong fella sleep. Hy-ah, mahster! Rum! You like'm rum? You catch'm rum any amount—my word! Plenty rum, mahster!"

But even this magic call, which never failed to rouse Pellett from his couch in the mornings, fell now on deaf ears. Pellett had had his skinful, and the fitness of things decreed that he should soak the clock around.

Karaki knelt beside him, pried him up until he could get a shoulder under his middle, and lifted him like a loose bag of meal. Pellett weighed one hundred and fifty pounds; Karaki not much more than a hundred. Yet in some deft coolie fashion of his own the little black man packed his burden, with the feet dragging behind, clear down to the beach. Moreover, he managed to get it aboard the proa. Pellett was half drowned and the proa half swamped. But Karaki managed.

No man saw their departure. Fufuti still dreamed on. Long before the agent awoke to wrath and ruin, their queer crescent craft had slipped from the lagoon and faded away on the wings of the trade.

The first day Karaki had all he could do to keep the proa running straight before the wind. Big smoky seas came piling up out of the southeast and would have piled aboard if he had given them the least chance. He was only a heathen who did not know a compass from a degree of latitude. But his forefathers used to people these waters on cockleshell voyages that made the venture of Columbus look like a ride in a ferryboat. Karaki bailed with a tin pan and sailed with a mat and steered with a paddle: but he proceeded.

Along about sunrise Mr. Pellett stirred in the bilge and raised a pea-green face. He took one bewildered glance overside at the seething waste and collapsed with a groan. After a decent interval he tried again, but this was an illusion that would not pass, and he twisted around to Karaki, sitting crouched and all aglisten with spray in the stern.

"Rum!" he demanded.

Karaki shook his head, and a haunted look crept into Pellett's eyes.

"Take—take away all that stuff," he begged pathetically, pointing at the ocean. . . .

Thereafter for two days he was very, very sick, and he learned how a small boat in any kind of a sea can move forty-seven different ways within one and the same minute. This was no trifling bit of knowledge, as those who have acquired it can tell. It was nearly fatal to Pellett.

On the third day he awoke with a mouth and a stomach of fumed leather and a great weakness, but otherwise in command of his few faculties. The gale had fallen and Karaki was quietly preparing fresh coconuts. Pellett quaffed two before he thought to miss the brandy with which his breakfast draught was always laced. But when he remembered the milk choked in his throat.

"Me like'm rum."

"No got'm rum."

Pellett looked forward and aft, to windward and to lee. There was a great deal of horizon in sight, but nothing else. For the first time he was aware of a strangeness in events.

"What name you come so far?" he asked.

"We catch'm one big fella wind," explained Karaki.

Pellet was in no condition to question his statement nor to observe from the careful stocking of the proa that they had not been blown to sea on a casual fishing trip. Pellett had other things to think of. Some of the things were pink and others purple and others were striped like the rainbow in most surprising designs, and all were highly novel and interesting. They came thronging up out of the vasty deep to entertain Christopher Alexander Pellett. Which they did.

You cannot cut off alcohol from a man who has been continuously pickled for two years without results more or less picturesque. These were days when the proa went shouting across the empty southern seas to madrigal and choric song. Tied hand and foot and lashed under a thwart, Pellett raved in the numbers of his innocent youth. It would have been singular hearing had there been any to hear, but there was only Karaki, who did not care for the lesser Cavalier poets and on whom whole pages of *Atalanta in Calydon* were quite wasted. Now and then he threw a dipperful of sea water over the white man, or spread a mat to keep the sun from him, or fed him with coconut milk by force. Karaki was a poor audience but an excellent nurse. Also he combed Pellett's whiskers twice every day.

They ran into calms. But the trade picked them up again more gently, so that Karaki ventured to make westing, and they fled under skies as bright as polished brass.

> "My heart is within me
> As an ash in the fire;
> Whosoever hath seen me
> Without lute, without lyre,
> Shall sing of me grievous things,
> even things that were ill
> to desire—"

Thus chanted Christopher Alexander Pellett, whose face began to show a little more like flesh and a little less like rotten kelp. . . .

Whenever a fair chance offered, Karaki landed on the lee of some one of the tiny islets with which the Santa Cruz region is peppered, and would make shift to cook rice and potatoes in the tin dipper. This was risky, for one day the islet proved to be inhabited. Two white men in a cutter came out to stop them. Karaki could not hide his resemblance to a runaway nigger, and he did not try to. But when the cutter approached within fifty yards he suddenly announced himself as a runaway nigger with a gun. He left the cutter sinking and one of the men dead.

"There's a bullet hole alongside me here," said Pellett from under the thwart. "You'd better plug it."

Karaki plugged it and released his passenger, who sat up and began stretching himself with a certain naïve curiosity of his own body.

"So you're real," observed Pellett, staring hard at Karaki. "By George, you *are*, and that's comfort."

He was right. Karaki was very real.

"What side you take'm this fella canoe?"

"Balbi," said Karaki, using the native word for Bougainville.

Pellett whistled. An eight-hundred-mile evasion in an open boat was a considerable undertaking. It enlisted his respect. Moreover, he had just had emphatic proof of the efficiency of this little black man.

"Balbi all same home b'long you?"

"Yes."

"All right, Commodore," said Pellett. "Lead on. I don't know why you shipped me for supercargo, but I'll see you through."

Strangely—or perhaps not so strangely—the whole Fufuti interval of his history had been fading from his brain while the poison was ebbing from his tissues. The Christopher Alexander Pellett that emerged was one from earlier years: pretty much of a wreck, it was true, and a feckless, indolent, paltry creature at best, but ordinarily human and rather more than ordinarily intelligent.

He was very feeble at first, but Karaki's diet of coconuts and sweet potatoes did wonders for him, and the time came when he could rejoice in the good salt taste of the spray on his lips and forget for hours together the crazy craving for stimulant. They made a strange crew, this pair—simple savage and convalescent drunkard—but there was never any question as to which was in command. That was well seen in the third week when their food began to fail and Pellett noticed that Karaki ate nothing for a whole day.

"See here, this won't do," he cried. "You've given me the last coconut and kept none for yourself."

"Me no like'm eat," said Karaki shortly.

Christopher Alexander Pellett pondered many matters in long, idle hours while the rush of foam under the proa and the creak and fling of her outriggers were the only sounds between sea and sky. Sometimes his brow was knotted with pain. It is not always pleasant to be wrenched back into level contact with one's memories. Thoughts are no sweeter company for having long been drowned. He had met the horrors of delirium. He had now to face the livelier devils of his past. He had fled them before.

But here was no escape of any kind. So he turned and grappled with them and laid them one by one.

When they had been at sea twenty-nine days they had nothing left of their provisions but a little water. Karaki doled it out by moistening a shred of coconut husk and giving Pellett the shred to suck. In spite of Pellett's petulant protest, he would take none himself. Again the heathen nursed the derelict, this time through the last stages of thirst, scraping the staves of the cask and feeding him the ultimate drop of moisture on the point of a knife.

On the thirty-sixth day from Fufuti they sighted Choiseul, a great green wall that built up slowly across the west.

Once fairly under its headlands, Karaki might have indulged a certain triumph. He had taken as his target the whole length of the Solomons, some six hundred miles. But to have fetched the broadside of them any-where in such a craft as the proa through storm and current, without instrument or chart, was distinctly a feat of navigation. Karaki, however, did no celebrating. Instead, he stared long and anxiously over his shoulder into the east.

The wind had been fitful since morning. By noon it was dead calm on a restless, oily sea. A barometer would have told evil tales, but Karaki must have guessed them anyway, for he staggered forward and unstepped the little mast. Then he bound all his cargo securely under the thwarts and put all his remaining strength into the paddle, heading for a small outpost island where a line of white showed beach. They had been very lucky thus far, but they were still two miles offshore when the first rush of the hurricane caught them.

Karaki himself was reduced to a rattle of bones in a dried skin, and Pellett could scarce lift a hand. But Karaki fought for Pellett among the waves that leaped up like sheets of fire on the reef. Why or how they got through neither could have said. Perhaps because it was written that after drink, illness, madness, and starvation the white man should be saved by the black man again and a last time from ravening waters. When they came ashore on the islet they were both nearly flayed, but they were alive, and Karaki still gripped Pellett's shirt. . . .

For a week they stayed while Pellett fattened on unlimited coconut and Karaki tinkered the proa. It had landed in a waterlogged tangle, but Karaki's treasures were safe. He got his bearings from a passing native fisherman, and then he knew that *all* his treasures were safe. His home island lay across Bougainville Strait, the stretch of water just beyond.

"Balbi over there?" asked Pellett.

"Yes," said Karaki.

"And a mighty good thing too," cried Pellett heartily. "This is the limit of British authority, old boy. Big fella mahster b'long Beretani stop'm here, no can go that side."

Karaki was quite aware of it. If he feared one thing in the world, he feared the Fiji high court and its resident commissioner for the Southern Solomons, who did sure justice upon all who transgressed in its jurisdiction. Once beyond the strait he might still be liable for the stolen goods and the broken contract. But never—this was the point—never could he be punished for anything he might choose to do over there in Bougainville.

So Karaki was content.

And so was Christopher Alexander Pellett. His body had been wrung and swept and scoured, and he had downed his devils. Sweet air and sunshine were on his lips and in his heart. His bones were sweet in him. As his vigor returned he swam the lagoon or helped Karaki at the proa. He would spend hours hugging the warm sand or rejoicing in the delicate tracery of some tiny sea shell, singing softly to himself, while the groundswell hushed along the beach, savoring life as he never had done.

"Oh, this is good—good!" he said.

Karaki puzzled him. Not that he vexed himself, for a smiling wonder at everything, almost childlike, filled him these days. But he thought of this taciturn savage, how he had capped thankless service with rarest sacrifice. And now that he could consider soberly, the why of it eluded him. Why? Affection? Friendship? It must be so, and he warmed toward the silent little man with the sunken eyes and the expressionless face from which he could never raise a wink.

"Hy, you, Karaki, what name you no laugh all same me? What? You too much fright 'long that fella stuff you steal? Forget it, you old black scamp. If they ever trouble you, I'll square them somehow. By George, I'll say I stole it myself!"

Karaki only grunted and sat down to clean his Winchester with a bit of rag and some drops of oil he had crushed from a dried coconut.

"No, that don't reach him either," murmured Pellett, baffled. "I'd like to know what's going on under that topknot of yours, old chap. You're like Kipling's cat, that walks by himself. God knows I'm not ungrateful. I wish I could show you—"

He sprang up.

"Karaki! He one big fella friend 'long you: savee? You one big fella friend 'long me: savee? We two dam' big fella friend, my word! . . . What?"

"Yes," said Karaki. No other response. He looked at Pellett and he looked away toward Bougainville. "Yes," he said, "my word," and went on cleaning his gun—the black islander, inscrutable, incomprehensible, an enigma always, and to the end.

The end came two days later at Bougainville.

Under a gorgeous dawn they came into a bay that opened before their prow as with jeweled arms of welcome. The land lay lapped in bright garments like a sleeper half awakened, all flushed and smiling, sensuous, intimate, thrilling with life, breathing warm scents . . .

These were some of the foolish phrases Pellett babbled to himself as he leaped ashore and ran up on a rocky point to see and to feel and to draw all the charm of the place to himself.

Meanwhile Karaki, that simple and efficient little man, was proceeding methodically about his own affairs. He landed his bolts of cloth, his tobacco, his knives, and the other loot. He landed his box of cartridges and his rifle and his fine tomahawk. The goods were somewhat damaged by sea water, but the weapons had been carefully cleaned and polished. . . .

Pellett was declaiming poetry aloud to the alluring solitude when he was aware of a gentle footfall and turned, surprised, to find Karaki standing just behind him with the rifle at his hip and the ax in his hand.

"Well," said Pellett cheerfully, "what d'you want, old chappie?"

"Me like," said Karaki, while there gleamed in his eyes the strange light that Moy Jack had glimpsed there, like the flicker of a turning shark; "me like'm too much one fella head b'long you!"

"What? Head! Whose—my head?"

"Yes," said Karaki simply.

That was the way of it. That was all the mystery. The savage had fallen enamored of the head of the beachcomber, and Christopher Alexander Pellett had been betrayed by his fatal red whiskers. In Karaki's country a white man's head, well smoked, is a thing to be desired above wealth, above lands and chiefship's fame, and the love of women. In all Karaki's country was no head like the head of Pellett. Therefore Karaki had served to win it with the patience and single faith of a Jacob. For this he had schemed and waited, committed theft and murder, expended sweat and cunning, starved and denied himself, nursed, watched, tended, fed, and saved his man that he might bring the head alive and on the hoof—so to speak—to the spot where he could remove it at leisure and enjoy the fruits of his labor in safety.

Pellett saw all this at a flash, understood it so far as any white could understand it: the whole elemental and stupendous simplicity of it. And standing there in his new strength and sanity under the fair promise of the morning, he gave a laugh that pealed across the waters and started the sea birds from the cliffs, the deep-throated laugh of a man who fathoms and accepts the last great jest.

For finally, by corrected list, the possessions of Christopher Alexander

Pellett were these: his name still intact; the ruins of some rusty ducks; his precious red whiskers—and a soul which had been neatly recovered, renewed, refurbished, reanimated, and restored to him by his good friend Karaki.

> "Thou shouldst die as he dies,
>   For whom none sheddeth tears;
> Filling thine eyes
>   And fulfilling thine ears
> With the brilliance...the bloom
>   and the beauty..."

Thus chanted Christopher Alexander Pellett over the waters of the bay, and then whirled, throwing wide his arms:
"Shoot, damn you! It's cheap at the price!"

THE POWER OF WORDS

Leo Rosten

They sing. They hurt. They teach. They sanctify. They were man's first, immeasurable feat of magic. They liberated us from ignorance and our barbarous past.

For without these marvelous scribbles which build letters into words, words into sentences, sentences into systems and sciences and creeds, man would be forever confined to the self-isolated prison of the scuttlefish or the chimpanzee.

"A picture is worth ten thousand words," goes the timeworn Chinese maxim. "But," one writer tartly said, "it takes words to say that."

We live by words: LOVE, TRUTH, GOD.

We fight for words: FREEDOM, COUNTRY, FAME.

We die for words: LIBERTY, GLORY, HONOR.

They bestow the priceless gift of articulacy on our minds and hearts—from "Mama" to "infinity."

And the men who truly shape our destiny, the giants who teach us, inspire us, lead us to deeds of immortality, are those who use words with clarity, grandeur and passion: Socrates, Jesus, Luther, Lincoln, Churchill.

Today, Americans, caught between affluence and anxiety, may again give thanks for the endless riches in the kingdom of print.

Suggestions for Study

1. Explain why you like or do not like mythology.

2. Imagine that you are taking a bus trip across country; write a diary for one day of your trip.

3. After reading "Spreading the News," write an essay in which you describe one of your own experiences with gossip or false rumors.

4. After reading "Borrowing in a New Settlement," write an essay in which you give your own ideas on borrowing. Make the essay as humorous as you can.

5. Write an essay on the "Man Question." Use examples from your own experiences.

6. From what you know of sickness in children, does the story "The Use of Force" impress you as true to life? Write an essay in which you discuss the "use of force" in another situation.

7. George Bernard Shaw, in his play "Man and Superman," says that shame motivates man's actions, thoughts, and deeds. Does the story by Crane agree with this philosophy? Do you agree? Write a sketch in which you show how young children treat each other.

8. Pretend that you are visiting the sea or the mountains for the first time; write a personal essay showing your impressions.

9. Re-examine the title of this section; then make a list of the selections which, in your opinion, best illustrate stature.

10. Choose one of the selections in this section and discuss the techniques that the author used in putting across his ideas.

Composition Topics

1. How much of a Handicap is Shyness?

2. A Very Unusual Place

3. The Hamburger's Place in Society

4. A Day's Frustrations

5. My Interest (Lack of Interest) in Science